Women and the Politics of Class

JOHANNA BRENNER

Monthly Review Press
New York

Columbia FLI Partnership
HQ1154. B83 2000

Library of Congress Cataloging-in-Publication Data
ISBN 1–58367–010–6 (paper)
ISBN 1–58367–009–2 (cloth)

Monthly Review Press
122 West 27th Street
New York, NY 10001

Designed and typeset by Illuminati, Grosmont
Manufactured in Canada

10   9   8   7   6   5   4   3   2   1

Contents

Acknowledgements

With profound gratitude I here acknowledge my friends. I am very fortunate to have engaged in an extended intellectual dialogue—sometimes not so simple or easy—with people who I love and respect. I owe special thanks to my co-authors Barbara Laslett and Nancy Holmstrom, astute thinkers and dear friends. The articles we've written together are full collaborations, expressing our shared political commitments and drawing equally on our different areas of knowledge. Thanks also to Barbara for being there in hard times and for her outstanding editorial skills. Thanks to Jan Haaken, true friend and comrade, for teaching me about psychoanalytic feminism and giving me tools for understanding emotional life, tools that have been crucial for me personally as well as intellectually. I thank Samira Haj for all the love and support we share and for challenging my thinking and drawing me into new intellectual terrains. My gratitude also to Bill Resnick, loved companion and intellectual sparring partner. How I understand the world is continually shaped by our conversations and by his often unique and compelling insights about contemporary politics. Thanks to Pat Kirkham for her enduring friendship and Gary Smith for his wise counsel. Perry Anderson and Erik Olin Wright have been generous colleagues; their encouragement over the years has been very important to me. I am grateful to Christopher Phelps, who commissioned the book when he was editor at MR Press, for his enthusiasm about the project and for helping me to shape the collection. I want to thank my editors Lucy Morton and Robin Gable for their help also. Always in my mind are my son Aaron Brenner and my brothers Adam, Louis, and Peter Seitchik. Their love and appreciation for me and mine for them is deep and abiding. Our relationship sustains me in everything I do, including writing this book.

Chapter 1, "Rethinking Women's Oppression" (with Maria Ramas), was first published in *New Left Review* 144 (March–April 1984). Chapter 2, "Gender and the State" (with Barbara Laslett), was first published as "Gender, Social Reproduction, and Women's Self-Organization: Considering the U.S. Welfare State" in *Gender & Society* 5, no. 3 (September 1991). Chapter 3, "Gender and Class in U.S. Labor History," was first published in *Monthly Review* 50, no. 6 (November 1998). Chapter 4, "The Feminization of Poverty, Comparable Worth, and Feminist Political Discourse," was first published as "Feminist Political Discourses: Radical Versus Liberal Approaches to the Feminization of Poverty and Comparable Worth" in *Gender and Society* 1, no. 4 (December 1987). Chapter 5, "The Politics of Welfare Reform," was first published as "Towards a Feminist Perspective on Welfare Reform" in *Yale Journal of Law and Feminism* 2, no. 1 (Fall 1989). Chapter 6, "Welfare Reform: Reframing the Debate," was first published in *Against the Current* 54 (January–February 1995). Chapter 7, "Socialist-feminism versus Communitarian Conservatism" (with Nancy Holmstrom), was first published as "Autonomy, Community, and Women's Rights" in Mike Davis and Michael Sprinter, eds., *The Year Left* (Verso, 1985). Chapter 8, "Democracy, Community and Care," was first published as "Utopian Families" in *Socialist Register 2000* (Merlin Press). Chapter 9, "Meeting the Challenge of the Political Right," was first published as "Feminism's Revolutionary Promise: Finding Hope in Hard Times" in *Socialist Register 1989* (Merlin Press). Chapter 10, "The Best of Times, the Worst of Times: U.S. Feminism Today," was first published in *New Left Review* 200 (July–August 1993). The author and publishers gratefully acknowledge permission to reprint this material here.

Introduction

The articles in this book were written out of my experience as a political activist, a socialist, and a feminist thinker and teacher. They are theoretical and practical, exploring Marxist-feminist questions but always with an eye toward doing politics. In this century feminism has made extraordinary gains, pushing back the boundaries of male domination within industrial capitalist societies. Now, though, the movement for women's liberation faces a political impasse. I try to account for feminism's gains and limits and suggest that old modes of organizing need to be transformed to meet new challenges.

I write about bringing anti-capitalist ideas and perspectives into feminism but also about bringing feminism into socialist politics. I explore the intersection of capitalist class relations with race/ethnicity and gender. I explore how economic life and politics interconnect with family life and sexuality. I argue that creating collective, democratic, and unalienated forms of family and community life are as central to socialism as revolutionizing work and politics. I insist on the value of imagining and discussing these alternatives even though they seem unattainable.

I belong to a socialist organization, Solidarity, that meets on Sunday. I joke sometimes that it's my church. But my politics do not rest on faith in an inevitable triumph, the final conflict, or History. However, I do believe in hanging in there, keeping socialist ideas and ideals alive, doing politics that are as pro-working class, liberatory, and democratic as possible, and in being part of that long tradition of struggle for an egalitarian and democratic world.

Themes that have been at the core of my intellectual and political commitments tie the articles in this book together. I start, as Marx did, with the capitalist mode of production and its distinctive social arrangements. I reject functionalist arguments—arguments that try to explain all the different institutions of capitalist societies by how they function to support the interests of the capitalist class. But I do think that what Marx called the social relations of production—class relations—constrain and shape politics, social life, culture, personal life, and much else.

I begin to trace these linkages in Part I, Toward a Historical Sociology of Gender. For me, historical materialist explanation begins with how societies organize the collective labor basic to human survival and with the power relations that are embedded in those institutional arrangements. Marxists have focused their attention almost entirely on the production of things. Marxist feminists have broadened this notion of necessary labor to include the care and nurturing of people—we use the term "social reproduction." Feminists early on identified the particular way social reproduction is organized in capitalist societies—through the nuclear family household—and the gender division of labor in social reproduction—women's assignment to the work of caring for people—as central to the oppression of women in capitalism. But where did the gender division of labor come from? Was it just "carried over" from the patriarchal households of the societies where capitalism originated? Was it determined by women's biology? Was it the product of capitalist interests in guaranteeing new laborers? Was it the product of working-class men's interests in securing their wives' sexual services and caring labor? Was it because capitalists and male workers shared in the domestic ideology that women's place was in the home and that women's wages ought to be lower than men's wages?

These are the questions Maria Ramas and I address in our article on rethinking women's oppression (Chapter 1). We argue that to understand women's oppression in capitalism, it is necessary to explain not only what men wanted but also what *women* wanted, how women defined their interests in relation to men's and what resources women had for contesting with men politically. We argue that in the nineteenth century, human biology *and* the structures of capitalist accumulation—the capitalist employers' drive for profit—powerfully constrained the choices open to working-class women. In the constraints of human biology we included not only women's role in biological reproduction (pregnancy, breast-feeding) but also children's long period of dependence on adults and their need for consistent attention to develop physical, emotional, and intellectual capacities. We argue that pregnancy and breast-feeding in themselves are perfectly compatible with women's involvement in production. But capitalist control over production, in general, and the exploitative sweatshop conditions of nineteenth-century industry, in particular, made combining wage work and motherhood extremely difficult. We argue further that there is a general tendency in capitalism to privatize reproduction—to force family households to shoulder much of the responsibility for caring work. These conditions shaped how working-class women saw their interests and how they engaged in working-class struggles with both capitalist employers and the emerging capitalist state. But we also look at another side of capitalism—a tendency toward lowering the costs of and increasing the range of consumer goods. In the twentieth century, we argue, expanding demand for women's labor and the availability of commodities that make it easier for women to work a double day laid the basis for new forms of working-class women's organization and struggle.

This emphasis on women's political self-organization and how it is both enabled and constrained by gender and class relations appears again in the article I wrote with Barbara Laslett on gender and the U.S. welfare state (Chapter 2). We show how different periods of capitalist development were associated with changes in the organization of social reproduction and in the levels of political organization and mobilization of middle class and working-class women. We consider how middle-class and working-class women's everyday responsibilities for the work of social reproduction shaped their capacities to organize and to intervene in three crucial periods of contestation over state policy: the progressive era, the 1930s and the 1960s. Comparing Black middle-class and white middle-class women's organizing in the Progressive Era and the 1930s, we show how race oppression shaped African-American women's relationship to their communities and families and thus their strategic choices and opportunities for political action.

This article entered into feminist debates about the nature of the capitalist state, another theme of my work. I approach the state as an arena of contest and struggle among groups with many different interests. But I also see the state as constrained and limited by capitalist class power. These constraints and limits operate directly, as capitalist employers and their organizations use their money and connections to influence politicians and political parties. But these constraints and limits operate also, and most fundamentally, *indirectly*—outside the political system itself. For example, they operate through the competitive, divisive structures of the labor market and hierarchically organized occupations.

And they operate through the final dependence of the state on the prosperity of the economy, which in turn depends on capitalist decisions about investment and production. How these limits and constraints express themselves in any given time and place—their effects—is a complex matter. In Parts II and IV and in the Conclusion, I trace out these interconnections between changing dynamics of the capitalist economy and the political climate, the capacities of state actors, the possibilities for self-organization by oppressed groups, the challenges and difficulties they face.

In Chapter 3 on gender and class in U.S. labor history, I return to the issue of working-class women's self-organization and working-class men's strategic choices, following out the complex connections between men's and women's gendered interests, emotions and identities. I argue that both in securing their place in the competitive labor market and in organizing their everyday work of caring for each other and children, working-class people have to group together to survive. In the normal course of things, survival projects create group loyalties and solidarities, lived interdependencies, whether at work or in family and community networks. And, also in the normal course of things, these group solidarities, reflecting existing racial/ethnic divisions, operate to repro-duce white working-class people's relative privilege as well as their loyalty to whiteness. Survival projects respond to material conditions—to the possibilities for and limits on working people's collective action. And they confer different resources, different capacities for self-organization, on women and men. In the group life that emerges out of survival projects men and women develop gender identities, define their inter-ests, and experience their emotional needs.

These explorations in theory and history arose from my participa-tion in socialist-feminist political organizations and feminist groups where questions such as the nature of the capitalist state, patriarchy, and capitalism, were hotly debated. Most of the articles in Parts II–IV emerged from my organizing experience. In the 1970s I entered a male-dominated blue collar occupation, telephone installation and repair, becoming a rank-and-file organizer and a student of how gender works at work and in unions. In the 1970s and 1980s I belonged to a grass-roots reproductive rights group which struggled to make the pro-choice movement a multi-issue movement, one that would go beyond abortion rights to represent the other pressing reproductive rights issues of working-class women, women of color, and queer women. In the late 1980s I became involved with a local welfare-rights group.

As a socialist active in struggles for reform, I have sought to define strategies that reflect a pro-working-class, feminist, and anti-racist politics. Key strategic choices in reform efforts are how claims are made, how problems are defined, how demands are justified and argued for, and how groups and movements are structured. In Chapter 4, on the feminization of poverty and comparable worth, I contrast different strategic approaches, showing what makes one a socialist strategy. Chapter 5, on the politics of welfare reform, is both an analysis of the causes of the great shift in federal welfare policy represented by the passage of the Family Support Act of 1988 and an outline of a socialist-feminist strategy for responding to the attack on single mothers represented by welfare reform. Chapter 6, on reframing the welfare reform debate, addresses an activist rather than an academic audience and argues for linking the needs of single mothers to those of all working-class parents.

The articles in Part III, New Politics of the Family (Chapters 7 and 8), emerge from my reproductive-rights activism. The increasing success of the right's "pro-family" anti-abortion and anti-gay politics led to a heated debate about feminism's own political stance toward the family. Some feminists began to argue that the mainstream feminist movement had overemphasized individual rights such as abortion. They identified themselves as "communitarians," critics of capitalism's individualistic and competitive values. Nancy Holmstrom and I were active in reproductive-rights work and engaged in these disputes about strategies for taking on the right. Our article (Chapter 7) challenges both the limited, single-issue politics of the mainstream movement and the communitarian critics' disparagement of women's struggle for individual freedom. We argue that these "new communitarians," influential social theorists in elite policy circles of the Democratic Party, are closer to social conservatives than to the radically democratic communitarian traditions in anarchism and socialism. I take up these questions again in Chapter 8. Invited to contribute to a symposium on "necessary utopias," I returned to thinking about alternatives to the family as we know it, about how to combine individual autonomy and more collective forms of living. The article is republished here in the hope that it will encourage readers to imagine life beyond the limited horizons of the present.

Part IV, Class Politics and Feminist Strategy, follows out the recent history of the women's movement, its political challenges and prospects. Chapter 9 lays out the general argument, explaining both the impasse of feminism and the drift to the right, while also assessing what Marxism and feminism still have to offer to each other. Chapter 10 assesses in depth the state of U.S. feminism in the early 1990s. The dilemmas I identify are still very much with us. In Part IV, I show how changes in the capitalist economy shaped the emergence of feminism in the 1960s, its spread and successful institutionalization in the 1970s and 1980s and its stalemate in the 1990s. I argue that the second-wave feminist movement completed the task begun by the first—to dismantle the system of legalized, intentional exclusion of women from key institutions in economic and political life. All women gain from this victory, but upper-middle-class women have reaped tremendous benefits, while working-class women find their lives in some ways worse, rather than better, than before. For most working-class women, transcending the constraints of the gender division of labor and the burdens of the double shift will require more than an end to discrimination. They need living wage jobs, paid family leave, and a broad range of affordable, quality services, especially to help with caring for children, the ill, and the elderly in their families.

But as capitalist economic power increases globally and locally, possibilities for shifting from private to more social responsibility for caregiving radically shrink. Indeed, with capital's empowerment come income stagnation, deterioration of work life, insecurity and more competition for jobs, withdrawal of company benefits except for upper-level employees, cuts in public services, as funding is diverted to the military and prisons, and corporations wage a successful assault on trade unions and on government intervention to protect workers on the job. In these circumstances white people try to save themselves at the expense of people of color, divisions among ethnic groups get more intense, and political life shifts decisively to the right, with the Democratic Party abandoning policies of income redistribution or support for the poor.

This environment is quite different from the period of the 1960s and 1970s when the second wave won its victories. Then, in the context of an expanding capitalist economy and a liberal welfare state, it was possible for feminism to make considerable gains for women without substantially challenging the distribution of wealth. The gender-only focus of the mainstream women's movement could be successful. In the future, progress for women will depend on challenging corporate capital's political and economic power. This challenge cannot be organized by feminists alone, nor with old forms of feminist organization.

In the concluding essay, written for this volume, I begin to incorporate analysis of race more fully into my work on gender and class. The essay takes off from the notion of "intersectionality." Developed primarily by feminists of color, intersectionality defines an analytic strategy that addresses the interrelation of multiple, cross-cutting institutionalized power relations defined by race, class, gender, sexuality (and other axes of domination). My essay analyzes the intersection of class, race, and gender in two ways. First, I consider class as a social location defined primarily in terms of access to occupations and the material and nonmaterial resources they confer on individuals within them. Drawing on a rich historical literature created by African-American scholars, I explore how class differences among Black women have created lines of conflict as well as alliance. And I explore how similar class position and different racial/ethnic locations of white women and women of color in the working class shape their experiences and gender identities. Second, I consider class at a more systemic level, tracing out the ways that the dynamics of the capitalist economy and the powers of the capitalist class today constrain the political prospects of both the Black civil rights and feminist movements. Finally, returning to a theme that percolates through my work, I conclude that the fate of these movements is now crucially tied to the rebuilding of the institutions of working-class self-organization: a serious and disruptive challenge to capital, a broad and militant "rainbow movement" linking social justice and environmental movements to renewed, more community-linked, more democratic, and more internationalist trade unions, and eventually to working-class political organizations that would challenge the corporate domination of politics.

Spanning a period of sixteen years, the articles in this book reflect my own intellectual development but also the shifting political conjunctures and intellectual currents of the 1980s and 1990s. Later articles build on earlier ones, as I extended and deepened my analysis in response to the extraordinary body of feminist intellectual work that has been done over these decades. The last two decades have also been a time of profound political and economic change both in the U.S. and globally. At the opening of the Reagan presidency, conservatism seemed still contested, and radical activist movements—such as the anti-nuclear movement, women's peace movement, queer politics, and international solidarity movements—were part of the political scene. The relationship between the "new social movements" and Marxist theories of revolutionary change continued to be a compelling political and intellectual issue. In the 1990s, the astonishing fall of communism, the defeat of the revolutions in Central America, and the clear hegemony of conservative discourse and policy in the U.S. seemed to make radical politics—and certainly any discussion of a "revolutionary subject"— irrelevant. Yet, by the turn of the twenty-first century, working-class people in the U.S., battered, undermined and on the defensive, are groping toward new, more collective responses to the global arrogance of corporate power. Class issues are back on the political agenda. And on the agenda, still, are the theoretical and strategic questions at the heart of the socialist-feminist project.

Part I

Toward a Historical Sociology of Gender

Chapter 1

Rethinking Women's Oppression

with Maria Ramas

The 1970s and early 1980s were witness to an extraordinary flowering of Marxist-feminist analysis and debate. Michèle Barrett's *Women's Oppression Today* is an ambitious attempt to present and synthesize this literature. Through a dialogue with the most influential currents in socialist-feminist thought, Barrett attempts to construct a Marxist analysis of the relationship between women's oppression and class exploitation in capitalism that is neither reductionist nor idealist. In this concern, Barrett's project is very much a part not only of Marxist feminism, but of the contemporary re-evaluations of Marxist theory as a whole, especially the renewed emphasis on the importance of ideology, the state, and class struggle. Two theoretical issues lie at the heart of the Marxist-feminist debates of the 1970s and early 1980s: (1) the degree to which women's oppression is constructed independently of the general operation of capitalist production; (2) the degree to which the oppression of women is located at the level of ideology. Barrett's critique identifies the central dilemma her analysis will seek to transcend. Marxist-feminist approaches such as domestic labor theory, she argues, which begin from the premiss that women's oppression is an integral part of capitalism and not independently determined, tend toward reductionism. It cannot be convincingly shown that privatized reproduction on the basis of domestic labor actually affords capital the cheapest method for reproducing labor power. Moreover, to view this system as an effect or precondition of capitalist class relations leaves untheorized why it is women who are in the home and fails to take into account male domination of women within the working class. Theories of this kind thus naturally lead to a political strategy which simply collapses the struggle for women's liberation into the class struggle: women's social position expresses their exploitation by capital, not a relationship of dependence and powerlessness vis-à-vis their husbands and fathers.

Marxist-feminist approaches that have adopted the concept of patriarchy as an analytical tool have been concerned to incorporate precisely this fact of male power into class analysis. The attraction of this concept is that it recognizes that men have privileges as men and wield power over women, even within the working class. The problem, however, has been to unravel the relationship between class and gender hierarchies. Are we speaking of two systems, one governing "production" and one "reproduction," or of a single system? Barrett points out that attempts to construct a single system tend toward reductionism and functionalism by arguing that patriarchy functions to the benefit of the capitalist class. Dual analyses, on the other hand, have not satisfactorily linked the two types of hierarchies. Are they in conflict or mutual accommodation? And, most importantly, what is the process by which this occurs?

The Elaboration of Barrett's Critique

For Barrett, the central flaw of dual systems theory is that it unnecessarily limits the scope of Marxist theory by attempting to compensate with the concept of patriarchy for the insufficiency of "sex-blind" Marxist categories. This resolution of the problem, however, is really no resolution, or at least it is not a Marxist-feminist resolution because it leads us away from the crucial insights of the Marxist theoretical framework and places us firmly back on the terrain of empirical sociology. Rather, Barrett sees the Marxist-feminist project as one that will revise and develop Marxist theory so that it can encompass and demystify the relationships between different social structures. By limiting Marxist theory to the realm of capitalist production, dual systems theory prevents us from building on what is absolutely essential to a materialist conception of society—the determinant relationship between different levels of human social organization and experience.

The final major Marxist-feminist approach Barrett assesses focuses on the creation of masculine and feminine subjectivity and the representation of gender difference in cultural production. This approach has been influenced considerably by the shift in Marxism's theoretical approach to ideology initiated by Althusser. The rejection of economism and the reprioritization of ideology have opened the way for Marxist-feminists to place problems of gender relations at the center of Marxist analysis and to avoid the problems of reductionism and empiricism that plague those approaches utilizing reproduction or patriarchy as central organizing concepts.

Barrett finds two interrelated problems with these approaches. First, drawing heavily upon psychoanalytic thought, they tend to be ahistorical. To date they have failed to present an analysis of gender ideology and subjectivity that demonstrates how these have changed over time or how they relate to specific historical social formations. Second, there is a tendency in these approaches to jettison Althusser's rather nebulous but necessary affirmation of the primacy of the material "in the last instance" in favor of a conception of ideology as absolutely autonomous. This tendency is best revealed in discourse theory, of which Barrett gives an extended critique. She argues that once ideology is severed from material reality, it no longer has any analytical usefulness, for it becomes impossible to posit a theory of determination—of historical change based on contradiction. These approaches, thus, like dual systems theory, ultimately lead us back to a bourgeois theory of multidetermination by different factors—political, ideological, economic, and so forth.

Having identified the major problems in current theoretical work, Barrett attempts to resolve them in an analysis that recognizes the importance of ideological elements—the construction of gendered subjectivity, its determinations and consequences—without severing ideology from its mooring in material relations. At the same time she proposes to utilize a historical analysis to steer between the Scylla of reductionism and the Charybdis of empiricism.

Capitalism and the Family Household

Barrett views the key to women's oppression as a complex she terms the "family-household system." The complex includes a given social structure—the household—and a given ideology—the family—which, while connected, are not parallel. The household structure is one in which a number of people, usually biologically related, depend on the wages of a few adult members, primarily those of the husband/father, and in which all depend primarily on the unpaid labor of the wife/mother for cleaning, food preparation, childcare, and so forth. The ideology of the "family" is one that defines family life as "'naturally' based on close kinship, as properly organized through a male bread-winner with a financially dependent wife and children, and as a haven of privacy beyond the public realm of commerce and industry."[1]

Barrett's crucial contention is that the family-household system is not inherent to capitalism but has come to form *a historically constituted* element of class relations. This structure was not inevitable, but rather emerged through a historical process in which an ideology that posited women's natural connection to domesticity was incorporated into capitalist relations of production. This ideology sprang in part from precapitalist conceptions of women's place, but was predominantly a bourgeois construction that fitted with bourgeois family relations. The ideology was accepted by the organized working class in the nineteenth century and was determinant in forming craft-union political strategy. The pivot in the formation of the family-household system, Barrett contends, was the mid-nineteenth-century struggle between a coalition of capitalists and male workers on the one hand, and female workers on the other, as a result of which the better-organized male craft unions and the bourgeois-controlled state were able to override the interests of female workers. The expulsion of women from craft unions and the protective legislation on women's working conditions passed in Britain in the 1840s–1860s effectively forced women into the domestic sphere and laid the basis for a sex-segregated wage-labor market. Once the family-household system was in place, a sex-segregated labor market was almost inevitable. The sexual division of labor within the household and within the labor market, once established, serve to reinforce each other. Women's low wages and their segregation in a limited number of occupations effectively consolidate their position in the family, and vice versa.

Working-class men fought for the family-household system because it was in their short-term interests. However, in the long run, Barrett argues, this represented a real defeat for the class as a whole because it split the interests of working men and women. Working-class men could have organized to raise women's wages, a strategy that would have unified and thereby strengthened the working class. Instead, they fought for a family wage and unions for men, and for protective legislation for women, in an attempt to eliminate low-waged competition and force women into the domestic sphere.

On the other hand, precisely because the family-household system divides the working class, and because the system is fundamentally a conservative social force, its adoption by the working class was in the long-term *political* interests of the bourgeoisie, if not necessarily in its economic interests. Hence, the capitalist class utilized its hegemonic position in the state to help construct the system through the protective legislation implemented in the nineteenth century, and continues to maintain the system today through the welfare state.

Barrett's analysis concludes that women's oppression, while not having any material basis in the period when the system was historically forming, "has acquired a material basis in the relations of production and reproduction of capitalism today." She explains:

> A model of women's dependence has become entrenched in the relations of production of capitalism, in the divisions of labor in wage work and between wage labor and domestic labor. As such, an oppression of women that is not in any essentialist sense pre-given by the logic of capitalist development has become necessary for the ongoing reproduction of the mode of production in its present form.[2]

Because women's oppression is not a prerequisite for capitalism, theoretically it would not be impossible for women to achieve liberation within capitalist society. Such liberation would require: (1) a redivision of labor and childcare responsibilities; (2) an end to the actual or assumed dependence of women on a male wage; (3) a transformation in the ideology of gender. These changes would be extremely difficult to achieve, however, given that they are so systematically interwoven into the fabric of capitalist social relations. As Barrett concludes:

> These divisions are systematically embedded in the structure and texture of capitalist social relations in Britain and they play an important part in the political and ideological stability of this society. They are constitutive of our subjectivity as well as, in part, of capitalist political and cultural hegemony. They are interwoven into a fundamental relationship between the wage-labour system and the organization of domestic life, and it is impossible to imagine that they could be extracted from the relations of production and reproduction of capitalism without a massive transformation of those relations taking place. Hence, the slogan "No women's liberation without socialism; no socialism without women's liberation" is more than a pious hope.[3]

Barrett's review of the state of feminist theory is impressive, particularly because it allows her to identify in a remarkably clear, if somewhat schematic, manner the impasse Marxist feminism has reached. And while we do not find that her analysis ultimately succeeds in breaking the impasse, it does indicate the direction in which we must move if we are to break through onto new terrain. Barrett's insistence that the family-household system, the crucial site of women's oppression, is not functionally determined by capitalist needs alone, and her concomitant emphasis on a historical approach which centers on how class struggle shaped the sexual division of labor, are absolutely essential to a successful Marxist-feminist analysis. Her commitment to the development of a nonreflexive but materialist theory of gender ideology is also crucial.

Problems with Barrett's Approach

However, in our view, Barrett's analysis falls short of its mark in that it ultimately fails to decipher the enigma of how the "sex-blind" dynamics of the capitalist mode of production described in Marxist theory and the profoundly sexist day-to-day operations of capitalist society fit together. One major reason for this is her failure satisfactorily to confront the major theoretical problem that any specifically Marxist feminist analysis must address: how is it possible, given the capitalist drive to accumulate and to use up labor power, that women are left out of capitalist production and remain in the home to the extent that they do? Domestic labor theorists offer the explanation that the family-household system is, in fact, generated by capital accumulation itself and that, therefore, this is really not the problem it at first appears to be. As we have seen, Barrett rejects this approach in her analysis of a single, historically developed system. But she does not really resolve the theoretical issue at stake. If the laws of capital accumulation are sex-blind, as Barrett agrees they are, then how are gender divisions perpetuated? Her image of these divisions as "embedded in the structure ... of capitalist social relations" is really simply that. What does it mean? What exactly are the mechanisms that *recreate* and reinforce the gender division of labor within the workforce? How are these mechanisms connected to the capitalist need to maximize profit? Looking at the historical process does not allow us to ignore the theoretical issue of how capitalism perpetuates rather than undermines gender divisions.

Barrett recognizes the problem in her contention that the domestic labor system is not necessarily in the economic interests of the bourgeoisie. But if it is in their political interests, as she claims, how does it happen that capitalists are able to subordinate their short-term interest in the largest possible profit to their long-term political interests? In the same vein, in order to argue that gender divisions are not located in a separate patriarchal system, Barrett is forced to redefine *relations of production*. This term does not refer simply to *class relations*, she argues, but "must comprise the divisions of gender, or race, definitions of different forms of labor, of who should work and at what."[4] But what is the relationship between *these* relations and *capitalist class relations?* Especially since, for Barrett, "it can plausibly be argued that the wage-labor relation and the contradiction between labor and capital—the defining characteristics of the capitalist mode of production—are 'sex-blind' and operate quite independently of gender."[5] Despite the sleight of hand, we are back to a dual systems framework—and to the same problem: How does the sex-blind contradiction between labor and capital connect with relations of production in which gender difference plays a very significant role? To say that these have evolved historically is not, in our view, sufficient.

To put our criticism slightly differently, Barrett's analysis, while materialist in approach, fails to identify any material basis for women's oppression in capitalism. She rejects not only explanations that root this development in capitalist exigencies of the reproduction of labor power, but also radical-feminist proposals that point to biological repro-duction as a material basis. Further, Barrett fails to find this system to be unambiguously in the vital material interests of any social group. Certainly it is not in the interests of women. Nor is it in the class interests of working-class men: (a) because it is not clear that women's domestic labor in the home raises the standard of living of the class as a whole; (b) because it divides the working class by creating competi-tion between men and women as wage laborers and within the family; and (c) because it has never really been thoroughly established anyway. Moreover, although working-class men have some interest in the family-household system as men, Barrett does not believe that this is as great as some feminists argue. The role of male as breadwinner (a) locks men effectively into wage labor; (b) has deprived them of access to their children; and (c) oppresses them by imposing a rigid definition of masculinity. Thus the husband cannot be viewed, as Christine Delphy proposes, as the "self-conscious appropriator of his wife's labour power, responsible for the exploitation of her labour in the home."[6]

Finally, the system cannot be viewed as unambiguously serving the interests of the capitalist class, although, in Barrett's view, capitalists benefit more than any other social group. For while the system is not perhaps in their best economic interests, it is very advantageous politically as it "divides and weakens the working class and reduces its militancy."[7] This is the primary reason why the bourgeoisie has invested enormous resources through the state in economic support of this form of household.

If the family-household system really is as tenuous a construction as Barrett's analysis suggests, it is difficult to explain why it has embedded itself so deeply in capitalist society. For, while it may be in the political interests of the bourgeoisie, it is not, at least in Barrett's analysis, essential to the survival of the bourgeoisie. Once again, Barrett must confront the problem of how capitalists as a class are able systematically to suspend their short-term interests in maximizing profit in favor of their political interests. Further, if the interests of working-class men, both as men and as proletarians, are not conclusively served by this system, and if no material basis in social relations of production and reproduction can be found which might push the working class to struggle for this system, it is hard to explain what has prevented the workers' movement from adopting a more enlightened strategy on this issue.

Barrett is well aware of this problem, and her solution is to give ideology great weight in the analysis. Gender ideology, she argues, must be viewed in this case as a material force. Because gender ideology becomes gender identity, it exists at the level of our very subjectivity. Thus, although the family-household system may not be in the interests of working-class men and women, "it does not follow that all women, or the entire working class, suffer from some simple false consciousness as to where their interests really lie. Gender identity and the ideology of the family are embedded in our very subjectivity and our desires at a far more profound level than that of 'false consciousness.'"[8] The suggestion is that gender ideology is powerful enough to counteract or withstand the battering of the "sex blind" tendencies of the law of capital accumulation.

Such a formulation, of course, necessitates an analysis of the production and dynamics of gender ideology itself, and the requirements for changing its content. Barrett does not address these questions in any detail in *Women's Oppression Today*. Perhaps she will explore them in further work.[9] As her analysis stands in this book, however, we are left with an account in which the ideology of gender difference, produced by mechanisms which we do not yet understand but which, we must hypothesize, operate independently of capitalist social relations, has been powerful enough historically to have had an autonomous effect on the shaping of capitalist social relations, and remains powerful enough to reproduce this situation on an ongoing basis. Such an analysis is, of course, subject to all the criticisms of dual systems approaches that Barrett herself makes so well.

Unions and Protective Legislation

We should now discuss in some detail, as it represents what may be considered an emerging Marxist-feminist consensus, Barrett's central historical account of the formation of the family-household system and the resulting ghettoization of women in low-paying sectors of capitalist production through protective legislation and trade-union exclusivism.[10] Protective legislation, which banned nightwork for women and prevented them from working in certain industries, helped to structure the sexual division of labor by disallowing competition with men on an equal basis for certain skilled jobs—for example, mining and printing— and by making unrestricted male labor generally more appealing to capitalists. Barrett argues that women's precarious position in capitalist production then conditioned the continuation of their domestic role within the family, and their dependence upon men.

Now, it is very difficult to make a convincing case that so precarious a social-political edifice could have played a major role in conditioning the sexual division of labor or the family-household system, either in England or in the United States. The U.S. example is particularly provocative because legislation barely existed until well into the twentieth century. The first women's hours law was a ten-hour regulation passed in Ohio in 1852. Twenty-five years later only two other states and one territory had maximum-hours regulations; by 1908 the total number of states with such laws on the books was only ten.[11] Furthermore, not only was the enactment of protective legislation an arduous and slow-moving process, but those laws that were passed were virtually unenforced in the nineteenth century and well into the twentieth. Before 1908 only five or six states had provisions in the laws for factory inspectors.[12] And even when such provisions were made, inadequate policing apparatuses and lenient treatment of offending manufacturers greatly weakened their impact.[13]

In Britain the issue is somewhat more complex because protective legislation was passed at the national level and appears to have been slightly better enforced. The first significant legislation was the famous Ten Hours Bill passed by parliament in 1847, which limited women's labor to ten hours per day in textile industries only. In the course of the next two decades modified versions of this legislation were applied to other industries, and in 1867 parliament extended protection to include workshops as well. In addition to these Acts restricting women's hours, the Mines Regulation Act of 1842 prohibited women from underground mine work.[14]

While the evidence is limited and somewhat impressionistic, what there is suggests that all of this legislation did not have any determining effect on the structuring of job segregation by sex. To the extent that the Ten Hours Bill was effective, it appears to have limited men's as well as women's labor hours.[15] Insofar as this was the case, it could not have adversely affected women's chances for employment within the industry. Indeed, it was precisely because a sexual division of labor already existed in the textile industry, such that male, female and child labor were utterly interdependent, that the Ten Hours Bill could win the shortening of the working day for all through the limitation of female and child labor. Nor does this legislation appear to have resulted in any significant replacement of male for female labor, either within the industry as a whole or within particular sectors. In fact, the proportion of women to men in the textile industry continued to increase during the latter part of the nineteenth century.[16]

It is probable that the extension of protective legislation to other industries in the course of the second half of the nineteenth century also failed significantly to affect the sexual division of labor. On the whole such legislation was both less stringent than that which regulated the textile industry, in most cases allowing longer hours, and not very effectively enforced. However, by the time these laws became effective, skilled male workers were generally working shorter hours than those called for by such legislation; for by the 1870s many unions had succeeded in limiting the working day in their trade to nine hours. By the turn of the century, protective legislation in this form was almost completely outdated, as the normal working day in most industries had fallen to 9½ hours.[17]

As with protective legislation, the impact of the skilled trades' exclusion of women cannot explain the sexual division of labor. There is no question but that trade unions followed a rigorous exclusionary policy vis-à-vis women in both Britain and the United States during the first three-quarters of the nineteenth century. It is also true that it was often justified by reference to a patriarchal ideology of gender difference. We are sceptical, however, that trade-union policy had the effect Barrett suggests. Even if trade unions had been wholly successful in excluding women from their trade, which they were not, it is difficult to see how this could have significantly contributed to the capitalist sexual division of labor as a whole, as the skilled occupations controlled by trade unions in the nineteenth century represented only a very small fraction of the capitalist division of labor.

The Record of Union Struggle

The historical evidence similarly undermines Barrett's contention that the way working-class men organized in the nineteenth century was determined primarily by precapitalist patriarchal ideology. The realms of both legislative reform and industrial organization offer disconfirming historical cases. The movement for the Ten Hours Bill is particularly revealing in this respect as it was one of the earliest and most successful reform efforts. The movement, from Barrett's point of view, embodied men's desire to exclude women from production as an expression of the precapitalist ideology of gender difference. However, many historians argue that the main goal of at least the working-class component of the movement was the shortening of the working day for all. Hutchins and Harrison, for example, suggest that the demand for the restriction of women's labor hours, which first surfaced in 1841, quite late in the movement's history, represented an alternative approach to the restriction of adult labor and was adopted only after earlier strategies focusing on the restriction of child labor and/or motive power had failed.[18]

The earliest and most consistent demand made by the working-class component of the factory movement was a call for the reduction of the working day for all.[19] However, the bourgeoisie's adamant opposition to any restriction of adult male labor, on the one hand, and the growing middle-class outcry against the condition of factory children, and later factory women, on the other, molded the strategy which emerged from the 1830s onwards.[20] The strategy was to reduce the adult working day indirectly, through legislation that would fix the hours of child labor in such a way as to make it impossible for adults to work longer hours. This would have been the effect of Sadler's movement-backed bill, introduced into parliament in 1832, which called for a limit of ten hours' labor per day for children under eighteen and the prohibition of nightwork for all under twenty-one. The government's bill, which was passed by parliament in 1833 in lieu of Sadler's, while providing for more stringent restrictions on child labor, actually represented a defeat for the Short-Time Movement because it allowed manufacturers to continue to employ adults for long hours by using children in relays.[21] The Short-Time Movement responded by agitating for restrictions on motive power and for a new factory act, eventually introduced by Lord

Ashley in 1837, that would have restricted the labor of all under twenty-one to ten hours. Parliament rejected both bills precisely because its members recognized them to be thinly veiled attempts to restrict the labor time of all.[22]

It was at this point that the agitation for the restriction on women's hours was first voiced by the Movement, which mounted an energetic campaign in the 1840s on behalf of this new demand. The vigor of this offensive, combined with the economic depression, was substantial enough to persuade parliament to vote the Ten Hours Bill into law in 1847.[23] Barrett is aware of this line of interpretation, though she ignores it in *Women's Oppression Today*. In an article coauthored with Mary McIntosh she writes:

> It has been said that the Ten-Hours Movement in a sense compromised with the philanthropists, seeing the restriction of women's and children's factory hours as the only way to achieve a reduction of hours for all. As Ray Strachey put it, the men were "hiding behind the petticoats of women" in pushing for the 1847 Ten Hours Act on compassionate grounds for women and young persons, knowing that it would force their own hours down to ten as well.... But the factory legislation did play a part in further differentiating men's from women's work and in reinforcing patterns of job segregation in which women were found mainly in a narrow range of low-paid occupations, especially outside of the factories themselves.[24]

Barrett and McIntosh do not seem to take issue here with the contention that the major motive of the factory movement was to limit all adult labor. Yet they maintain that regardless of motive the effect of the legislation was to contribute to a discriminatory sexual division of labor. Of course, the argument that protective legislation "further differentiated men's from women's work" and "reinforced patterns of job segregation" is quite different from the proposition of *Women's Oppression Today*—that this legislation was primarily responsible for job segregation by sex.

Trade-union history poses similar problems for Barrett's analysis. While one can cite numerous cases in which trade unions practiced discriminatory policies toward working women and justified them by waxing eloquent on woman's "proper sphere," there are also many examples of trade-union support for women's organizational and strike activities, and one can even upon occasion find trade-union journals and conferences supporting feminist viewpoints.[25] We do not point out that male trade unions often supported women as workers in order to paper over their unquestionable, substantial history of discrimination.

But we would suggest that an explanation of trade-union activity vis-à-vis women that hangs on the power of patriarchal ideology is clearly inadequate. It would indicate a history of trade unions far more homogeneous on this issue than was in fact the case.[26]

The almost complete unanimity with which trade unions virulently opposed the entry of women into their craft was part and parcel of a general attempt to limit potentially ruinous competition from labor willing to work at reduced rates. The "dishonorable trades," the euphemism for unapprenticed labor, were, even more than mechanization, the major threat to the privileged craft workers during the first two-thirds of the nineteenth century, and control of entry into the trade was the major weapon used by unionists to preserve their relatively privileged position in the labor market. This was attempted either by enforcing traditional craft apprenticeship regulations, or, in the case of new factory trades such as mulespinning, by creating an artificial apprenticeship system.[27]

It is entirely unnecessary to resort to ideology to explain why trade unions were particularly adamant in their opposition to female entry into their trades. It is quite clear that when unions were unable to exclude women, a rapid depression of wages and general degradation of work resulted. Barbara Taylor's account of the London Journeymen Tailors Union (LJTU) strike against homework in 1833 well illustrates this dynamic.[28] The LJTU was in fact one of the strongest unions in Britain during the eighteenth century, strictly controlling hours, prices, and labor recruitment. By the early nineteenth century, the privileged position of the tailors was threatened by a reorganization of production that made it possible for capitalists to replace the relatively expensive labor of the male tailors with the cheaper labor of women working at home. The LJTU attempted to block this by preventing production outside of workshops and was fairly successful as late as the 1820s. The growth of the ready-made clothing industry, however, which centered on women engaged in homework for pitifully low wages, broke the back of the union in the 1830s. The 1833 strike against homework (female tailoresses) was the tailors' last attempt to preserve their position.

In mid-century, a tailor summarized the effect of female labor thus.

When I first began working at this branch [waistcoat-making], there were but very few females employed in it. A few white waist-coats were given to them under the idea that women would make them cleaner than men ... But since the increase of the puffing and sweating system, masters and sweaters have sought everywhere for such hands as would do the work below the regular ones. Hence the wife has been made to compete with the husband, and the daughter with the wife.... If the man will not reduce the price of his labor to that of the female, why he must remain unemployed.[29]

This scenario was repeated in many other industries during the course of the nineteenth century: Edinburgh printing, Scottish tailoring trades, pottery and cigar-making.[30]

That competition, rather than ideology, was the crucial determinant of male exclusivism is underscored by the fact that in cases where women were not competing with men, or where women were in the industry from the start, unions tended to include women and even gave substantial support to their attempts at organization and strike activity.

Sometimes the very same unions that barred women from their trades supported women's organizing and strike efforts in other industries or sectors of their own industry. Thus, the London Union of Journeymen Bookbinders supported women folders and sewers in their dispute with the Bible Societies in the 1830s and 1840s, and the Glasgow Mule-spinners campaigned for equal wages for women in the 1830s.[31] A famous U.S. example is that of the Iron Molders who, while strictly excluding women from their union, provided substantial financial support to the Troy laundresses' strike in 1869.[32] Another impressive U.S. example is that of the male shoemakers of Lynn, Massachusetts who consistently supported female shoemakers throughout the 1830s and 1860s.[33] In unskilled trades that included women, unions almost always followed a policy of including women; the earliest unions of this type in Britain were the weaving unions. The New Unions which organized unskilled workers in the latter part of the nineteenth century generally included women on an equal basis with men.[34] In the U.S. the prime example is, of course, the Knights of Labor, the only national union in the nineteenth century to organize on an industrial rather than a craft basis.[35]

Again, we do not wish to suggest that male trade unionists or male workers in general supported women's right to equality in work as well as in all other aspects of social life, or to deny that they held sexist ideas about women. Rather, these examples suggest that if the history of trade-union attitudes toward women is to be properly understood, we require a far more complex analysis of the socioeconomic background than that which Barrett and other proponents of her general standpoint tend to offer. Furthermore, the fact that (i) trade unions were not wholly successful in their attempts to bar women from their trades, and (ii) that working-class men, especially in unskilled unions, often did support women workers, suggests to us that something more than trade-union behavior underlay the formation of the sexual division of labor in the nineteenth century. Indeed, trade-union strategies, like protective legislation, cannot be explained without recognizing that women came into the capitalist labor market at a disadvantage. The organizing strategies of working-class men appear to have been a response to, rather than a cause of, the marginalization of women in wage work.[36]

The Material Basis for the Family-Household System

In sum, the problems we have identified in Barrett's interpretation can all be traced to one major lacuna in her analysis: the absence of a material basis for the historical development and reproduction of the family-household system, the sexual division of labor, and women's oppression in capitalism. We do not take issue with the contentions that such a system may serve the bourgeoisie's political interests, that working-class men (at least those in skilled jobs) wanted to exclude women from higher paying sectors of production, or that all men had an interest in maintaining control over women's lives for both practical and emotional reasons. In fact, we would even contend that their short-term interests in such a situation are greater than Barrett allows. However, the crucial question, in our view, is how men were able to accomplish this against the opposition of women, given the "sex-blind" tendencies of capitalist accumulation which were pushing in the opposite direction.[37]

In the remainder of this essay we would like to suggest an alternative analytical and historical interpretation that places considerable weight on the exigencies of biological reproduction. This is a somewhat heretical stance for socialist feminists. Most—Barrett among them—are extremely reluctant to acknowledge any role for biological differences in determining women's social position. Underlying this reluctance is a healthy concern that any such focus may inadvertently lead down the path to biological determinism.[38] Let us be clear at the outset. We do not wish to argue that biological facts of reproduction in themselves determine social relations, in capitalism or in any other social formation. We do propose, however, to take seriously Timpanaro's suggestion that the *relationship* between the natural and the social must be built into the analysis.[39] In our view, a materialist account of women's oppression simply must consider the way in which the class-structured capitalist system of production can incorporate the biological facts of reproduction, and the extent to which biological differences, considered in such a context, condition women's participation in economic/political life, their capacity for self-organization in defense of their interests and needs, and so forth. Furthermore, this problem must be approached in a historical way. We must consider how the historical development of capitalism may have altered this relationship.

We propose to analyze the development of the sexual division of labor in capitalism and the formation of the family-household system within the context of the contradiction between the capitalist dynamics of production and the exigencies of biological reproduction. On the one hand, as Marx and Engels argued, there is the distinct tendency of capital accumulation to pull women into wage labor and thus to lay the material basis for their independence from men. On the other hand, however, the exigencies of biological reproduction have historically posed a significant barrier to the full development of this tendency.

The contradiction seems to us to be apparent. Biological facts of reproduction—pregnancy, childbirth, lactation—are not readily compatible with capitalist production, and to make them so would require capital outlays on maternity leave, nursing facilities, childcare, and so on. Capitalists are not willing to make such expenditures, as they increase the costs of variable capital without comparable increases in labor productivity and thus cut into rates of profit. In the absence of such expenditures, however, the reproduction of labor power becomes problematic for the working class as a whole and for women in particular.[40]

In what follows we will explore the impact this contradiction has had on women's position in capitalism in the nineteenth and twentieth centuries. Our analysis is in three parts. In the first part we will argue that both the sexual division of labor and the family-household system, as they developed in nineteenth-century England and the U.S., were crucially conditioned by the exigencies of biology and class structure. As Barrett points out, while capital leaves the problem of the reproduction of labor power to the working class, it does not require that this be accomplished within a set of hierarchical gender relations. Nor does it require that women be primarily responsible for childrearing and domestic labor. We will argue, however, that the biological facts of reproduction, insofar as they conditioned both sexual divisions of labor *and* power balances between men and women, made this outcome likely if not inevitable.

In the second part we will consider how capitalist development in the twentieth century affected this situation. We will argue that the rapid development of the forces of production under capitalism has laid the basis for women to transcend the constraints of biological reproduction, but that at the same time capitalist relations of production continue to limit the development toward equality. This is the case not because gender divisions are "embedded" in capitalist relations of production, as Barrett argues; indeed, there is a real tendency within capitalism to threaten and undercut these divisions and to restructure the labor force. Rather, the tendency of capitalism toward periodic crises, and therefore toward cuts in the standard of living of the working class, prevents a break from the family-household system and reinforces the subordination of women.

We will conclude by briefly considering the role of the state and ideology in the creation and reproduction of women's oppression. We will argue that once the material basis for women's oppression has been located, it becomes possible to construct a framework for analyzing the respective roles of the state and ideology that grants both relative autonomy while recognizing their ultimate connection to material relations.

Biological Reproduction and Class Structure in the Nineteenth Century

The assignment of women to reproduction and their marginalization in wage work was prior to, rather than an effect of, protective legislation or trade-union policy. All studies of women's work in the nineteenth century indicate that for the most part women withdrew from full-time work in factories and shops with the birth of their first child. Long before protective legislation or union contracts, married women were shaping their employment around their domestic responsibilities. Along with their children, women made crucial economic contributions to their households. However, whereas their sons and daughters went into unskilled wage work, women with children gained income in those employments that fitted with the demands of childcare and housework: part-time work, homework, seasonal work, taking in boarders, and so on.[41] The exception proves the rule: where women could work with their children, their participation rate rose—for example, Italian mothers in the New York canneries, immigrant mothers in New England textile mills and early English cotton factories.[42] Married women who took factory work, most commonly in the textile and garment industries, belonged to families whose husbands were employed in highly seasonal work or were extremely low-waged.[43] Even in the textile towns where opportunities for women to work were far greater than for their husbands—a relatively unusual case—the wives' participation rate was low: 17 percent in Roubaix in 1872, of whom 54 percent were factory workers; 26 percent in Preston in 1851, two-thirds in factories.[44] In the United States in 1887, well before any significant legislation, only 4 percent of all women factory workers were married.[45]

This raises two issues. First, why did certain aspects of working-class reproduction—in particular childcare—remain outside capitalist production, so that a division of labor developed in which one person in the household became primarily responsible for this necessary labor? Second, why were women relegated to this position of domestic laborer rather than men?

In the pre-industrial economy, reproduction could be accommodated to the demands of production because the organization of production remained in the hands of the artisanal or home-based workers themselves.[46] The rise of factory production fundamentally altered this situation by robbing the workers of control over the production process. The increasing determination of work rhythms by complex, coordinated machine production posed difficulties in matching productive and reproductive work. However, in the abstract, the organization of production itself does not prevent the reconciliation of these two kinds of work. Capitalist class relations of production—the capitalist control of the workers' time and the constant squeezing out of surplus value that accompanies it—in fact determined that the rise of factory production would pose a severe threat to the survival of the working class. The family-household system emerged as the resolution to this crisis. Barrett's contention that this particular resolution was determined by an ideology of gender difference that predated capitalism assumes that alternatives to locating the reproduction of labor power in the household existed—an assumption that must be addressed and justified.

The elimination of the household as a site for reproducing the labor force on a daily and intergenerational basis requires relatively cheap goods and services to be available through the market—sending out laundry, hiring servants to clean, eating out or buying prepared meals, paying for childcare, and so forth. If wages are not sufficient to purchase the whole range of these services, domestic labor has to be done in addition to wage work to make up the difference. The evidence is overwhelming that the income of several earners was necessary to provide even the bare necessities for the majority of working-class families in the first half of the nineteenth century and even in the second half, when wages did rise.[47] Therefore a sizeable amount of domestic labor remained to be done under extremely primitive conditions which made it physically arduous and time-consuming.[48] At the same time, the working day was long in capitalist production outside the home—from twelve to fourteen hours, sometimes more. Given these circumstances, a division of labor in which one person undertook domestic labor along with supplementary wage work, while another earned wages full time, was preferable to a division of labor in which two adults worked long factory hours and then returned home to do additional labor.

The determining factor, however, was the incompatibility of child-care and work outside the home. In theory it might have been possible for both husbands and wives to work and pay for childcare, but in practice the survival of their children was jeopardized when both parents worked. Wages were generally low, and the additional cash for child-care could not be generated if both adults were working just to purchase the necessities of life. In many working-class districts women often could not make provision for childcare. They left children on their own, under the care of slightly older siblings, or under the supervision of a neighbor who looked in from time to time.[49] Engels reported that children were killed by domestic accidents twice as often in Manchester where factory work prevailed for women, as in Liverpool where mothers found other employment.[50] The demands of childcare were particularly difficult to reconcile with the long and exhausting hours of wage work demanded by the capitalist employers. The need for care and supervision of older children cannot, however, account for why the mother was assigned to the home; but women's biological role in reproduction can.

Many nineteenth-century observers considered that factory work was especially unhealthy for women. Engels reported that female factory workers experienced more difficult childbirth than other women and that miscarriages were more frequent among them than the average.[51] The issue here is not so much the physical demands placed on preg-nant women, since women in precapitalist society combined physically demanding work with pregnancy, nursing, and so on. However, where this had been done successfully, women retained control over their participation in production. They were able to regulate their work so as to take account of their different physical needs in pregnancy—for example, by taking more frequent rest periods.

While the consequences of factory work were harmful for women, they appear to have been disastrous for their children because working mothers could not nurse. Bottle-feeding was not an acceptable substitute for most of the nineteenth century. Sterilization techniques were unknown and bottle-feeding appreciably increased the risk of infant mortality. The only other alternative, wet nursing, was also generally unacceptable for the working class, as infants had to be sent long distances to board with poor women who took in far too many babies and generally could not feed them all adequately. Here again, infant mortality rates were quite high.[52]

Because the nursing of infants was necessary to guarantee their survival, and because employers would not make provision for the needs of pregnant women and infants, it made sense for the woman to stay at home if the family could afford it, while her husband went to work. When women spent much of their married life bearing and nursing children, as they did throughout the nineteenth century, the logic of the sexual division of labor embodied in the family-household system was overwhelming.

In order to participate fully in production, women required a range of support services—most crucially, job-site care for infants, nursing breaks for working mothers, paid maternity leave. Yet where working conditions in general were barely supportable, where employers were consistently hostile to unions, where unemployment insurance, workmen's compensation, occupational safety, and so on, were unknown, the provision of such services could only be a utopian dream. A working class barely strong enough to establish simple weapons of defense was in no position to wrest these enormous concessions from capital. In the absence of these necessary supports, equal wages for women and equal access to skilled trades would not have solved women's problems, even had the labor movement adopted a much less ambiguous stance toward women's work for wages. Even a skilled woman worker would have had to withdraw from work once her childbearing began. Moreover, most female workers, like most male workers, were neither highly skilled nor highly paid. Thus, it simply cannot be assumed that the combined incomes of two equally paid full-time workers would have generated enough income to allow them to purchase acceptable substitutes for the mother's reproductive labor. Far more than equal pay would have been necessary in order to construct a non-patriarchal form for reproducing the working class.[53]

To argue that the sexual division of labor had a material base is not to say that either the precapitalist ideology of the patriarchal family or the "dual spheres" ideology of the bourgeoisie had no role in the construction of the family-household system within the working class.

It is also not to deny that men had a material interest in a family where men retained control over women and children, were given respect and power, and where men's needs came first. But working-class men did not have the means to impose this form of household over the opposition of women. Nor are we satisfied to explain the ascendance of the family-household ideal as "false consciousness" within the working class. Rather, given the historical conditions under which the system emerged, the forces and relations of capitalist production imparted a coercive charge to biological reproduction. Where pressures on the wage level of the working class were great, where the low level of development of the forces of production made domestic work exhausting and time-consuming, and where the proletariat struggled just to eke out survival, the necessity for women to bear and nurse children seriously constrained the alternatives open to the working class for organizing its reproduction.

The Class Basis of High Fertility

It may be asked, of course, whether women had any choice but to have many pregnancies and many children. The techniques available for contraception throughout the eighteenth and nineteenth centuries— primarily abstinence and coitus interruptus—were not highly reliable. Interfering with sexual activity and requiring the cooperation of men, these techniques were difficult to practice except under tremendous pressure. However, they were effective enough to allow American women to cut their birthrate in half over the course of the nineteenth century.[54] Nonetheless, up until the 1920s American women continued to have large numbers of children, and fertility rates among immigrant and working-class families remained high. For the cohort of mothers born in 1890, 43.5 percent had four or more children, 60 percent had three or more.[55] In 1910 native-born married women had 3.4 children on average, while immigrant women had 4.2.[56] Working-class fertility appears to have remained high through the nineteenth century in France and England as well.[57] After 1920, without any substantial increase in the use of newer birth-control mechanisms, American fertility rates were sharply reduced. Therefore, to understand why women did not limit the number of years in which they were bearing and nursing children, we have to take into account not only the inadequacy of birth-control techniques but also how high fertility fitted into an overall strategy for survival within the working class.

Studies of fertility in relation to economic change have shown that opportunities for young couples to find work, or land in the rural economy, and the usefulness of child labor point in the direction of large families. The possibility of establishing a household independent of one's parents early in life encourages earlier marriage. The demand for child labor depresses the incentive to practice birth control during the early years of marriage. Together these factors produce high fertility levels. This pattern was especially typical of domestic industry.[58] The same argument that has been used to explain the greater fertility and family size associated with proto-industrialization can be applied to the nineteenth-century working class. Opportunities for wage work for both men and women allowed young couples to set up house at an early age. Probably even more important in determining high fertility rates, however, was the value of child labor combined with the very high levels of infant and child mortality that prevailed in many urban quarters throughout the nineteenth and even into the twentieth century.[59] While the utility of very young child labor declined by the end the nineteenth century, it seems that the labor of older children and teenagers remained an important source of family income well into the twentieth century.[60] In the absence of social security or pension systems, teenagers' wages provided crucial old-age security, perhaps allowing the parents to accumulate savings or property.[61] Since it was necessary for the family to have a large number of surviving children, and since infant and child mortality rates were high, there was little reason for couples to limit the number of births.

Sexual Division of Labor and Wage Differentials in Capitalist Production

Barrett contends that women's low wages and the uneven distribution of women in certain segments of the labor force cannot be explained without reference to a precapitalist sexual division of labor and a concomitant ideology of women's work. From the beginning men, as employers and co-workers, have accepted women only in jobs which correspond to familial roles. "Occupations such as charring, domestic service, spinning, weaving, millinery and so on were very common for women, while their major engagement in factory and mining work lasted only for a short while."[62] Capitalist competition and the drive for capital accumulation, she argues, produced the sexual division of labor, for example, by skill, but these fundamental processes did not construct a *sexual* division in which women were the less skilled workers and some skills are defined as male, some as female. Moreover, Barrett argues, the category of skilled work itself is ideological. Whether a particular trade is recognized as "skilled work" and is paid accordingly depends on its members' ability to insist on that differential. Thus female work, though not always less skilled, is always lower paid than male work because female skills are culturally devalued. Barrett concludes that "because the wage-labour relation and the contradiction between labour and capital ... are 'sex-blind' and operate quite independently of gender,"[63] the gender division of labor can only be explained in terms of a historical development in which precapitalist ideology crucially conditioned the outcome: men reserved certain kinds of highly paid work for themselves and accepted women only in those jobs that reflected and reinforced their domesticity.

In our view, however, it is both possible and preferable to explain the origins and reproduction of sex segregation in the occupational structure precisely in terms of the "sex-blind" operation of the capitalist labor market, in which capitalists compete to hire labor for the least cost and workers search for the highest-paid work available. Sex-segregation of jobs and low female wages are intimately connected. Both have their roots in the barriers women face in defending their pay and working conditions. Women are disadvantaged on the labor market because of their family responsibilities. Women's skills are less "valued" not because of an ideological devaluation of women, but because women are less likely to be unionized, less mobile in making job searches, more constrained in general by their domestic duties.

Barrett argues that "the entire history of women's work, including their function as cheap substitutes for male labor, rests on the fact that from the earliest years of capitalist production it has been possible to insist on this differential. This discrepancy can be related to ideological definitions of the basic element of food consumption."[64] From the precapitalist division of labor within the home, it was assumed not only that women needed less food and could subsist on lower wages, but also that they often sacrificed their own needs to those of husbands and children. This ideology of women's sacrifice allowed employers to pay women less.

In our view, ideology concerning women's lower costs of reproduction may have encouraged employers to pay women less and may have made it more difficult for women to organize themselves to demand more. But all else being equal, ideology alone could not have forced women to accept lower wages. Of course, all else was not equal—women's intermittent participation in waged labor, the supplementary character of their wage earning, their ultimate destination as wives and mothers, distinguished them from men. If we remember which women were working and why, we can see how women could be utilized as cheap competitors with men. Adult women workers usually had children to support, were widows or married to men with unstable incomes. These women constituted a particularly defenseless and desperate labor pool. Their home burdens made it difficult for them to find the time or energy to organize; their lack of mobility made it difficult for them to search for better work.[65]

The other group of working women, young women living in the parental home, did not face the same constraints. And it is clear from the history of female unionization that young single women were the backbone of the union organization that did take place.[66] Where young single women made up the majority of the workforce, the chances of organized struggle were improved. There were cultural and ideological barriers which hindered women from defending themselves, but these were often overcome. Nonetheless, on the whole, because young women were usually living at home and could expect to remain working for only a short period of their lives, they were also more easily exploited and less motivated to defend their skills or to learn the higher-paying skills which required a fight to break into male industries.

Knowing that she was likely to leave work once married, and having opportunities for steady albeit lower-paid "women's work," a young woman might have been reluctant to make the kind of fight required to enter and remain in skilled male work. Many working-class daughters may have preferred the feminine support of the garment factory to the hostility of the printshop. And, given that women's wages were quite low even when they did factory work, young women might have reasonably chosen the new jobs in retailing and clerical work which did not pay enough to attract men.

Underlying the sex-segregation of jobs, then, are the material difficulties women face in striking a wage bargain with their employers. These difficulties are fundamentally related in turn to the sexual division of labor within the family, itself conditioned by women's role in biological reproduction. The place of ideology in this determination is secondary. Barrett contends that the ideological origins of sex-segregation are evidenced in the fact that women's jobs replicate their domestic pursuits. This, however, puts the cart before the horse. Historically, the sex-typing of jobs has been fairly flexible. Weaving and spinning were male and female respectively in domestic industry, but in the factories mule-spinning became a male job, powerloom weaving a female job. Two of the most important fields for women's waged work today—teaching and office work—were originally male jobs. On the other hand, medicine was largely women's work and became an exclusively male profession in the course of the eighteenth century. In the sexual changeover, the character of the jobs also changed. Medicine was redefined as a "science"; the secretary became a handmaiden instead of an administrative assistant. But these changes followed rather than preceded the change from one sex to the other.

In all the instances of feminization, the availability of women as cheap workers and men's inability or disinclination to defend their jobs were key elements. For example, in the United States in 1840, 60 percent of schoolteachers were men, but by 1860 only 14 percent were men.[67] The redefinition of the schoolteacher as a substitute mother for young children paralleled the increasing emphasis on the mother's moral training in child development. But the major motivation for the feminization of teaching was economic. As one contemporary observed: "It is true that sentimental reasons are often given for the almost exclusive employment of women in the common schools; but the effective reason is economy.... If women had not been cheaper than men, they would not have replaced nine-tenths of the men in American public schools."[68]

The history of the textile workforce in New England provides another example. The first factory hands were young, single farm women recruited when male labor was scarce and expensive. As the female operatives became leading militants and organizers in the 1830s and 1840s, the employers turned to Irish men and their families to replace the women. In the immigrants employers found large numbers of men and boys willing to work for "women's wages."[69] The low wages and poor working conditions of the industry ultimately forced the farm girls out, following the failure of their organizing efforts. Unlike the Irish men and their children, the Yankee women had options: to return to their family farms, or to enter new fields then opening up. During the mid-nineteenth century, at the same time that immigrant men were replacing women in the cotton mills, women were replacing native-born men in teaching.[70]

Many jobs that are "women's work," such as charring and dress-making, were taken up because they could more easily be combined with family responsibilities than could factory work. They remained female not because of their connection to domesticity, but because they were also among the lowest-paid jobs. Men do janitorial work where it pays a competitive wage. Female jobs have tended to stay female because they are low-paid; once a female job begins to pay relatively high wages, it also begins to attract male labor—for example, work in nursing or libraries.[71]

In sum, whereas Barrett argues that a precapitalist ideology of female dependence played a major role in determining the family-household system, we suggest that biological facts of reproduction conditioned the sexual division of labor. Because factory production in particular, and capitalist production in general, could not accommodate childbearing and early nurturing, married women were forced to seek more marginal, lower-paying kinds of work. Already in the 1830s and 1840s—the crucial period when, according to Barrett, class struggle shaped the sexual division of labor—few married women were working in anything other than the most marginal forms of waged work.

The formation of the family-household system must be viewed within this context. Given that a sexual division of labor and wage differentials favoring men already existed, the most logical and indeed only real alternative for resolving the crisis of working-class reproduction was the family-household system. For any meaningful alternative would have demanded the wresting of substantial concessions from the capitalist class, concessions they could not afford to make. In any case, the working class was in no position to win them, given the balance of class forces prevailing during the period.

This resolution was tragic for women because it made possible the continuation of female dependence and subordination. Insofar as it amplified the tendency for women to be placed in a precarious position in the labor market, it increased the power imbalance between men and women, allowing men to exert control over women's sexuality, to shift a major portion of the burden of domestic labor onto women, and to make unreciprocated emotional demands.

The Family-Household System in the Twentieth Century

While the nineteenth century saw the emergence and consolidation of the family-household system, the twentieth century, especially after the Second World War, witnessed a very different trend—the disappearance of the full-time housewife. This is a consequence of one side of capitalist development. The drive to accumulate pulls married women into wage labor by increasing the demand for women workers, as production expands faster than the labor supply (in, for example, clerical work after the Second World War), and by increasing the supply of women able to work. Increased productivity of capital allowed for higher working-class incomes without jeopardizing accumulation. Through struggle over the social and the private wage, the working class captured some of the benefits of their higher productivity. In turn, social security, pensions, improved health, and so on, encouraged lower marital fertility, both by decreasing infant mortality and by increasing old-age security, thereby decreasing the parents' need for their children's labor.

Correlatively, in the search for new markets, capital commodified reproduction and expanded the array of goods and services available and necessary for an acceptable standard of living. By cheapening commodities used in domestic production and lowering fertility, capitalist development has reduced the domestic labor time necessary for reproduction, allowing women to work at two jobs.[72] Women have been brought back into wage labor to replace their teenage children as the major source of income required to supplement the male wage.[73] This change has laid the basis for the re-emergence of feminism and a challenge to the traditional family. On the other hand, the incorporation of women into wage labor on an equal basis with men has been limited by their continued responsibility for childrearing. In the U.S., for example, only 15 percent of married women with children under six work full-time, and only 27 percent of married women with school-age children work full-time, compared to 48 percent of married women without children.[74] The number of years in which women work full-time is still conditioned by the number of children they have. As women have fewer children, they have more available years to work, but, unless they have no children and therefore no responsibility for childcare, their wages will be lower than men's. So long as women earn less than their husbands, they will be less able to force men to take equal responsibility for family care, reinforcing their inequality in the labor market.[75]

In the nineteenth century, the assignment of women to domestic labor was biologically determined. But how can we account for it today, when women have few children and there are alternatives to maternal childcare?

While the capitalist development of the forces of production tends to undermine the family-household system by pulling women into wage labor, capitalist class relations set up a counter-tendency reinforcing the sexual division of labor. This is not, as Barrett argues, because gender divisions are "embedded" in capitalist relations of production. It is because one consistent tendency of the capitalism system is to reduce working-class living standards and to force working people to accomplish the labor necessary for their reproduction in their "own" time. The amount of this labor depends on how high wages are relative to services available on the market. This relationship is partly a matter of the development of the forces of production—increasing efficiency and lowered costs of prepared meals and foods, household appliances, domestic services such as laundry.[76] However, while sufficient for reproducing adult labor, capitalist methods of cheapening production are generally inappropriate to the care of people. Adequate substitutes for family care through the market have to be labor-intensive and therefore relatively expensive.[77]

To provide quality childcare and to allow parents to organize their work around the demands of childrearing—flexitime, infant care at the worksite, parenting leave, after-school care, paid time off for family responsibilities—would represent a substantial increase in the wage bill. The amount of necessary labor workers have to perform in addition to waged work, therefore, will also depend on the class struggle: on whether the working class can force capitalists to underwrite the labor involved in childrearing (and incidentally, the care of older people, the sick, disabled, etc.) by raising the social or the private wage, or both. Up to now, even in the most advanced capitalist economies, the working class has not been able to achieve such gains.

Because individual families have to take responsibility for their dependent members, and because for most families even two incomes are not sufficient to purchase adequate substitutes on the market, a substantial amount of work remains to be done within the household. In this context, the traditional sexual division of labor retains its force. This is partly an effect of gender ideology (the apparently natural connection between women and children) and socialization—even today women will be more likely to have the necessary skills. But in addition to this cultural and psychological inheritance, present economic realities force women into the mother role. Women earn less than men. Recurrent economic crises intensify the uncertainty facing working people even in good times. With secure and high-paying employment always in short supply, it is important for families to protect the higher paying job. If one person has to stay home or organize their work around children's needs, it is in the interest of both wife and husband that she, not he, subordinates wage work to home responsibilities.[78]

The capitalist drive for profit creates the conditions under which men and women negotiate the division of labor within the household. In this process men have an incentive to protect their traditional family roles, which, however burdensome, also confer important privileges. For men to share childcare and housework equally would substantially decrease their (already small) leisure time, since domestic work has be done along with a normal work day. Moreover, men have a claim on their wives' emotional support, respect, deference, and sexuality while the family-household system sustains a more generalized sexist culture in which even working-class men enjoy rights to social honor and respect that women do not have. It is hardly surprising, then, that even when their wives work, husbands do not expand their domestic labor. The traditional ideology ("domestic life is her responsibility") strengthens men's position and undermines women in the conflict over who will have how much free time. But this ideology is underpinned by the reality that even when she works, he makes more money and she cannot afford to push him too hard. If the marriage breaks up she will end up financially worse off.[79]

Ultimately, then, the "sex-blind" operations of the relations of capitalist production create the framework within which the working class organizes its reproduction. The decisions to have children at all, how many children to have, how to care for them, how to define their needs, are neither purely economic nor purely instrumental. On the other hand, they are not exclusively cultural or ideological. In constructing a life, in developing a strategy for survival, working-class people make choices, both individually and collectively, which have to take into account the material constraints shaped by capitalist class power.

The sexual division of labor still has a logic. But the complex of forces pressing women into their domestic role is far more contingent today than in the nineteenth century. A minority of women have already been able to break out of the vicious cycle in which home responsibilities reinforce low wages and vice versa. These women have reaped the gains of the feminist movement to enter professional/managerial jobs with high incomes. Their higher incomes allow them to challenge traditional roles, especially because they have less to fear from being on their own. On the other hand, they can compete with men because their high incomes allow them to buy out of their domestic responsibilities. These women have resolved the problem on an individual basis—but the majority of women cannot. For them, a breakthrough depends on collective struggle: the self-organization of women within the working-class movement to change the conditions of daily life so that they can take men on inside the family. This means primarily changing the organization of reproduction by expanding collective responsibility for dependent people, especially children. Reducing the individual household's responsibility depends on the class struggle and the capacity of the feminist movement to organize within that struggle to ensure that childcare, paid parental leave, and so forth, would be demands.

These gains may be difficult to win in a recession. Recessions do draw more women into work, increasing their potential for self-organization. But recessions also intensify the material pressures that reinforce the sexual division of labor. Women pay high penalties when they work, simply in order to maintain the family's previous standard of living. Their income is required to buy the same wage goods as before, so they can't afford market services to substitute for their own domestic labor. Employers have no reason to make concessions such as childcare, since female labor is oversupplied as more wives are forced to seek work. State service-cuts further increase the pressure on the household. The capitalist response to contraction—to attack the working-class standard of living—puts distinct limits on how far working-class families can reorganize the division of labor within the household by aggravating the dynamics which created the rationale for the traditional division of labor in the first place. The more desperate women are to work, the more burdened they are by home responsibilities, the more difficult it is for them to organize against their employers, and the more intractable income inequalities between men and women remain.

Moreover, in a contracting economy, the qualitative changes that would solve the problem collectively by relieving the family of care for dependants could be gained only at the expense of capitalist profitability—and they will therefore meet consistent resistance from employers. On the other hand, feminist organization can make a difference to the demands raised by social movements and substantially shift the terrain of the class struggle. But it is unlikely that the movement will actually win these demands, short of revolution.

Should the capitalist system manage to survive the crisis, renewed prosperity may open the way for significant gains. An expanding economy allows the capitalist class greater flexibility in responding to working-class movements, and therefore creates the conditions under which, through struggle, the working class can go beyond the family-household system. While the cyclical return of depressions may limit how far this tendency can go, we cannot foreclose the possibility of significant changes in the way reproduction is carried out and of a long-term development toward sexual equalization within capitalism.

Women and the Welfare State

Barrett argues that the capitalist state "props up" the family-household system through its welfare provision, protective legislation, and other avenues of state regulation. Left to itself, the private economy tends to deprive the working class—or at least broad sections of it—of the means to establish the male breadwinner/female housewife family. By providing a material base for the working class to adopt the middle-class form of the family, the welfare state allowed the bourgeoisie to "hegemonize the working-class family under its own rubric" and helped "forge a major link in the chain of women's dependence."[80]

State welfare policies assume a male breadwinner and male responsibility for wife and child, thereby encouraging women to rely on men economically and reinforcing the bourgeois ideal of the family within the working class, Barrett contends. For example, in England a wife's unemployment benefit covers only herself, while her husband's is raised above that of the single man to take account of wife and children. The family income supplement for low wage earners is available only where the husband, not the wife, is in full-time, low-paid work. As Mary McIntosh argues, "policies like this make it unwise for a couple to rely too heavily on the wife's income." Similarly, "provisions like widow's pensions ... make it less necessary for a wife to be able to support herself alone."[81]

We find this approach to the welfare state, the dominant one in the Marxist-feminist literature, entirely unconvincing. In the first place, the legislation and programs which Barrett and others[82] see as the basis for the "male breadwinner" family form did not develop until after the Second World War. Yet large sections of the working class had organized households around a dependent housewife long before this. In only the most abjectly poor and insecure working-class families did wives go out to full-time wage work.

Second, Barrett lays far too much stress on state policies which reinforce women's dependence on men and ignores the contradictory trend within the welfare state toward social responsibility for children and other dependants, freeing women who would otherwise shoulder the burden. Barrett is right that income maintenance programs are regarded as temporary substitutes for, or supplements to, the husband's wage. It is assumed that the mother will stay at home to take care of the children, and that intact families rely primarily on the man's wage. On the other hand, during its rapid expansion in the 1950s and 1960s the welfare state developed services to care for dependent adults and, to a lesser extent, children outside the family—mental hospitals, convalescent hospitals, pensions and retirement homes for the elderly, pre-school and after-school programs such as Headstart in the U.S.

If we compare welfare legislation before and after the Second World War, we see not a firmer location of responsibility for dependants within the family, but a halting, grudgingly given movement toward the narrowing of familial responsibility. Most important, we see in the postwar years the extension of state support to husbandless mothers—a benefit which is justified on the grounds of women's special responsibility for children, but one which in fact makes women far less dependent on men than they have previously been.

In England, for example, the state's reluctance to relieve the family of its responsibility for dependants was clearly evident in prewar welfare policies. The Poor Law Act of 1927 mandated: "It shall be the duty of the father, grandfather, mother, grandmother, husband or child of the poor, old, blind, lame, or impotent person or other person not able to work if possessed of sufficient means, to relieve and maintain such a person."[83] On the other hand, since 1948 financial dependence has been assumed solely between husband and wife and parents and minor children. Children are no longer legally required to support their elderly parents, and parents are not responsible for their incapacitated adult children.

So, far from reinforcing the male breadwinner family, some early welfare provisions refused to recognize that men *had* dependants. The National Insurance Act of 1911 provided sickness and unemployment benefit only for the male worker and not for his wife or children. Today in England, benefits make allowance for a man's, though not a married woman's, dependants.[84] Did the prewar policies encourage female independence? Or did they simply further impoverish working-class women's lives?

Similarly, it makes little sense to argue that widow's pensions encourage women to rely on men rather than prepare to be self-supporting. Widow's pensions were demanded to meet the needs of older women and women with children who already could not support themselves. In the U.S. at the turn of the century, roughly one out of every five husbands was dead before the age of forty-five.[85] Yet, also at this time, the vast majority of working-class wives did not work for wages outside their homes. Prior to the development of pensions, women were not more likely to be "self-sufficient," but widows were more impoverished, more insecure, more burdened.

Despite the obvious need of abandoned women with children, before the Second World War both British and U.S. governments were very reluctant to provide adequate support. Generally, opponents argued in terms of the need to prevent desertion and to force men to shoulder their responsibilities. But it should be remembered that, rhetoric notwithstanding, full support for women with children would have been expensive, and governments no doubt feared that deserted women and children would become permanent burdens on the community instead of on the men in their families—brothers, fathers, uncles, and so on.[86] A 1909 Commission on the Poor Laws reported that "relatively low relief is granted and the mother is expected to earn something in addition."[87] In the U.S. also, husbandless women with children received meager assistance or none. Aid to Dependent Children, established in New Deal legislation in 1934, paid benefits to children but not support to mothers. Even so, it was hedged with so many eligibility restrictions that it was available only to a small minority of the women in need.[88] Again, did these policies encourage women to remain on their own? Or would they not have made women even more anxious to find another male breadwinner?

In contrast since the Second World War, the trend in both the U.S. and Britain has been to provide a minimal state subsistence allowing mothers of young children to stay home. Benefits are inadequate but they do tend to reduce women's dependence on men.[89]

Finally, Barrett's approach to the relationship between the welfare state and the family gives too much weight to functionalist and conspiratorial views. It contradicts her own conclusion that the state is a "site of struggle."[90] Neither Barrett nor the major sources on which she bases her claim that the bourgeoisie had a pressing political interest in remaking the working-class family in its own image[91] demonstrate that welfare reforms which helped the working class to maintain its families originated with, or found widespread political support within, capitalist circles. The common contention that advanced elements of the bourgeoisie supported the welfare state in order to guarantee the reproduction of the working class (Hartmann) or render it conservative and divide it remains substantially unproved. It must be shown not only that some individuals spoke of the need for the state to step in—this is the bulk of the "evidence" to date—but also that they envisioned something other than a meager supplement, grudgingly given, which they were willing to grant in the absence of a serious working-class political challenge. Confronted with the alternative of a potentially revolutionary working-class movement, some capitalists *were* willing to support some welfarist concessions—hardly proof that capitalists wanted or preferred such policies for the achievement of their own economic or political aims.

The welfare state is a major arena of class struggle, within limits imposed by capitalist relations of production. Those limits can accommodate substantial reforms. However, these reforms have not been handed down from above as part of a strategy to impose the bourgeois family form on the working class. Welfare state policies have been achieved as political concessions to working-class movements and middle-class reformers. On the other hand, to regard the welfare state as a direct expression of working-class needs would be to ignore the constraints within which reform movements have operated. It is obviously beyond the scope of this article to show precisely how different social forces interacted to shape the modern welfare state. But it is necessary to emphasize that, despite important gains in the most advanced capitalist societies, welfare provisions have been hedged with restrictions and only establish a bare subsistence floor for working-class living.

As political outcomes, state policies have necessarily reflected the balance of power, not only between classes, but between men and women in the working class. Insofar as state policies aim to shore up rather than substitute for the family-household system, this is, in part, because men have been better organized within the working-class movement. Men's point of view, men's needs, and men's assessment of priority demands have dominated the struggle: for example, state-supported quality childcare at the bottom of the agenda, high wages for men at the top. But more fundamentally, we would argue, the capitalist class has consistently resisted expanding state responsibility for children and other dependent persons. While recognizing the need to provide for the poor in order to retain legitimacy and to control the lower orders, the ruling class is also quite concerned to maintain work incentives. State subsidy above a bare minimum threatens to draw the sting of unemployment and undermine labor discipline. Protection of capitalist accumulation demands, therefore, a welfare policy that is cheap (does not cut into profits) and minimal (does not undercut the necessity to labor).[92]

Middle-class reformers, always anxious to defend their programs in terms of the long-run needs of the capitalist system, often spoke as representatives of the capitalist class, but we should not confuse them with their rulers. The reformers' vision of the welfare state, often elitist and technocratic, sought through education and the conditional provision of support to encourage the working-class family to achieve the "male breadwinner/female housewife" standard. Like the reformist labor leaders who emphasized that they were not denying the employers' property rights but asking for the workers' fair share, middle-class reformers affirmed the bourgeois ideals of self-reliance and the work ethic at the same time as they insisted that individuals had a claim on the community, when they were in need, due to forces beyond their control.[93] Despite these assurances, the capitalist class remained substantially unmoved: in both England and the U.S. through the interwar years, the working-class family and the women in it continued to bear the burden of dependants unaided by the state.

In the face of this array of forces, we can understand how the demand for the family wage and for a welfare policy supplementing rather than replacing the family as the primary site for the care of dependants might have arisen within the working class. State services have always been seriously underfunded and understaffed, and therefore of poor quality, bureaucratic, and inaccessible to their clients. As a result, working-class people have had a fundamentally ambivalent attitude toward state substitutes for home care. Moreover, because a thoroughly socialized system of care is enormously expensive and apparently out of reach, a welfare program which substitutes for the family only temporarily appears to be a more realistic and pragmatic goal—and one that can win support from middle-class allies.

We do not wish to deny that broader ideological assumptions affected the direction of reform demands. The bourgeois ideal of individual self-reliance and the patriarchal ideal of the male breadwinner surely informed many working people's vision of the good life. Nonetheless, we would also contend that the strength of these ideals can only be accounted for in the context of the social and political forces that marginalized alternative visions—most particularly the circumstances in which very militant and generalized working-class struggles were necessary to make even small gains toward state support for the reproduction of the working class. In the face of this consistent resistance, the working class, including working-class women, has been forced to choose *not* between programs that acknowledge community responsibility for all dependent people and those that merely supplement a system of privatized familial care, but between a welfare state that assumes the male-breadwinner family and no state help at all.

The Role of Gender Ideology

The crux of Barrett's analysis is that the development of women's oppression in capitalism must ultimately be laid at the door of ideology. The ideology of gender, quite simply put, shaped capitalist social relations of production. Barrett makes this clear in a number of passages. For example, writing of protective legislation:

> Protective legislation represented a material defeat of the interests of working women and, furthermore, a defeat that is not simply explicable in terms of a proposed logic of capitalist development. It involved an assumption, shared by the labour movement among others, that the relegation of women to domesticity and childcare was natural and desirable. In this respect the eventual outcome was the product of an ideology of gender division that was incorporated into the capitalist division of labor rather than generated by it.[94]

As we suggested earlier, gender ideology is Barrett's *deus ex machina*, her means of escape from the vexing dilemma of the Marxist–reductionist/dual systems–idealist impasse of socialist feminist thought. However, to give gender ideology so determining a role without slipping into an idealist formulation requires that certain questions be answered. What, for example, is the relationship between this ideology and others? Is it alone so autonomous and determining, or do all ideologies have this capacity? How is gender ideology produced and reproduced, and what allows its autonomy? What, if anything, is the material basis of gender ideology?

Barrett attempts answers to some of these questions, but, in our view, with little success. She suggests that gender identity is created "in an ideology of family life" rather than within actual concrete families, and is "continually recreated and endorsed, modified or even altered substantially, through a process of ideological representation."[95] But how exactly one appropriates gender identity and how it is reinforced or transformed in adult life, remain untheorized. Barrett argues that gender ideology is culturally reproduced through mechanisms of stereotyping, compensation, collusion, and recuperation.[96] But where exactly these mechanisms are located, why they occur, and how they affect the process by which individuals develop a gender identity, remain unclear.

Ultimately, Barrett treats the appropriation of gender ideology as the relatively passive internalization of an already defined set of ideas about men and women that exists at the level of "culture." This seems clear in her explanation of the adoption of "familial ideology," by the working class. She argues that this ideology has little connection to actual social relations. "Familial ideology" is at odds with the working class household structure in which women provide necessary income; moreover, "familial ideology" serves no individual interests—that is, holding such ideas meets no one's needs.[97] In this approach, ideology can only be conceived as a mysterious, powerful, unchanging phenomenon—one that imposes itself upon individuals who accept it passively and for reasons that are really not very clear.

In our view, ideology and consciousness are processes in which individuals actively, creatively, engage. The "imaginary relationship of individuals to their real conditions of existence" is the work of human creativity.[98] Thus we would argue that gender ideology, like all ideology, is rooted in and shaped by women's and men's actual experience and practice in everyday life. We agree with Barrett that the relationship between experience and consciousness, between social relations and ideology, is not an unmediated one. To define the relative autonomy of ideology is precisely to decipher these mediations. However, such explorations must be placed within a general framework of levels of determination—of the limits to "autonomy"—if we are not to risk granting powers to ideology that we did not originally intend. One way to understand these levels of determination is to place the creative process of ideological construction within historically defined limits. Historically developed social relations construct the possibilities within which women and men imagine and order their existence.

For example, the determined nature of the sexual division of labor and the family-household system in the nineteenth and early twentieth centuries entailed that the ideas of "male breadwinner"–"female childrearer/dependant" (the key components in Barrett's "familial ideology") were not really negotiable. These ideas retained their force precisely because they were underpinned by an inescapable social reality. Because the family-household system imposed itself on individuals with unrelenting logic, women and men had to take these social relationships into account when forming their ideas about themselves and their world. This was true not only for the bourgeoisie but also for the working class.

However, the very intricate, complex web of ideas constituting gender ideology that was in continual process of definition and redefinition during the nineteenth century cannot be explained solely by reference to necessary social relations. This is easily seen in the case of nineteenth-century bourgeois gender ideology. Many excellent works in middle-class women's history have recently been written by feminist historians who argue that the bourgeois ideology of domesticity was not simply imposed upon women but was in good part shaped by women themselves. In this way they created a world view, out of circumstances not of their choosing, that explained their experience and was forged by their needs. For example, in her interesting essay on the origins of the Victorian sexual ideology of female "passionlessness," Nancy Cott argues that this notion, initially tied to the rise of evangelical religion, was pivotal in the transformation of the female image from sexual to moral being, and was embraced and further developed by women because it allowed for the construction of an improved view of women's character and social purpose.[99] This idea was, of course, just one element in a cluster of related ideas, loosely defined as the ideology of domesticity, that legitimized a host of varied social campaigns by middle-class women in the nineteenth century. These ideas, rather than merely reflecting social reality, helped to transform it by widening bourgeois women's spheres of influence and activity. In this sense, the creation of gender ideology is a continual social, political act.[100]

However, this formidable creativity always rested upon the bedrock of a seemingly inescapable sexual division of labor. During the nineteenth century, feminists and anti-feminists alike accepted the notion of "dual spheres"; feminists based their demands for greater social and familial power in part on the importance of women's domestic/mothering role. Nineteenth-century feminists could not escape the seeming inevitability of domesticity. Only in the twentieth century did feminists really begin to challenge the sexual division of labour—particularly in childrearing and domestic labor. But then again, only in this century has the possibility of transforming the sexual division of labor become real.

Conclusion

We have argued that historically developed capitalist class relations of production, in combination with the biological facts of reproduction, set up a powerful dynamic toward the family-household system, assuring women's continued subordination to men and their exaggerated vulnerability to capitalist exploitation. While emphasizing that women's oppression in capitalism emerged from the confrontation between the demands of capitalist accumulation and the structures of human reproduction, our analysis nevertheless places the self-organization of women and the development of a working class women's movement at its center. For while capitalist development in the twentieth century has laid the basis for alternatives to the family-household system, the implementation of these requires political struggle. Capitalist class relations, especially the drive for profit, will continue to push in the direction of privatizing reproduction and forcing the working class family to shoulder responsibility for its dependants. It is this tendency, and the inability of the working class thus far to counter it significantly, that underlies the persistence of the sexual division of labor and gender inequality.

Thus, gender divisions are not so much embedded in the capitalist division of labor or relations of production, as produced by a complex balance of forces at a given point in the history of capitalism. Most crucial among these are the development of the forces of production, the organization of the working class, the self-organization of women, the state of the economy. Any significant alteration in working class women's position requires the expansion of collective responsibility for dependants—especially children. Because the current system benefits men, at least in the short run, a change depends upon the capacity of the feminist movement to shape working-class struggle to include such a vision. Thus it appears to us that Marx and Engels were correct about a tendency toward sexual equalization with capitalism. Of course, sexual equality within capitalism is not the same as women's liberation; that would require the transcendence of capitalism. Nor do we contend that equalization is an inevitable consequence of capitalist development. Rather, we view capitalism as a dynamic system, changing the conditions of daily life and making possible new forms of struggle and consciousness. The outcome of its history, and ours, will be shaped by political struggle for which we need to understand its contradictory tendencies.

[1984]

Notes

1. Michèle Barrett, *Women's Oppression Today* (London, 1980).
2. Ibid., 249.
3. Ibid., 254–55.
4. Ibid.
5. Ibid.

6. Ibid., 217.
7. Ibid., 222–23.
8. Ibid., 226.
9. Unfortunately, Barrett and McIntosh do not do this in their collaboration, *The Anti-social Family* (London, 1982).
10. Heidi Hartmann, "The Unhappy Marriage of Marxism and Feminism: Towards a More Progressive Union," *Capital and Class*, Summer 1979; Heidi Hartmann, "Capitalism, Patriarchy and Job Segregation by Sex," Zillah R. Eisenstein, ed., *Capitalist Patriarchy and the Case for Socialist Feminism* (New York, 1979). Also Sally Alexander, "Women's Work in Nineteenth-Century London," in Juliet Mitchell and Ann Oakley, eds., *The Rights and Wrongs of Women* (Harmondsworth, 1976); Alice Kessler-Harris, "Where Are the Organized Women Workers?", in Nancy F. Cott and Elizabeth Pleck, eds., *A Heritage of Her Own* (New York, 1979).
11. Judith A. Baer, *The Chains of Protection* (Westport, Conn., 1978), 30–32; Elizabeth Faulkner Baker, *Protective Labor Legislation* (New York, 1925).
12. Baer, *The Chains of Protection*, 30.
13. New York State is perhaps a typical case. New York first made provisions for factory inspectors in 1886. In 1911, a state investigative committee found the enforcement of protective legislation to be entirely inadequate. The committee's findings had little impact on improving enforcement, however. As late as 1921–1922, the New York Labor Department had only forty-three inspectors for 35,000 factories, And even when these identified offenders, the punishment was light. Between 1915 and 1923, an estimated 50–70 percent of cases brought before the New York court went unfined, and in cases where fines were meted out, they were generally too small to have any impact. Baer, *The Chains of Protection*, 285, 289, 296, 297, 304, 312–33, 314, 315, 339.
14. For a summary of factory legislation during the nineteenth century, see B. L. Hutchins and A. Harrison, *A History of Factory Legislation* (London, 1903).
15. Ibid.; J. T. Ward, *The Factory Movement, 1830–1855* (London, 1962).
16. Hutchins and Harrison, *A History of Factory Legislation*, 110. Norbert C. Soldon, *Women in British Trade Unions, 1874–1976* (Dublin, 1978), cites statistics indicating that the ratio of women to men in the textile industries increased over the second half of the nineteenth century from 131:100 in 1861 and 148:100 in 1871, to 164:100 in 1881.
17. Hutchins and Harrison, *A History of Factory Legislation*, 197–98, 174, 193. Also see Barbara Drake, *Women and Trade Unions*, Labour Research Department, Trade Union Series No. 6 (London, 1920). The 1842 Mines Regulation Act, prohibiting women from underground labor in the mines, did take away jobs for women. However, these were almost exclusively confined to the unskilled and low-paid job of carrying coal from the pit to the surface. Women almost never did the skilled work of hewing. See Jane Humphries, "Protective Legislation, the Capitalist State, and Working-Class Men: The Case of the 1842 Mines Regulation Act," *Feminist Review* 17 (Spring 1981), 10. It is not clear precisely what impact the restriction on nightwork had on women's labor opportunities. It does not appear to have displaced women in the printing trades in Britain, however, as most female compositors worked in shops which prepared weekly or biweekly journals, where nightwork was not the rule. J. R. Ramsay MacDonald, *Women in the Printing Trades* (London, 1904), 75.

18. Hutchins and Harrison, *A History of Protective Legislation*.
19. For example, in 1818 the Operative Cotton Spinners of Manchester petitioned Parliament for a universal 10½ hour day with nine hours of actual work. Hutchins and Harrison, *A History of Protective Legislation*, 43–44. In 1831, when workers' short-time committees were taking the first steps towards forming an alliance with Oastler and other middle-class reformers to agitate for the regulation of child labor reform, the Lancashire Trades Unions were campaigning for a short-time bill for all classes of workers in all trades. Sidney and Beatrice Webb, *History of Trade Unionism* (London, 1950), 123. In their public rallies and demonstrations, operatives continually demanded an act that would directly or indirectly limit adult labor. See Hutchins and Harrison, *A History of Protective Legislation*. Also Cecil Driver's very interesting account, *Tory Radical: The Life of Richard Oastler* (New York, 1946).
20. Driver, *Tory Radical*.
21. J. T. Ward argues that the government bill was passed only to prevent a Ten Hours Bill that would have effectively limited adult as well as child labor. Ward, *The Factory Movement*, 115. Also see Ward's "The Factory Movement," in J. T. Ward, ed., *Popular Movements, 1830–1850* (London, 1970), 68.
22. Hutchins and Harrison, *A History of Protective Legislation*, pp. 60–61. From 1833 to 1855, the Short-Time Movement periodically attempted to win a restriction on motive power as the ultimate means for enforcing factory acts and limiting adult labor. All attempts were unsuccessful. Ward, "The Factory Movement," p. 68; Hutchins and Harrison, *A History of Protective Legislation*, 52, 104, 108–09, 110–12.
23. Both Ward and Hutchins and Harrison attribute the success of the Movement to a series of factors: the force of its organized campaign, Tory–Whig conflict, and the trade depression of 1847 which temporarily weakened the textile masters' resistance to the measure. With the return of favorable trade, manufacturers began to evade the Act through the use of relay systems, as well as to organize for its repeal. As a result, the Act was amended in 1855 to allow for 10½ hours' labor within a set working period, thus making evasions more difficult. The 10½ hour day remained in effect in the textile industries until 1874, when it was reduced to 10. See Ward, *The Factory Movement*.
24. Michèle Barrett and Mary McIntosh, "The Family Wage: Some Problems for Socialists and Feminists," *Capital and Class*, 11 (1980).
25. For example, in 1829 the Mechanics Union of Trade Associations of Philadelphia, the first central labor body in the United States, invited Francis Wright to deliver the Fourth of July Address. The address, on women's equality, was reprinted by the Associations and distributed to their workers. Particularly in the 1830s, several labor journals took a very progressive stance towards the issue of women's labor and women's rights—the *National Laborer* of Philadelphia, the New York *Daily Sentinel*, and *Working Man's Advocate* among them. One labor party in the 1830s, the Association of the Working People of New Castle, Delaware, even demanded enfranchisement for women. Philip Foner, *Women and the American Labor Movement* (New York, 1980), 51–52.
26. The same argument applies to dual systems accounts. While Barrett stresses the role of ideology in shaping male responses to women's employment, Hartmann, for example, emphasizes male material interests. Hartmann argues that the trade unions' decision "to exclude women rather than to organize

them is explained ... by patriarchal relations between men and women: men wanted to assure that women would continue to perform the appropriate tasks at home." Hartmann, "Capitalism, Patriarchy and Job Segregation by Sex," 219.

27. W. H. Fraser, "Trade Unionism," in Ward, ed., *Popular Movements*. Unions often utilized kinship and sometimes regional criteria to limit access to their trade. National conferences of cotton-spinners held on the Isle of Man in 1829 and at Manchester in 1830, for example, resolved that spinners were to be allowed to train only their own families and poor relations of mill owners. Glasgow spinners, on the other hand, attempted to prevent mobility by excluding those who had not started as a piecer in Glasgow. Fraser, "Trade Unionism," p. 97.

28. Barbara Taylor, *Eve and the New Jerusalem* (New York, 1983). Barrett cites this case as an example of how male trade unions organized to exclude women from high-paying skilled work. Interestingly, they overlook two of the most important points of Taylor's research: first, that the Tailors' Union was entirely unsuccessful in this attempt, and second, that the consequence of their failure was the destruction of the union and the degradation of their trade.

29. Quoted in Taylor, *Eve and the New Jerusalem*, 106.

30. Drake, *Women and Trade Unions*, 31–38.

31. Ibid., 4–6

32. Foner, *Women and the American Labor Movement*, 155. Printing unions, building trades, iron work, and shoemaking unions also supported the strike with financial donations.

33. In 1834 the men's cordwainers' union supported Lynn female shoemakers in their strike for higher wages. The union raised funds for the strike and boycotted manufacturers not supporting the strike. Foner, ibid., 47. In 1859–1860, male cordwainers and women shoebinders together created the famous strike of 20,000 in Lynn. Foner, ibid., 90.

34. Drake, *Women and Trade Unions*, 5.

35. Foner, *Women and the American Labor Movement*, 185–212.

36. For an interesting study of the shifting strategies (and conditions leading to their adoption) by which male printers tried to cope with the employers' use of cheap female labor, see Ava Baron, "Women and the Making of the American Working Class," *Review of Radical Political Economics* 14, no. 3 (Fall 1982).

37. It should be clear that *working class* women's oppression poses the key theoretical problem here; for, unlike women's subordination in feudal society or within the bourgeoise, it cannot be related to male control of property.

38. Barrett, *Women's Oppression Today*, 250.

39. Sebastiano Timpanaro, *On Materialism* (London, 1975), 29–54; but see also Barrett, *Women's Oppression Today*, 74.

40. For a more extended discussion of this point and its relationship to Marx's contention that labor power must be paid the cost of its reproduction, see Johanna Brenner, "Women's Self-Organization: A Marxist Justification," *Against the Current* 1, no. 1 (Fall 1980), 25–27.

41. See, among others, Alice Kessler-Harris, *Women Have Always Worked* (New York, 1981), 73; Robert Smuts, *Women and Work in America* (New York, 1971), 2–3, 23, 56; Louise A. Tilly and Joan W. Scott, *Women, Work and Family* (New York, 1978), 123–29; Carol Gronemann, "She Earns as a Child, She Pays as a Man,"

in Milton Cantor and Bruce Laurie, eds., *Class, Sex, and the Woman Worker* (Westport, Conn., 1977), 89–98; Barbara Mayer Wertheimer, *We Were There* (New York, 1977), 209–13; Theresa M. McBridge, "Women's Work and Industrialization," in Renate Bridenthal and Claudia Koonz, eds., *Becoming Visible: Women in European History* (Boston 1977), 285–87; Mary Lynn McDougall, "Working-Class Women During the Industrial Revolution," in Bridenthal and Koonz, eds., *Becoming Visible*, 267–68, 273; Tamara K. Harevan, *Family Time and Industrial Time: The Relationship between the Family and Work in a New England Industrial Community* (New York, 1982), 198; Mary P. Ryan, *Womanhood in America: From Colonial Times to the Present*, 2d ed. (New York, 1979), 125.

42. Virginia Yans-McGalughlan, "Italian Women and Work," in Cantor and Laurie, eds., *Class, Sex, and the Woman Worker*, 109–11; Smuts, *Women and Work in America*, 57.

43. Tilly and Scott, *Women, Work and Family*, 129–31; Elizabeth Pleck, "A Mother's Wages," in Nancy F. Cott and Elizabeth H. Pleck, eds., *A Heritage of Her Own* (New York, 1979), 376–82. High wages also seem to pull women into the labor market. Thus Pleck notes for the early twentieth century that Italian women married to low-waged men were far more likely to work in cities where wages for women (in the garment industry) were relatively high (p. 382).

44. Tilly and Scott, *Women, Work and Family*, 87–88.

45. Smuts, *Women and Work in America*, 19.

46. This is not to argue for some idyllic precapitalist past for women, but only to explain the more attenuated division of labor between men and women in precapitalist society. Feudal serf and proto-industrial households could be forced by ruling-class exactions to labor so intensively as to endanger the health of the entire family. But this pressure could only be exercised indirectly through the level of surplus demanded, allowing producers an important degree of flexibility in how they would meet that demand. Therefore, except at a very extreme point, women could regulate their work to take account of children's needs, for example by taking nursing breaks while working in the fields.

47. Susan Estabrook Kennedy, *If All We Did Was Weep at Home: A History of White Working-Class Women in America* (Bloomington, 1979), 52; Kessler-Harris, *Women Have Always Worked*, 71; Susan M. Strasser, "An Enlarged Human Existence? Technology and Household Work in Nineteenth-Century America," in Sarah Fenstermaker Berk, ed., *Women and Household Labour* (London and Beverly Hills, 1980), 44–45. The proportion of the weekly wage spent on food by a Massachusetts laborer was 85.8 percent in 1830; 76 percent in 1860, according to Strasser, "An Enlarged Human Existence?" For income in relation to basic necessities in England and France, see Tilly and Scott, *Women, Work and Family*, 137–38.

48. On the conditions of housekeeping, which had not improved for many women as late as the 1920s, see Kessler-Harris, *Women Have Always Worked*, 44–45; Ryan, *Womanhood in America*, 129; McDougall, "Working-Class Women," 274; Strasser, "An Enlarged Human Existence?", passim; Leslie Woodcock Tentler, *Wage-Earning Women* (New York and Oxford, 1979), 149.

49. On childcare arrangements, see Kennedy, *If All We Did Was Weep at Home*, 167; Ryan, *Womanhood in America*, 128; Harevan, *Family Time and Industrial Time*, 204–07; Tentler, *Wage-Earning Women*, 153–60.

50. Friedrich Engels, *The Condition of the Working Class in England* (Palo Alto, Calif.,

1969), 160; McDougall, "Working-Class Women," 274, reports that in the 1870s working mothers in Bradford, England, lost 68.8 percent of their children.

51. Engels, *The Condition of the Working Class in England*, 182.

52. Tilly and Scott, *Women, Work and Family*, 132–33. Ann Oakley, *Women's Work* (New York, 1976), 48–49, argues that wet-nursing was not particularly dangerous, apparently contradicting Tilly and Scott. However, since her figures are for Britain, where, unlike in France, wet-nursing was not a common practice among the working class, class differences may explain the different findings.

53. Jane Humphries argues that the family wage for men was both a necessary demand and ultimately in the interests of the working class as a whole. "Class Struggle and the Persistence of the Working Class Family," *Cambridge Journal of Economics* I, no. 3 (September 1977). As will soon be clear, we do not agree with the second part of her argument.

54. Daniel Scott Smith, "Family Limitations, Sexual Control and Domestic Feminism in Victorian America," in Cott and Pleck, eds., *A Heritage of Her Own*, 226.

55. *Perspectives on American Fertility*, U.S. Bureau of the Census, Current Population Reports, Special Studies, Series P-23, no. 70, 11.

56. Ryan, *Womanhood in America*, 130.

57. Tilly and Scott, *Women, Work and Family*, 99–102; Ellen Ross, "Fierce Questions and Taunts: Married Life in Working-Class London, 1870–1914," *Feminist Studies* 8, no. 3 (Fall 1982), 578.

58. D. Levine, *Family Formation in an Age of Nascent Capitalism* (New York, 1977); also Hans Medick, "The Proto-Industrial Family Economy: The Structural Function Household and Family during the Transition from Peasant Society to Industrial Capitalism," *Social History* 3 (October 1976), 291–315.

59. Ryan, *Womanhood in America*, 129; Levine, *Family Formation in an Age of Nascent Capitalism*, 68–71; Tilly and Scott, *Women, Work and Family*, 91.

60. Hareven, *Family Time and Industrial Time*, 189–91; Ryan, *Womanhood in America*, 124–26. Dublin reports that in Lowell in 1860, the average son or daughter worked a minimum of eight years while living at home. Given the average family size, families could count on seventeen years in which children's earnings would supplement family income. Thomas Dublin, "Women, Work, and the Family: Female Operatives in the Lowell Mills, 1830–1860," *Feminist Studies* 3, no. 1/2 (Fall 1975), 36. In Chicago in 1920, nearly 80 percent of unskilled workers' teenage children living at home were working; 70 percent of all 16–17 year olds living in Chicago and in New York in 1920 were not in school. Throughout the early decades of the twentieth century, a large proportion of working-class families were forced to withdraw their younger children illegally from school. School systems, not particularly anxious to meet the expenses of expanding school places, turned a blind eye to truancy, while child labor laws were unenforced. Only in the 1930s did school attendance among working-class teenagers begin to rise significantly. Miriam Cohen, "Italian-American Women in New York City, 1900–1950: Work and School," in Cantor and Laurie, eds., *Class, Sex, and the Woman Worker*, 128–33; Tentler, *Wage-Earning Women*, 93–95, 100–101; Winifred D. Wandersee, *Women's Work and Family Values, 1920–1940* (Cambridge, Mass., 1981), 60–62. For France and Britain,

see Tilly and Scott, *Women, Work and Family*, 178–81.

61. Cohen, "Italian-American Women," 125; Ross, "Fierce Questions and Taunts," 576.
62. Barrett, *Women's Oppression Today*, 181.
63. Ibid., 99.
64. Ibid., 182–83.
65. Smuts, *Women and Work in America*, 51; Tentler, *Wage-Earning Women* , 143–46.
66. Alice Kessler-Harris, "Organizing the Unorganizable," in *Class, Sex, and the Woman Worker*, 161 n.2. For contemporary data, see Kate Purcell, "Militancy and Acquiescence Amongst Women Workers," in Sandra Burman, ed., *Fit Work for Women* (New York, 1979), 112–33, 128–29.
67. Margery Davie, "Woman's Place Is at the Typewriter: The Feminization of the Clerical Labor Force," in Eisenstein, ed., *Capitalist Patriarchy and the Case for Socialist Feminism*, 251.
68. Ibid.
69. Dublin, "Women, Work, and the Family," 34–35.
70. Kessler-Harris, *Women Have Always Worked*, 65.
71. Cultural and ideological elements do affect the distribution of men and women into certain kinds of jobs. For example, employers hire men or women for some jobs in order to use the power and authority relationships which prevail in the society. Lazonick argues that factory employers preferred men for spinning because they were better able than women spinners to discipline the children working under them as piecers and helpers. Women's cheaper labor was preferred in powerloom weaving where only a single operator was required. W. Lazonick, "The Subjection of Labour to Capital: The Rise of the Capitalist System," *Review of Radical Political Economy* 10, no. 1 (Spring 1978), 8–9. In general, of course, men have been favored for supervisory and management positions, especially when the workforce is male. Men are preferred as waiters in high-class restaurants because more symbolic power is conferred on the patron who is served by a man than by a woman, etc. Finally, men may resist "women's work," even when it pays comparably, and women may not enter "men's jobs" for fear of being unfeminine. Nonetheless, the evidence does not support the view that ideological elements are the major cause of sex segregation.
72. Many feminists have argued that changing household technology cannot account for women's work outside the home. They cite time-distribution studies showing that the total hours per week housewives devote to housework and family care have remained the same since the 1920s. But this is only true of full-time homeworkers, and, more important, the time is spent differently. Time devoted to childcare has increased, while the time spent on preparing and cleaning up after meals has declined. Laundry and housecleaning time has remained the same, because standards have risen—which means that by lowering standards a woman can reduce the burden. With washers and dryers, laundry hours may be distributed over an entire week; our grandmothers had to devote an entire day. Flexibility in planning housework is greater, and the physical energy expended is less. See Susan Strasser, *Never Done: A History of American Housework* (New York, 1982), for descriptions of the various housework tasks in the nineteenth and early twentieth centuries.
73. It has also been argued that women had to re-enter wage work because the

economic penalties to teenagers of early school-leaving became too high. In the U.S. in 1920, only 30 percent of children 16–19 years old were in school; by 1970, only 35 percent were working for wages. Bonnie Fox, "Women's Double Work Day: Twentieth-Century Changes in the Reproduction of Daily Life," in Bonnie Fox, ed., *Hidden in the Household* (Toronto, 1980), 200–02.

74. "Full-time" means 35 hours or more per week for 50–52 weeks. The category of married women without children includes only those whose husbands are under the age of 55. In 1978, 56 percent of married women with children under 6 worked, 15 percent full-time, 41 percent part-time (20 percent full-time for part of the year, 21 percent part-time for part or all of the year). Among married mothers of school-age children, 65 percent worked, 27 percent full-time, 38 percent part-time (13 percent full-time for part of the year, 25 percent part-time for part or all of the year). Among married women without children, 77 percent worked, 43 percent full-time, 34 percent part-time (19 percent full-time for part of the year, 15 percent part-time for part or all of the year). U.S. Bureau of Labor Statistics, *Marital & Family Characteristics of the Labor Force, March 1979*, Special Labor Report No. 237, January 1981. Part-time work for married women appears to be even more prevalent in Europe. See, for example, Alice M. Yohalem, *Women Returning to Work: Policies and Progress in Five Countries* (Totowa, N.J., 1980), 114.

75. Divorce, separation, and single parenthood are multiplying the households in which women are the primary breadwinners. Still, a heterosexual couple and their children remain the fundamental living unit. Even at the current high divorce rate, a half of all marriages endure. Moreover, high rates of divorce are matched by high rates of remarriage. Five out of six men and three out of four women remarry, generally rather quickly—about a half of remarriages take place within three years following divorce. Andrew Cherlin, *Marriage, Divorce, Remarriage* (Cambridge, Mass. and London, 1981), 29–30.

76. Contrasting the lives of migrant workers and traditional working-class households, Maxine Molyneux suggests that domestic production represents a higher standard of living for workers than going to the market ("Beyond the Domestic Labour Debate," *New Left Review* 116 (July–August 1979), 10–11). This is an important point, but misses two issues. First, in some cases the market can provide a higher standard of living by making it possible to buy out entirely of domestic work—witness the lifestyles of urban middle-class professionals. Second, the case of migrant workers does not solve the problem of intergenerational reproduction within capitalism, since the next generation of workers is produced outside the capitalist system.

77. Like the definition of working-class subsistence, quality childcare has both a biological and a "moral and historical" element. What is acceptable care in one era may fall well below standard in another. Moreover, the "needs" of character formation, intellectual development, and so forth vary greatly between societies and historically. A society which intends to utilize the capacities of its people to the fullest would surely define adequate child rearing very differently than a capitalist society does. On the other hand, advanced capitalism may require a more labor-intensive and extended period of dependency (education) among children than did precapitalist society. The assumption that only an intense bond between mother and child can produce a healthy personality, the extended period of dependency in children that pre-

vails today, are surely socially/historically and not biologically determined. Nonetheless, it seems beyond doubt that in human development there is a biological limit to how short the period of dependency can be and a biologically determined need for a substantial investment in labor time by adults (although not necessarily the biological parents) in order for children to develop.

78. Married women's rate of absenteeism from work is significantly higher than that of single women and married men. (Among Blacks, both single and married women have much higher rates than married men, probably because single Black women are much more likely than single white women workers to have children.) Daniel E. Taylor, "Absences from Work Among Full-Time Employees," *Monthly Labor Review*, March 1981, 69.

79. A 1973 U.S. study of divorced people married in 1968 found that when household income was adjusted for needs (number of persons, age of children), divorced men gained 17 percent in household income, divorced women lost 7 percent. Cherlin, *Marriage, Divorce, Remarriage*, 82.

80. Barrett, *Women's Oppression Today*, 229.

81. Mary McIntosh, "The Welfare State and the Needs of the Dependent Family," in *Fit Work for Women*, 164–65.

82. Elizabeth Wilson, *Women and the Welfare State* (London, 1977). Hilary Land, "Who Cares for the Family?", *Journal of Social Policy* 7 no. 3 (1978); Mary McIntosh, "The Welfare State," for the English case.

83. McIntosh, "The Welfare State," 167.

84. Ibid., 166.

85. Smuts, *Women and Work in America*, pp. 51–54.

86. Blanche D. Coll, *Perspectives on Public Welfare*, U.S. Department of Health, Education and Welfare (Washington, D.C.: U.S. Government Printing Office, 1969), 13–15, 54.

87. Barret, *Women's Oppression Today*, 232.

88. W. Norton Grubb and Marvin Lazerson, *Broken Promises: How Americans Fail Their Children* (New York, 1982), 190–91, 200; on the "employable mother" rule, low level of payments, restrictive eligibility, see Coll, *Perspectives in Public Welfare*, 77–81.

89. In the U.S., very few intact families receive support. Grubb and Lazerson, *Broken Promises*, 199.

90. Barrett, *Women's Oppression Today*, 246.

91. Ibid., 222–23. For a nuanced presentation of this position which recognizes the contradictory tendency within capitalism to undermine the traditional family-household, see Irene Breugel, "What Keeps the Family Going?", *International Socialism*, Series 2, no. 1 (July 1978).

92. Grubb and Lazerson, *Broken Promises*, 190; Coll, *Perspectives in Public Welfare*, 15; Frances Fox Piven and Richard Cloward, *Regulating the Poor: The Function of Public Welfare* (New York: 1971), chaps 1 and 4.

93. While disagreeing with his overall interpretation, we agree with Zaretsky's characterization of middle-class reform ideology. Eli Zaretsky, "The Place of the Famiy in the Origins of the Welfare State," in Barrie Thorne with Marilyn Yalom, eds., *Rethinking the Family: Some Feminist Questions* (New York, 1982), 188–224.

94. Barrett, *Women's Oppression Today*, 137–38.

95. Ibid, 206.
96. Ibid, 205, 108.
97. Ibid, 205, 213–25.
98. The quote is, of course, Althusser in "Ideology and Ideological State Appa-
    ratuses," in *Lenin and Philosophy* (New York, 1971), 162.
99. Nancy Cott, "Passionlessness: An Interpretation of Victorian Sexual Ideology,
    1790–1850," *Signs: A Journal of Women in Culture and Society* 4 (1979), 210–36.
    See also N. Cott, *The Bonds of Womanhood* (New Haven, 1977); Linda Gordon,
    "Voluntary Motherhood: The Beginnings of Feminist Birth Control Ideology
    in the U.S.," in Mary Hartman and Lois Banner, eds., *Clio's Consciousness Raised*
    (New York, 1974), and *Woman's Body, Woman's Right* (New York, 1976); Mary
    P. Ryan, *Cradle of the Middle Class* (Cambridge, 1981); and Kathryn Kish Sklar's
    masterful *Catherine Beecher: A Study in American Domesticity* (New York, 1976).
100. It is beyond the scope of this essay to assess the potential contribution that can
    be made to understanding gendered subjectivity by psychoanalysis, but we
    believe this to be underestimated by Barrett.

Chapter 2

Gender and the State

with Barbara Laslett

The end of the 1970s brought formal recognition that things were not well between Marxism and feminism; there was, to use Heidi Hartmann's phrase, an "unhappy marriage" between them. Women's oppression and feminist struggles, she argued, had consistently been subordinated to class oppression and class struggle. Women's issues were seen "at best [as] less important than class conflict and at worst divisive of the working class." To resolve the dilemma, Hartmann proposed that patriarchy and capitalism be seen as separate systems of domination, each of which has to accommodate the other.[1] In this essay, we take issue with this "dual-systems" approach as it has been used to account for the gendered character of the welfare state.

Within the dual-systems—or capitalist-patriarchy—framework, socialist-feminists have argued that the state mediates between the conflicting interests of male capitalists and workers, on the one hand, and their common interests as white men, on the other. They point out that state policy with regard to both services (education, welfare, health care, etc.) and regulation (labor legislation, public health and housing laws, etc.) reflects and perpetuates women's marginalization in paid labor and their assignment to unpaid labor in the home. From this perspective, state provision for women and children is understood as a "negotiated settlement" among contending groups of men. The development of the welfare state, rather than giving women access to income and services as an alternative to their dependence on men, established a "public patriarchy" that reinforced women's dependence on the male-breadwinner family and on a male-controlled state.[2] This analysis, however, ignores the impact and existence of women's political agency and misses the possibility that state programs provide women with resources as well as constraints.

A second interpretation of the gendered character of the welfare state does recognize women's agency. Skocpol argues that women were architects of the welfare state in late-nineteenth- and early-twentieth-century America, especially through state-level political activities. Indeed, she argues that in the Progressive Era, white middle-class women were more effective than working-class men in implementing reforms.[3] And Nelson points out that from its beginning social welfare in the United States has been a gendered, two-track system. Protective legislation was implemented for women but not men. Contributory, non-means-tested programs such as pensions and workmen's compensation, considered to be entitlements, have been directed toward men as workers. Noncontributory, means-tested programs such as mothers'/widows' pensions and maternal and child health care, understood as public charity, have been directed toward women, primarily as mothers. This two-track system of social benefits, and its legitimating ideology, was embedded in state structures during the Progressive Era. Since that time, Nelson observes, it has been expanded and elaborated but not substantially changed.[4] Also working within a state-centered approach, Orloff, while agreeing with Nelson that programs were gendered, argues that in the Progressive Era "social contribution" was the basis of entitlement for both men and women.[5] She contends that the emergence of differential legitimations connected to contributory programs for men and noncontributory programs for women did not emerge until the 1930s.[6]

While incorporating women's historical agency, this approach, which focuses more than does the capitalist-patriarchy framework on political institutions and processes, also has problems. First, it does not theorize why middle-class women were organized and effective as political actors in the Progressive Era. Nor does it explain why they organized for programs that substantially institutionalized a male-breadwinner family model. Second, the emphasis on the timing and institutionalization of particular policies draws attention away from the possibility of continued contestation over them. It neglects variation in women's capacities for political organization or changes in what women organized to achieve.

In this essay we present an alternative to both the capitalist-patriarchy and state-centered frameworks that builds upon them but attempts to transcend the shortcomings we have identified. Our approach draws on Marxist and feminist theory, but we are part of that strand within the socialist-feminist project that seeks to develop a "single-system" rather than a "dual-systems" model.[7] In line with state-centered approaches, we recognize the importance of political structures and political activity. State policy outcomes cannot be "read off" the interests of social groups—of men as men or as workers and employers. But, in line with the capitalist-patriarchy analysis and in contrast with the state-centered approach, we argue that women act with resources and under constraints set by gender and class relations. For this reason, Marxist analysis that concentrates on the ways in which the dynamic of the capitalist mode of production sets limits on and opens opportunities for political action has to be expanded to include the structures of social reproduction—the socially organized labor necessary to renew life. In analyzing the development of state policy, then, we focus on how the organization of social reproduction and, in particular, the gender division of labor within it, affected women's political self-organization: why women organized, with what goals in mind, within what range of alternatives, and with what capacities to affect outcomes. We begin with the observation that, not only in the Progressive period but also in the 1960s and 1970s, women were engaged in political action on their own behalf, while in the other major period of contestation over state policy, the 1930s, women's political self-organization was substantially absent.

By political self-organization we mean any collective action in which women as activists and leaders define goals and construct strategies, not only self-consciously feminist organizing. Thus the "woman movement" at the turn of the century that helped establish models of social welfare and industrial regulation based on the assignment of women to unpaid labor in the family is an example of women's political self-organization. So, too, is the organization of a new generation of women activists in the 1960s and 1970s who saw their interests quite differently and challenged those very models that Progressive Era women had worked to institutionalize. In both eras, "women's needs and rights" entered the political discourse concerning the obligations of the state. In the New Deal, by contrast, the debate over state policy focused overwhelmingly on men, particularly men as workers and family providers.

This variation in women's self-organization has to be accounted for. We do so by asking about the ways in which women's responsibilities as mothers and wives provided resources for, but also imposed constraints on, their capacity for collective action. Changes in the organization of social reproduction in the twentieth century, we believe, account for differences in women's political self-organization across the three periods. By social reproduction we mean the activities and attitudes, behaviors and emotions, and responsibilities and relationships directly involved in maintaining life on a daily basis and intergenerationally. It involves various kinds of socially necessary work—mental, physical, and emotional—aimed at providing the historically and socially, as well as biologically, defined means for maintaining consumption, how the maintenance and socialization of children is accomplished, how care of the elderly and infirm is provided, and how sexuality is socially constructed.

The organization of social reproduction varies over time and across societies, but a gender division of labor has always been central to it.[8] Yet the content and context of women's work in social reproduction in the United States has not been static. In our analysis, we look at how social reproduction and gender relations were reorganized over the course of the twentieth century and the implications of that reorganization for women's political activity. Our discussion looks at two pivotal periods: the turn of the twentieth century and the years between the Second World War and the 1970s, although we present a less full empirical account of the latter than the former.

In the late nineteenth century and through the Progressive Era, the conditions under which white middle-class women carried out their responsibilities for social reproduction provided organizational resources and legitimation for their collective action. Their political reform activities were based in voluntary associations and institutions built in their separate "female world" and were justified in terms of their special responsibilities as mothers. African-American middle-class women, usually denied entrance to white women's groups, formed their own organizations that operated under a similar charge, although their concerns and ideologies were broader and less likely to be on behalf of women and children only.[9]

Although the gender division of labor persisted, the reorganization of social reproduction, begun at the turn of the century, brought a new focus on nuclear family relations and heterosexuality in psychological, cultural, and behavioral terms. These changes, substantially completed by the 1920s, opened up new possibilities for women as individual actors in the modern world, but undermined the women-centered institutions and maternalist ideology on which their previous self-organization had been based. In the post-Second World War decades, another reorganization of women's responsibilities for social reproduction—including the increased access of young middle-class women to higher education and the increased entry of married middle-class women into paid labor as an extension of their responsibilities to their families—laid the groundwork for women's political self-organization, but on a very different institutional basis and with a correspondingly different set of legitimations. Most centrally, it became possible for women to challenge the gender division of labor itself.

Gender and Social Reproduction

Relations of gender and generation are fundamental properties of how social reproduction is organized. Often naturalized around age and sex differences, all known systems of social reproduction have been based on a gender division of labor. Although this pattern appears to be mandated by the relationship between procreation, sexuality, and the needs of infants, the distribution of the work of social reproduction between families, markets, communities, and states—and between women and men—has varied historically. Systems of social reproduction are the historical outcomes of class and gender struggles—struggles that are often about sexuality and emotional relations, as well as political power and economic resources. Furthermore, although social reproduction can be viewed conceptually as an organized system, its components stand in a problematic relationship to each other. Women's claim to equality with their husbands, embedded in the twentieth-century notion of companionship marriage and motherhood as career, for example, was contradicted by their continued economic and social subordination within the male-breadwinner family.

In this essay we contend that continuities and changes in the organization of social reproduction and the social construction of gender in the early twentieth century substantially altered the lives of middle-class women, who had been the backbone of women's political self-organization in the Progressive Era. Increasing participation in education and wage work, especially for unmarried women, encouraged a greater emphasis on middle-class women's sexual and personal autonomy. Women's low wages, however, put economic autonomy out of reach even for many single women and certainly for mothers. Despite declining fertility, the continuing demands on women for domestic labor and childcare, along with the rising standards of household maintenance and childrearing, made it extremely difficult for most women to combine paid and unpaid work. Thus women, especially with children, continued to have few alternatives outside dependence on a male breadwinner. This discrepancy between middle-class women's possibilities as single women and their limitations as mothers/wives helps to explain why women participated in a new emphasis on sexuality and companionship in marriage.[10] But this participation affected women's identities and sense of themselves—steering them in the direction of heterosexual rather than homosocial interests and ties.

In contrast to nineteenth-century beliefs about women's sexual passionlessness, in the early twentieth century there was a celebration of sexuality, including women's, as a source of pleasure, personal fulfillment, and personality development, but only if it was a sexuality of the right sort—if it was heterosexual.[11] Other sexual relationships—lesbianism, in particular—were now labeled perverse and selfish; these labels were used to denounce the political reform activities that had been central to women activists in the Progressive Era.[12]

Celebration of sexuality—of heterosexuality—as a central dimension of the new youth culture, was also connected to the emerging norms of companionship in marriage—norms that undermined the "separate spheres" justification of women's political activities in at least two ways.[13] On the one hand, it increased and bestowed a certain sacred aura on relations between husbands and wives in the name of "normalcy" and "adjustment," a sharp contrast to the moral authority that relations among women had in the nineteenth century. On the other hand, the new emphasis on women's heterosexual relationships undermined bonds between women that had previously been central to women's culture. It also emphasized women's links to their own husbands and children—to their nuclear families—rather than to women's responsibility for morality within the society as a whole.

Other institutional and cultural shifts worked in the same direction—in particular, the development of domestic consumerism and new ideas about childrearing. For the modern housewife of the 1920s, consumerism was connected to a new definition of domestic work, to new ways for middle-class women to guard the health and well-being of their families, to the new material standards for middle-class family life—changes identified with increasingly available consumer goods.[14] The continuing supply of an exploitable pool of women workers, particularly immigrant and Black women, to help carry the burden of attaining the higher standards for domestic health and comfort, encouraged most middle-class women to accept rather than challenge the work involved in maintaining the modern household.[15] In the face of their continuing exclusion or marginalization in other fields of achievement, and despite the occasional woman exemplar of the capacity to combine career and family, it is not too surprising that, where resources permitted, middle-class women sought to elaborate the value and meaning of their work in the one arena were they had some control: the home.

The new standard of living to which middle-class U.S. families aspired involved more than material goods alone. It carried certain implications for family relationships in general and involved new definitions of desirable family relationships—between mothers and children as well as between husbands and wives. Shaped by changing economic conditions that affected the intergenerational transmission of social status—particularly the greater importance of education for occupational placement—new, class-specific definitions of maternal adequacy and inadequacy developed.[16] This shift was reflected in the parent education movement. To the PTA in the Progressive Era parent education was a means for changing society by organizing mothers of the nation in common cause. By the 1920s, parent education "referred by and large to the instruction of middle-class women in ways they could rear their own children in accordance with new behavioral science dictums."[17] Special emphasis was put on pre-school children, especially those aged two to six. Although efforts were made to proselytize mothers at all social levels, the audience for parent education was, inevitably, the increasing number of educated women in the population, particularly college-educated women.[18] It is also likely that educated women's family activities were elaborated and became implicated in husbands' careers in new ways at this time. Although more historical research is needed on this point, the important contribution made by wives to middle-class husbands' success, observed by Whyte in the 1950s and by Kanter in the 1970s, may also have absorbed middle-class women's energies.[19] All of these developments turned home and family into a different kind of space for women. They were not simply the place where domestic goods and services were provided, where women did their duty, fulfilled their obligations; nor were they seen as a moral retreat, a "haven in the heartless world" from the commercialism and amorality of nineteenth-century economic relations. They had become, rather, the center of women's creative life, of their fulfillment.

Critical for understanding how these changes affected the organization of social reproduction is the decline in fertility that occurred for all occupational groups in the United States in the first part of the twentieth century.[20] Although class differences can be observed with a sharper and earlier decline among middle- compared to working-class families, smaller families became characteristic of the entire population.[21] This decline in fertility not only freed mothers to participate in a companionate marriage and create a "quality" home but also made it more possible for them to aspire to raising "quality" children. These changes defined family responsibilities and relationships in new ways, but presented no challenge to the gender division of labor that had been so central to social reproduction in the Progressive period. They did, however, change the focus and goal of middle-class white women's activities. The new standards for middle-class family life—mutual enjoyment of sexuality and companionship in marriage, attention to child development and educational achievement, rising expectations for standards of living, comfort and pleasure in family life, and the relationship between lifestyle and status—all focused women's attentions on their own individual families.

It is important to recognize that this increasing focus on nuclear family affairs was not simply forced upon middle-class white women by human services professionals—often other women who had begun to establish themselves as experts in professions such as social work, child development, home economics, education—or by the sellers and advertisers of consumer goods. The increasingly professionalized activities of service workers such as teachers, social workers, and nurses not only provided some middle-class women with occupations but also made it possible for other middle-class women, the very women who had been the backbone of reform politics in the Progressive Era, to affiliate themselves to the culture of modernity that was developing around them. Given the limited range of their alternatives, it is, perhaps, not too surprising that middle-class women followed this course.

While it is impossible to consider this question at any length here, changes in the economy and education in early twentieth-century America are also crucially linked to changes in the organization of social reproduction. Expanded opportunities for women to work in white-collar jobs, elaborated standards for personal appearance and recreation, possibilities for commercial education in secondary and business schools all contributed to the growing youth culture in the high schools and women's choices in young adulthood.[22] But even when women were successful in overcoming previous occupational segregation, as in clerical work, or when they were victorious, however temporarily, in organizing trade unions to protect their interests, as telephone operators did, the opportunities they carved out for themselves rarely provided sufficient resources for a comfortable, middle-class life.[23] Marriage as women's best career option had not yet begun to be challenged on any wide scale. Rising expectations for family life and personal comfort, however, did lead an increasing number of middle-class women to join the labor force.[24]

In contrast to the maternalist ideology that had existed earlier, the new culture with which middle-class women were now identifying and helping to construct was legitimated by rationalist values of modern science rather than moral values of a more communitarian culture. And this new culture was male, not female, dominated. Although women like Lucy Sprague Mitchell were important figures in developing this culture, particularly in fields such as child development, and women were unusually prominent in constructing the new psychiatry of family relationships, developments in the social sciences meant that scientific educators such as Lawrence K. Frank and scientific sociologists like William F. Ogburn were the experts whose voices dominated the new discussions of sexuality, education, and family relationships.[25] As a consequence, the culture of expertise in family affairs developed, in the first instance, as primarily male professions and most of the women involved in them affiliated and identified themselves with men's worlds and practices. Each of these developments underscored women's dependence on men—on the male wage, on male culture, and on the nuclear family. It is this economic and psychocultural dependence, we believe, and the decline in women's political self-organization associated with it, that helps explain the absence of women's voices in the Great Depression.

During the 1930s, married women came under pervasive attack for wage work outside the home despite their increased participation in the labor force. The Depression undercut any rationale for women's employment except family economic need and reinforced the traditional division of labor in which men were breadwinners and women were wage spenders and household workers on behalf of their families.[26] While it is important to remember that not all U.S. families experienced extreme loss of income during the Depression, Elder concludes that the economic hardship experienced during the 1930s contributed to the increased value of the family and children for both women and men.[27] Indeed, the experience of U.S. families during the Depression seems to have strengthened norms about the gender division of labor within the family, regardless of how behavior may have contradicted them. Whatever incipient critique of gender inequalities the ideal of companionship in middle-class marriage or the reality of married women's increased labor force activity may have presented in the 1920s, norms about the gender division of labor that would become central to feminist challenge in the 1970s were firmly rerooted in the family and gender culture of the 1930s.

The organization of social reproduction for middle-class white families in post-First World War America was inherently unstable. Gender relations and identities based in companionate marriage and full-time motherhood as career raised women's aspirations and modern capacities and then denied them the possibility of achievement. But these contradictions only exploded in the 1950s and 1960s.

Of particular importance were the changing demographics of family formation and fertility and the rising standards for family comfort begun in the 1920s.[28] Lowered fertility, earlier ages at marriage, and lower age at the birth of the last child from the 1950s onward meant that women were freed from full-time mothering at a relatively young age.[29] Married women were now able to consider interests outside the family at younger ages, and such interests were particularly legitimate if they were pursued in the name of family well-being. Oppenheimer's analyses of the demand for female labor in the postwar period and her analyses of the family "life-cycle squeeze" demonstrates the economic and demographic components of these dynamics. She shows that for all occupational groups, although more strongly among lower- than higher-status ones, women's participation in the paid labor force corresponded to the period of the family life cycle when family expenses were highest—that is, when there were adolescent children in the home—and the husband's earning had not risen to meet them.[30] In order to maintain the same standard of living, married women entered, or re-entered, the labor force. Smaller families and the availability of household appliances and consumer goods and services meant that it was now possible for women to do a double day, combining domestic and childrearing responsibilities with paid work.

The rising demand for women's paid labor, especially in clerical work and the service professions, was thus met with an increasing supply of educated women looking for employment.[31] The resulting massive re-entry of women into the labor force was inherently explosive around issues of gender inequality. Although women could work outside the home without fundamentally challenging the reigning gender ideology, nonetheless once women were working they had access to new experiences and resources that could support their political organization. Both the increasing number of married women in the paid labor force and the increasing number of their daughters attending college created the structural conditions for a mass base to a new women's movement. The political movements of the 1960s and 1970s—in the United States, the civil rights and antiwar movements—were its catalyst.[32]

Women's Political Self-organization

From the late nineteenth century through the First World War in the United States, white middle-class women were major political actors in formulating and winning reforms that, however limited in scope and funding, did expand state responsibility for social reproduction. In analyzing the relationship between women's self-organization and state policy, we focus particularly on white middle-class women. First, although African-American middle-class women were organized and played crucial political roles in their own communities in this period, they were excluded from the organizations and activities of the "woman movement." Second, while working-class women appear to have supported many of the goals of the women reformers at the turn of the century, it was more difficult for them, especially once married and mothers, to participate in the organization-building through which middle-class women exercised influence within the male-dominated political system.[33] Even when working-class women participated in reform organizations and campaigns, these tended to be dominated by middle-class women who set the reform agenda in ways that both represented and denied the needs of their working-class allies.[34]

Middle-class white women's political influence was accomplished through organized educational, research, and lobbying activities based in the women's club movement, settlement house movement, and child welfare and mother's groups—all organizations whose mandate for action was grounded in the nineteenth-century doctrine of separate spheres. The great irony of this period is that the same gender division of labor that marginalized white middle-class women from paid labor and mandated their economic dependence on men also provided them with an institutional base from which to organize politically. For it was through voluntary associations that grew out of their responsibilities for social reproduction (for managing homes and raising children) that white middle-class women developed the political resources necessary for collective action. This collective action had two dimensions: the demand for political equality and the demand for social protection and support for motherhood. Its apparently contradictory elements were integrated in the claim that women's responsibilities as mothers justified, indeed demanded, their access to political power.

The maternalist politics so central to middle-class women's political activism in the Progressive Era reflected the social position and experience of the women who put it forward. Campaigns for state intervention had allowed some middle-class women to carve out alternatives to marriage and motherhood by taking up work as providers of social services in the new "female" professions—schoolteaching, home economics, social work, public health, and nursing.[35] Many of these women, and the single-sex institutions they built, provided leadership and organizational resources to the movement.[36] But in calling for the state to increase the resources available to women, including working-class and immigrant women, to fulfill their maternal role, the vast majority of middle-class activist women were reflecting their own life experience and goals as married mothers dependent on a male breadwinner.

Whatever the limits of the Progressive Era women's movement (including its class and race biases and the powerful political opposition it faced), advocates for women had an impact on law and public policy outcomes. In the 1930s by contrast, and despite African-American and white women's continuing involvement in voluntary and political organizations, feminism was fundamentally marginalized in political organization and political discourse.[37] There was, as a consequence, no challenge to the institutionalization of the gender division of labor in relief programs, education and job training, social security legislation, unemployment insurance, labor relations law, and of course Aid to Families with Dependent Children.[38]

Several explanations have been put forward for why the broad-based "women's rights" movement declined in the 1920s. Splits in the movement between "equal rights feminists" and "social-feminists," the increasingly single-issue focus on suffrage and the consequent emphasis on electoral politics that left the movement without political influence once a women's voting block failed to materialize, the postwar repression of the left, and the increasingly conservative political climate—all contributed to undermining feminist organization.[39] We would agree that the conservative political climate and sectarian divisions of the 1920s would have discouraged political activism and made it more difficult to recruit new members during that decade. But, all else being equal, we would also expect a resurgence of activity and organization as the political climate changed in the 1930s. Certainly, this was the case for the African-American movement, which recovered from the decline suffered during the late 1920s and early 1930s as a result of political repression and the impoverishment of the African-American community.[40] Indeed, during this decade, migration northward and to the cities increased African-American capacity for organization and mobilization.[41] In contrast, we would argue, the changing organization of social reproduction had undermined the development of gender solidarities among white, middle-class women and their potential for self-organization.

Unlike their white counterparts, African-American middle-class women could not hope to advance the careers of sons and husbands through an exclusively private strategy. Traditions of women's political self-organization remained strong, and their organizations played leadership roles in the political defense of the African-American community.[42] White middle-class women's rights activists and organizations also continued into the 1930s, and women who saw themselves as advocates for women gained influence in the Democratic Party and the New Deal administration.[43] Although this elite of professional and activist women was better positioned than ever before within political institutions, they had lost their access to a mass base. The changing material conditions of married white middle-class women's lives undermined the information networks, social solidarities, and self-definitions that had facilitated their political mobilization. Without that potential mass support, advocates for women within the New Deal administration and the Democratic Party, no matter how well placed, could not turn their personal influence and expertise into legislative and policy victories. A different set of circumstances constrained the activities of working-class women.

During the 1930s, working-class communities waged historic struggles and women played important roles in both community and labor movements. Yet their activism rarely took the form of women's self-organization, either within these movements (as in the case of women in the African-American movement) or outside them (as in the cross-class alliances of women in the Progressive Era). It might be argued that in the face of the economic hardships of the Depression, working-class women would be concerned more with survival than "equality," or that the need for class solidarity demanded by the community and labor struggles of the decade prevented alliances with the middle-class women and organizations who continued to advocate for women in the 1930s. Yet the experience of the African-American movement demonstrates that it was possible to participate in working-class protest and organize for equality at the same time. Indeed, the activity of a cross-class movement based in race solidarity was critical to the inclusion of

African-American working people in the organizations of working-class struggle and political representation.

Of course, the movement for African-American equality was hardly victorious in this period. Racist policies of segregation, exclusion from labor law protection, and discrimination in relief and social services persisted at both federal and local levels. But, taking the period as a whole, the New Deal and Second World War brought tremendous steps forward in consciousness and political organization for African Americans. For women, however, things were quite different. Reform demands and state policies in the 1930s revolved around the assumption that families were or should be supported by male breadwinners.[44] Women's rights organizations and women trade-union activists protested bans on married women's employment, the exclusion of unemployed women from relief programs, under-representation of women in work programs, and the exclusion of women's jobs from Fair Labor Standards legislation.[45]

To understand why organized women were so unsuccessful in winning support for these demands, we have to consider that, while women's labor force participation increased during the decade, the vast majority of married women did not work for wages. In 1940 only 15 percent of married women were in paid labor; even at the lowest levels of family income, only 25 percent worked for pay.[46] In addition, working-class women who did work for pay were doubly burdened by their domestic responsibilities. Women trade-union activists tended to be young and single or older women whose children were also older.[47] Domestic burdens did not keep women from participating in bursts of militant action but they were a barrier to participation in day-to-day organization building. Yet, without an organizational base, the women trade-union activists were limited in how successfully they could challenge male domination within the labor movement. In contrast to the issue of racism, feminist concerns remained marginal within the organizations leading the social movements of the 1930s: the Congress of Industrial Organizations (CIO) and the Communist Party.

While increasing numbers of women entered paid labor in the 1930s, the majority of workers were still men—88 percent of employed workers nationally and 78 percent in manufacturing. African-American workers were also a minority within the labor force. But whereas occupational gender segregation meant that organizing men usually did not require organizing women, organizing white men did require organizing African-American men, especially in the mass-production industries that were the focus of the CIO.

The trade-union movement began to recognize that it had to identify itself with African-American civil rights—not just the inclusion of Blacks in unions but, more broadly, the struggle for equal opportunity in employment and against discrimination in education, housing, and the legal system. Pressure for this recognition came from two directions: from the importance of African-American men in the mass-production industries and from the political self-organization of African Americans in the communities where the CIO was organizing. Some of the individuals leading the CIO had personal histories of support for African-American equality. Communist Party unionists were especially active in pushing for anti-racist policies and the inclusion of African Americans in leadership positions. But their ability to win the point with the rank and file in the CIO rested in part on the reality of the conditions for organizing in the mass-production industries—the often pivotal role of African-American men in the labor process and the employers' use of African-American workers as scabs. White workers in the CIO were by no means immediately won over to support African-American workers' rights, but although racism was persistent and pervasive throughout the 1930s and the war, it was at least contested within the CIO, while sexism went substantially unchallenged.

In some times and places, the CIO unions became significant allies of the movement for civil rights.[48] For example, African-American workers constituted 12 percent of Ford employees, concentrated at the strategic River Rouge plant in Detroit. The United Auto Workers (UAW) became the most vocal advocate in the labor movement of anti-lynching and anti-poll tax legislation, the most lavish contributor to Negro rights associations, and the most constant lobbyist in Congress for legislation favorable to African Americans. Civil rights spokesmen in return marched in UAW picket lines around the Rouge plant. This was crucial for the union, because up to this point Ford's "welfarist" policies toward institutions in the African-American community had recruited the Black community leadership to his side. Ford capitulated in 1941, recognizing the UAW and agreeing to wage increases.[49]

As women's share of the labor force increased during the war and as women workers began to organize, they were able to force the CIO unions to take greater recognition of their needs.[50] But even where working women were able to win over their local unions, they were still operating in a political and social climate in which the male breadwinner ideology was hegemonic. Without a broader social movement that effectively challenged the gender division of labor and supported their rights to work, women workers found themselves politically isolated. In contrast, African-American men could rely on a movement, such as the NAACP, that had increased in membership and militancy. Thus African-American men workers and women workers fared very differently in the postwar[51] industries that they had entered during the war.[52]

The militancy and self-organization of African Americans affected not only the unions but also the revolutionary left, which gave important, although not always consistent, support to their organizing efforts. Whereas the struggle against African-American oppression was at the center of Communist Party politics, the party's relationship to feminism remained ambivalent, if not hostile. Since the Communist Party dominated the left and its culture during the 1930s, the Party's organization and politics constituted another barrier to the development of women's self-organization.

Although never dominant, a socialist-feminist politics had emerged in the Progressive Era. Many of the first generation of "new women," such as Jane Addams and Florence Kelly, identified with the socialist movement.[53] And the "sex radicals" of the Bohemian world of Greenwich Village, Paris, and Berlin in the 1920s also provided an alternative vision of gender possibilities.[54] These traditions were suppressed within the Communist Party. The hierarchical structure of the party made it extremely difficult to challenge official program and policy. Without norms of free debate and discussion, women on the left had little space to raise questions that were not on the leadership's agenda.[55]

The Communists' emphasis on workplace organizing and on the historic center of trade unionism—male blue-collar workers—tended to marginalize issues of concern to women. Nevertheless, and despite the lack of interest from their party, Communist women spearheaded women's organization as workers and as members of working-class communities.[56] On the whole, however, this organizing focused primarily on public discrimination rather than on the gender division of labor and male power in the household. While defending women's rights to work and demanding help for women workers to negotiate a double day, the Communist Party never questioned that home and family remained primarily a woman's responsibility.

While the political culture and structure of the Communist Party restricted women's opportunities for challenging the dominant view, many women members, like the majority of adult women outside the Party, were also housewives dependent on men for economic support. For them, for much the same reasons as for other women, the notion that the key issue in the defense of the working class was the demand for employment, unionization, and higher wages for men would have been quite compelling. Thus neither the women nor the men within the Communist Party could articulate a critique of the gender division of labor in both working-class and middle-class families.

Had there been a feminist movement in the 1930s as radical in its critique of domestic life as the Communist Party was of capitalism, Communist women might well have organized on their own behalf and developed a "communist-feminist" politics. In the 1930s, however, in the absence of feminist movements and organizations in the larger society, it was impossible for women on the left to envision, let alone organize, a new way of accomplishing the work of social reproduction.

In the 1960s, the political ideas of the civil rights and student movements, challenging inferiority based on biological difference and demanding democratic and egalitarian forms of governance, provided a powerful intellectual framework that women could adapt to their own ends. In comparison to left culture of the 1930s, the 1960s counterculture legitimated the search for individual self-expression as a political goal, opening up more space for women to question sexism in personal as well as political life.[57] While these differences are important in explaining the emergence of feminism in the 1960s, we would also emphasize the changing conditions of middle-class women's lives.

Whereas turn-of-the-century women's organization found a mass base in middle-class homemakers, second-wave feminism was based on social networks and institutional and economic resources that grew out of middle-class women's increasing participation in employment and higher education. While suburban housewives swelled the ranks of recruits, the mainstream movement developed from preexisting networks and organizational resources of women professionals, trade-union officials, and political party activists.[58] With one in five women enrolled in higher education, the radical organizations of the second wave found a mass base, facilities, and institutional resources in and around colleges and universities.[59]

Older married women may have re-entered paid labor in fulfillment of their responsibilities to their families and younger women may have entered college expecting to follow their mothers' life courses, but within a short time of its emergence, second-wave feminism had begun to challenge the gender division of labor in social reproduction itself. This challenge originated in the young women of the movement, a generation for whom the contradictions of companionate marriage and phallocentric and compulsory heterosexuality were especially explosive.[60] Since that time, and partly through the articulation of the interests of working-class women and women of color in the welfare rights, civil rights, and trade-union movements, the gender division of labor and the role of the state in fostering or undermining women's social and sexual autonomy has come to be a political issue.[61]

This challenge to the gender division of labor responds to the change in women's labor-force participation over the 1970s and 1980s—that now the vast majority of women do a "double day." However, the political response is accounted for not by the problem of the double day itself, but by women's increased resources for self-organization. In part because of the previous gains of the women's movement and in part because of the continued demand for women's labor (their growing share of trade-union membership, their presence in the upper-level professions), women's self-organization has been institutionalized in professional associations, trade unions, and political organizations. While no longer a radical movement, feminism has maintained a political presence through a loose network of organizations advocating for women.[62] No battles have been definitely won, and some may be temporarily lost, but men's responsibility for childcare and domestic work, the privileging of heterosexual marriage in the provision of employee benefits and state services, and the legitimacy of women-headed families are now matters of political debate as well as personal conflict.

Conclusion

We have argued that the development of welfare state policy cannot be explained by its functions in protecting the interests of men as a group or capitalists as a class but has to be explained historically as the outcome of political conflict and political interventions, including the collective action of women. But, drawing on Marxist and feminist theory, we emphasize the ways in which the political goals and resources of contesting groups are historically constrained, and we locate those constraints in structures of gender as well as class. We argue that the organization of social reproduction and the gender division of labor central to it not only has placed limits on but also, at times, has provided resources for women's self-organization.

Our approach is a historical materialist one, for we take as a starting point the socially necessary and socially organized labor through which humans reproduce themselves—not only the production of things but the work involved in using those things to renew life. In addition to what we consider a more comprehensive historical analysis, our approach also aims at developing a single-system theory, based on the recognition that production and social reproduction are two domains of an integrated process of species reproduction. Although a full account of the interrelationship has not been possible here, our analysis indicates the ways in which the changes in the organization of social reproduction that were so crucial to the presence and absence of women's self-organization in twentieth-century United States were related to qualitative changes in the capitalist economy (the rise of corporate capitalism, mass production, and the beginnings of mass consumption in the early twentieth century; the rise of multinational firms, the spread of mass education, and mass consumption and the consequent demand for women's labor after the Second World War).

The advantages of our framework are clear in its ability to cut through the counterpositions in feminist analysis of the welfare state between those that emphasize women's political agency (and, therefore, the ways in which the state conferred resources on women) and those that emphasize women's political powerlessness (and, therefore, the ways in which the welfare state has reinforced women's economic marginalization and dependence on the male-dominated nuclear family). We have tried to show that although the gender division of labor remained constant, its implications for women's political self-organization changed quite radically over the course of the twentieth century. Qualitative shifts in the organization of social reproduction, material and ideological, explain why middle-class women achieved self-organization during the Progressive Era and during the 1960s and 1970s, but not in the 1930s. These changes also explain why white middle-class women organized around a maternalist politics that helped to institutionalize the ideal of the male-breadwinner family in state policy, while second-wave feminism has contested the gender division of labor in the state, family, and the economy.

In considering the impact of the organization of social reproduction on women's collective action, we have also argued that the differences in the politics of self-organized African-American and white middle-class women reflected the different demands and possibilities African-American women faced in carrying out their responsibilities for social reproduction. In particular, African-American middle-class women could not rely on the individualized strategies of upward mobility available to the white middle class. Further, we have argued that continuities in the organization of social reproduction, especially the substantial privatization of the burdens of caregiving that fall especially heavily on working-class women, also explain outcomes. The gender division of labor diminished working-class women's capacities for self-organization and limited their ability to challenge either the working-class men or middle-class women who dominated political movements and organizations purporting to represent them in the contest over state policy.

Our account is by no means a finished one that fully incorporates class, race, and gender into an explanation of the welfare state. But we hope we have demonstrated the potential of our conceptual framework and the value of pursuing a single-system socialist-feminist analysis.

[*1991*]

Notes

We would like to thank the American Sociological Association Committee on Problems of the Discipline for supporting the conference at which this article was discussed and the conference participants for their responses and suggestions. We would also like to thank Chris Bose and Barrie Thorne for their helpful readings.

1. H. Hartmann, "The Unhappy Marriage of Marxism and Feminism: Towards a More Progressive Union," *Capital and Class* 8 (1979), 1–33.
2. Mimi Abramovitz, *Regulating the Lives of Women: Social Welfare Policy from Colonial Times to the Present* (Boston: South End Press, 1988); E. Boris and P. Bardaglio "The Transformation of Patriarchy: The Historical Role of the State," in I. Diamond, ed., *Family, Politics, and Public Policy: A Feminist Dialogue on Women and the State* (New York: Longman, 1983); E. Boris and P. Bardaglio, "Gender, Race and Class: The Impact of the State on the Family and the Economy, 1790–1945," in N. Gerstel and H. E. Gross, eds., *Families and Work* (Philadelphia: Temple University Press, 1987).
3. T. Skocpol, *Protecting Soldiers and Mothers: The Politics of Social Provision in the United States, 1870s-1920s* (Cambridge, Mass.: Harvard University Press, 1992).
4. B. Nelson, "The Gender, Race and Class Origins of Early Welfare Policy and the U.S. Welfare State: A Comparison of Workmen's Compensation and Mothers' Aid," in L. Tilly and P. Gurin, eds., *Women, Politics and Change* (New York: Russell Sage, 1990).
5. A. Orloff, "Gender in Early U.S. Social Policy," *Journal of Policy History* 3 (1991).
6. A. Orloff, *The Politics of Pensions: A Comparative Analysis of the Origins of Pensions and Old-age Insurance in Canada, Great Britain and the United States, 1880s-1930s* (Madison: University of Wisconsin Press, 1993).
7. H. J. Maroney and M. Luxton, "Feminism and Political Economy to Feminist Political Economy," *Feminism and Political Economy: Women's Work, Women's Struggles* (Toronto: Methuen, 1987); and D. E. Smith, "Feminist Reflections on Political Economy," *Studies in Political Economy* 30 (1989) 37–59.
8. For further discussion, see J. Brenner and B. Laslett, "Social Reproduction

and the Family," in U. Himmelstrand, ed., *Sociology from Crisis to Science? Vol. 2, The Social Reproduction of Organization and Culture* (London: Sage, 1986); and B. Laslett and J. Brenner, "Gender and Social Reproduction: Historical Perspectives," *Annual Review of Sociology* 15 (1989), 381–404.

9. E. B. Brown, "Womanist Consciousness: Maggie Lena Walker and the Independent Order of Saint Luke," *Signs* 14 (1989), 610–33; G. Mink, "The Lady and the Tramp: Gender, Race, and the Origins of the American Welfare State," in L. Gordon, ed., *Women, the State, and Welfare* (Madison: University of Wisconsin Press, 1990).

10. B. Laslett, "Women's Work in Los Angles, California: 1880–1900: Implications of Class and Gender," *Continuity and Change* 5 (1990), 417–41.

11. Nancy Cott, "Passionlessness: An Interpretation of Victorian Sexual Ideology, 1790–1850," *Signs: A Journal of Women in Culture and Society* 4 (1979), 210–36; and J. D'Emilio and E. B. Freedman. *Intimate Matters: A History of Sexuality in America* (New York: Harper & Row, 1988).

12. C. Smith-Rosenberg, *Disorderly Conduct: Visions of Gender in Victorian America* (New York: Oxford University Press, 1980).

13. P. Fass, *The Damned and the Beautiful* (New York: Oxford University Press, 1977); J. Modell, *Into One's Own: From Youth to Adulthood in the United States* (Berkeley: University of California Press, 1989).

14. R. S. Cowan, "Two Washes in the Morning and a Bridge Party at Night: The American Housewife Between the Wars," in L. Scharf and J. M. Jensen, eds., *Decades of Discontent: The Women's Movement, 1920–1940* (Westport: Greenwood Press, 1983).

15. P. Palmer, *Domesticity and Dirt: Housewives and Domestic Servants in the United States, 1920–1945* (Philadelphia: Temple University Press, 1989).

16. I. Wrigley, "Children's Caregivers and Ideologies of Parental Inadequacy," in E. Abel and M. K. Nelson, eds., *Circles of Care* (Albany: State University of New York Press, 1990).

17. S. L. Schlossman, "Before Home Start: Notes Toward a History of Parent Education in America, 1897–1929," *Harvard Educational Review* 46 (1976), 436–67.

18. S. L. Schlossman, "Philanthropy and the Gospel of Child Development," *History of Education Quarterly* 21 (1981) 275–99.

19. W. H. Whyte, Jr., *The Organization Man* (New York: Doubleday, 1957); and R. Kanter, *Men and Women of the Corporation* (New York: Basic Books, 1977).

20. W. H. Grabill, C. V. Kiser, and P. K. Whelpton, *The Fertility of American Women* (New York: Wiley, 1958).

21. See, for example, K. Mason, M. Weinstein, and B. Laslett, "The Decline of Fertility in Los Angeles, California, 1880–1900," *Population Studies* 41 (1987), 483–99.

22. S. H. Norwood, *Labor's Flaming Youth: Telephone Operators and Worker Militancy, 1878–1923* (Urbana: University of Illinois Press, 1990); D. Tyack and E. Hansot, *Learning Together: A History of Co-Education in American Schools* (New Haven: Yale University Press, 1990).

23. M. L. Fine, *The Souls of the Skyscraper: Female Clerical Workers in Chicago, 1870–1930* (Philadelphia: Temple University Press, 1990); Norwood, *Labor's Flaming Youth*; S. P. Breckinridge, "The Activities of Women Outside the Home," *Recent Social Trends, Volume 1*, Presidential Research Committee, eds. (New York:

McGraw–Hill, 1933).

24. W. D. Wandersee, *Women's Work and Family Values: 1920–1940* (Cambridge, Mass.: Harvard University Press, 1981).

25. J. Antler, *Lucy Sprague Mitchell: The Making of a Modern Woman* (New Haven: Yale University Press, 1987); Nancy Chodorow, "Seventies Questions for Thirties Women: Gender and Generation in a Study of Early Women Psychoanalysts," in N. Chodorow, ed., *Feminism and Psychoanalytic Theory* (New Haven: Yale University Press, 1989); B. Laslett, "Unfeeling Knowledge: Emotion and Subjectivity in the History of Sociology," *Sociological Form* 5 (1990), 413–34; D. Ross, "The Development of the Social Sciences," in A. Oleson and J. Voss, eds., *The Organization of Knowledge in Modern America: 1860–1920* (Baltimore: Johns Hopkins University Press, 1979).

26. L. Scharf, *To Work and to Wed: Female Employment, Feminism and the Great Depression* (Westport: Greenwood Press, 1980); but see A. Kessler-Harris, *A Woman's Wage: Historical Meanings and Social Consequences* (Lexington: University Press of Kentucky, 1990), chap. 3.

27. G. H. Elder, *Children of the Great Depression: Social Change in Life Experience* (Chicago: University of Chicago Press, 1974).

28. Wandersee, *Women's Work and Family Values*; and P. C. Glick, "Updating the Life Cycle of the Family," *Journal of Marriage and Family* 39 (1977), 5–14.

29. Glick, "Updating the Life Cycle of the Family," 5–14.

30. V. K. Oppenheimer, *The Female Labor Force in the United States* (Berkeley: University of California Press, Population Monograph Series No. 5, 1970); V. K. Oppenheimer, "The Life-Cycle Squeeze: The Interaction of Men's Occupational and Family Life Cycles," *Demography* 11 (1974), 227–45.

31. Oppenheimer, *The Female Labor Force in the United States*.

32. S. M. Evans, *Personal Politics: The Roots of Women's Liberation in the Civil Rights Movement and the New Left* (New York: Knopf, 1979).

33. J. Jones, *Labor of Love, Labor of Sorrow: Black Women, Work, and the Family from Slavery to the Present* (New York: Basic Books, 1985); L. Tilly, "Paths of Proletarianization: Organization of Production, Sexual Division of Labor, and Women's Collective Action," *Signs* 7 (1981), 400–17.

34. Meredith Tax, *The Rising of Women: Feminist Solidarity and Class Conflict: 1880–1917* (New York: Monthly Review Press, 1980).

35. P. M. Glazer and M. Slater, *Unequal Colleagues: The Entrance of Women into the Professions, 1890–1940* (New Brunswick: Rutgers University Press, 1997); R. M. Morantz-Sanchez, *Sympathy and Science: Women Physicians in American Medicine* (New York: Oxford University Press, 1985), 282–315; S. M. Reverby, *Ordered to Care: The Dilemma of American Nursing, 1850–1945* (Cambridge: Cambridge University Press, 1987), 109–10.

36. E. B. Freedman, "Separatism as Strategy: Female Institution Building and American Feminism 1870–1930," *Feminist Studies* 5 (1979), 512–29.

37. N. F. Cott, "Across the Great Divide: Women in Politics Before and After 1920," and E. B. Higginbotham, "In Politics to Stay: Black Women Leaders and Party Politics in the 1920s," in Tilly and Gurin, eds., *Women, Politics, and Change*.

38. Abramovitz, *Regulating the Lives of Women*; E. Faue, "Women, Family, and Politics: Farmer-Labor Women and Social Policy in the Great Depression," in Tilly and Gurin, eds., *Women, Politics, and Change*; S. Ware, *Holding Their Own:*

American Women in the 1930s (Boston: Twayne Press, 1982).

39. N. F. Cott. *The Grounding of Modern Feminism* (New Haven: Yale University Press, 1987); C. M. Mueller, "The Empowerment of Women: Polling and the Women's Voting Bloc," in C. M. Mueller, ed., *The Politics of the Gender Gap* (Newbury Park: Sage Press, 1989); J. M. Jensen, "All Pink Sisters: The War Department and the Feminist Movement in the 1920s," in Scharf and Jensen, eds., *Decades of Discontent.*

40. H. Sitkoff, *A New Deal for Blacks* (New York: Oxford University Press, 1978).

41. E. Clark-Lewis, "This Work Had an End: African-American Domestic Workers in Washington, D.C., 1919–1940," in C. Groneman and M. B. Notion, eds., *To Toil the Live Long Day: American Women at Work, 1780–1980* (Ithaca: Cornell University Press, 1987).

42. P. Giddings, *Where and When I Enter: The Impact of Black Women on Race and Sex in America* (New York: William Morrow, 1984); R. Terborg-Penn, "Discontented Black Feminists: Prelude and Postscript to the Passage of the Nineteenth Amendment," in Scharf and Jensen, eds., *Decades of Discontent.*

43. S. Ware, *Partner and I: Molly Dewson, Feminism, and New Deal Politics* (New Haven: Yale University Press, 1987); Cott, *The Grounding of Modern Feminism.*

44. Kessler-Harris, *A Women's Wage.*

45. L. Scharf, "The Forgotten Woman: Women, the New Deal, and Women's Organizations," in Scharf and Jensen, eds., *Decades of Discontent.*

46. Ware, *Holding Their Own.*

47. L. Frankel, "Southern Textile Women: Generations of Survival and Struggle," in K. Sacks and D. Remy, eds., *My Troubles are Going to Have Troubles with Me* (New Brunswick: Rutgers University Press, 1984); R. Meyerqwitz, "Women Unionists and World War II: New Opportunities for Leadership," Paper delivered at the meeting of the Organization for American Historians, San Francisco, 1980.

48. Sitkoff, *A New Deal for Blacks*, 184–85.

49. Ibid., 186.

50. R. Milkman, *Gender at Work* (Urbana: University of Illinois Press, 1987); S. H. Strom, "Challenging 'Woman's Place': Feminism, the New Left, and Industrial Unionism," *Feminist Studies* 9 (1983), 361–96.

51. P. S. Foner, *Women and the American Labor Movement* (New York: Free Press, 1979); Sitkoff, *A New Deal for Blacks.*

52. Milkman, *Gender at Work.*

53. Jensen, "All Pink Sisters."

54. K. E. Trimberger, "Feminism, Men, and Modern Love: Greenwich Village: 1900–1925," in A. Snitow, C. Stansell, and S. Thompson, eds., *Powers of Desire* (New York: Monthly Review Press, 1983).

55. R. Shaffer, "Women and the Communist Party, USA, 1930–1940," *Socialist Review* 93 (1979), 73–118; K. E. Trimberger, "Women in the Old and New Left: The Evolution of a Politics of Personal Life," *Feminist Studies* 5 (1979), 432–61.

56. Strom, "Challenging 'Woman's Place'."

57. Trimberger, "Women in the Old and New Left."

58. N. F. Gabin, *Feminism in the Labor Movement: Women and the United Auto Workers, 1935–1975* (Ithaca: Cornell University Press, 1990); A.S. Rossi. *Feminists in Politics* (New York: Academic Press, 1982).

59. M. M. Ferree and B. B. Hess, *Controversy and Coalition: The New Feminist Movement* (Boston: Twayne Press, 1985).
60. D'Emilio and Freedman, *Intimate Matters*.
61. D. Balser, *Sisterhood and Solidarity: Feminism and Labor in Modern Times* (Boston: South End Press, 1987); G. West, *The National Welfare Rights Movement: The Social Protest of Poor Women* (New York: Praeger Press, 1981).
62. Chapter 9 in this volume.

Chapter 3

Gender and Class in U.S. Labor History

The relationship between gender and class, central to understanding the history of the labor movement, raises important issues for Marxist analysis in general. Grappling with the complexities of this relationship forces us to confront a wide range of theoretical and practical questions. What is the connection between "material conditions" and "identity"? What role do culture, discourses, sexuality, and emotions play in shaping people's responses to their material conditions? How are the varieties of consciousness of class related to other identities and affiliations? These questions challenge us theoretically and politically, as we seek to develop a working-class politics that incorporates struggles against all forms of oppression.

We can approach these questions historically by asking how and why working-class men have, throughout the history of the labor movement, often chosen forms of trade-union organization and strategies that systematically disadvantaged women workers—excluding women from their unions and, when they did organize with women, accepting, even demanding, gendered occupations and wage differentials. Feminist explanations originally focused on how working-class men's strategies reflected their gendered material interests or their psycho-sexual needs. These analyses illuminated how union strategies underwrote working-class men's gender privilege, but they also tended to attribute a fixed set of motivations to men as a group. Material interests and emotional needs may be powerful wellsprings of human action. However, it is also important to contextualize them historically. How people understand their interests and experience their needs varies tremendously and is shaped by the possibilities and constraints of a given historical moment.

More recent feminist approaches, drawing on poststructuralist theory, have moved away from an attribution of gendered interests/needs to more historically specific accounts of, in Ava Baron's words, "the construction of gender identity and its role in shaping workers' lives."[1] Here, explanations focus on how cultural meanings of sexual difference, expressed in discourses of gender, affected action. Efforts to secure a stable gender identity underlay men's job choices, the ways they defined and did their work, and the strategies they chose to fight their employers, decisively shaping the gendered division of waged labor and the structure of work and unions.

Nevertheless, recognizing that many different meanings of sexual difference circulate at the same time, we must explain why some discourses of gender and not others took the stage; why certain gendered identities were mobilized in workplace and communal struggles; and how particular definitions of gender came to be institutionalized in workplaces, families, and communities. This question points toward an analysis of relations of power between employers and workers and between men and women within working-class households, communities, and workplaces. It brings us back to looking at interests that arise as working-class men and women attempt to survive within the competitive structures of a capitalist economy. And it brings us back to the socio-emotional needs that individuals develop in the context of organizing daily life on and off the job. Rather than counterposing explanations which draw on interests, needs, and discourses, I want to suggest some ways to understand how they are linked.

Survival Projects

I would start with the concept of *survival projects*, the ways people group together in order to live in capitalist society. These projects take different forms, from the most narrow and individualistic modes of striving to mass collective action. Individuals may be very conscious of making strategic choices, or they may adopt them more or less unconsciously. In either case, people must enter into various kinds of affiliation to secure the basic necessities of life. These patterns of affiliation are fundamental to how individuals define the boundaries of their solidarities, how they position themselves in relation to others, how they organize a worldview, and how they develop their various definitions of self, including their gendered identities.

I want to use the notion of survival projects because it is a way of talking about material life that recognizes the importance of individuals' motives and action, while placing these in specific social and historical contexts. We can conceptualize resistance and accommodation as outcomes of a process that is simultaneously cultural, individual, psychological, collective, and social. Individuals are situated in workplaces and communities, within which they develop understandings, feelings, and intentions. Through groups, individuals try to establish some control over their situation in the labor market as well as vis-à-vis particular employers. And because most working-class people (in contrast to more affluent professionals and managers) cannot reproduce themselves entirely through the market, groups are also constituted by exchanges (of money and unpaid labor) outside the capitalist economy.

There is no such thing as an identity abstracted from social practice. Like other identities, gender is negotiated and renegotiated in the practices of everyday life. Strategies that working-class people adopt for economic survival within the rules of the capitalist game shape these everyday practices in fundamental ways. These survival strategies will necessarily include forms of mutual support, not only in the workplace but outside of waged work—relations of sharing and solidarity across households, in neighborhoods, in kinship and friendship networks, in communities, and so on. Key resources include sharing cash income, bartering services such as childcare, and sharing living space.

Although historically women have predominated in creating social networks outside the workplace, I am not at all suggesting that we should locate gender in community while class belongs at work. Rather, I am suggesting that households, survival networks (of kin, fictive kin, and friends), neighborhoods, and workplaces are interrelated. Until well into the twentieth century, communal ties created a base of support for worker protest and trade-union organization, as well as women's community organizing (the co-operative movement, rent strikes, and so forth). But communal ties can also be sources of ethnic and racial hostility as communities, formed through particularistic and local sharing networks, compete with each other for scarce resources (jobs, better neighborhoods, and the like).

In contemporary capitalism, personal survival networks may not be as centered within spatial communities as they once were (although this might be debated). Yet they remain crucial resources, determining the level of individual and family well-being. And, operating in a normal everyday way, they reproduce distributions of relative privilege among groups within the working class. The role that friends and kin play, for example, in facilitating access to employment is well documented and an important source of racial and ethnic segregation in the occupational structure.

Many feminists have rightly argued that identities are multiple (one is never simply a worker) and that different identities are not lived separately. One is not a worker here, a woman there, and a person of color elsewhere. Feminist labor historians have also emphasized that women, like men, develop identities as workers. Further, while feelings mobilized by workplace-based identity, the intense commitment to a particular self-definition, have a gendered character, these feelings and commitments do not arise only from meanings of gender.

This is important to emphasize from the start. When we talk about gendered workers, we risk associating with gender the emotional components of identity in which gender "modifies" workers, as if workers' identities reflect rational calculations of material interest, while gender arises from sexuality, culture, and emotion. But workers' identities, in their many variations, also have unconscious and emotional components. They mobilize feelings as much as gender does. And, on the other side, gender identities, while drawing on cultural meanings and mobilizing sexuality, are constructed within material relations, relations defined by the survival strategies through which people accomplish their basic life tasks.

Cultural meanings of gender, like cultural meanings of class, are produced by men and women within group life, on and off the job. However, because the production of meaning is itself a group process, it is also intensely political. The choices that groups of people make about such matters as how to organize their survival, how to represent themselves, how to resist and where to accommodate, and who within the group has rights to what valued goods, is a product of negotiation and struggle. The outcome, therefore, reflects the different kinds and levels of resources that men and women bring into the process (as, for example, skilled craft workers, unskilled workers, legal or undocumented immigrants, married women, or single mothers).

How men and women affiliate—at work and outside it—both reflects gender identities and creates them. Group affiliations respond to a complex set of constraints and opportunities. These constraints and opportunities cannot be reduced to the operations of the capitalist economy, but neither can they be divorced from them. In what follows, I give some examples of how we might make the connection.

Sectorial Strategies and Market Competition

Workers in capitalism are pulled apart as much as (perhaps even more than) they are pushed toward collective action. The operations of the capitalist market constrain the strategies of both employers and workers and tend to reproduce particularistic group identities and exclusionary strategies. If workplace relations tend to enhance workers' recognition of their common condition, competition in the labor market tends to encourage individualistic strategies for survival. That workers have been able to overcome individualistic tendencies through unionization should not blind us to the very real difficulties and barriers that have to be faced and overcome.

An analysis of gender and strategic choices ought to take these difficulties sufficiently into account, acknowledging that the competitive structure of the labor market threatens to undermine solidarity and divide groups of workers from each other. Although trade unions are common strategies for countering employers, trade unions have often organized on a relatively narrow basis, hardly constituted as organizations of the working class as a whole. Organizing to secure immediate, short-run economic advantages often runs counter to organizing based on longer-run possibilities for challenging employers on a more class-wide basis. From this point of view, working men's individualistic or narrowly based group strategies for survival may have been the source for certain kinds of masculine identities as much as a consequence of them.

The fact that male workers have adopted exclusionary and elitist attitudes toward other men and not just toward women further supports this idea. Control over a craft, for instance, required control over apprenticeship and employment. Skilled workers narrowed the potential labor pool by using many different criteria for entry into their trade: not only gender, but kinship (training only sons or close relatives), geography (city printers' refusal to unionize country printers who undercut them), ethnicity, race, and so forth. Faced with employers' efforts to avoid established apprenticeship systems and to use lower-paid skilled male workers (immigrants, rural workers, etc.) to undercut their rates, craft unions followed the same exclusionary tactics, striking against the employment of non-union workers rather than attempting to unionize them. Masculinity of a certain sort (e.g., white or native-born) was produced and mobilized to delimit the areas of labor belonging to unionized men and to justify their exclusionary strategies.

In following sectorial strategies, male craft workers were not unique. Competition among workers over jobs and as members of different occupations and industries can and often does overwhelm and obscure the common interests that they have as a class. The skilled disregard the unskilled, the organized disregard the unorganized, the stronger unions disregard the weaker ones—and this happens among workers who share ethnic identity or gender as well as those who do not. Sectorial organization, narrow strategies in which some sets of workers secure their immediate economic interests even to the detriment of others, can characterize industrial as well as craft unions. (Conversely, skilled craft workers are as capable as industrial workers of developing very broad-based conceptions of solidarity—for example, the Knights of Labor in 1884–1887.) The point is that when we look at labor history we don't necessarily see "working-class identities" arising out of trade-union organization. We may see a range of understandings, organizations, and practices within trade unions, reflecting very different conceptions of what it means to be a worker and even very different views of whether all workers belong to a "working class."

When working women have organized on the basis of craft exclusion rather than industrial organization, they have, like nineteenth-century male craft workers, adopted patronizing attitudes toward other workers and profound emotional commitments to maintaining occupational boundaries and divisions of labor in the workplace.[2] Registered nurses have been no more willing to take "less credentialed" hospital workers into their unions than male craftsmen were willing to assimilate the "lesser skilled" women workers into theirs. Unionized women teachers have often made separate contract deals with school administrations and failed to support the demands and organizing of clerical workers and teachers' aides.

If craftsmen clung to masculine craft identities rather than adopt new strategies as their industries changed and women entered their workplaces, so have women workers developed feminine craft identities embedded in particular strategies for organizing against their employers. Conflicts among women workers can look very much like those between women and men. Waitresses successfully organized along gender-segregated craft lines in the 1920s and 1930s, developing fierce commitments to an identity as female workers, doing work that was different from that of men but equally skilled. In the 1960s, they clung to these identities, and to the forms of organization that had served them so well as against a younger generation of waitresses, working under very different conditions in an expanding and reorganizing food service industry.

By the early 1970s, at the height of the feminist movement, younger waitresses turned to the courts to demand access to jobs (elite food service, bartending) that had previously been closed to women. They also sought to change union strategy, abandoning craft unionism for a more industrial mode. According to historian Dorothy Sue Cobble, older waitress leaders experienced this challenge as an assault on their identities as skilled craft workers as well as on their leadership positions, reacting with anger and mobilizing to squelch the opposition. The highly factionalized political situation starkly counterposed strategies which otherwise might have been melded together and, preserving some of the older strategies, strengthened waitress organizing even in the new conditions.[3]

Gender Divisions of Labor and Strategic Choices

More privileged workers can choose to protect themselves on the labor market by organizing to establish or defend a racial or gendered occupational structure. But whether workers can successfully carry out this kind of strategy depends upon employers being willing to accommodate the particular distribution of relative privilege and upon marginalized groups being in a position to challenge these strategies. To understand whether and when women successfully resist, we need to consider both how they construe their interests and what resources for contestation are available to them at different times and places. We must look beyond the workplace and labor market to survival networks organized around a gendered division of labor, networks which have been and continue to be primary strategies for working people to secure their conditions of life.

Women's responsibilities for caregiving have provided resources and posed limitations. They have structured women's interests as well as their identities. On the one hand, women have used these responsibilities to make successful claims on men and on their communities. In the past (and even today, to a certain extent), women's sharing networks enabled mothers to participate in wage work. And out of these networks women developed solidarity for political action—as community members and as trade-union activists.[4]

On the other hand, caregiving responsibilities are also constraints. They hamper women's collective self-organization, especially in organizations and struggles which extend beyond the community level. Historically, the more localized and communal a working-class organization is, the easier it has been for women to participate in action and organization, to take on leadership roles, to develop their own demands and ways of representing themselves, and to contest with men. The more centralized, bureaucratic, and trans-local working-class organizations are, the easier it is for men to monopolize decision-making and marginalize women. Limitations on women's participation were cultural (definitions of leadership, and notions of masculine authority and the role of women in the public sphere) but also material. In the first instance, caregiving responsibilities restricted women's leadership beyond the local level. Until quite recently most women union leaders and organizers were single, childless, or had grown children. But even when individual women fought their way into leadership at the regional or national level, they were isolated, lacking a collective political base.[5]

Caregiving responsibilities shaped working-class women's interests, creating potentials for both solidarity and conflict. Single women, daughters of working-class families, single mothers, and married women have adopted different survival strategies, which in turn shape their own as well as their family members' participation in work and workers' protest. Married women dependent on a male breadwinner and young single women workers living in male-headed households had very different real interests from those women workers who were sole or primary wage-earners for themselves or their families. In many instances, married women supported the efforts of predominantly young and single female workers to unionize and receive higher wages. And at times female solidarity has been built across significant divides—for instance, between married women home workers and single women factory workers.[6] On the other hand, in struggles where men have promoted their own interests at the expense of single female workers, cross-cutting alliances have sometimes undermined female solidarity, as married women have thrown their support behind the men of the community.[7]

Conflicts surfaced between married and single women workers in the electrical industry in the years immediately following the Second World War over who had more "right" to hold onto their wartime jobs. This division occurred in the context of pervasive fears about postwar unemployment, unions dominated by men numerically and politically, and a hegemonic male-breadwinner ideology unchallenged by a feminist organization either inside or outside the trade unions.[8]

Women's strategic choices are, like men's, shaped by a complex set of constraints and resources, needs and opportunities. These, again, reflect not only their position in the labor market (e.g. their levels of skill, the demand for their labor) but also how they are positioned within the communities on which they depend for their survival and how their communities are positioned in relation to others. Some of the key factors here are the degree of political support for women's claims to wage work, the degree to which women can actually rely on male breadwinners for support, and, in relation to the former, their community's norms of motherhood and womanhood. The different strategic choices of white and Black women workers in one case study illuminates this point.

After the Second World War, the predominantly male unionized bartenders mobilized to drive women, who had entered bartending during the war, from the trade. Most of the white women unionists, who had in fact fought men for the right to serve liquor (previously a male preserve), did not mobilize to hold onto bartending work. But three hundred Black women bartenders in Chicago launched a strong protest. Their all-Black union local leadership conceded to the women, continuing to dispatch women bartenders from the hiring hall. In 1961, however, when a city ordinance banning women from bartending was finally enforced, 400 women lost their jobs. The male-dominated local (as well as the international) refused to help, so the barmaids turned to the community for support and picketed city hall. Black community newspapers ran stories sympathetic to the women; however, the ordinance was allowed to stand.[9]

Black women and white women workers pursued different strategies because discrimination in the food service industry limited Black women's access to higher paid employment as waitresses at the same time that industry growth was expanding white waitresses' opportunities. Black women, although faced with opposition from Black men, also had more space to assert their own "breadwinner" claims since their right to living-wage work was more supported in the Black community. Where white waitresses found their main support for their identities as craft workers inside the union, Black women belonged to a racially oppressed community which generated its own oppositional organizations, including Black newspapers. Perhaps because the women bartenders' struggle focused more on the white-dominated city council than on their own Black union local, it was easier for the women to win community support. Although many white waitresses were also single mothers, they did not have the same sorts of community institutions to turn to and so were under more pressure to come to terms with the men in their union.

Thus, the different sources of group support for women both at and outside of work shaped the ways in which they developed gendered work identities and structured the risks they faced and the resources they had available to contest with men about what was and was not gender-appropriate work for women. White women had stronger ties to the union, fewer resources outside it than Black women, and, perhaps most important, far less economic need than Black women had to challenge men's attempts to define bartending as inappropriate work for women.

Politics of Struggle and Discourses of Gender

Discourses of gender were always entailed in trade-union struggles, as workers sought to justify their demands to each other, to a general public, and to potential allies in the middle class. Strategies of self-representation are political choices, sometimes self-conscious, sometimes unreflective, but always choices. Differing modes of making a case are always available. How male trade unionists represented themselves or women workers shifted, depending on how necessary they thought it was to appease middle-class allies and how pressured they were by their female colleagues who had a different vision of how they wished to be spoken of and seen.

For example, throughout the late nineteenth century and into the 1920s, the majority of the female factory labor force remained young and single. Male trade unionists and middle-class reformers, male and female, attempted to win support for striking women workers by drawing on anxieties about young women's sexuality, an intense focus of public discourse in the period. Trying to picture factory girls as sympathetic victims, these discourses emphasized the differences between working men and women by defining women's low wages as a problem of sexual victimization (the cause of the working girl's "fall" into prostitution). When working women could make their voices heard, they strongly objected to this line of defense, rejecting its patronizing tone and advancing very different images. Shifting attention away from the issue of their virtue, young women strikers asserted their similarity with men, appealing for support on the ground of their breadwinner roles, their reliance on wage-earning to support themselves and their families.[10]

The process of choosing organizing strategies is both conscious and unconscious. Men's and women's individual identities as workers are created, then reproduced and solidified, in daily life in informal workgroups and formal workers' organizations, producing deep commitments to ways of understanding oneself and feelings about others. Defining the boundaries of "us" and "them" is part of everyday resistance to managerial authority on the job and certainly crucial to all kinds of confrontational challenges to management. While necessary for protection, group boundaries have their own rigidities and defensive sides.

The passionate feelings that leak through the minutes of both nineteenth- and twentieth-century union meetings where the employment of women was discussed demonstrate that craftsmen experienced lower-waged women's entry into their workplaces as an attack on their masculinity, their sexual and social selves. The economic threat that lower-paid women workers represented was certainly real. But much more than wage levels was at stake. Women's presence also threatened the practices, feelings, and relationships through which men had constructed a culture of solidarity within their organizations.

Solidarity involves defining and maintaining group loyalties to defend against the threat of both real and imagined betrayals. Organizing against a powerful (and seductive) enemy can be frightening. Gender difference (the obsessive demarcation of masculinity) could be, and often was, mobilized to manage these anxieties. But a defensive masculinity was only one strategy, and not the only one possible. Where the turn of the century Cigar Makers' Industrial Union (CMIU) pursued exclusionary strategies and very reluctantly organized women workers into a separate and secondary section of the union, male Cuban émigrés in Tampa's cigar industry, radicalized by the struggle for independence, rejected craft organization in favor of an anarcho-syndicalist union, La Resistencia, which sought to organize all workers throughout the city. Prominent among them were women tobacco strippers, who represented over one-quarter of Resistencia's membership. Attacked as both un-American and unmanly by the CMIU, the male leadership of La Resistencia characterized the CMIU as "a barn of white livered dung hill cocks," proclaiming themselves "the voice of virile labor."[11] In the context of a politicized community and an industry where men and women labored in the same factories and received equal pay for the same work (although men tended to monopolize the most highly paid jobs), strategic choices required working men to redefine the boundaries of gendered work and the meaning of masculinity.

Periods of labor radicalism and mass struggles were the most hospitable environment for challenges to hegemonic cultural constructions
of gender. The movements' radically democratic ideology encouraged
claims for gender equality and respect for women as partners, not
subordinates. The actual organizing and solidarity of workers in conflict
with employers encouraged women workers to organize and encouraged working-class men to support them. Organized feminism,
while predominantly middle class in membership, helped working-class
women to develop the language and political resources to articulate
demands for political and economic equality within their trade unions
and communities. (The contrast between the 1930s and earlier
moments of widespread class mobilization is especially striking along
these lines.[12])

In the nineteenth century, when labor radicalism was tied to a
broader political movement and goals of revolutionary change, such as
the vision of cooperative commonwealth at the heart of Owenite socialism in England in the 1830s and the Knights of Labor in the United
States in the 1880s, women could be full members of organizations,
participating not only as workers but as members of working-class
communities. This was especially important because women were a
numerical minority in the paid workforce. Insofar as women were included, there was at least a potential base of support for feminist ideas.
At the height of their militancy, and responding to pressure from women
delegates (mostly textile operatives and shoe workers), the Knights'
national convention endorsed woman suffrage in 1886.[13]

Greenwald's comparative study of conflicts over women's entry into
male jobs during the First World War suggests how men's strategic
choices were affected by generalized class struggle and middle-class
feminist alliances with working-class organizations. In Kansas City, a
city-wide and week-long general strike in support of striking men and
women laundry workers preceded the introduction of women as conductors on the streetcars. A strong branch of the Women's Trade Union
League (WTUL) had cooperated with the union movement around the
laundry strike, proving their reliability as working-class allies. When the
streetcar company sought to hire women as conductors for lower pay,
the Amalgamated Transit Union went out on strike, with newly hired
women, demanding equal pay for equal work. Their strike won the
support of the Kansas City labor movement and the WTUL. In
Cleveland and Detroit, by contrast, the male-dominated unions struck
against the employment of women.[14]

The conditions that encouraged challenge to gender norms were not part of everyday life and organizing. Radical movements' defeat brought demoralization about the possibilities of broad-based challenges to capital, encouraging better-placed workers to fall back onto more narrow, sectorial forms of trade-union organizing, and prompting others to seek more privatistic routes to economic survival.

Implications for the Present

Today the lines of conflict and solidarity between men and women workers have shifted in profound ways. The question of women's place in trade unions, of women's ability to labor and to lead, is, if certainly not settled, no longer the fundamental axis of gender relations. Forty percent of all trade-union members are women, and their representation within leadership, especially in unions with large numbers of women, is growing significantly.[15] With feminism as a strong current in the trade unions, women workers have organized for new bargaining issues like comparable worth, family leave, sexual harassment policies, and to redefine the scope of trade-union politics, forcing their unions to take positions on abortion rights and lesbian and gay rights.

Unfortunately, these gains are outweighed by the sustained corporate assault against all workers' wages and working conditions. The unionized portion of the labor force is at its lowest point in fifty years, mainly because men's rates of unionization have fallen dramatically. Unions are on the defensive economically and politically. As various forces search for strategic counter-offensives, the drumbeat against "special interests" and "identity politics" has become very loud, expanding well beyond the right and the center. There is, of course, something real here: working people's distress and the concentration of wealth have become too great to ignore. However, this particular rediscovery of workers as a forgotten middle has counterposed "identity" to class politics, even holding the left responsible for the current weakness of progressive forces.[16]

Here, I think, is the new "fault line" of gender (and racial) conflict, posing the question of whether working-class institutions of struggle will adopt inclusive political strategies. Tragic losses suffered by blue-collar men threaten to overshadow, politically, the double day, the low wages, and the job insecurity faced by many working women. Broad political support for Clinton's assault on single mothers in the name of welfare reform reflects deep divisions within the working class between employed workers and chronically unemployed and underemployed workers, between married women with children and single mothers.

The history I have outlined demonstrates that how trade unions will respond to the employers' offensive depends, at least in part, on the political self-organization of marginalized groups. Declining male wages in the context of a hyper-competitive labor market, pervasive economic insecurity, and disappearing public services have destabilized the old gender order, but not in ways that clearly improve the lives of working-class women and men. Whether men will respond in a defensive re-assertion of their lost male privilege depends on whether women will have the political resources to challenge men, forcing them to redefine masculinity in more egalitarian terms. In turn, how women come to define their own gendered interests depends on whether men and women together will opt for more collective rather than individualistic solutions to current dilemmas. Counterposing "identity" to "class" politics, there-fore, is absolutely mistaken. Rather, as many movement activists and trade unionists are already doing, we have to build a coalition politics through struggles that creatively address (rather than wishfully disregard) divisions within the working class and support (rather than undermine) the efforts of oppressed people to represent themselves, their interests, and their needs.

[*1991*]

Notes

1. Ava Baron, "Gender and Labor History: Learning from the Past, Looking to the Future" in Ava Baron, ed., *Work Engendered: Toward a New History of American Labor* (Ithaca: Cornell University Press 1991), 31. In addition to the articles in this collection, see for the English case Anna Clark, *The Struggle for the Breeches: Gender and the Making of the British Working Class* (Berkeley: University of California Press, 1995), and Sonya Rose, *Limited Livelihoods: Gender and Class in Nineteenth-Century England* (Berkeley: University of California Press, 1992).

2. Mary H. Blewett, *Men, Women and Work: Class, Gender, and Protest in the New England Shoe Industry, 1780–1910* (Chicago: University of Illinois Press, 1988), chap. 8, esp. 242–49.

3. Dorothy Sue Cobble, *Dishing It Out: Waitresses and Their Unions in the Twentieth Century* (Chicago: University of Illinois Press, 1991), 192–200.

4. Ardis Camerion, "Bread & Roses revisted: Women's Culture and Working-Class Activism in the Lawrence Strike of 1912," in Ruth Milkman, ed., *Women, Work, and Protest* (Boston: Routledge, 1985); Karen Brodkin Sacks, *Organizing at Duke Medical Center* (Chicago: University of Illinois Press, 1988), chap. 5.

5. Elizabeth Faue, *Community of Suffering and Struggle* (Chapel Hill: University of North Carolina Press, 1991), chap. 5; Carol Turbin, *Working Women of Collar*

City (Chicago: University of Illinois Press, 1992), chap. 3.

6. Eileen Boris, "'A Man's Dwelling House is His Castle': Tenement House Cigar Making and the Judicial Imperative," in Baron, ed., *Work Engendered*, 139.

7. Blewett, *Men, Women and Work*, 123–33.

8. Ruth Milkman, *Gender at Work: The Dynamics of Job Segregation by Sex during World War II* (Chicago: University of Illinois Press, 1987), 145.

9. Cobble, *Dishing It Out*, chap. 7.

10. Blewett, *Men Women and Work*, 284–85; Jacquelyn Dowd Hall, "Private Eyes, Public Women: Images of Class and Sex in the Urban South, Atlanta, Georgia, 1913–1915," in Baron, ed., *Work Engendered*, 260–69.

11. Patricia A. Cooper, *Once A Cigar Maker: Men, Women and Work Culture in American Cigar Factories, 1900–1919* (Urbana: University of Illinois Press, 1987), esp. 114–17, 151–52; Nancy A. Hewitt, "'The Voice of Virile Labor': Labor Militancy, Community Solidarity, and Gender Identity among Tampa's Latin Workers, 1880–1930," in Baron, ed., *Work Engendered*, 142–67.

12. For a fuller discussion of this point, see Chapter 2 above.

13. Susan Levine, *Labor's True Woman: Carpet Weavers, Industrialization, and Labor Reform in the Gilded Age* (Philadelphia: Temple University Press, 1984), chap. 5; Barbara Taylor, *Eve and the New Jerusalem: Socialism and Feminism in the Nineteenth Century* (New York: Pantheon Books, 1983).

14. Maurine Weiner Greenwald, *Women, War and Work: The Impact of World War I on Women Workers in the United States* (Ithaca: Cornell University Press, 1990), chap. 4, esp. 172–80.

15. Cynthia Costello and Barbara Kivimae Krimgold, eds., *The American Woman, 1996–97* (New York: W. W. Norton, 1996), 69.

16. See, for example, Richard Rorty, *Achieving Our Country: Leftist Thought in Twentieth Century America* (Cambridge, Mass.: Harvard University Press, 1998), and Todd Gitlin, *The Twilight of Common Dreams* (New York: Metropolitan, 1995).

Part II

Women and Social Policy

Chapter 4

The Feminization of Poverty, Comparable Worth, and Feminist Political Discourse

Feminization of poverty and comparable worth have become feminist issues in the United States in part to include in feminist politics the central concerns of working-class women and women of color. In both cases, women social scientists have played an important part as scholars producing data to attest to the social reality of gendered inequality and as technical advisers to organizations and governments concerned with remedying economic inequities.[1] Because of the role feminist social scientists play in both campaigns, we need to consider carefully the broader politics within which feminization of poverty and comparable worth are inserted.

I contend that situated within a liberal political discourse, both the feminization of poverty and the comparable worth campaigns, in practice, and often in rhetoric, fail to bridge class and race divisions among women and, instead, reinforce the separation of feminism from the movements of other subordinated groups. While appearing to speak to problems that women share, they have tended to unite only through a denial of race and class differences. My point is not that these campaigns and the issues they raise are mistaken. Rather, it is that the current organization of these campaigns, in particular the policy demands and their accompanying justifications, may not constructively address differences in the situation and needs of all classes of women. I will suggest an alternative framework that does not court the danger of strengthening the ideological and social underpinnings of women's subordination.

Liberal Discourse on Equality

A liberal discourse on equality operates with two interrelated assumptions. The first assumption involves issues of organization and allocation: that is, how necessary social functions—governance, education, the production of goods, services, and knowledge—should be organized (hierarchy) and how resources and labor time should be allocated (differential rewards). The second assumption involves the issue of dependence and the related separation of the public and private spheres. Liberal thought assumes that social relationships of economy and polity are created by autonomous, independently contracting individuals. I will lay out each of these assumptions and then show how they are fundamental to feminist political discourse on women's poverty and gendered pay inequity.

A liberal discourse on equality centers on the ideal of meritocracy. Liberal political thought accepts the notion of inequality and hierarchy: some will have more, some less; some will command, others follow; some will create, others only implement. Equality is defined as equal opportunity, and thus, from a liberal perspective, fairness exists when the distribution of individuals within unequal positions reflects their individual qualities—their differential motivation, talent, intelligence, and effort—and not their gender, race, religion, or family background. Liberal demands have changed over time—in the eighteenth century, they were tied to the free market and unregulated competition; in the twentieth century, they were compatible with state intervention in the economy. But there is a continuity in liberal goals and argument. The free market was rejected when it became clear that the market alone would not distribute people in a meritocratic way. Inequalities in familial economic and social status and historic prejudices led to unfair outcomes for meritorious individuals. State intervention was required to ensure equality of opportunity. The goal of liberal social and economic policy is still a just distribution of individuals within a hierarchy of rewards and power.

The compelling character of this view is not surprising, since its crucial assumptions about social organization and human nature are widely accepted in advanced capitalist society. These assumptions are that there are large and significant differences among individuals in talent and potential; that a complex industrial society requires hierarchies; that competition and differential rewards for various positions within the hierarchies will motivate the most talented people to fill the most central and important positions.[2] A radical critique challenges these assumptions, claiming that most individuals are capable of making valuable contributions to society and, collectively, of governing it.

In contrast to the assumptions underlying liberal political thought, socialists (and many radical and socialist feminists) have contended that hierarchy brings out the worst, not the best, in individuals, and that while those at the bottom suffer particularly, everyone is distorted and narrowed by competitive striving. They also contend that collective decision-making and responsibility are workable alternative forms of social organization, even in an advanced industrial society, and that such forms promote the full development of individual talents and offer the greatest individual freedom.[3]

The second fundamental assumption of liberal political thought is that dependence belongs in the private sphere—there is no place for dependent individuals either in the notion of economic contract or in the concept of the citizen. Indeed, political citizenship is defined by independence, by the capacity to make choices based on individual self-interest, free from control by others on whom one is dependent. Similarly, wage laborers own their own persons and can sell their labor power as independent contractors. As Daniel Bell so nicely puts it:

> The liberal theory of society was framed by the twin axes of individualism and rationality. The unencumbered individual would seek to realize his own satisfactions on the basis of his work—he was to be rewarded for effort, pluck, and risk—and the exchange of products with others was calculated by each so as to maximize his own satisfactions. Society was to make no judgments between men—only to set the procedural rules—and the most efficient distribution of resources was the one that produced the greatest net balance of satisfactions.[4]

The contribution of women within the family in reproducing the male breadwinner and replacing his labor over a generation is of course hidden in liberal economic theory. The dependence of the whole society, the economy, and the political system, on the family and women's work within the family is ignored. As Linda Gordon argues, "Liberal political and economic theory rests on assumptions about the sexual division of labor and on notions of citizens as heads of families."[5] A society of "freely contracting" male citizens relies on the prior existence of the noncontractual relationships of the family. Women and children (and other nonearners) are regarded as dependants of men. How they fare depends on the "effort" and "pluck" of their male protector. Barrett and McIntosh argue that "in order to elevate the morality of the market into an entire social ethic it is necessary to ignore all those members of society who do not themselves enter the market.... Those who cannot earn a living are subsumed under those who can."[6] Women's dependence within the family makes them noncitizens, and their family commitments make them politically suspect.[7]

Welfare-state intervention is justified within a political framework that retains the notion of the independent citizen. Just as the society has an obligation to promote the conditions for a free and fair exchange between competing individuals but no obligation to secure their livelihood, the society has a collective obligation to care only for those individuals who cannot legitimately be asked to care for themselves and who, through no fault of their own, cannot be cared for within the family system. Welfare policy has generally been constructed so as to restore the male-breadwinner family, not to substitute for it.[8] Thus men and women have had a very different relationship to the welfare state and different ways of legitimating their claims to state support. Women have had to prove they are morally deserving (their dependence is assumed); while men have to prove they are legitimately dependent (their independence is assumed). For example, the rules and regulations of workmen's compensation, disability programs, and unemployment insurance, developed primarily in response to the demands and needs of male workers, require that workers prove either that they are no longer "able-bodied" (in the first two instances) or that they are without work through no fault of their own.[9]

Alternative Frameworks

The radical alternative to the liberal framework has argued for interdependence and the legitimate claim of each individual on the community to meet his or her needs for good and productive work, physical sustenance, emotional support, and social recognition. Radical and socialist feminists have further argued that men are as dependent on women's unpaid labor (including women's emotional work) as women are on men's income and that parenthood is a social contribution and should be recognized as such. Socialist feminists have envisioned a society in which the right to contribute and the right to be cared for are equally shared by men and women. This depends on a reformulation of individual and collective responsibilities and the redistribution of material resources such that the care of dependent individuals is no longer primarily a private responsibility of the family.[10]

Feminists have of course been divided on how to approach the state: whether to demand "a fair field and no favor" or "protection."[11] The comparable worth campaign is organized around the first approach: it is essentially a campaign to rectify distortions of the market, which has failed to reward women according to the value of their work. It therefore appeals directly to the liberal principle of meritocracy. The feminization-of-poverty campaign is organized around the second approach—it aims to rectify men's failure to provide for their wives through refusal of child and spousal support (in the case of divorced women) or through lack of life insurance (in the case of widows). Women's claims on the state for support are justified by their lack of a male breadwinner. In the rest of this essay, I will discuss the ways in which the feminization of poverty and comparable worth campaigns reflect a liberal political discourse, outline the likely consequences, and suggest an alternative approach.

Feminization of Poverty

Two central assertions of the feminization-of-poverty campaign— "Divorce produces a single man and a single mother," "40 percent of ex-husbands contribute nothing to their children's support"—link women's poverty primarily to men's failure to support their families. They also picture women's poverty as something that happens even to good middle-class people. In this regard, the campaign shares with earlier feminist campaigns, such as the campaigns for women's legal right of separation and for mothers' pensions, an imagery of female victimization. While attempting to provide women an alternative to marriage, these campaigns operated within ideological terms and political limits that assumed rather than undermined the male-breadwinner family.[12]

Like those campaigns, the feminization-of-poverty campaign responds to a real problem facing women and has a potentially radical side. On the other hand, also like those campaigns, in seeking to legitimize their demands and to be most effective in gathering political support, feminists have appealed to broadly held liberal political values and assumptions. As Folbre argues, the increasing pauperization of motherhood reflects a consensus that AFDC mothers are not among the "deserving" poor.[13] The feminization-of-poverty campaign attempts to change this perception. Portraying poor women as innocent victims of men's irresponsibility may win sympathy for the plight of poor women but at the cost of failing to challenge deeply held notions about feminine dependence on a male breadwinner and distinctions between the deserving and the non-deserving poor, in particular between the "good" woman who is poor because her husband refuses support and the "bad" woman who is poor because she has had a child outside of marriage or has married a poor man who cannot provide.

The feminization-of-poverty literature often assumes that women of all races and classes have a common destiny as poor single heads of families following divorce or widowhood. It is true that generally women's standard of living declines after divorce, while their ex-husbands' standard of living rises.[14] But relative deprivation is not impoverishment. Some women—for example, those with more affluent ex-husbands, those employed during marriage, and those with marketable job skills—are less likely to end up poor or near-poor.[15] Race and ethnic differences are quite striking in this regard. In 1983 the median income for Black and Hispanic women maintaining families was only 60 percent of the median income of white women maintaining families— $7,999 and $7,797 compared with $13,761. The unemployment rate for Black and Hispanic women maintaining families is double that of white women—18.7 percent and 16.7 percent compared with 8.6 percent.[16] While many white women are "only a husband away from poverty," many minority women with a husband are poor: 13.8 percent of all Black married-couple families were below the poverty level, compared with 6.3 percent of all white married-couple families.[17]

A study comparing separated and divorced women with children whose family income when married had been in the upper, middle, or lower thirds of the income distribution showed that while divorce and separation had a leveling effect, significant differences in post-divorce or separation income remained among women even after five years. Women who when married had a family income in the top third lost the most (50 percent of family income); women in the poorest third experienced the least drop (22 percent of family income). But women from the highest third income bracket had post-divorce or separation incomes twice that of women from the lowest third, and 131 percent of the income of women from the middle third, because women from more affluent marriages were more likely to receive alimony and child support.[18] Women from the lowest third income bracket were most likely to be eligible for welfare and food stamps (71 percent in the first year). In the first year, only one-fourth of the women from marriages in the middle third income bracket received welfare or food stamps, dropping to one-eighth by the fifth year.

In addition to ignoring class and race differences among women, the feminization-of-poverty campaign denies the poverty of men, especially minority men. Women make up an increasing proportion of the poor because more women are falling into poverty, not because more men are getting out. As Malvaux argues, the slogan that "by the year 2000 all the poor will be women and children," made sense only if genocide (or full employment) was planned for minority men.[19]

One reason poor women outnumber poor men is that men have a shorter life span: after age sixty-five there are 1.5 women for every one man. However, older Black men are twice as likely to be poor as older white women (and three times more likely to be in poverty than older white men). Hispanic men over sixty-five are also more impoverished than white women—20.7 percent compared with 7.2 percent. In 1984, white widows had a mean family income of $23,469 and an average income per family member of $8,331, compared with a mean family income of $13,464 and $3,663 per family member for widowed Black women, and $15,503 and $4,515 per family member for widowed Hispanic women.[20]

The astonishing growth in families headed by a woman (from 11.5 percent in 1970 to 22.9 percent in 1984 overall, and from 33 percent to 56 percent among Blacks) and the consequent increasing poverty of women may be the result, at least in part, of the economic structure rather than men's neglect of their familial responsibilities. Many Black men do not have access to steady employment and higher-paid work. Stack describes the cross-household survival networks that organize family life among poor Blacks.[21] Black fathers may contribute to their children's support while living in a different female-headed household. In 1979, 15 percent of Black men aged twenty-five to sixty were living in households in which they were not the head, compared with 6 percent of white men in the same age group.[22] For those near the bottom of the economic pyramid, minority or white, poverty is not simply a problem of women without men—it includes their sons, husbands and ex-husbands, and fathers.

When the feminization-of-poverty campaign focuses on the increased standard of living of divorced men compared with that of their ex-wives and looks to child-support enforcement legislation as a solution to women's poverty, it fails to address this reality. By 1984, in the United States, never-married women constituted one-half of the household heads among Black women-headed families. Sixty percent of these women are under 30; Black men between the ages of fifteen and twenty-nine (who are most likely to be the fathers of these women's children) do not earn enough money to support them—a substantial proportion have no income and a majority earn less than \$10,000 a year.[23] A California study found that half of the ex-husbands of women in the welfare system earned incomes under \$15,000 a year.[24]

There is surely a fine but very important line between the feminist demand that men take responsibility for their children and the anti-feminist demand that men have the obligation to be the family bread-winner. Conservatives recognize the poverty of abandoned women. Their solution is to force men to support women and children by making divorce more difficult (in order to tie men to their families), to force women on welfare to name the child's father and how to find him, and so forth.[25] The claim that women's poverty is caused by dead-beat fathers, similar to the claim that Black poverty is caused by teen-age mothers, is not only factually incorrect but looks to the restoration of the nuclear family as the solution to the problem of dependent care.[26]

In the face of political opposition and constricted government budgets, expanded public services for single mothers—increased eligibility for benefits, inexpensive quality childcare—will not be easy to win. The desperate need of poor women may seem to justify the use of whatever arguments appear politically effective. However, we ought to be alerted to the dangers of this temptation by the way that previous reform campaigns (for example, for protective legislation for women workers) appealed to prevailing gender ideals and thereby contributed to perpetuating a gender ideology that justified women's exclusion from public life.[27]

The alleviation of women's poverty ought to be incorporated in a broader program of social and economic change. The familistic ideology and state policy that deny collective responsibility for dependent individuals, force women to take on the burdens of caring, and assume that only men have a claim to economic independence and citizenship, must be transformed. For instance, a comprehensive system of supplements to low-income households, regardless of their composition, would benefit all the poor and near-poor, including women-headed families. Paid parental leave (for meeting the needs of older children as well as infants) would benefit single mothers and help men and married women to combine wage work and caregiving.

In the longer run, a living wage, quality childcare, and good work are necessary for everyone, but especially for women who choose not to share childcare with a man. A program that incorporates short-term reforms into the larger goal of expanded social responsibility for caring would counteract both the stereotypical dependence of women as caregivers and the stereotypical independence of men as citizen-workers. This approach would frame the feminization-of-poverty issue in a way that connects it to the movements of working-class people and people of color.[28]

Comparable Worth

As its proponents have argued, comparable worth focuses attention on the systematic devaluation of women's work and the roots of that devaluation in a general cultural denigration of women and womanly activities. Unlike equal pay and affirmative action programs, comparable worth offers the possibility of raising the wages of the vast majority of women working in jobs that have traditionally been held mostly by women. Trade unions, especially in the public sector, have embraced comparable worth as a strategy for raising their members' wages, and many working women have been brought into union activities around the issue.

Because it has been taken up by trade unions and because it has met resistance from employers, employer organizations, and conservatives, comparable worth advocates have tended to assume that the issue has radical or potentially radical force. Hartmann and Treiman argue: "Claims of comparable worth force explicit discussion about relative pay rates. As such, they politicize wage setting in a new, possibly even revolutionary, way."[29] Similarly, Feldberg argues that comparable worth "has radical implications because it initiates an end to women's economic dependency and questions the market basis of wages."[30]

Comparable worth is often referred to as the civil rights issue of the 1980s. Yet the significance of comparable worth as a remedy to women's low pay and to occupational segregation is limited. Its application has been most effective in public-worker settings because these workers are often unionized and because it is possible for these unions to bring pressure through legislatures or elected officials. The State of Washington finally bargained a comparable worth settlement with the American Federation of State, County and Municipal Employees even though the union's comparable worth lawsuit had lost on appeal. San Francisco was forced to give comparable worth raises to women and members of minority groups, a step Mayor Diane Feinstein resisted, after voters approved a ballot measure directing city officials to resolve the pay inequities.[31] Without such political pressure, the chances for imposing comparable worth on the private sector through the courts are slim, at least in the near future, since such suits are rarely won and only a small proportion of women employees in the private sector are unionized.[32]

While a demand for recognition of the value of their work and higher pay is a possible strategy for all women workers, raising wages by equating women's and men's wages in comparable jobs will not work in industries, such as insurance, in which men are employed mostly at the top and middle, and women at the bottom.[33] Affirmative action remains crucial to encouraging women's employment in nontraditional occupations and management. Furthermore, as even its supporters point out, comparable worth will not improve the access of women of color to jobs and education.[34]

As a political discourse, comparable worth's fundamental claim to legitimacy reinforces an existing ideology: the necessity and validity of meritocratic hierarchy. Rather than questioning the market as an arbiter of wages, comparable worth attempts to

> pay a fair market wage to jobs historically done by women. This means that the wage rate should be based on the productivity-based job content characteristics of the jobs and not on the sex of the typical job incumbent.... Comparable worth advocates seek to disentangle and remove discrimination from the market.[35]

Job evaluations use wage surveys to fix a dollar value to the factor points for benchmark jobs, which are then used to establish a salary scale. Job evaluations measure only the traits of jobs; the money value of the traits is determined by the wages prevailing in the labor market. Thus comparable worth aims primarily to rationalize the existing sorting and selecting of individuals into unequal places and does not eliminate market criteria from job evaluation.[36]

From this point of view, comparable worth is a relatively conservative approach to women's low pay in that it situates its rationale firmly within the hegemonic liberal political discourse. A radical approach to women's low pay would not only challenge the existing inequalities between women's and men's pay for comparable jobs, but would also contest the notion that people's income should be determined primarily by where they fit in an occupational hierarchy. If jobs are assessed in terms of their necessity to an integrated labor process, it is equally important that all jobs be done consistently and well. Anyone who contributes his or her best efforts in a particular job is as deserving as any other individual.

Western contemporary society will not accept "from each according to his/her ability, to each according to his/her need" as a standard of fairness. Nonetheless, the claim that everyone who labors deserves to live decently has been, particularly in periods of working-class mobilization, a central value. Of course, historically, the trade-union movement appealed to the right of the working *man* to make a family wage. Perhaps because the strategy has served to institutionalize women's marginalization in wage labor, feminists have preferred to address the problem of women's low pay in terms other than women's life needs as individuals and as mothers. Perhaps also because it relies on broadly shared meritocratic values, comparable worth may appear to be a practical approach to raising women's pay. But so long as comparable worth efforts remain within that liberal discourse, they risk eventually increasing racial and occupational divisions among working women.

The heart of the comparable worth strategy is the job evaluation. Certain dimensions of every job are measured and given a numerical rating: knowledge and skill, effort, responsibility, and working conditions are the major dimensions used. These dimensions are weighted. Typically, skill and responsibility are given higher weights than working conditions. In the Hay study on which an Idaho State employee's comparable worth adjustment was based, the weight given the dimension of responsibility was forty-two times the weight given to working conditions.[37] Supervision of other people and responsibility for money or expensive equipment are measures that may not reflect responsibilities typical of women's jobs.

McArthur argues that important dimensions of jobs are left out of most job evaluations. Opportunity for advancement, job security, and how boring a job is might also be considered as compensable factors; jobs might deserve higher compensation not only for poor physical working conditions but for poor psychological conditions. Of course, as she also reports, the more desirable a job is, the higher people judge its monetary worth, not the other way around.[38] Therefore the impact of a job evaluation scheme on a given workforce will depend on how the evaluations are constructed. Treiman demonstrates that evaluation methods that put a low value on working conditions and physical strength will tend to assign higher scores to jobs typically done by whites. He concludes:

> The choice of factors and factor weights in job evaluation schemes should not be regarded as a technical issue beyond the purview of affected parties but rather as an expression of the values underlying notions of equity and hence as a matter to be negotiated as part of the wage-setting process.[39]

To evaluate the probable impact of comparable worth, then, we need to consider who will participate in the negotiations over the factors and factor weights and with what sorts of assumptions. Since less than one-fifth of the U.S. workforce and only 13 percent of all U.S. women workers are unionized, we can expect that in most cases, technical experts and management will formulate the evaluation policies.[40] We can further expect that existing cultural biases in factors and factor weights will be replicated. Acker demonstrates how difficult it is to overcome experts' and managers' resistance to altering evaluation systems even in a unionized and public setting, especially when alterations might change the rank order of jobs or undermine pay differentials between management and nonmanagement employees.[41]

Malvaux contends that Black men and women will benefit from comparable worth adjustments, because the jobs held by Black women and men tend to be even more underpaid relative to comparable white men's jobs than are white women's jobs.[42] However, the implementation of a job evaluation scheme that all parties agree is equitable may legitimize large differences in pay among employees by race and occupation. Even after the implementation of comparable worth among Washington State employees, one of the highest nonmanagement women's jobs will pay 149 percent of one of the lowest women's jobs.[43] Estimating the impact of comparable worth adjustments under different conditions, Aldrich and Buchele found the earnings gap between women workers by quintiles would be reduced by at most 6.5 percent.[44] Since women are not distributed proportionately by race within job categories, large inequalities by race will remain, but will appear to be reflections of differential merit and thus ultimately be difficult to challenge.

Comparable worth may also exacerbate hierarchies in women's jobs. For example, hospital administrations do not currently award differential salaries among nursing specialties, although there is a clear hierarchy of rewards to medical specialties. Remick predicts that job evaluation systems may expose "internal squabbles that will have to be dealt with by the nursing profession."[45] At hearings conducted by the U.S. Equal Employment Opportunities Commission in 1980, the American Nurses Association testified to the similarities between intensive-care unit nurses and doctors.[46] Comparable worth adjustments may encourage nurses with such specialties to claim higher pay.

Comparable worth may very well open up discussion of how society values work, but that discussion must be framed by a broader challenge to the prevailing culture. The superior value of mental over manual skills and the greater importance of supervisory over other kinds of responsibility should not be assumed but questioned. Otherwise, we can expect comparable worth to readjust women's and men's pay but to change very little, perhaps even to solidify, the existing divisions in the workforce: divisions between whites and minority workers, between designated professionals and nonprofessionals, between white-collar and blue-collar workers. These divisions cut across gender and have been an important source of trade-union disunity. Yet any radical potential for "politicizing the wage-setting process" depends on the strength of worker organization.

Gender divisions within the workforce have played an important part in perpetuating women's low pay. Male-dominated trade unions have been willing to take up the issue only as women workers have become organized. The kind of strategies used for raising the pay of women workers can undermine or aggravate men's resistance, increase or decrease the possibilities for overcoming employer opposition, and create a more unified—or more divided—workforce.

Job evaluation studies often find men's job classes "overpaid" for the content of their jobs, especially craft jobs, which tend to be held by white men.[47] Since market realities may be felt to require relatively higher wages in order to recruit and hold those workers and it may be illegal to equalize pay scales by lowering men's wages, most plans attempt to achieve equity over the long run by gradually increasing women's wages. Some plans freeze men's wages; others simply raise men's wages more slowly—for example, giving all workers a cost-of-living raise and women workers an equity bonus. The plan selected influences the impact of a comparable worth settlement on relationships between the men's and women's sections of a workforce. Freezing men's wages is divisive, but because it is cheaper, comparable worth adjustments will probably take that route, except when worker organization and union leadership mount effective opposition.

A less divisive strategy is to adjust women's wages to a level commensurate with the intrinsic value of their work. In the strike by women clericals at Yale, the union demanded higher pay on the ground that the women made an important contribution to the university, a contribution that has historically been undervalued because they were women. The union did not center its strategy on a direct comparison with men's wages or claims about the comparative value of men's and women's work. The women were well-organized; the unionized, predominantly blue-collar men had nothing to lose and much to gain from a united workforce, so the men were willing to honor the women's picket line for the entire ten weeks of the strike. The women reciprocated and supported the men when their contract came up, which allowed the men to make gains that they had unsuccessfully struck for in the past.[48] In short, although the women's and men's pay scales were adjusted separately, not in relation to each other, the gender gap was narrowed.

In sum, comparable worth seems to offer an immediate remedy to a pressing problem, but it may institutionalize divisions among women and between women and men that will make future collective campaigns difficult. While some supporters of comparable worth themselves signal potential dangers, such as the dominance of technocrats and managers in wage setting or divisions among women workers, they tend to minimize the risks and overestimate its radical potential.[49] Unless a very different kind of organizing is done concerning the issue, this potential is not likely to be realized.

Comparable worth has been presented as a demand for removing discrimination and improving women's position within an existing system. The demand for equity could, however, be put forward as part of a broader set of longer-range goals that challenge the terms of the system itself. A radical strategy would argue for raising the pay of the lowest-paid workers, most of whom are women and minorities, on the grounds that everyone who contributes his or her labor deserves a comfortable and secure existence. This strategy would not only protest the undervaluation of women's work but also argue that existing salary differentials among jobs, especially between management and non-management jobs, are unnecessarily large. And it would argue that if we are looking at the work people do, then we should ask whether that work is productive, safe, and interesting, and whether it allows people to use their talents and skills and to develop new ones.

Feminist historians have written at length about the ways that the dual spheres ideology of the nineteenth and early twentieth centuries shaped feminist politics and blunted the radical potential of the women's movement.[50] Liberal political discourse has similarly shaped contemporary feminist thinking. The feminization-of-poverty and comparable worth campaigns argue their case in terms of claims that reflect and in turn reinforce the assumptions of a liberal political framework.

A radical framework contests these assumptions, challenges the hierarchical organization of work and the privatization of care giving, and generates a more inclusive set of claims. A language of rights does not have to be limited to a narrowly defined meritocratic standard but can be expanded to include the rights to contribute one's best efforts, to do work that enriches, and to receive in return a decent standard of living. It can also include the right of children to care from their community and the right of parents to economic and social support in carrying out their responsibilities to their children.

Neither the feminization of poverty nor comparable worth are inherently radical concepts. Their impact will depend on how solutions are conceptualized, how they are implemented, and how they are used politically.

[1987]

Notes

1. Pamela S. Cain, "The Role of the Sciences in the Comparable Worth Movement," in R. Shotland and M. Mark, eds., *Social Science and Social Policy* (Newbury Park: Sage Press, 1985); Diana M. Pearce and H. McAdoo, *Women and Children: Alone and in Poverty* (Washington, D.C.: National Advisory Council on Economic Opportunity, 1981); D. Treiman and H. Hartman, eds., *Women, Work, and Wages: Equal Pay for Jobs of Equal Value* (Washington, D.C.: National Academy Press, 1981).
2. Kingsley Davis and W. E. Moore, "Some Principles of Stratification," *American Sociological Review* 10 (1945), 242–49.
3. Kathy E. Ferguson, *The Feminist Case Against Bureaucracy* (Philadelphia: Temple University Press, 1984); Ronald Mason, *Participatory and Workplace Democracy: A Theoretical Development in Critique of Liberalism* (New York: Basic Books, 1982); Joyce Rothschild-Whitt, "The Collectivist Organization: An Alternative to Rational Bureaucratic Models," *American Sociological Review* 44 (1979), 509–27.
4. Daniel Bell, "On Meritocracy and Equality," *The Public Interest* 29 (1972), 29–68, 58.
5. Linda Gordon, "Feminism and Social Control: The Case of Child Abuse and Neglect," in Juliet Mitchell and Ann Oakley, eds., *What is Feminism: A Reexamination* (New York: Pantheon, 1986), 81.
6. Michèle Barrett and Mary McIntosh, *The Anti-Social Family* (London: Verso, 1982), 48–49.
7. Suan Okin, *Women in Western Political Thought* (Princeton: Princeton University Press, 1979); Carole Pateman, "'The Disorder of Women': Women, Love, and the Sense of Justice," *Ethics* 91 (1980), 20–34.
8. Jane Lewis, ed., *Women's Welfare / Women's Rights* (London: Croom Helm, 1983); Eli Zaretsky, "The Place of the Family in the Origins of the Welfare State," in Barrie Thorne with Marilyn Yalom, eds., *Rethinking the Family: Some Feminist Questions* (New York: Longman, 1982).
9. Barbara Nelson, "Women's Poverty and Women's Citizenship: Some Political Consequences of Economic Marginality," *Signs* 10 (1984), 209–31.
10. Barrett and McIntosh, *The Anti-Social Family.*
11. Alice Kessler-Harris, *Out To Work: A History of Wage-Earning Women in the United*

States (New York: Oxford University Press, 1982); J. Lewis, "Feminism and Welfare," in Mitchell and Oakley, eds., *What Is Feminism?*.

12. Eileen Boris and P. Bardaglio, "The Transformation of Patriarchy: The Historic Role of the State," in Irene Diamond, ed., *Families, Politics, and Public Policy* (New York: Longman, 1983); Elizabeth Pleck, "Feminist Responses to 'Crimes Against Women,' 1868–1896," *Signs: Journal of Women in Culture and Society* 8 (1983) 451–70.

13. Nancy Folbre, "The Pauperization of Motherhood: Patriarchy and Public Policy in the United States," *Review of Radical Political Economics* 16 (1984), 72–88.

14. Lenore J. Weitzman, *The Divorce Revolution: The Unexpected Social and Economic Consequences for Women and Children in America* (New York: Free Press, 1985).

15. Robert S. Weiss, "The Impact of Marital Dissolution on Income and Consumption in Single-Parent Households," *Journal of Marriage and the Family* 46 (1984), 115–27; Weitzman, *The Divorce Revolution*.

16. J. Brenner, *Poverty: Not for Women Only* (San Francisco: Alliance Against Women's Oppression, 1983).

17. Bureau of the Census, *Characteristics of the Population Below the Poverty Level: 1984*, Current Population Reports, Consumer Income, Series P-60, no. 152 (Washington, D.C.: U.S. Government Printing Office, 1984).

18. Weiss, "The Impact of Marital Dissolution."

19. Julianne Malvaux, "The Economic Interests of Black and White Women: Are They Similar?", *Review of Black Political Economy* 14, no. 1 (1985), 4–27.

20. Bureau of the Census:, *Characteristics of the Population Below the Poverty Level: 1984*, and *Money Income of Households, Families, and Persons in The U.S.: 1984*, Current Population Reports, Consumer Income, Series P-60, no. 151 (Washington, D.C.: U.S. Government Printing Office, 1984).

21. Carole B. Stack, *All Our Kin: Strategies for Survival in a Black Community* (New York: Harper & Row, 1975).

22. Bureau of the Census, *Detailed Population Characteristics: U.S. Summary* (Washington, D.C.: U.S. Government Printing Office, 1980).

23. Margaret Simms, "Black Women Who Head Families: An Economic Struggle," *Review of Black Political Economy* 14 (1985/1986), 140–51.

24. Women's Economic Agenda Project, *Women's Economic Agenda* (Oakland, n.d.).

25. Barbara Ehrenreich and Karen Stallard, "The Nouveau Poor," *Ms.*, July–August 1982, 217–24.

26. William Darity, Jr. and Samuel L. Myers, Jr., "Changes in Black–White Income Inequality, 1968–1978: A Decade of Progress," *Review of Black Political Economy* 10 (1980), 167–77; Wendy Sarvasy and J. Van Allen, "Fighting the Feminization of Poverty: Socialist-Feminist Analysis and Strategy," *Review of Radical Political Economics* 16 (1984), 89–110.

27. Johanna Brenner and Maria Ramas, "Rethinking Women's Oppression," Chapter 1 of this volume; Kessler-Harris, *Out to Work*.

28. Sarvasy and Van Allen, "Fighting the Feminization of Poverty."

29. Heidi Hartmann and Donald J. Treiman, "Notes on the NAS Study of Equal Pay for Jobs of Equal Value," *Public Personnel Management* 12 (1983), 404–17, 416.

30. Roslyn L. Feldberg, "Comparable Worth: Toward Theory and Practice in the United States," *Signs: Journal of Women in Culture and Society* 10 (1984), 311–28, 313.

31. "San Francisco Agrees to Pay Raise for Women," *New York Times*, March 20, 1987.

32. Frances C. Hutner. *Equal Pay for Comparable Worth: The Working Woman's Issue of the Eighties* (New York: Praeger, 1986); "Union Membership for Employed Wage and Salary Workers, 1985," *Monthly Labor Review* 109 (1986), 44–46.

33. Helen Remick, "Major Issues in *a priori* Applications," in Helen Remick, ed., *Comparable Worth and Wage Discrimination: Technical Possibilities and Political Realities* (Philadelphia: Temple University Press, 1984).

34. Feldberg, "Comparable Worth"; Malvaux, "The Economic Interests of Black and White Women."

35. H. Remick and Ronnie J. Steinberg, "Technical Possibilities and Political Realities: Concluding Remarks," in Remick, ed., *Comparable Worth and Wage Discrimination*.

36. Mark Aldrich and Robert Buchele, *Economics of Comparable Worth* (Cambridge, Mass.: Ballinger Press, 1986).

37. Donald Treiman, "Effect of Choice of Factor and Factor Weights in Job Evaluation," in Remick, ed., *Comparable Worth and Wage Discrimination*.

38. Leslie Zebrowitz McArthur, "Social Judgment Biases in Comparable Worth Analysis," in H. I. Hartmann, ed., *Comparable Worth: New Directions for Research* (Washington, D.C.: National Academy Press, 1985).

39. Treiman, "Effect of Choice of Factor and Factor Weights in Job Evaluation," 89.

40. "Union Membership for Employed Wage and Salary Workers, 1985," *Monthly Labor Review* 109 (1986), 44–46.

41. Joan Acker, "Sex Bias in Job Evaluation: A Comparable Worth Issue," in Christine Bose and Glenna Spitze, eds., *Ingredients for Women's Employment Policy* (Albany: University of New York Press, 1986).

42. Julianne Malvaux, "Comparable Worth and Its Impact on Black Women," *Review of Black Political Economy* 14 (1985/6), 47–62.

43. Calculated from Remick, "Major Issues in *a priori* Applications."

44. Aldrich and Buchele, *Economics of Comparable Worth*.

45. Helen Remick, "Dilemmas of Implementation: The Case of Nursing," in Remick, ed., *Comparable Worth and Wage Discrimination*, 97.

46. Lorraine D. Eyde, "Evaluating Job Evaluation: Emerging Research Issues for Comparable Worth Analysis," *Public Personnel Management* 10 (1983), 425–44.

47. Robert L. Farnquist et al., "Pandora's Worth: The San Jose Experience," *Public Personnel Management* 12 (1983), 358–68.

48. Molly Ladd-Taylor, "Women Workers and the Yale Strike," *Feminist Studies* 11 (1985), 465–91.

49. Feldberg, "Comparable Worth"; Remick, "Dilemmas of Implementation."

50. See, for example, Linda Gordon and Ellen Dubois, "Seeking Ecstasy on the Battlefield: Danger and Pleasure in Nineteenth Century Feminist Sexual Thought," *Feminist Studies* 8 (1983) 451–70.

Chapter 5

The Politics of Welfare Reform

Provisions for the poor have always been a contentious political issue in the U.S. For good reason. Welfare policy engages conflicting economic interests, clashing worldviews, competing social needs. Critical analyses of social welfare practice have centered on the ways that policies function to regulate the labor market and to preserve social order and discipline. In this approach, conflicts and interests structured by class and race take center stage.[1] Recently, feminist scholars have argued that social welfare policy also reflects structures of gender inequality.[2] This essay engages the theoretical debate by examining a "welfare reform" initiative, the Family Support Act of 1988.[3] But this essay also has a practical political purpose: to offer a strategy toward welfare policy that promotes women's independence as individuals and supports them as mothers.

The centerpiece of the Family Support Act is its expanded work requirements for single mothers with young children. Its passage represents a significant shift in the liberal position on welfare policy, since conservatives have always favored programs in which mothers are required either to find work or to work in exchange for welfare benefits. In the past, liberals opposed these "workfare" programs but supported voluntary training and work experience programs that would help mothers become self-supporting once their children reached school age. Since 1971, Congress has required the states to register women with school-age children in training, work experience, or job search programs.[4] But until this act, women with children under six have generally been exempt from these requirements.[5] The 1988 Act requires states to enroll mothers with children over three years old in training, work experience, and job search programs and allows states to make participation in such programs mandatory for mothers of children as young as one year old.[6]

Advocates of the Family Support Act argue that it will cut the welfare rolls and end poverty by making single mothers "self-sufficient." But the Family Support Act is no more likely to cure poverty than previous welfare reforms. Indeed, welfare families' conditions of life will continue to deteriorate, since cash benefits are very low and not indexed for inflation (unlike, for instance, social security).[7] Benefit levels in most states are, and will no doubt remain, well below the poverty line, because the Family Support Act does not set a federal minimum benefit standard.[8] Indeed, a federal minimum benefit was never seriously considered in the discussion of welfare reform.[9] Few welfare recipients remain on welfare for long periods and many already leave welfare for paid work.[10] However, they remain poor, because their low-paid jobs do not cover their job-related expenses (e.g. transportation, childcare) or health-care needs.[11] And fully 40 percent of all women who leave welfare with an earnings increase eventually return.[12] To end poverty for working single mothers requires decently paid jobs, affordable quality health care and childcare.

Many critics of the Family Support Act argue that its major thrust is not to improve the lives of poor women but to reduce welfare expenses and welfare rolls by making welfare increasingly less attractive as an alternative to low-paid work and by making fewer people eligible for assistance. Promises that single mothers will get real skills or training will not be fulfilled, critics predict. Instead, states will offer only minimal services to welfare recipients, who will be forced to work at minimum-wage service-sector and manufacturing jobs, filling the labor needs of local employers.[13] They have a point. All previous experience with "welfare to work" programs demonstrates that high-quality programs are very expensive and reduce costs only over the long term.[14] Thus, whatever the reform promises, programs are likely to be underfunded and in practice end up doing little to reduce the caseload or increase the skills and education of recipients.[15]

Feminists have been divided over the issues raised by the Family Support Act. In the debates leading up to passage of the Act, most agreed with the critics, but they disagreed about the alternatives feminists ought to support. Some argued against the goal of making single mothers economically "self-sufficient." The proposed reforms, they argued, would leave single mothers even worse off. Poor women would be forced to put their children in inadequate daycare while they worked at dead-end, low-paid jobs. These feminists assert the value of women's work as mothers and defend their entitlement to state supports.[16] They consider it a mistake for women to embrace male-defined notions of "independence." Men, they point out, are not really "independent," for they "depend" on women's unpaid labor in the home to care for them and for their children. Moreover, they note that while poor women on welfare are stigmatized for failing to be "self-sufficient," it is perfectly acceptable for married women to "choose" full-time motherhood and dependence on their husbands over wage work.[17]

Other feminists, who recognized the limitations of the reforms being debated, nonetheless argued for proposed legislation providing the most benefits, protections, and services (education, job training, childcare) to help women on welfare enter paid work.[18] "Marriage to the state," they asserted, is no better than dependence on husbands for economic support. The "motherhood mystique" ("children need mother's care"; "women are natural caregivers") could be used to legitimate single mothers' claim to income from the state.[19] But by defining women primarily as caregivers, the "motherhood mystique" also perpetuates the gender division of labor in the family, encourages women's reliance on men for economic support and justifies discrimination against women in paid employment.[20]

Feminist differences on welfare policy reflect a real, sometimes seemingly intractable, difficulty that characterizes many feminist reform efforts: the conflict between a "politics of equality" and a "politics of difference." I will argue that this counterposition is not inevitable, and that it is possible to craft a strategy that combines both.

Theoretical Perspectives

The most interesting feminist work on the welfare state has analyzed state policy in terms of the intersection of capitalism and patriarchy.[21] The state, it is argued, mediates between competing needs of capital— for women's low-waged labor on the one hand and for women's unpaid domestic labor on the other—and the interests of men. The rise of industrial capitalism threatened men's control over women by undermining the economic and political basis of male authority within the family. At the same time, the employment of women threatened the adequate reproduction of wage labor. On the other hand, to subsidize women's reproductive labor through the state threatened male control over women within the family—by offering women an alternative to dependence on a male breadwinner—and undercut the availability of women, particularly working-class women and women of color, as a low-waged labor force for capitalist employers. Tracing the history of welfare policy, Mimi Abramovitz argues that distinctions between "deserving" and "undeserving" women have allowed the state to support some women who followed the dominant family ethic—those who were widowed or caring for injured or sick husbands—while excluding others—those who appeared to "choose" single motherhood. Similarly, local control over eligibility and benefit levels has been used to force working-class women, and especially women of color, into paid work where local industries rely on their low-paid labor.[22] In general, Abramovitz says, welfare policy has balanced competing needs by allowing some mothers to support themselves outside the labor market and the male-breadwinner family, while forcing many others into wage work in the lowest-paid and least secure jobs and ultimately back into marriage. Feminists have also argued that in addition to class and gender, racial inequality has structured welfare policy, particularly in the ways it differentiates among women—women of color are more likely than white women to be defined as "undeserving."[23]

While this body of work has laid a foundation on which to build, the capitalist-patriarchy approach has not sufficiently recognized that welfare state policy toward single mothers has had a contradictory rather than unitary impact and that women have been agents as well as victims in its creation and implementation. The establishment and expansion of state support to single mothers reflected the political organization of women, not only the actions and interests of men or capitalist employers. And the growth of the welfare state after the Second World War tremendously enlarged women's alternatives to dependence on men by increasing women's employment and providing services which, however minimal, are far better than those previously available.[24] True, the miserly benefits, demeaning rules and regulations, harassment and surveillance by caseworkers diminish the attraction of welfare as an alternative to the male-breadwinner family, even for those women who are deemed eligible for benefits. True, also, that white, middle-class women active in lobbying for welfare legislation have often failed to represent the interests and needs of the working-class women and women of color in whose names they claim to speak. Nonetheless, welfare policy has tended to undermine the male-breadwinner family, rather than simply upholding it. Such contradictory outcomes challenge an explanation of welfare policy in terms of its function for reproducing either capitalism or male domination.[25] An analysis of the political process through which welfare legislation was passed also raises questions about the adequacy of this theory.

For instance, among the many groups testifying to Congress for or against the welfare reform bills, there were only a handful of business organizations—the U.S. Chamber of Commerce and the National Business Alliance, as well as some individual businesses.[26] Moreover, none of the major corporate think-tanks, such as the Committee for Economic Development or the Conference Board, has issued a policy statement on welfare for half a decade.[27] The prominent voices among those advocating reform before Congress belong to social service administrators, state and local government executives, charitable organizations, social service professionals, and lobbies for the poor.[28]

Federal government policy toward single mothers reflects diverse pressures: middle-class reformers (such as church-affiliated activists, volunteers in charitable organizations, political party activists) and growing numbers of service professionals who argue the need to provide for the poor in order to prevent class polarization and unrest and to ensure the reproduction of skilled and socialized worker/citizens; federal government administrators interested in maintaining social order, economic prosperity and the legitimacy of the party in power; politicians looking for re-election; political organizations representing workers and subordinated groups, such as trade unions, civil rights organizations and women's organizations; sometimes explosive political and social movements of the poor; special interest business groups; and state and local governments anxious to reduce their own costs by transferring them to the federal level or resisting federally mandated expansions. The history of welfare policy since the Second World War reflects this diversity of interests and the shifting political coalitions among them.

Aid to Families with Dependent Children (AFDC) offers one example of how political coalitions shape welfare policy. While the value of AFDC benefits declined in the 1970s, in-kind benefits, particularly food stamps and medical care, increased. While popular attitudes toward welfare are generally negative, voters tend to prefer in-kind benefits to cash handouts. Gender ideology also shapes popular preferences for in-kind programs. Cash grants replace wages and are typical of programs developed for men, such as unemployment insurance, whereas in-kind grants allow the donor to retain control over the behavior of the recipient and are more common in programs developed for women.[29] Most important, however, in-kind programs are vigorously supported by provider groups with political resources, such as farm organizations, construction and real-estate industries, hospitals and the American Medical Association.[30]

The capitalist state is an arena of political struggle for all kinds of organized groups; policy outcomes, shaped by an historically determined balance of forces, are almost always double-edged. There are instances, of course, where organizations representing capitalist employers directly engage in the policy-making process and wield considerable influence over the outcome. And at times, male-dominated organizations such as skilled trade unions or professional associations have attempted to use the state to exclude women from their occupations or otherwise to protect male privilege in the labor market. But very often—and this is the case with regard to state policy toward single mothers—the politically organized groups involved in fighting over policy and the issues that engage them do not reveal direct intentional intervention by capitalist employers as a group. Moreover, the major proponents of legislation are often not men but women. Welfare policy reflects structures of class and gender, but not because the state functions to reconcile the interests of men with those of capitalist employers. Rather, welfare policy is shaped by class and gender, because the class structure and the social organization of gender set limits to and create opportunities for those particular interest groups who at any given time participate in the policy-making process. This process of setting limits and creating opportunities occurs both outside and inside the political process itself. In the capitalist economy, investment decisions are privately controlled and primarily determined by profitability. Consequently, state policies which threaten or appear to threaten profit levels, by undermining work incentives, redistributing income and wealth, or cutting too deeply into profits through taxation, will trigger reduced investment, capital outflows, lowered exchange rates, and other responses that can lead to an economic downturn. Capitalist class interests are imbedded in the imperatives of the capitalist economy. These imperatives set the context within which decisions about taxation and spending must be made, and they operate regardless of who holds office or directly controls government decision-making. Further, interest groups contesting state policies seek political goals and rhetoric that are realistic and will tend to limit themselves to policies compatible with a "positive business climate." In this way, the postwar era of prosperity and growth did not create the expansion of the welfare state, but made it possible. The qualitative changes in the scope and level of government spending reflected the political organization of different interest groups and most spectacularly the Civil Rights movement of the early 1960s. But the way the political system responded to the mobilization of this new constituency also depended on the opportunities provided by an expanding and prosperous economy. Correlatively, economic decline and the end of the era of growth did not create the conservative backlash, but undermined the political economy on which the welfare state had been based. Increasing conflicts over shrinking political and economic resources drove a broad wedge into the coalition of interests that had constituted the base of postwar liberalism.

Women's self-organization as a political force has varied in time and by class over the period during which the modern welfare state and social policy has been constructed. We cannot understand the evolution of state policy apart from an account of the presence and absence of women in the political process. For example, white, middle-class women's organizations played a crucial role in the passage of income-maintenance, public health, and other social legislation in the Progressive period but not during the New Deal.[31] And it was not until the 1960s that poor women, particularly Black women who were the clients of welfare programs, organized themselves to contest social policy. To understand not only when women mobilized, but also which women mobilized and for what ends, and with what strategies and political rhetoric, requires an analysis of the changing social organization of gender and especially the sexual division of labor within the household and the economy. Responsibility for caretaking as unpaid work within private households has been both a political resource and a disadvantage for women. And the changing circumstances under which women take up this responsibility explains both their self-organization and their political marginalization.[32]

The next section will review the history of Aid to Families with Dependent Children (AFDC) and the context of the current welfare reform, showing how changes in the capitalist economy, and in gender relations, shaped policy outcomes.[33] The last section of this essay will discuss feminist responses to the Family Support Act of 1988.

Class and Gender in the Development of Welfare Policy

Until the early twentieth century, it was common for children of poor single women to be removed from their mothers' care. Between 1911 and 1921, forty states enacted legislation that allowed local authorities

to award grants to those destitute single mothers who were considered
to be "proper guardians," so that the family could stay together. Many
women reformers rationalized the idea of mothers' pensions in terms of
children's need for their mothers' care: state support would make it
possible for poor women without husbands to live like women with
husbands. They could specialize in motherhood, so to speak.

It has been argued that this "politics of protection" reflected more
the patriarchal gender ideology and class interests of reformers than the
real needs of poor women.[34] It is true that the women militants of the
child welfare movement, primarily responsible for developing welfare
programs and organizing for their enactment, were overwhelmingly
white, middle-class volunteers and members of emerging social welfare
professions. Most of them unquestioningly accepted the notion that men
ought to take primary responsibility for their families' economic support,
while mothers should depend on a male breadwinner. On the other
hand, some working-class women, predominantly women trade unionists,
defended working mothers and argued for higher wages and unionization, so that women could adequately care for their families. They
resisted a politics of protection, claiming that it disadvantaged women
in the labor market, reinforced the idea that women could not be both
good mothers and paid workers, and institutionalized women's
dependence.[35]

Assumptions about proper family life shaped the way that mothers'
pension programs were organized, defended, and implemented.[36]
Mothers' right to support was conditional on whether or not they
conformed to accepted gender roles and sexual codes. In withholding
support to mothers who were "undeserving," lawmakers, charitable
organizations, social workers and courts reinforced a gender ideology
that defined independent women as suspect and defined motherhood as
a full-time job. But why did so few women challenge that ideal or
organize successfully around alternative programs? One explanation may
lie in the social reality of the time: the majority of married women with
children, in both working-class and middle-class families, did not work
for pay full-time *outside* their homes.[37] Working-class women, and especially women of color, had to contribute to their families—but they did
so primarily by work that could be combined with childbearing and
childrearing, such as working at home, working only during certain
seasons, and taking in boarders.[38] In all classes, men were the primary
family breadwinners, and the loss of their income left women, particularly those with children, in dire poverty. Low levels of women's trade-

union organization, women's exclusion from skilled work and from many professions, and the unavailability of childcare meant that dependence on the state for support was the only realistic alternative for most women to dependence on fathers, male relatives, or charity.

In addition to limiting the alternatives open to single mothers, women's economic dependence on men also restricted their capacity for political organization and representation. While some middle-class women did organize, and thus played an important part in the creation of the welfare state, the majority of women, from any class, were only marginally represented in the balance of organized political forces. This fact shaped the political discourse—the voices of working-class women and women of color generally were silenced. It also shaped reformers' strategies, which had to adapt to political reality, to what might be winnable.

"Mothers' pensions" created a policy framework that shaped the later establishment of federal income-maintenance programs for single mothers.[39] The criteria differentiating "fit" from "unfit" mothers were vague and arbitrary. Once deemed eligible, mothers were often supervised by caseworkers to ensure that they provided a "suitable home." Although legislation in many states covered women who were deserted, divorced, or never-married as well as widows, in practice these mothers tended to be regarded as "unfit" and ineligible for support. Because local governments were unwilling to spend much money on the programs, grants were very small and most women were expected to supplement their grants with wage work.[40] On the other hand, paid work that took them away from home was frowned upon and could result in termination. Home work (sewing or taking in laundry, for instance) was a common solution—but one that did little to pull these women out of poverty.

Mothers' pensions established the principle of government's responsibility for single mothers (or, more accurately, perhaps, for the children of single mothers). However, narrow eligibility requirements, along with accompanying distinctions between the deserving and the undeserving, low funding, and successful political resistance at the local level excluded many women from benefits. Most programs did not constitute a real alternative to dependence on male support.[41] By the early 1930s, widows constituted 82 percent of recipients, 96 percent of all families served were white, and less than 3 percent of all female-headed families received aid.[42]

In 1935, the federal government entered the picture with the creation of Aid to Dependent Children (ADC), which for the first time offered federal funds to states to establish financial assistance programs for needy children.[43] Women reformers, well-placed in the Roosevelt administration, were key players in crafting the legislation and ensuring its inclusion in the Social Security Act of 1935.[44] However, although personally influential, they had no political base. There was no "women's movement," no feminist organization among the organizations and grassroots forces that formed the New Deal coalition. It is not surprising, then, that New Deal policies incorporated the assumptions of the male-breadwinner family ideal: mothers ought to depend on male wages, the cure for poverty was male employment, men should have priority in training and work programs.

In 1939, amendments to the Social Security Act effectively separated widows from other single mothers by establishing benefits for widows and their children until the children reached age sixteen.[45] Social security benefits to widows were set by the federal government. But in ADC the level of benefits and determinations of eligibility for widows of uncovered male workers, and for deserted, divorced or unmarried mothers, remained in the hands of local authorities.[46] The superiority of social security benefits to those in ADC reflected differences in political influence by gender and by race. Widows' pensions rewarded faithful wives as part of a system of benefits to white men.

During the 1950s, as the ADC caseload changed to include more divorced, separated and unmarried mothers and more women of color, many states tightened up eligibility requirements and increased harassment of recipients. "Substitute father" rules made a single mother's male companion responsible for supporting her and her children. Surprise raids were made on welfare mothers to search out the "man in the house" whose presence would automatically disqualify them.[47] "Suitable home" rules based on vague and discretionary definitions of moral fitness were often used to deny aid to unmarried mothers, whose "illegitimate" children automatically defined them as morally unfit.[48]

Throughout the 1950s, social workers and social scientists had proposed, without much success, an increase in services to the poor, including single mothers. By arguing that poor families needed counseling in order to secure and retain jobs, social service professionals blamed the poor for their condition and claimed a rehabilitative role for themselves. They appeared to have won their point with the Kennedy administration. Kennedy's 1962 "social service amendments" to the Social Security Act encouraged states to establish social services and hire caseworkers, for example, by permitting states to claim 75 percent rather than 50 percent federal reimbursement for administrative costs in AFDC cases where rehabilitation services were given.[49] These amendments were developed by two welfare reform commissions appointed in 1961, which included many prominent social workers.[50]

ADC was changed to AFDC in 1962, and for the first time two-parent families became eligible for assistance through AFDC–UP (Unemployed Parent). Only half the states actually established AFDC–UP programs, but, with the inclusion of "able-bodied" men, Congress amended AFDC to allow states to force recipients to work in exchange for their benefits. However, since states were required to provide a 50 percent match for the Community Work and Training programs, as compared with a 25 percent match for social services to AFDC recipients, only a few states actually instituted "workfare" programs.[51] In principle, however, husbands were expected to work or search for work, while only "deserving" mothers who lacked men to support them would be eligible for aid without either working or proving they were seeking work. Still, many localities found ways to keep single mothers off the rolls.[52]

The history of AFDC up to this point reveals that gains for single mothers reflected political efforts of women reformers, who were predominantly white and middle-class. Working-class women participated in the mass movements that forced the expansion of the welfare state at the turn of the century and in the 1930s. However, working-class women organizers were marginalized in those movements and even in the coalitions that they sometimes formed with middle-class women reformers. This situation changed in the 1960s, when poor Black single mothers organized a movement to convert welfare from a miserly, begrudged, and demeaning charity to a secure entitlement.

In alliance with professionals and middle-class reformers, especially those from the federal poverty program (and within the context of the civil rights movement) grassroots groups of welfare mothers, organized in the National Welfare Rights Organization (NWRO), won a major expansion of AFDC in the late 1960s.[53] The NWRO organized to demand expanded benefits, to inform more poor women about their eligibility for benefits, and to extend the rights of women recipients in relation to state bureaucracies.[54] Between 1950 and 1965, the number of AFDC recipients had increased approximately 6 percent a year. But between 1965 and 1970, the annual rate of growth jumped to 18 percent. By 1975, the number of recipients had reached 11 million, compared to only 3 million in 1960.[55]

Community legal service lawyers from the poverty program were especially important allies for NWRO activists.[56] Between 1967 and 1971, 368,000 families headed by unwed mothers became eligible for welfare due to court rulings that overturned home eligibility checks, man-in-the house rules, and midnight raids. In 1969 the Supreme Court declared residency requirements illegal, adding 800,000 to the AFDC rolls by 1970.[57] In addition to using the courts to expand poor women's access to support, the welfare rights movement forced welfare departments to establish formal grievance procedures that made arbitrary terminations more difficult. NWRO groups informed poor women of their eligibility for assistance, produced welfare rights handbooks for recipients, and succeeded in eliminating some of the more intrusive and demeaning aspects of the welfare system.[58] By the end of the 1960s, poor women had won rights and protections that gave them a more secure claim to state support.[59] Between 1965 and 1970 states increased AFDC benefit levels by 36 percent.[60] The proportion of eligible families headed by women who actually received benefits increased from 60 percent in 1967 to nearly 90 percent in 1971.[61] Real expenditures for public benefits increased by 69 percent between 1965 and 1970. By 1970 welfare costs were expected to "exceed the budgeted amount by $1 billion.[62]

The welfare rights movement not only increased the level of benefits but helped to reduce the stigma of welfare and to secure women's entitlement to state support. Almost from the first, however, this right came under attack. In 1967, Congress considered amendments to the Social Security Act to penalize mothers of children born outside marriage or mothers deserted by their husbands. The amendments proposed to freeze federal aid to the states for such mothers, denying additional funding to states that increased the proportion of unwed or deserted mothers in their caseloads. Opposition from the social service establishment and civil rights and welfare rights organizations forced withdrawal of the amendments by 1969.[63]

Also in 1967, Congress began to consider the issue of moving recipients off the rolls and into paid work. Wilbur Mills, chairman of the Ways and Means Committee, asked, "What in the world is wrong with requiring these people to submit themselves, if they are to draw public funds, to a test of their ability to learn a job?"[64] This conservative backlash was fairly well countered by the welfare advocates. While Congress did establish the Work Incentive Program (WIN), most of the provisions aimed at punishing welfare mothers were removed. WIN's "earned income disregard" allowed recipients to earn a certain amount without affecting their grant.[65] Previously, any dollar earned had been deducted from the AFDC award, effectively penalizing recipients for working. In addition to the earned-income disregard, WIN allocated federal funds for states to develop programs aimed at placing recipients in jobs. Participants were required to register for work, accept referrals to training or work experience programs, and take any bona fide job offer. WIN participation was mandatory for men in AFDC–UP, but only voluntary for single mothers of children six years old or more, for whom childcare was to be available while they were in training or searching for a job.[66] Mothers of younger children were not expected to participate.

The gains of the 1960s could not continue. Benefits to single mothers would not have increased without the mobilization of poor Black women in the NWRO, the urban rebellions of the early 1960s, and the civil rights and Black Power movements. But the welfare expansion was also made possible by the postwar prosperity. In the context of an expanding economy, state managers could respond to political pressures by increasing taxation and spending without threatening capital accumulation. Indeed, the post-Second World War welfare state was funded predominantly by increasing taxation on personal incomes and individual households, not corporate revenue.[67] The entire edifice of liberal welfare state politics relied on economic expansion—rising real incomes took the sting out of the increasing tax burden on wage and salary workers.

From the early 1970s, economic pressure on corporate profits led to an increasingly well-organized employers' offensive against working-class standards of living. Over the 1970s, median real family income declined by 16 percent, while regressive taxes were rising.[68] Existing social and economic divisions—between the unemployed and the employed, between public and private workers, between whites and people of color—were aggravated as groups scrambled to improve their incomes, generally at the expense of one another. In this economic context, political liberalism and support for the welfare state unraveled.

The shift in political climate was already clear in 1976, when Carter campaigned for the Democratic Party nomination as a Washington outsider opposed to the "bloated federal bureaucracy," sounding themes that Reagan was to use against him in 1980. The passage of Proposition 13 in California began a "tax-payers' revolt," which swept into many states in the late 1970s. Although expansion was no longer on the agenda, through the mid-1970s liberals and conservatives essentially forced a stalemate around welfare policy. The political and economic climate made it difficult to pass new programs that increased spending, so conservatives were able to defeat initiatives such as Carter's proposal to create public service jobs for welfare recipients, which promised to add as much as $12.4 billion to the federal budget.[69] On the other hand, the 1960s had created a much larger and better organized social welfare lobby, including organizations such as the American Public Welfare Association, the National Council of Local Public Welfare Administrators, the National Association of Social Workers, the Children's Defense Fund, the National Child Support Enforcement Association, the Coalition for Human Needs, and the Child Welfare League. This lobby, together with civil rights and trade-union organizations, was sufficiently influential in Congress to contain, although not entirely prevent, conservative schemes—for example, proposals to make the Work Incentive Program mandatory for women with children under six.[70]

In 1971, for the first time, Congress broke with the principle of supporting single mothers to stay home with their children. Amendments to the Work Incentive Program (WIN II) expanded the definition of the able-bodied poor to include mothers with children six or older, required their registration in the program, and refocused the program from education and vocational training to employment services and subsidized employment.[71] However, because the state was required to provide childcare to mothers participating in WIN II, many recipients were registered but placed in a "hold" category and never in fact participated.[72] *De facto*, mothers were exempted.

WIN II blurred the distinction between forcing recipients to work in exchange for benefits ("workfare") and providing training and services. Under the guise of "work experience" programs, states could require WIN II participants to work in public service jobs or else lose their eligibility.[73]

Because the welfare state relied on redistributing resources among wage and salary workers rather than reallocating resources from capital to labor, liberal proponents of welfare were increasingly on the defensive during the 1970s. Declining productivity and competitiveness in the U.S. economy required policies to create a positive business climate, such as corporate tax breaks and the diversion of investment resources to the private sector.[74] The need to restore corporate profitability on the one hand, and the resistance of large numbers of voters to tax increases on the other, left administrations and legislatures little choice but to trim taxes and spending. The Reagan landslide and Republican control of the Congress in 1980 opened the way for a successful conservative offensive against social expenditures and forced welfare advocates to design a new strategy.

In passing the Omnibus Budget Reconciliation Act of 1981 (OBRA), Congress launched an assault on AFDC which managed to cut the rolls by 8 percent in one year.[75] Ironically, while Reagan's rhetoric emphasized putting recipients to work, in fact the vast majority who suffered benefit cuts or who were declared noneligible were the working poor.[76] The Act cut funding for WIN programs in half between 1979 and 1984; limited the earned income disregard provision to four months' support; and established a cap on eligibility for gross income at 150 percent of the state's need standard.[77] Seven hundred thousand households with working parents were cut from the welfare rolls or had their benefits reduced, and the proportion of all poor families with children under eighteen receiving AFDC dropped from an average of 83 percent during the 1970s to 63 percent by 1983.[78]

Abramovitz argues that the cuts were designed to drive more women into the wage labor market to fill the demand for low-paid female labor. In addition, she suggests that the increasing numbers of recipients indicated that welfare had become too attractive an alternative to marriage.[79] This assertion makes little sense. First, the rapid increases in AFDC recipients had ended; enrollment had stabilized by the mid-1970s. Second, most of the recipients affected by the legislation already participated in the labor force. Unemployment remained relatively high; no real evidence of a shortage of low-paid labor, including women's labor, existed (except in a few especially high-wage areas, like Massachusetts). It may be true that even though the value of cash and in-kind benefits averaged well below the poverty line in most states, welfare was a better deal than paid work for most single mothers of young children. Even so, the OBRA cuts did not target those women, driving them into the workforce. If anything, the cuts might have forced women back on welfare, because they lost the benefits which supplemented their low wages.[80]

While able to cut federal funds for the working poor, even the Republican Congress could not pass the mandatory "workfare" programs that Reagan wanted. The forces opposed to "workfare" programs include public employee unions adamantly opposed to placing recipients in jobs that otherwise would be done for a union wage, welfare rights groups contesting what they call "welfare slavery," and social service lobbies, such as the National Association of Social Workers (NASW) who oppose any mandatory program.[81] While not requiring "workfare," Congress for the first time allowed states to use federal funds for such programs.[82] However, most states which did not already have "workfare" programs did not establish them, preferring instead to experiment with training, work experience, and employment (WIN Demonstration) programs. These state programs provided the model for the Democratic House and Senate welfare reform bills introduced in 1987.[83] Essentially, welfare reformers conceded the ground on single mothers' employment in order to craft a program that they hoped would increase federal funding for state programs and benefits for women on welfare. Disputes over the specific provisions of the welfare reform legislation reflected this goal. Republican proposals were punitive, provided few benefits, and were therefore cheaper. Democratic versions varied from those with least protections and benefits for clients (S. 1511, Moynihan's bill) to those with more (H.R. 1720 was estimated to cost $2.3 billion more than Moynihan's bill). The most liberal proposal, H.R. 1720, as amended by the Education and Labor Committee, responded to many of the objections opponents had raised against previous proposals for "putting welfare women to work." For example, H.R. 1720 emphasized voluntary over mandatory placement in training, work experience, job search or paid work programs, and limited the participation of women with children under six years old to twenty hours per week. It placed further restrictions on Community Work Experience Programs (CWEP). It protected recipients from being forced to take a job if they would end up with real family income lower than their income on welfare. The bill subsidized poor working mothers' childcare expenses for up to a year[84] and required states to provide education as well as vocational training, while permitting states to use federal funds for post-secondary education for welfare mothers.[85]

Even the most generous proposal, of course, did not come close to providing the range of services necessary to move women out of poverty. Moreover, none included what many reformers see as the major need: the creation of a national benefit standard and an increase in federal funding levels, so that benefits allow families to live above the state poverty level. Finally, no welfare reform bill addresses the major cause of poverty—low wages and unemployment.

The political conjuncture that created support for the Family Support Act was shaped by fundamental changes in the economy and in gender relations. The structural economic shifts affected the politics of welfare in two ways. First, the fading of U.S. world economic hegemony and the crisis of profitability, which produced an employers' offensive on workers' standards of living and required state subsidies to the private sector, placed relatively stringent limits on the "guns and butter" welfare state expansion of the 1950s and 1960s. Second, the restructuring of the U.S. economy undermined the male-breadwinner family. Declining male wages and greater demand for women workers, especially in low-paid clerical and service jobs, sent increasing numbers of women into wage work. In a period where the vast majority of women with young children work for wages, a welfare policy that pays women to stay home is anachronistic.

Most single mothers, including those with children under six, are in full-time paid work. But many *married* mothers are also in the labor force. Almost 33 percent of married mothers with children under three and 40 percent of married mothers with children three to five work full-time outside of the home. Well over half of all married mothers of children under six are employed either full- or part-time.[86] That even mothers in two-parent families are in paid work fundamentally undermines traditional definitions of motherhood. Full-time motherhood appears to be more a sign of affluence, a kind of luxury spending, than a biological necessity. While economic restructuring has somewhat worsened the conditions of life of many working-class women (and especially women of color), opportunities for paid work, however unequal they are in comparison to those for men, have improved women's alternatives to depending on men for economic support. Women's increasing access to income, although still limited, has underwritten a feminist challenge to traditional gender ideology. This challenge has been conducted predominantly in the service of the middle-class and affluent working woman rather than the working-class and poor woman. Nonetheless, the 1988 consensus on welfare reform reflects the political impact of feminism. Feminists have not only significantly changed attitudes but also established a permanent representation of women within the political system. However fragile, the emergence of a "women's policy network" connecting women in Congress to a large array of groups which can craft and lobby for legislation and mobilize constituencies has given liberal feminism a political voice.[87] That voice made women's impoverishment a political issue and shaped proposed solutions.

The Emergence of the Welfare Reform Consensus

By shifting costs for welfare onto the states and at the same time subsidizing welfare-to-work demonstration programs, OBRA provided much of the impetus behind welfare reform.[88] Governors and their welfare administrators responded to the increasing burden by utilizing welfare reform to re-federalize welfare costs. Within an ideology of promoting "independence," governors and state welfare administrators lobbied Congress intensively for increased funding of work incentive programs as a vehicle for getting money back into the states.[89] Perhaps it is not surprising that state managers accepted a trade-off in which increasing funds were purchased at the cost of further undermining single mothers' entitlement to state support. But the most significant development in the emerging welfare reform consensus was that groups and organizations which had fought to defend this right for a long time now gave it up.

The absence of any radical, grassroots women's organization (or at least the extreme political marginalization of such organizations) affects the development of policy in two ways: (1) it narrows the parameters of politically winnable reforms, and (2) it encourages technocratic solutions, which aim to manage poverty as a social problem without empowering women. Middle-class allies of the poor—social service professionals, policy analysts, lobbyists and legislators—are encouraged by their education, professional formation, and social structural position to explain poverty in terms of cultural and personal disabilities rather than the structure of economic opportunity.[90] But these tendencies can be challenged by organized groups and social movements or reinforced when the movements decline.

During the 1980s, the discourse around welfare shifted as the social welfare lobby attempted to adapt to the prevailing political climate.[91] In the 1950s and 1960s, social workers and policy planners used a culture of poverty analysis to justify increased spending on benefits and services to poor families—to intervene in the *intergenerational* transmission of poverty by rehabilitating mothers and providing more security and opportunity for children. Welfare rights and civil rights organizations, on the other hand, contested the culture of poverty and claimed benefits as a right that women had as mothers and as human beings. Although service professionals and welfare rights activists did not speak the same language, they both argued for increasing benefits to welfare mothers.

In the context of the civil rights and Black Power movements, the organization of the urban poor in welfare rights and other community organizations, and the consequent threat of political and social disruption, social work professionals provided the legitimating arguments for a policy of increasing benefits that was being forced on the legislature anyway.

In the late 1970s and especially in the 1980s, concerned to justify their programs and positions and freed from any pressure from below, social policy experts began to emphasize work incentives and the need to move individuals, including single mothers, out of "dependency." Job training and placement are defended in terms of educating young mothers—who are the heart of the "hard core" welfare population—so that they can become self-supporting. Welfare reform targets teenage parent families and families receiving AFDC for two or more years. Advocates argue that by spending more on these families, the intergenerational cycle of poverty can be broken and current costs lowered as the 15 percent to 25 percent of the welfare recipients who require long-term support move into the workforce.[92] This political discourse revives the culture of poverty analysis on a new basis: teenage girls, or more specifically Black teenage girls, not adult women as in the 1960s, have been forced to shoulder the blame for poverty. If, at the turn of the century, the "backward" immigrant woman and her "drunkard" husband peopled the victim-blaming discourses on poverty, since the Second World War, Blacks have been the icons of the poor. The 1960s' paradigm was the "matriarchal" Black mother and her "shiftless street-corner" husband; in the 1980s it becomes the "promiscuous" Black teenager and her "drug-gang" boyfriend.

This shift in political discourse has spread far beyond the social layers in which it originated. Even groups and organizations that had attacked the Moynihan Report and the culture of poverty in the 1960s have begun to adopt it. In the 1960s, civil rights organizations countered the Moynihan Report by arguing that the end of institutionalized racism and the creation of decent and well-paid jobs for Black people (or, more accurately, Black men) were the solution to poverty. But by 1987 the Black Family Summit, convened by the Urban League and the NAACP, emphasized strategies of self-help. John Jacobs, president of the Urban League, asserted: "In concentrating on the wrongs of discrimination and poverty we have neglected the fact that there is a lot we can do about our problems ourselves."[93] Black leader Eleanor Holmes Norton, former Chair of the Equal Employment Opportunity

Commission, has written on the theme of restoring the traditional Black family. "The family's return to its historic strength," she argues, "will require the overthrow of the complicated predatory ghetto subculture, a fact demanding not only new government approaches, but active Black leadership and community participation and commitment.[94]

The demoralization and disorganization of urban Black ghettos cannot be denied. And perhaps it is not surprising that, in the wake of the political defeat of full-employment programs (such as Humphrey–Hawkins) and the dismantling of the legislative and judicial attack on institutionalized racism, Black organizations have adopted a rhetoric of self-help as a way to funnel some money into social services for the Black community.

Because the analysis of poverty in terms of family disorganization seems to succeed in attracting foundation and corporate funds to community programs run by Black organizations, organizers are tempted to use it. For example, the Black Family Reunion Celebration, organized by the National Council of Negro Women, was funded by Proctor & Gamble, Eastman Kodak, and Coca-Cola. This turn in Black politics has also helped to create a climate for welfare reform as a "solution" to Black poverty.

The new "culture of poverty" politics does acknowledge institutionalized racism in pointing out that declining job opportunities for working-class young men, and because of racism, especially for young Black men, are responsible for the rise in single-parent families. Young mothers are on welfare because the fathers of their children cannot support them.[95] This argument contains an important truth. But it also draws on and promotes a male-breadwinner ideal: the solution to women's impoverishment is to recompose the nuclear family. Indeed, pro-family discourse permeates the advocacy of welfare reform, evident in arguments for requiring all states to fund the AFDC–UP program. It is clearly a step forward for unemployed fathers to be seen as legitimate recipients of support. The difficulty lies in arguing for AFDC–UP as a "solution" to the rise of women-headed families, which denies the reality that, as the Black feminist Barbara Omolade has put it, single motherhood is "both a chosen and an imposed condition."[96]

Mainstream feminist organizations (NWPC, NOW, Congressional Women's Caucus, Women's Equity Action League, etc.) have not made the welfare reform debate a priority.[97] In the year when welfare reform was a major issue, the Congressional Women's Caucus and other feminist organizations focused on a package of legislation primarily aimed at the problems of working parents, problems such as parental leave and childcare.[98] Their major initiative against the impoverishment of single mothers has been Child Support Enforcement legislation, not raising AFDC benefits or expanding eligibility.[99] Women's groups have pressed for automatic withholding of child support, higher monetary awards, and state help in tracking down delinquent fathers. The Family Support Act responded to some of these demands. The major beneficiaries of increased enforcement, however, are not AFDC mothers, because the fathers of children on AFDC are generally working in very low-paid jobs or unemployed. According to federal projections by the Health and Human Services Agency, higher child-support payments would lift fewer than 10 percent of families off the welfare rolls.[100]

A more positive effect of feminism on the welfare reform consensus is the agreement that moving women into paid work requires childcare and health benefits for transition periods. In these provisions, the Family Support Act recognizes that women workers have needs different from those of men, needs which the state has an obligation to meet. It is no accident that this recognition has occurred in a period when feminist groups have been targeting work/family issues for legislative action. Without the feminist challenge to traditional roles and its demands for social supports for working women, women's increasing labor force participation alone would have produced a very different legislative climate, one in which the special needs of women workers may have been ignored.

While able to mobilize grassroots support around certain issues, such as legalized abortion, most advocates for women are not connected to a radicalized grassroots constituency. Yet without such a constituency, it is easy enough for feminist organizations to ignore welfare reform's threat to poor women and to accept the apparently narrow limits of what might be "winnable."[101]

The Family Support Act of 1988

The Family Support Act follows previous policy in allowing states wide flexibility. Thus we can expect the usual pattern in which the more liberal and prosperous states will have programs that are less punitive and provide more services than those in the more conservative and poorer states. But in general, services will be underfunded and offices will continue to be understaffed; recipients will continue to have to negotiate a bewildering array of rules and regulations; some individuals who are eligible for benefits will have them routinely terminated; and so forth.

The Act seems to be the usual mix of trade-offs and compromises. Conservatives maintained federal funding for "workfare" (CWEP), while liberals added education to the services that states must provide in the JOBS program (the WIN replacement). Participation in the JOBS program will be mandatory for women with children over three, and states may make it mandatory for women with children as young as one. On the other hand, women with children under six cannot be required to participate more than twenty hours per week, and first consideration for enrollment must be given to volunteers.[102] Evidence from the demonstration programs on which JOBS is based indicates that there have generally been more volunteers than slots when appropriate services are provided, so the program might in fact be voluntary for quite some time. While the Reagan administration pressured Congress to set high participation goals, the Act sets relatively modest goals. States need to provide slots for only 7 percent of their eligible caseload by 1991 and for only 20 percent by 1995. Still, in the more punitive states the work requirements could be enforced arbitrarily in order to push more mothers of children under six into paid work and off the rolls. On the other hand, for mothers of children six or over, who were already subject to a work requirement under the WIN programs, the JOBS program offers some improvements. For instance, recipients must have achieved a basic level of literacy before they can be forced into job search or job training. In California's GAIN (the WIN Demonstration Program) over 55 percent of participants needed remedial education.[103] Recipients can be required to look for work for only two to four months out of the year. And there are firm restrictions preventing states from forcing recipients to take jobs which lower their standard of living.[104] The Act provides childcare and health care subsidies for one year after an individual leaves the welfare rolls for employment, makes these benefits available to all recipients, and requires states adequately to inform individuals of their entitlement.[105] In this area, the Act substantially increases subsidies to poor working women.[106] However, the cap on childcare subsidies, which is negotiated individually by the states and the federal government, may still be set too low to provide quality care.

Whether, overall, these different trade-offs will leave poor single mothers better or worse off than before is difficult to assess. It is clear, however, that this reform will not diminish the impoverishment of single mothers, the vast majority of whom will remain marginalized, low-paid workers.[107]

Defining a Feminist Stance toward Welfare Reform

Disagreement about welfare reform highlights the tension between "different treatment" and "equal treatment" strategies in feminist politics. In a competitive market society, living standards are expected to reflect individual effort. State provisions are legitimate only to guarantee the bare minimum. Therefore state support for full-time mothers can only be justified if mothers' care is a necessity, not a choice. But to make this claim is to assert a natural and intense relationship between mothers and their children and between women and nurture. A politics of difference thus appears to reinforce traditional constructions of womanhood. On the other hand, a politics of equality, which argues that women and mothers have a right to economic independence, to be "family breadwinners" just like men, appears to reinforce conservative attempts to force welfare mothers into work without childcare or other support. Conservatives argue that women on welfare need to be "weaned" from dependence into independence. Welfare handouts, they claim, breed psychological dependency, a lack of self-discipline, and promiscuous pleasure-seeking rather than responsible self-control.

Feminists who attack the reforms fear the more punitive proposals. They have accused supporters of adopting a "middle class" and male-identified perspective which ignores the real needs and conditions of working-class and poor women, devalues motherhood as work, and cooperates in state schemes to cut the welfare rolls by producing a captive pool of low-waged female labor for the growing service industries.[108] Those feminists who defend the reforms look to the more generous options. In response to the critics, they argue that dependence on a male-controlled state represents no real improvement for women, that benefits will never be high enough to offer full-time mothers a reasonable standard of living, and that most working-class women in fact want to work and to be economically independent.[109]

The feminist debate on welfare policy reflects the real difficulty in developing a strategy for reforms that are both achievable and emancipatory. The costs required to move women out of poverty—increased training and education, subsidized childcare, medical benefits, and decent jobs—are far beyond what can now be won. Neither poor people nor their potential allies are well-organized. Under these conditions, any attainable reform might leave poor women worse off—they risk losing their claim to income maintenance without moving any closer to economic self-sufficiency.

Despite the dangers, I would argue for a strategy centered on providing working mothers with support rather than demanding payments for women to stay home with their children. There is much in the current legislation to oppose: requirements that teenage mothers live with their families in order to be eligible for state support; continuation of federal subsidies to state workfare programs; excessive flexibility to local governments in implementing programs; inadequate grievance procedures and protections for recipients; and no national benefit standard which would ensure income above the poverty line. On the other hand, the new legislation offers a substantial infusion of new federal money to poor families in some of its features, particularly the continuation of childcare and health benefits for a year after an individual leaves welfare for employment, and the requirement that all states introduce AFDC–UP. One can support those provisions of the Act which mandate training and education programs and which target services to teenage mothers, without supporting the new "culture of poverty" politics. It is true, as critics argue, that many poor single mothers in fact need nothing more than well-paying jobs—their poverty can be cured better through a jobs program than a social service program. But an adequate jobs program is not imminent. In the meantime, states should not be allowed to fill their JOBS programs with employable individuals who are likely to leave welfare for low-paid jobs anyway. It may be practical, under current circumstances, to require states to concentrate services on those most in need of them, primarily teenage mothers and long-term recipients. But to promise that providing teenage mothers with work, education, and training programs will cure poverty is not only impractical, it is harmful. Such claims reinforce the victim-blaming discourses on poverty and undermine the arguments for full-employment programs.

In entering the welfare reform debate, feminists must emphasize the need to go much further in providing high cash benefits and a guaranteed standard of living to all households. A program of jobs and support provides possibilities for movement-building and alliances. Welfare families' needs should be aligned to those of the working poor and nonpoor by arguing for an increase in the range and quality of services provided to all families, including families with single mothers: nationalized medical care, quality parent/teacher controlled daycare and after-school programs as part of public education, and subsidies for adequate housing. Ultimately an approach that emphasizes employment can argue for the provision of well-paid, useful, and productive work, while showing that the costs are affordable and the benefits enormous.

At the turn of the last century, it may have been progressive to argue for poor mothers' right to withdraw from wage work. Combining wage work and domestic work was extremely difficult under any circumstances, and expanding state support for daycare or forcing employers to make concessions to women's family responsibilities was not a possibility. But these conditions no longer apply.[110]

To argue that the state should support women to stay home (rather than to combine work and parenting) concedes ground to the dominant conservative gender politics. In the current debate over childcare legislation, for example, conservatives are proposing "wages for housework": they advocate using tax credits and vouchers to pay women, even women in "intact" families, to stay home with their children. The Hatch Childcare Bill would give triple tax exemptions to families for each child cared for by a parent at home, while funding daycare at a level far below that proposed by the Democrats.

Poor and working women themselves would prefer to combine work and parenting.[111] Women leaders in the National Welfare Rights Organization opposed categorizing single mothers along with the aged and disabled as "economically immobile"—that is, unable to be self-supporting. While arguing for an adequate income for women who chose to work in the home, these women also argued for jobs, educational opportunity, and childcare for single mothers, and they often challenged male organizers who gave priority to jobs for unemployed men and who tended to ignore the childcare issue.[112] A renewed poor women's movement is much more likely to form around demands for jobs and service support than increased welfare alone.

The growing organization of women workers, and their increasing influence within the trade-union movement, makes possible alliances between employed and unemployed women and between better-paid workers and the working poor. Such alliances, while not simple, will be easier to make today than in the past when men dominated trade-union politics and the problems of combining work and family responsibilities were entirely marginal to trade-union organizing. As union women mobilize around demands for federal action to help both two-parent and single-parent families with childcare, they have the potential to become allies for women on welfare who also need quality childcare so they can work.[113] Indeed, the extension of subsidized childcare would solve one of the primary difficulties faced by single mothers: income from their low-paid jobs does not cover the costs of working, especially childcare costs. Similarly, while the number of working women with health care benefits has grown, many are without coverage. State legislation requiring employers to provide medical benefits for all workers, or state subsidization of health insurance for all, would also make it much easier for women on welfare to move into paid work.

A politics that emphasizes combining work and parenting for all families can directly challenge the false distinction between "dependent" families (those that rely on the state) and "independent" families (those that rely on their own resources). This distinction has been the foundation of AFDC policy. While working parents have different needs, almost all working parents need help from the state. Affluent two-earner families may be able to generate by themselves the high levels of income and flexible working conditions necessary to combine successfully waged work, parenting and caregiving. But most families, even those with two earners, cannot solve work/family dilemmas alone. Because caregiving and parenting remain primarily a familial, private responsibility rather than a social and community responsibility, and because men generally earn higher incomes than women, the traditional gender division of labor which assigns caregiving tasks to women continues, even where women work for wages. Single-earner families, especially those headed by a woman, are especially disadvantaged. At a minimum, good jobs at a living wage for *women* as well as for men, a shorter workday, and publicly funded programs providing high-quality care are necessary to meet the pressing needs facing the majority of men and women.[114]

The entry of women into the labor force and the increasing influence of women trade unionists, the impact of feminism on the perception of women's family roles, and the increasing organization of professionals and grassroots constituencies around family/work issues, make it possible for the first time since the emergence of industrial capitalism to challenge women's assignment to unpaid caring work. We can reasonably argue for households' universal need for social provisions that will help them carry out their responsibilities for raising children and caring for adults.

[*1989*]

Notes

I would like to thank Lynne Butler for her assistance with the research for this article. I would also like to thank Karen Van Meter and Ursula Werner for their help in editing it.

1. See, e.g., M. Katz, *In the Shadow of the Poorhouse: A Social History of Welfare in America* (New York, 1986); C. Offe, *Contradictions of the Welfare State* (Cambridge, Mass., 1984); F. Piven and R. Cloward, *Poor People's Movements* (New York, 1977); F. Piven and R. Cloward, *Regulating the Poor: The Functions of Public Welfare* (New York, 1971).

2. See, e.g., M. Abramovitz, *Regulating the Lives of Women: Social Welfare Policy from Colonial Times to the Present* (Boston, 1988); G. Pascall, *Social Policy: A Feminist Analysis* (Boston, 1986); Gordon, "What Does Welfare Regulate?", *Social Research* 55 (1988), 609–30.

3. Family Support Act of 1988, Pub. L. No. 11–485, *102* Stat. 2343 (1988).

4. Prior to 1971, Congress had mandated the enrollment of women with school-age children in the Work Incentive Program (WIN), but allowed states to set their own regulations. Thus, liberal states like New York registered very few mothers, whereas Utah forced most to register for the program. S. Law, "Women, Work, Welfare, and the Preservation of Patriarchy," *University of Philadelphia Law Review* 131 (1983), 1249–1339. However, even after 1971, most of the Work Incentive Programs were funded at levels too low to accommodate all recipients. Although the state must register all recipients, programs have tended to serve the most employable recipients who need the least services: men, women with older children who do not require childcare or after-school care, and volunteers. J. Handler, "The Feminization of Poverty and the Malen-ization of AFDC," *New York University Review of Legal and Social Change* 17 (1989).

5. The original House bill, H.R. 1720, the Family Welfare Reform Act of 1987, also exempted women with children under six. However, it was amended in the House Ways and Means Committee to require participation by women with children aged three years or older, and to allow states to require mothers of children one year or more to participate. Mothers of children less than six could not be required to participate in work or training more than 20 hours per week and only when childcare was provided.

6. The Family Support Act does, however, limit their required participation in training or wage work to 20 hours per week. For a description of the shifting liberal position and emerging consensus, see Reischauer, "Welfare Reform: Will Consensus Be Enough?", *Brookings Review*, Summer 1987, at 3.

7. Rovner, "Welfare Reform: The Next Domestic Priority?", *44th Congress Questions* 2281, 2283 (1986).

8. Combined welfare and food stamp benefits still leave recipients substantially below subsistence in almost four-fifths of the states. M. Sklar, "Welfare Reform and Youth Unemployment Policy Options," *American Family* 11 (1988), 9–11.

9. Opposition to a national benefit standard was almost universal in the Congress, except for a handful of liberal democrats. See D. Moynihan, "Letter to the Editor," *New York Times*, August 6, 1987, A26, col. 4.

10. More than 50 percent of single mothers leave welfare within two years and only 17 percent stay on welfare for more than eight. Roughly 21 percent of eligible single mothers leave welfare for paid work. Nichols-Casebolt and

McClure, "Social Work Support for Welfare Reform: The Latest Surrender in the War on Poverty," *Social Work: Journal of the National Association of Social Workers* 34 (1989) 77–80.

11. Almost two-thirds of households in poverty receive no cash assistance at all; over 40 percent do not receive any means-tested benefits. Handler, "The Feminization of Poverty," 13. In 1985, 41.5 percent of the poor population over fifteen years old were working. Rovner, "Welfare Reform," 2283.

12. M. Bane and D. Ellwood, *The Dynamics of Dependence: The Routes to Self Sufficiency* (Cambridge, Mass., 1983).

13. See B. Ransby, *Agenda*, December 1988, 3; Handler, "The Feminization of Poverty," 121–25.

14. For a review of "welfare-to-work" programs, see Y. Hasenfeld, *Welfare and Work: The Institutionalization of Moral Ambiguity*, University of California Institute of Industrial Relations Working Paper No. 147 (1987), 39–56.

15. California's GAIN, one of the model programs for the Family Support Act, was projected to remove no more than 3 percent of the caseload from the welfare rolls. A national review of welfare-to-work programs found that more than 50 percent of those recipients who found work had to remain on welfare because their wages were so low. L. Udesky, "Workfare: It Isn't Fair and It Doesn't Work," *The Progressive* 51 (1987), 14–17.

16. W. Sarvasy, "Reagan and Low-Income Mothers: A Feminist Recasting of the Debate," in M. Brown, ed., *Remaking the Welfare State: Retrenchment and Social Policy in America and Europe* (Philadelphia, 1988).

17. Gordon, "What Does Welfare Regulate?"

18. National Coalition on Women, Work and Welfare Reform, *Changing Welfare: An Investment in Women and Children in Poverty* (1987)

19. On the "motherhood mystique," see M. Hoffnung, "Motherhood: Contemporary Conflict for Women," in J. Freeman, ed., *Women: A Feminist Perspective*, 4th edn. (Palo Alto, 1989).

20. S. Hartmann, "Changes in Women's Economic and Family Roles in Post-World War II United States," in L. Beneria and C. Stimpson, eds., *Women, Households, and the Economy* (New York, 1987), 33–65.

21. See Abramovitz, *Regulating the Lives of Women*; Pascall, *Social Policy*; M. Barrett, *Women's Oppression Today* (rev. ed, London, 1988); E. Wilson, Women and the Welfare State (London, 1977); E. Boris and P. Bardaglio, "The Transformation of Patriarchy: The Historic Role of the State," in I. Diamond, ed. *Families, Politics and Public Policy: A Feminist Dialogue on Women and the State* (New York, 1997), 132–152; M. McIntosh, "The State and the Oppression of Women," in A. Kuhn and A. Wolpe, eds. *Feminism and Materialism: Women and Modes of Production* (London, 1978), 254; C. Pateman, "The Patriarchal Welfare State," in A. Gutmann, ed., *Democracy and the Welfare State* (Princeton, 1988), 231.

22. Abramovitz, *Regulating the Lives of Women*, passim.

23. G. Mink, "The Lady and the Tramp: Gender, Race and the Origins of the American Welfare State," in L. Gordon, ed., *Women, the State, and Welfare* (Madison, 1989).

24. Pateman, "The Patriarchal Welfare State," 255–58.

25. Hasenfeld makes a similar point with regard to workfare programs in particular. Against those who analyze workfare as a mechanism of labor supply regulation and social control, he argues that these programs are expensive, hard

to administer and generally ineffective. Since there are better and cheaper ways to achieve the same ends, the programs have to be explained in other terms—in his view, the "moral ambiguity" in cultural values and norms about welfare and work, Hasenfeld, *Welfare and Work*.

26. CIS/Annual 1998 Legislative Histories of U.S. Public Law 464–75. Interestingly, their testimony primarily opposed mandatory work requirements for welfare recipients and instead supported training and job placement programs with voluntary participation. Unlike the ideological conservatives, these groups seem less concerned about curing a "pathology of dependence" through forced work and more interested in state programs that are directly crafted to subsidize employment of the more able and willing welfare recipients in low-waged local industry. The proposed legislation continued or expanded programs that pay employers to hire and train welfare recipients and allow low-paid workers to continue receipt of benefits. On the other hand, they considered as unrealistic proposals to establish a minimum national benefit or move the "hard to employ" recipients into work, because that would require excessive levels of spending. See, e.g., Hearings on Welfare Reform: H.R. 30 Fair Work Opportunities Act of 1987 and H.R. 1720 Family Welfare Reform Act of 1987, 100th Cong., 1st Sess, 252 (1987) (testimony of William Kohlberg, President, National Business Alliance).

27. On the other hand, a broad array of initiatives on welfare reform were taken by others in the period leading up to the introduction of legislation. Major actors were government officials, policy institutes, and foundations. They included the "Matter of Commitment Project" of the American Public Welfare Association (an organization of state human service commissioners); the National Governors' Association Task Force on Welfare Prevention, Governor Cuomo's Task Force on Poverty and Welfare; the Project on the Welfare of Families, chaired by Bruce Babbitt and Arthur Fleming; the Ford Foundation (which funded several different projects, including a Project on Social Welfare and the American Future); the Brookings Institution; the Urban Institute; and, for the conservatives, the White House Domestic Policy Council and the Working Seminar on the Family and American Welfare Policy, staffed by the American Enterprise Institute. See Children's Defense Fund, *National Welfare Reform Initiatives* (Washington, D.C., 1986).

28. Work, Education, and Training Opportunities for Welfare Recipients: Hearings Before the Subcommittee on Public Assistance and Unemployment Compensation of the House Committee on Ways and Means, 99th Congress, 2nd Session (1986).

29. For a discussion of the ways that gender ideology is expressed in the differences between welfare state programs directed toward men and toward women, see Abramovitz, *Regulating the Lives of Women*, *passim*; Law, "Women, Work, Welfare," *passim*; B. Nelson, "The Gender, Race, and Class Origins of Early Welfare Policy and the U.S. Welfare State: A Comparison of Workmen's Compensation and Mothers' Aid," in L. Tilly and P. Gurin, eds., *Women, Change, and Politics* (New York, 1989).

30. The National Association of Homebuilders, long an opponent of federal social welfare initiatives, emerged in the 1960s as a major source of support for housing subsidy measures. See L. Salamon, *Welfare: The Elusive Consensus* (New York, 1978), 90. Similarly, the growing and well-organized lobbies of childcare

providers have helped to put work plus childcare on the agenda for welfare reform. Although organizations such as the National Association for the Education of Young Children have focused on the various bills expanding the federal government role in childcare, they support any increase in federal payments for childcare services, including in welfare programs. Their efforts have helped not only to legitimate daycare and to undermine conservative opposition to a federal government role in childcare, but also to impress upon Congress the broad constituency for support to working mothers.

31. On the impact of the "Women's Lobby" on federal legislation in the early 1920s, see Mueller, "The Empowerment of Women: Polling and the Women's Voting Bloc," in C. Mueller, ed., *The Politics of the Gender Gap* (Newbury Park, 1988), 16, 18–21. For the New Deal period, see S. Ware, *Beyond Suffrage: Women in the New Deal* (Newbury Park, 1981). A "women's network" wielded influence within the New Deal administration, but there was no significant mass mobilization of women as there had been during the Progressive Era.

32. For an elaboration of this point, see "Gender and the State", Chapter 2 above.

33. This analysis focuses mainly on the impact of class and gender, but also indicates the points at which race inequality shaped the development of welfare policy.

34. Boris and Bardaglio, "The Transformation of Patriarchy," 85–86; see also Abramovitz, *Regulating the Lives of Women*, 190–95.

35. S. Lehrer, *Origins of Protective Labor Legislation for Women, 1905–1925* (Albany, 1987), 162–68.

36. For a discussion of how racist ideologies also shaped early welfare state programs, see Mink, "The Lady and the Tramp."

37. In 1900, 3 percent of native-born white married women, and 3.6 percent of foreign-born married women worked outside the home. By 1920, only 6.3 percent of married native-born white women and 7.2 percent of foreign-born wives were in the workforce. Even as late as 1940, only 12 percent of white married women worked outside the home. Labor force participation of Black wives was much higher—around 32 percent. C. Degler, *At Odds: Women and the Family in America from the Revolution to the Present* (New York, 1980), 384.

38. See J. Jones, *Labor of Love, Labor of Sorrow: Black Women, Work and the Family from Slavery to the Present* (New York, 1985), 125–26, 162–65; A. Kessler-Harris, *Out to Work: A History of Wage-earning Women in the United States* (New York, 1982), 122–26.

39. Analyzing the two major income-maintenance programs of the Progressive era—mothers' pensions and workmen's compensation—Barbara Nelson argues that the welfare state was characterized from the beginning by a two-track system that sharply differentiated programs for women (and for men of color) from those for white men. In workmen's compensation programs, eligibility was determined on straightforward decision criteria in the service of highly routinized decision-making. Routinized decision rules and concomitantly simpler application procedures contributed to client satisfaction with insurance programs and reinforced the social legitimacy of the clients as being deserving of their benefits. Mothers' pensions, by contrast, used moralistic, diffuse decision criteria and allowed high levels of bureaucratic discretion. Nelson, "The Gender, Race, and Class Origins." While Nelson's identification of differences in programs directed to men and to women is appropriate, her distinction

perhaps divides male and female programs too sharply. For instance, as Handler points out, unemployment insurance also has many continuing tests of "deservingness" (e.g., proof of looking for work) and only temporary protection from coercion (e.g., beneficiary cannot be forced to take "unsuitable" work). Handler, "The Feminization of Poverty," 67–68. On the other hand, an important difference remained, at least up until the 1970s: men's eligibility rested on whether or not they were able to work; women's rested on whether or not they were morally deserving.

40. Perhaps one reason state legislatures so easily passed mothers' pension legislation was that, generally, funding was left entirely to the local governments. Most localities refused to expand taxation or shift spending from other activities, so the mothers' pensions programs remained quite small. In many localities, the availability of benefits was keyed to local labor market demands, for instance, suspending payments during harvests in order to assure a supply of labor for the fields. Racism played a role also—poor Black women were more likely to be expected to work than white women. See note 41.

41. On local resistance, especially in areas where Black women were an important source of wage labor, see Abramovitz, *Regulating the Lives of Women*, 194, 317–18. Opposition from local businesses has continued to be a source of resistance to federal efforts to expand benefits. For example, a 1977 task force of the National Governors' Conference found substantial opposition from several state governments to a national payment standard set at even 75 percent of the poverty level because it would have "an unacceptable detrimental effect on the economics of those states by discouraging work by those with low earnings levels or potential." Salamon, *Welfare*, 122. On the other hand, local governments also have been a source of political pressure on the federal government to increase welfare spending. In the recent debates over welfare reform, the American Public Welfare Association (APWA), representing state welfare administrators, pushed for a new national minimum benefit standard roughly around the poverty line, to be indexed to inflation. Where the federal government paid 50 percent to 78.5 percent of state costs, with poor states getting the higher share, the APWA proposed a uniform federal share of 75 percent—an overall increase in the federal match. *Washington Post*, April 15, 1987, A21, col. 1.

42. See Handler, "The Feminization of Poverty," 34.

43. Payment levels were very low, and there was no provision for a grant to the mother. A federal matching grant for the mother was finally added in 1950 under pressure from state governments that were facing increasing caseloads and rising expenditures on the program. W. Trattner, *From Poor Law to Welfare State: A History of Social Welfare in America*, 3rd edn (New York, 1984), 291.

44. According to Edwin Witte, Executive Director of the Committee on Economic Security (CES), which crafted the Social Security legislation, there was little interest in Congress in the ADC program. "The major impetus for ADC came from the Children's Bureau whose proposals, based on the Mothers' Pensions programs, CES accepted with little comment." Abramovitz, *Regulating the Lives of Women*, 315. Susan Ware identifies twenty-eight women who formed the New Deal women's network, among them Grace Abbott, chief of the Children's Bureau; Mary Anderson, head of the Women's Bureau; Molly Dewson, director of the Women's Division, Democratic National Committee and

member of the Social Security Board; Frances Perkins, Secretary of Labor; and Jane Hoey, director of the Social Security Administration's Bureau of Public Assistance. Ware, *Beyond Suffrage*.

45. Since so many Black men worked in jobs not covered by Social Security, many Black widows were not eligible for the more generous and less restrictive Support through Social Security. Abramovitz, *Regulating the Lives of Women*, 250. The establishment of Old Age Insurance moved older white male workers into the ranks of the "deserving poor." Opponents of old-age pensions had always argued that they undermined the work ethic and rewarded profligacy, because men would not have to rely on their own efforts in order to provide for themselves and their families in old age. By tying eligibility to a lifetime of continuous paid employment and by making the program contributory, proponents could argue that Old Age Insurance would not undermine the necessity to labor. Further, the provision of widows' pensions did not violate the assumptions of male responsibility and female dependence, allowing white men as family breadwinners to provide for their wives and requiring women to stay married in order to collect benefits in their old age.

46. By 1961, widowed families comprised only 7.7 percent of the ADC caseload, down from 43 percent in 1937. Abramovitz, *Regulating the Lives of Women*, 321.

47. Law, "Women, Work, Welfare," 1259.

48. Abramovitz, *Regulating the Lives of Women*, 323–26.

49. Trattner, *From Poor Law to Welfare State*, 299.

50. The commissions recommended first and foremost the provision of rehabilitative services by professionally trained personnel and federal funding for social worker training. Ibid., 299–300.

51. Differential matching requirements reflected the influence of social work professionals within the Democratic administration and Congress at this time.

52. Even as late as 1967, only 60 percent of poor single mothers were receiving benefits. Handler, "The Feminization of Poverty," 73.

53. On the role of poverty program workers in supporting the organization of poor single mothers, see Piven and Cloward, *Regulating the Poor*, 320–30.

54. On the successes of direct action by NWRO in expanding benefits, see N. Kotz and M. Kotz, *A Passion for Equality: George Wiley and the Movement* (New York, 1977), 307–28.

55. Hasenfeld, *Welfare and Work*, 28.

56. See Trattner, *From Poor Law to Welfare State*, 302; Piven and Cloward, *Regulating the Poor*, 306–20.

57. *Shapiro v. Thompson*, 394 *U.S.* (1969) 618; see also *Regulating the Lives of Women*, 327, 335.

58. Piven and Cloward, *Regulating the Poor*, 306–20.

59. Sylvia Law calls this the "legalization of welfare." Law, "Women, Work, Welfare," 1267–71.

60. I. Garfinkel and S. McLanahan, *Single Mothers and their Children* (Washington, D.C., 1986), 110–14.

61. Ibid.

62. G. West, *The National Welfare Rights Movement* (New York, 1981), 295–99.

63. Salamon, *Welfare*, 89. The NWRO also played a role in defeating Nixon's Family Assistance Plan. The Plan's guaranteed minimum family income was so low that it would have reduced support to welfare recipients in high-benefit

states. Ibid., 91–97.

64. Abramovitz, *Regulating the Lives of Women*, 340.

65. Individuals can continue receiving aid if their monthly income (after deducting actual work expenses such as childcare, transportation, and uniforms), plus one-third of the remaining gross, is less than the state-defined need standard.

66. In the case of the WIN regulations, we can see how a politics of protection that considers men but not women "able-bodied" and thus expects men, but not women, to work, discriminates against women as workers. As Law argues, men were given preference in assignment to training programs, although many single mothers also volunteered to be trained. Law, "Women, Work, Welfare," 1286–87.

67. The effective tax rate on corporate income declined steadily from a high of 40 percent in the early 1950s to 13 percent in 1982. J. Pechman, *The Rich, the Poor, and the Taxes they Pay* (Washington, D.C., 1986).

68. Not surprisingly, acceptance of state spending for programs decreased among some groups, such as union households, which had previously supported them. See Brown, "The Segmented Welfare System: Distributive Conflict and Retrenchment in the United States, 1968–1984," in Brown, ed., *Remaking the Welfare State*, 182, 197–98.

69. Budget limits were not the only problem with Carter's program. It was opposed by the AFL–CIO and public employee unions because it proposed to pay welfare recipients placed in public jobs the minimum wage rather than the prevailing wage. Salamon, *Welfare*, 203.

70. The visible role of Black women in the welfare rights movement and the increasing proportion of Black women among welfare recipients helped to fuel the conservative backlash.

71. Congressional conservatives had tried unsuccessfully in 1967 to force all states to require mothers of school-age children to register for WIN programs. Interestingly, policy toward the work participation of welfare mothers parallels the general experience of mothers not on welfare. By the early 1970s, the majority of mothers of school-age children were in the labor force.

72. This was still true in 1980 when 39 percent of all adult AFDC recipients were registered, but only 19 percent ever participated, only 2 percent were enrolled in training, and only 1 percent found a job through WIN. Hasenfeld, *Welfare and Work*, 43–44.

73. However, Congress still would not fund straightforward "work for relief" programs. States establishing such programs had to use state funds.

74. Between 1966 and 1985, the effective tax rate on capital was cut in half. J. Pechman, *Who Paid Taxes: 1966–1985?* (Washington, D.C., 1985), 73.

75. Abramovitz, *Regulating the Lives of Women*, 358.

76. Moffitt and Wolf estimate that 35 percent of working welfare recipients lost eligibility. Moffitt and Wolf, "The Effects of the 1981 Omnibus Budget Reconciliation Act on Welfare Recipients and Work Incentives," *Social Services Review* 61 (1987), 247–260.

77. Sarri, "Federal Policy Changes and the Feminization of Poverty," *Journal of the Child Welfare League of America* 64 (1985), 235–247.

78. Abramovitz, *Regulating the Lives of Women*, 358.

79. Ibid., 353.

80. The same argument applies to the 1971 legislation making the WIN program

mandatory for women with school-age children. It passed in a recessionary period, not a time of labor shortages. Its proponents argued it would cut costs, but like the previous WIN program, WIN II moved few recipients off welfare, and appears to have raised, rather than lowered, overall costs. M. Rein, *Dilemmas of Welfare Policy: Why Work Strategies Haven't Worked* (New York, 1982); see also Law, "Women, Work, Welfare," 1336–37. It is difficult to demonstrate the legislation's economic or social effectiveness, even in mediating conflicting needs of capital and patriarchy.

81. NASW opposed Moynihan's bill because it did not require all state employment and training programs to include an "employability plan, client–agency contract and case management." National Association of Social Workers, Legislative Alert, Oct. 29, 1987. The final bill mandated the plan, but not case management.

82. Although the original House bill proposed to limit all Community Work Experience Program (CWEP) assignments to six months, the final House bill and the 1998 Family Support Act allowed states to use CWEP as part of the new training, job search and employment program. The Family Support Act also included rules to protect existing public jobs and wage rates from being undermined by the use of welfare recipients. *See* House of Representatives Conference Report No. 998, 100th Cong., 2d Sess. 144, *reprinted in* 1989 U.S. Code Cong. and Admin. News 2879, 2932 (hereinafter H.R. Conf. Rep. No. 998).

83. Gueron, "Reforming Welfare with Work," *Public Welfare* 45 (Fall 1987), 14–25.

84. However, the bill set a low cap on expenses—$175 per month for a child over two, and $200 per month for a child under two. Still, this cap was higher than the $160 per month cap in S. 1511.

85. The Moynihan bill did not require states to provide the more costly training and education programs, encouraging a continuation of the meaningless "make-work" activities that have thus far characterized much of the WIN program.

86. Department of Labor, Bureau of Labor Statistics, Marital and Family Characteristics of the Labor Force 1987 (unpublished table on file with author).

87. Costain, "Representing Women: the Transition from Social Movement to Interest Group," in E. Bonaparth, ed., *Women, Power and Policy* (New York, 1982), 19–37; see also S. Hartmann, *From Margin to Mainstream: American Women and Politics Since 1960* (Philadelphia, 1989), chaps 5 and 7.

88. Federal funding for WIN declined from $365 million in FY 1981 to $93 million in FY 1988. H.R. Conf. Rep. No. 998. By 1985, total spending for WIN approximated the level of funding in 1981, although federal spending had dropped. On average for all Work Programs, states paid 25 percent of the costs. Hasenfeld, *Welfare and Work*, 51.

89. For instance, the American Public Welfare Association's National Council of State Human Service Administrators called for welfare-to-jobs programs to be funded with a 75 percent federal share not subject to appropriations ceilings, whereas WIN allocations were capped. American Public Welfare Association and National Council of State Human Service Administrators, *One Child in Four* 20 (n.d.). They were successful in part. Although Congress rejected an open-ended entitlement, the Family Support Act significantly raises the cap on federal matching funds for the new welfare-to-work program (JOBS) above

what it had been for WIN and the other welfare-to-work programs (from $365 million in 1987 to $600 million in 1989). Whereas federal matching funds for childcare were subject to appropriation under WIN, the Act provides open-ended entitlement with a federal matching rate of 50 percent to 80 percent, and sets the allowable reimbursement at the applicable local market rate. H.R. Conf. Rep. No. 998, at 161–62.

90. J. Ehrenreich, *The Altruistic Imagination* (Ithaca, 1985).
91. Nichols-Casebolt and McClure, "Social Work Support for Welfare Reform."
92. For an excellent review of the literature on whether single motherhood causes intergenerational poverty, see S. McLanahan and K. Booth, "Mother Only Families: Problems, Reproduction, and Politics", Discussion Paper, Institute for Research on Poverty, University of Wisconsin–Madison, 1988.
93. "Welfare in Focus at Urban League," *New York Times*, July 22, 1997, A3, col. 1.
94. Norton, "Restoring the Traditional Black Family," *New York Times*, June 2, 1985, 6 (Magazine), 43; see also Black columnist William Raspberry's approval of conservative Stuart Butter's assertion that "if you begin with the idea that to father a child is to take on responsibility for that child, then you are likely to get serious about child support. You won't allow AFDC to allow a teen-age mother to set up a separate home and thereby be virtually condemned to poverty." Raspberry, "Begin Welfare Reform at Grass Roots," *Oregonian*, May 1988. For a critique of this approach, see A. Davis and F. Davis, "The Black Family and the Crisis of Capitalism," *The Black Scholar* 17 (September–October 1986), 33–40.
95. See, e.g., M. Wright-Edelman, *Families in Peril: Agenda for Social Change* (Washington, D.C., 1987); W. Wilson, *the Truly Disadvantaged* (Chicago, 1987).
96. B. Omolade, *It's a Family Affair: The Real Lives of Black Single Mothers* (Latham, N.Y., 1986).
97. Black organizations (National Urban League, NAACP, National Council of Negro Women, etc.) have been much more involved in lobbying for and crafting alternative programs. This may reflect their larger constituency among the poor and the fact that social service entrepreneurship among Black professionals is more concentrated in programs to deal with poverty.
98. One feminist organization, Wider Opportunities for Women, did initiate and direct an important intervention in the Congressional consideration of welfare reform. Their National Coalition on Women, Work and Welfare Reform crafted an alternative reform program which was presented in Congressional hearings, press conferences, and letters to legislators. Their proposal accepted the goal of transforming the welfare system into one which enables recipients to become economically self-sufficient. But they argued for making employment and training programs voluntary, increasing and standardizing minimum benefits, extending support services and subsidies to those who leave welfare for low-paid work, and effectively enforcing child support. Along with other advocates for the poor, their efforts no doubt helped to blunt some of the more conservative proposals. See National Coalition on Women, Work and Welfare Reform, *Changing Welfare: An Investment in Women and Children in Poverty* (Washington, D.C., 1987).
99. For a critique of "feminization of poverty" campaigns that target child-support enforcement, see Chapter 4.

100. Some estimates of the impact of child support enforcement on poor women's incomes are higher. Assuming relatively high childcare awards (17 percent of father's income for one child, 25 percent for two), those estimates indicated that the poverty gap—the difference between the incomes of poor families headed by single mothers and the amount of money they would need to move above the poverty level—would be reduced by 27 percent. Garfinkel and McLanahan, *Single Mothers and their Children*, 25.

101. Although they put their resources and attention elsewhere, many women's organizations did ultimately take a position on welfare reform during the last months of debate on the welfare reform legislation. They focused predominantly on making the work and training provisions voluntary rather than mandatory and on strengthening child support enforcement. See, e.g., C. Deyss (Social Policy Director, League of Women Voters), Letter to the Editor, *New York Times*, May 19, 1988.

102. Here, again, we see a parallel between the labor force participation of married mothers and the demands made on welfare mothers. Of married mothers with young children, the great majority who work do so part-time.

103. Handler, "The Feminization of Poverty," 87.

104. Recipients in high-benefit states fare better under these restrictions. In California, a high benefit state, a mother of two would have to get a job earning $7.00 an hour for 40 hours a week to approximate her living standard on welfare. Hasenfeld, *Welfare and Work*, 88. In Oregon, a low benefit state, the JOBS program requirement that mothers of children under six may not be forced to work more than 20 hours a week will result in a major increase in caseload levels and client eligibility for benefits. Adult and Family Services Division, *Impact of the Family Support Act on Oregon* (Salem, Or., 1988).

105. Previously, although recipients who left welfare for work were eligible for four months of transitional medicaid benefits, many states did not inform recipients of this benefit. Since the Congressional Budget Office based its estimate of the costs of the new Act on current levels of use, it probably underestimated the level of new funding that transitional benefits will require.

106. However, under the new Act, child and health care benefits end after one year, raising the possibility that individuals will not be able to continue in employment and will return to welfare. Conservatives were extremely concerned about this possibility and attempted to introduce various punitive schemes to prevent it. Liberals were able to counter these attempts in the area of medicaid benefits. The Act now says that the Secretary of Health and Human Services (HHS) must conduct a study of the impact of transitional medical assistance on welfare dependency. For childcare subsidies, the Act empowers the Secretary of HHS to issue restrictive regulations if a study finds such "recycling" is occurring. According to one informant, the difference in the two clauses reflects the difference in seniority and power of the respective committee chairs.

107. Forty percent of all AFDC recipients who leave AFDC have incomes below the poverty level in the years following AFDC support. Sarri, "Federal Policy Changes and the Feminization of Poverty," 237.

108. F. Piven and B. Ehrenreich, "Workfare Means New Mass Peonage," *New York Times*, May 30, 1987, A31, col. 2.

109. Bader, "Will Workfare Do the Job?", *New Directions For Women* 17 (January–

February 1988), 9.

110. See generally Chapter 2 above.

111. On poor women's attitudes, see Milwaukee National Welfare Rights Organization, *Welfare Women Speak Out* (New York, 1972); Coalition on Human Needs, *How the Poor Would Remedy Poverty: Interview with 50 Low-income Persons in Washington, D.C.* (July–August 1986). On working-class women's attitudes, see M. Ferree, "Working Class Jobs: Housework and Paid Work as Sources of Satisfaction," *Social Problems* 23, no. 4 (April 1976), 431–41.

112. West, *The National Welfare Rights Movement*, 93.

113. For example, the Coalition of Labor Union Women's American Family Celebration held a demonstration in Washington, D.C. on May 14, 1988 which demanded federal action on childcare, health care, pay equity, and paid parental leave.

114. In recasting the debate on welfare, Wendy Sarvasy similarly argues the need to associate programs for poor mothers with programs for all families. She calls for revaluing and ultimately restructuring caretaker work, in which both men and women would be rewarded for performing the important roles of taking care of other people. Trying to get poor mothers into paid work, she argues, simply legitimizes the assumption that poor mothers must have a privatized double burden. Instead, we should recognize that women are providing a socially necessary activity which needs to be rewarded, not stigmatized. Sarvasy, "Reagan and Low-Income Mothers." While I support much of her argument, I remain concerned that paying women to be full-time caretakers and domestic workers in their own homes, even reformulated so that it potentially includes men in the role, reinforces conventional ideas about children's needs, adequate mothering, and women's association with caretaking as well as reinforcing the belief that privatized care within the family household is necessarily preferable to more socialized forms.

Chapter 6

Welfare Reform:
Reframing the Debate

The myths, stereotypes, and just plain lies that circulate around welfare reform are outrageous; yet they seem to be impervious to reasoned argument. The only politics that comes close to welfare reform in its level of irrational myth-making is the politics of crime. And of course they are linked through the fundamentally racist and sexist organizing concept that teen mothers raise criminal sons, and more specifically that young African-American mothers (and their irresponsible male lovers) are the main cause of poverty and violence.

One of the truly fascinating (horrifying) aspects of this politics is the increasing use of the term "illegitimacy" to characterize the pregnancies of unmarried women. Following the sexual revolution, the word illegitimacy had practically disappeared from our political and journalistic vocabulary, along with that moralizing bad girl/good girl discourse on sexuality which had been used to control young women's sexual behavior. Of course, the new vocabularies of sexuality were not uniformly women-friendly—for instance, the identification of sexual freedom with sexual availability. And, as anyone familiar with young women's heterosexual experiences knows, many negotiate intimacy, contraception, and sexual pleasure with men under difficult, if not entirely restrictive and unequal, conditions. Still, lifting the stigma on unwed pregnancy as well as motherhood, along with expanding access to income support (AFDC, food stamps) for single mothers in the period from the 1960s to the mid-1970s, did expand women's sexual autonomy and reduce their dependence on men. Now, in op-ed pieces, editorials, journalistic accounts, political statements, we are confronted once again with a language of shame in which unwed motherhood is recast from a legitimate choice to a moral failing. (There is also a more subdued attack on divorce, filled with exaggerated claims about the emotional damage sustained by children whose parents selfishly divorce, putting their own happiness ahead of their children's needs. However, proposals to make divorce more restrictive do not fall on such fertile ground, probably because divorce cuts across race and class boundaries in a way that teen pregnancy and motherhood do not.) Clearly, targeting teen mothers in welfare reform proposals expresses a range of anxieties—about women's sexuality, about gender relations, about security, especially economic security—displaced onto the convenient and conventional scapegoats of a racist society (young Black women and men).

What makes the current situation especially difficult for those of us organizing against the attack on single mothers is that it comes from so many different directions at once: from the political right, from the Clinton administration, from Democrats as well as Republicans, from state governors and welfare system bureaucrats. And, perhaps most frustrating, almost no one—even from among the many supposed advocates for poor single mothers—is challenging the assumption that *welfare is itself the primary problem*, an assumption that Clinton reinforced with his campaign pledge to "end welfare as we know it."

The reigning consensus of the welfare reform debate is that there are too many people on welfare, that receiving welfare is bad for you, that teen pregancy is epidemic and responsible for many other problems, that families in general can and ought to be "self-sufficient," that being responsible means being completely self-supporting through paid work even if you are a single mother with a young child. (The corollary of the last point, explicitly stated by right-wingers and communitarians alike, is that since so few single mothers can support themselves and their children on one paycheck, welfare as an alternative to the market lets men—and communities—off the hook. While not all of them would go so far as to say this, many appear to support punitive policies such as denying young mothers the right to live independently or refusing additional benefits to a child born to a mother on welfare. These policies, they claim, will discourage out-of-wedlock births because they will force families/communities to police young people's sexual behavior more closely and reinstate that great regulatory institution: the shotgun marriage.)

This consensus is not simply a rightward backlash in response to the large social and cultural changes of previous decades, although it is that in part. It is not simply the brainchild of the secular and religious right, although it is also that. This consensus is the result of a more-than-decade-long campaign by social service professionals, social scientists, educators, population controllers, health professionals, and other moral entrepreneurs seeking state funding for their programs and research dollars in a hostile political climate. Reagan's election in 1978 definitively extinguished the already faltering war on poverty and its fundamental legitimating idea—that social and economic problems were the result of institutionalized social and economic inequalities.

Faced with increasing competition for a shrinking public spending pie, program advocates adjusted to the new conservative rhetoric which located causes in individual behavior and dysfunctional families/communities. It was not the right wing, but planned parenthood which first sounded the alarm about an epidemic of teen pregnancy with the slogan "children having children." It was not the right wing, but the community colleges and other social service contractors who promised to reduce "welfare dependency" and promote "self-sufficiency" through "life skills" classes for single mothers. It was not the right-wing, but mainstream feminists, lawyers, social scientists, and social workers who identified "dead beat dads" as the cause of single mothers' impoverishment. Promising to solve complex social and economic problems by modifying individual behavior, advocates got money into some programs, but reinforced the overall conservative drift.

Of course, poor single mothers who rely on AFDC know that it doesn't meet their needs with its punitive rules, arbitrary enforcement, and contradictory policies. There is no doubt that the welfare system should be changed. But welfare rights activists want to shift the focus and reframe the debate about welfare. In Oregon, where I work, there are three strands to this strategy: (1) to argue that the problem is poverty not welfare, and the solution economic reform not welfare reform; (2) to identify the difficulties facing single mothers as work/family conflicts that face many other working parents; (3) to challenge the use of federal waivers for "experimental" state programs on the ground that they violate poor people's basic human rights.

First, we are arguing that the main difficulty facing single mothers is not a character flaw ("welfare dependency") but lack of access to living-wage jobs. The vast majority of single mothers on welfare are working women who cannot earn sufficient to support themselves and their families. Over half of the women who leave welfare to work are driven back onto welfare. Their needs could be met through welfare reforms that allow families to combine paid work with cash assistance (for example, the EITC or "fill the gap" plans, which allow people to work and keep their AFDC benefits so their overall income is above poverty), and in-kind subsidies (universal health care, subsidized and thus affordable childcare).

Work is no answer to poverty in an economy that increasingly relies on minimum-wage jobs, where employers are cutting wages, slashing benefits or getting around them entirely by employing part-time, temporary, subcontracted workers, impoverishing families and communities. Providing education and training on a voluntary basis to single mothers will help some move higher up the occupational ladder. But many single mothers will inevitably be employed in minimum wage jobs. Raising the minimum wage substantially would help single mothers escape poverty through paid work—and force employers to share responsibility for ensuring that no one has to live in poverty. Other policies that would stanch the tide of low-wage employment are requiring state and local governments to contract only with employers who pay benefits to part-time as well as full-time employees, who stay neutral in union organizing campaigns, who pay above the median wage, and so on.

A second strategy for reframing the debate is to challenge the myth that families can or should be self-sufficient. Raising children well requires resources which most families, including many two-parent families, cannot provide on their own. Government policies already recognize this in the dependent tax exemption and deductions for childcare expenses and mortgage payments, not to mention public education. Of course *these* government subsidies, unlike AFDC, are not stigmatized for creating pathological "dependence." Rather than pretending that single-mother households can or should be self-sufficient, we are calling for an expansion of support to all parents. The fact is that the ability to be a caregiver to your own children when they are young is increasingly a privilege of the affluent. Only women married to high-income earners can afford to work part-time or take time off work when their children are little. There is a "crisis of caregiving" in the U.S. that is undermining the lives of children whose parents work far too many hours, whose childcare providers are underpaid and overworked, whose public schools are falling apart, and whose neighborhoods provide fewer and fewer supervised recreational services.

Single mothers want the right to work part-time while their children are young. They also want the difficulties they face as mothers, and therefore their right to refuse work when necessary, acknowledged. Their children may have emotional or physical disabilities, often the legacy of poverty, homelessness, abuse; they may live in dangerous neighborhoods where unsupervised children are especially unsafe; they may have to care for other family members. The question is, how to assert these needs without giving ground on single mothers' rights also to living-wage jobs and on the claim that children can thrive when cared for in quality childcare settings. And yet, again, there is something unsettling about the evolution of this debate over women's work. While "family values" types want to meet children's needs by putting women back into the home, neo-liberals, like Clinton, are blithely serving up men, women, and children to the maw of capitalist employment. Affluent professionals either find qualified help (often undocumented women) to care for their children, or take time off to do it themselves, but most working parents are being squeezed unmercifully. It is no wonder that the proportion of working women saying they would prefer to be full-time homemakers is inching up. As one writer put it, working mothers talk about sleep the way a starving person talks about food.

Often, when we propose that single mothers should not be forced into low-waged jobs, we are told that lots of other mothers have to put their children in childcare and work full-time. We respond that society should be supporting mothers (and fathers) through a range of subsidies—for example, quality, well-supervised, free before- and after-school programs, quality childcare including a living wage for childcare providers, and state-mandated employment policies (such as paid parental leave for men and women, flexible hours and paid leave for family responsibilities). Furthermore, single mothers, because they are raising families on one income, will require some "fill the gap" income support in addition to paid parental leave to ensure they live above the poverty line.

A third strand of our strategy for reframing the debate is to challenge the increasing use of waivers which allow states to ignore federal laws regulating the provision of benefits. At first, applications for waivers were carefully scrutinized and were intended to support relatively small pilot programs. Now they are practically routinely granted. Under the pretense of freeing the "creativity" of local government, the feds have basically allowed states to institute behavior-modification programs that deny benefits to enforce compliance. The waivers are undemocratic because with the stroke of a pen they unravel the guarantees (entitlements) and protections that advocates managed to get passed in Congress. They are also immoral. They are justified as "experiments," to test out the consequences of various policies—for instance, whether cutting benefits to single mothers whose teenagers are truant will raise graduation rates. But the experimental "subjects" do not have a choice about participating in this experiment. Every science that studies human beings recognizes that it is unethical to experiment on people without their permission. Imagine whether this kind of arbitrary punitiveness could be implemented as an experiment on any other group, or on the children of any other group. After all, we are talking here about depriving children of food or heat in order to control the behavior of their parents; or depriving parents of basic necessities in order to control the behavior of their children. How about, say, an experiment in an affluent school district to see if students became more responsible when they received mild electric shocks for failing to turn in their homework? It would be unthinkable.

Of course, none of these arguments will immediately stop the engine of welfare reform, now hurtling at top speed down the legislative track. But they are necessary to shift the way that people understand the issue. And they can be effective in the longer term. These arguments appeal to basic ideals of fairness and justice; they speak to the realities of all working-class parents; and they challenge the logic of contemporary capitalism.

[*1995*]

Postscript

The 1996 welfare reform took the waiver issue off the table by removing most of the federal regulation and oversight which had constrained state programs. The name switch from Aid to Families with Dependent Children (AFDC: the old name for cash payments) to Temporary Assistance for Needy Families (TANF) and the title of the 1996 Act, "Personal Responsibility and Work Opportunity Reconciliation Act," aptly capture the historic nature of this final step in the dismantling of single mothers' entitlement to federal income support. The political forces coming together to contest the current "forced work" state and federal policies are broader than they were before the passage of PRWORA. The strategic focus on organizing around living wage jobs and especially raising the wages of caregiving has brought new allies, such as Jobs With Justice and ACORN, to welfare rights organizing.[1] However, this last period of activism has also demonstrated, in my view quite decisively, that the political space for claiming the unique right of single mothers for income support to be full-time caregivers to their children is closed. As a short-run strategy it is unworkable. And, as I argued above, as a long-run strategy, it is not even preferable. On the other hand, I would argue that as the frenetic scramble to stay economically afloat increases, pressuring parents into long hours of paid work, there is more political space for challenging the dominance of corporate capital over people's needs. Thus, we should continue to talk about demands such as fully paid parental leave. Additionally, the unpaid, voluntary, and crucial community and caregiving work that women used to, and can no longer, provide must be replaced. The way to value this work is not to pay women to stay home with children so they can continue to perform it, but to create both new public/community services and support for men and women to take time off from their paid jobs so they can participate in doing community work. We can and should speak of the right to give care (as well as the right to receive care) as fundamental human rights which are currently being overridden and denied.

[2000]

Note

1. For an excellent overview of the players and the strategies in current welfare rights activism, see Mimi Abramovitz, *Under Attack, Fighting Back: Women and Welfare in the United States* (New York: Monthly Review Press, 2000).

Part III

New Politics of the Family

Chapter 7

Socialist-Feminism versus Communitarian Conservatism

with Nancy Holmstrom

In recent years, some of the theoretical precepts and political demands formerly taken as fundamental to feminism have come under attack on the left and within the feminist movement itself: (1) the struggle for women's right to control their own bodies; (2) a critique and rejection of the nuclear family in favor of full integration of women into the public domain; (3) the assertion of sexual liberation as fundamental to women's liberation. Ranging from Jean Bethke Elshtain and Christopher Lasch, on the right, to Betty Friedan and "Friends of the Family," on the left, these critics, despite their differences, have a common thrust which we will call "left" conservative-feminism.[1] While meeting fairly consistent opposition, they have also pushed socialist-feminists onto the defensive. This is especially the case for Elshtain, who uses the idiom of feminism and calls upon understandings that socialist- and radical-feminists share.

Elshtain, if rather cavalier about the subordination of women, is thoroughgoing in her indictment of liberal feminism for its hyper-valuation of male-defined success, its acceptance of the competitive and hierarchical structures of capitalist society, and its elitist commitment to the technocratic welfare state. Elshtain's affirmation of the traditional family and critique of state services and childcare pays homage to "woman's sphere" and traditional feminine values of nurturance, intimacy, and commitment, thereby appealing to a strong strain within feminism itself.[2]

While few socialist-feminists accept Elshtain's celebration of the traditional family, we find a deepening skepticism about the possibility of nonfamilial (non-kin, nonhousehold) forms of solidarity, adult relationships, and childraising. We see a retreat from that side of feminism that has emphasized women's need for fulfilling work, intellectual challenge, and sexual exploration, as well as a growing unease about the demand for women's rights.

This re-evaluation of feminist politics occurs in the midst of a larger public debate and struggle. The combination of social changes of the 1960s, employment recomposition, and economic crises have undermined the traditional family. The political response has been contradictory, but at present momentum is with conservatives. Fundamentalist organizations like the Moral Majority and the anti-abortion movement may be most visible, but pro-family politics and familial ideology have more sophisticated and more important sources and constituencies. While the Democrats ran the first woman vice-presidential candidate, and while more women are working for pay outside their homes, weddings are big again, family is celebrated in the media, and most Americans surveyed agree that strengthening the family is an important goal of social policy. A new ideal of a two-earner family and more consensual marriage is replacing the old male-breadwinner/female-housewife form. The effort to resuscitate the family is understandable. It remains the primary institution for caring for children. And as public life becomes more competitive and brutal, the family becomes an even more important source of emotional and economic survival at the same time as its capacity to provide them diminishes.

Feminists have not been exempt from these pressures. Given the decline of the left and women's movements, given also the tremendous difficulty of building collective and communal forms for sharing economic resources and providing for our social/emotional needs, most have returned to couple-based households (both heterosexual and lesbian) and motherhood (many with a live-in co-parent). While this is partly the 1960s' generation coming up against the biological clock, these choices, however positive, make women more open to a critique of feminism which denigrates the rewards of public life—work, political organizing, and so on.

Though seductive, this critique is intellectually barren, resting on a series of false counter-positions. In each area—family, sexuality, rights, abortion—the critique insists that we choose between bourgeois individualism and traditional forms. If we value commitment, then we need to give up feminist demands for autonomy. If we seek the rewards of raising children, then so much for full social participation. If we want security, then we can't hope for full self-development. While conflicts between autonomy and community and between private and public life are quite real under capitalism, and some trade-offs may be required in any society, these are not universally counterposed. Moreover, even within the limits capitalism imposes, we can win reforms that increase the social space for resistance and allow us, at least partly, to transcend these conflicts in our own lives.

The struggle for women's rights—that is, the language of rights and the goal of autonomy—is neither individualistic nor male-identified. While neither rights nor reforms constitute a full program for women's liberation, the struggle for rights is necessary to the women's movement and can be integrated into a politics of socialist transformation. Furthermore, the concept of rights will remain pertinent to any socialist society.

Equality and Commitment

In the Manichean world of left conservative-feminism, we have two choices. We can live in the traditional family, based on long-term commitment, an ethic of obligation and sharing, a recognition of others' needs and their claims on us. Or we can choose partnerships of "freely contracting" individuals, negotiating the terms of their "non-binding commitment," obligated only to satisfy their own needs in a life of aimless striving. Over against the social contract ideology of a capitalist society based on possessive individualism, Elshtain poses the social compact of traditional family and community.[3]

Elshtain does not mention the patriarchal character of this traditional family and its consequences—wife battering, exploitation, women's forced self-sacrifice, compulsory heterosexuality and the denial of women's sexual pleasure; nor does she recognize the advantages to women of the social and economic changes (expanded access to paid work, the welfare state, the sexual revolution, etc.) that have brought the traditional family into question and allowed women to change the terms of their personal relationships with men.

Admittedly the demise of traditional marriage (in which male economic support is exchanged for female domestic and sexual services) has been two-edged: while increasing women's freedom, it has left women in some ways more vulnerable to sexual and economic exploitation. But it is impossible to return to the traditional family, and most women don't want to. Many women who work—even in blue-collar and clerical jobs, generally out of economic necessity—want to keep their jobs. They appreciate the friendships and expanded sense of their own efficacy that working outside the home brings. They also want shorter hours, more time off, and an end to their double day—but they don't want to become housewives.[4] They recognize the value of their work lives to their personal relationships—daughters of working mothers are far more likely than daughters of housewives to mention their mothers as among the women they most admire.[5] The way to appeal to these women is not to celebrate the traditional family, but to show how women's supposedly selfish need for individuality actually builds relationships and long-term commitment.

Instead of simply invoking community, we have to determine the conditions under which women can give and expect commitment without sacrificing their own needs. We contend that despite the distortion effected by capitalist society on this concept, the liberal-feminist demand for full participation of women in the public domain of work and politics is essential. The object is not to free ourselves from commitment and obligation, but to enter these compacts from a position of equality. The fact that liberal-feminists speak the language of contracts and limited liability does not justify ignoring the material basis of mutuality. No one is or ever can be truly independent, so there is nothing categorically wrong with dependence, which is simply a condition of human existence. But for relationships to be equally fulfilling, dependence has to be equal, and that requires women's having equal access with men to economic survival and political power.

Ultimately, mutually rewarding relationships between men and women require broad social changes—control over reproduction, quality childcare, equal work, the socialization of the so-called private responsibilities of women in the family. Anthropological data support this point. Relationships are more egalitarian in societies where women are more equally empowered in the public domain.[6] In capitalist social formations, women gain power by earning income; the closer the spouses' incomes, the more equal their roles in decision-making.[7] People of equal power surely have a better chance of creating relationships that combine commitment and unity with autonomy.

Individuality and Solidarity

In opposition to the contemporary "obsession with self" and the bourgeois conception of "self-actualization" as occurring only when the self is free from obligations to others, left conservative feminism proposes the traditional community in which self-identity is always constructed in relational terms. The "I" is always defined as part of a "we" that pre-existed it and will continue to exist beyond it in the future. Against the rootless superficial individualism of an increasingly atomized society, left conservative-feminism counterposes the grounded identities of participants in a dense web of social ties.[8]

Left conservative-feminism forgets that with all its defects, bourgeois individualism represented an advance over feudalism, in which social ties were based on force, on necessity, and on the suppression of everyone, women most brutally. But there are alternatives to the either/or of the identity, obligation, and support provided by oppressive community, and the insecurity of free market individuality. The ahistorical, atomistic individualism based on market values that defines the self in bourgeois thought is not the only way to define autonomy. In our view, the value of non-traditional communities consists in their being freely chosen but also premissed on mutual obligations and individuals' right to expect group support.

The women's movement ideally, and to a certain extent in practice, represents a community in which the conflicts between individuality and community can be transcended. The group is expected to support and encourage each woman's individual development. Yet, each member is also understood to share important interests with other women—not because of biology primarily, but because of the history and society we unfortunately share. Through the recognition of mutual interests and a collective struggle around them, a sense of we, not just I, emerges. But this sense of collectivity is not based on obedience and conformity, does not require unconditional subordination. No one is forced to belong to the group, so people cannot be constrained in the same way as in the traditional family and community where one's daily survival depends on participation. Moreover, the group's long-term goals (equality, self-determination) and daily activity (political action) support structures and interactions (education, discussion, decision) that help each member become a critical and self-confident thinker, capable of preserving an independent point of view.

The group persists only so long as it continues to meet individual needs. But, as individuals participate, their needs also change—they develop commitments and ties to the group. This kind of solidarity is found in other movements as well: workers' movements, socialist movements, Black liberation although it may be called by different names—sisterhood, brotherhood, comradeship.

Constructing a group life that preserves this balance between individuality and collectivity is not simple. People fail in their commitments, dissent is treated as disloyalty. The women's movement has had plenty of failures along with notable successes. But the lessons of both provide the basis for new commitments. With all the failures, our experience still validates the possibility of reconciling autonomy and community.

Sexual Freedom and Intimacy

The counterposition between self-expression and commitment, autonomy and community, permeates feminist debate over sexuality. Elshtain's critique is echoed by Irene Diamond and Lee Quinby when they argue, in a *Signs* symposium, that the demand for control over our bodies slips too readily into a language of domination, and that instead of demanding "sexuated pleasure," feminists should seek to foster "the pleasure of intimacy, citizenry, cooperation, community, and communion."[9]

The feminist challenge to a heterosexual ideal based on dominance/submission and the double standard has cut in two directions. On the one hand, the hyperindividualism of the dominant ideology within which sexual freedom and consent are defined constructs sexual equality in terms of a bourgeois contract. Men and women are to be equally consumers and providers of sex. Women can take the same predatory stance toward men that men have taken toward women. In reality, the gross economic and social inequalities between men and women ensure that women end up the losers in such bargains. On the other hand, the recognition of women's right to demand sexual pleasure, to initiate sexual interactions, to be lustful, to be lesbian, has crucially improved many women's lives.

Those who see in the sexual revolution only new forms of domination and sexual exploitation of women are forced to retreat into a narrow ideal that excludes the pleasures of sexual experimentation and play. To emphasize "intimacy and communion" rather than "sexuated pleasure" is to deny our potential for a wide variety of sexual/affectional relationships, which range from casual sexual encounters to sexual friendships to deeply felt, long-term sexual intimacy. On the other hand, those who ignore the dangers of sexual freedom in the context of a male-dominated society simply open the door to the right-wing critique. In this society, long-term commitments do offer protection, however tenuous, for many women in heterosexual unions. Rather than allowing conservatives to force us into a choice between the protection and repressiveness of traditional heterosexual relationships (or of coupling modeled after them) and the freedom and danger of life lived outside them, we need to define a more historicized approach. This approach would hold on to a vision of sexual liberation while criticizing its degraded and manipulative versions in (capitalist) pornography, advertising, "swinging" lifestyles, and so on. It would require us to identify with the ideals of consensual sexual pleasure and experimentation as we organize for changes in the social, economic, and political context within which we engage in sexual practices and which inevitably define their meaning.[10]

Who Cares for the Children?

While socialist-feminists, until recently, regarded the privatized world of the family as fundamentally anti-social and a prison for women, left conservative-feminism centers on the family as the locus of nurturance, as the source for personalities capable of loyalty and commitment, and as one point of resistance to the imperatives of bureaucratic, technocratic state power.[11] On this view, private and public are treated as universal, counterposed entities, rather than historically created and thus potentially merged ways of organizing human interaction and social life.

It is easy enough for feminists to reject Lasch's claim that responsible and independent adults can only be produced by a successful resolution of the Oedipal drama, since that necessitates the subordination of women to the authority of men within the family and outside it.[12] It may be more difficult to reject Elshtain's claim that it is only within the bonds and loyalties of the family, the intense ties to particular others (especially our mothers) that we develop the capacity to make other commitments.[13]

In the evolution of feminist thinking, motherhood and mothering have moved from the periphery to the center, perhaps even replacing sexuality as the primary issue for analyzing women's oppression. Many feminists share in Elshtain's derision of the liberal-feminist ideal of the career woman and her co-parenting husband, spending "quality time" with their child, produced in her thirties when her career is well established. This is a lifestyle that few can achieve in capitalism; moreover, it leaves in place both the heterosexual, marriage-based household and the capitalist workplace as the primary institutions for organizing reproduction and production. Elshtain's attack on collective childcare as children cared for by no one in particular strikes a responsive chord.[14]

Daycare is often understaffed and chaotic, with high turnover and inadequate space. Many women have too little time for themselves or their children.[15] But perhaps more important, the pleasure of parenting and the value of the work mothers do, as well as the nurturant values associated with mothering, to all of which Elshtain appeals, are significant elements in feminist visions of a good society.

Insofar as socialist-feminism defines nurturance as it arises in the intense relationship between mothers (or parents) and children within the nuclear family, we remain vulnerable to Elshtain's critique. Left conservative-feminism imbues "good" childrearing with the characteristics of motherhood institutionalized in this society. There is no appreciation here for the need to liberate women and children from each other—to liberate parents not only from the continuous responsibility which depresses and impoverishes their lives but also from the excessive investment in their own children that privatized families encourage. Ignored entirely is the need to liberate children from excessive dependence, emotional and physical, on one or two adults in order to enable their more extensive participation in social life. Public experience teaches children to share, work together, appreciate the claims of others and the limits of individual autonomy, to develop a capacity for decision and leadership.

Children need security, attention, and guidance in relationships with loving adults—but no one has proven their absolute need for exclusive relationships mandated by nuclear family households. Children may require continuity in their lives but we already know that something is very wrong in the often overprotected and smothered childhoods of children with stay-home mothers (nor is there any reason to assume that things would improve with stay-home fathers).

The data thus far overwhelmingly support the conclusion that in most areas children in daycare do as well as, and in many areas do better than, children raised at home. Alice Clarke-Stewart argues that children in preschool daycare are more precocious intellectually and socially, less compliant and more assertive, than children raised at home.[16] Rather than seeking to preserve the privatized isolation of the nuclear family, why not favor the open and fluid network of adults and children cooperating across households that Stack found in her study of poor Black families?[17] Indeed, why not envision such networks based on friendship rather than kinship ties?[18]

The most radically collective modern childrearing system that we know much about are the left kibbutzim. Children lived in communal settings from several days after birth, though mothers breastfed on demand for the first five to six months. Parents visited daily throughout childhood and retained close relationships with their children. The major caregiver was the "metaplot." The child grew up in a dense web of caring personal relationships; mothering was described as "multiple."[19] Two early and quite limited studies (small groups and "observational" methods) by researchers committed to traditional forms reported some strengths but stressed deficiences in kibbutz children.[20] Later work, much of it large-scale, empirical, and longitudinal, found kibbutz children and kibbutz-raised adults to be very effective in terms of motivation, independence, psychological health, and worldly success.[21] There is no persuasive evidence that kibbutz childrearing has disabled children, and much reason to believe it has enhanced human development. At the very least, such collective experiments deserve our whole-hearted support. They could hardly do worse than the present system.

No Haven, No Heartless World

Even expressed in its weaker form as "the place you come home to," the image and idiom of the family privilege ties of solidarity based on personal life and denigrate those based on other kinds of relationships. If we envision, for example, a radically democratized organization of production which allows individuals to "be themselves" at work, which breaks down the division between work and play, which makes work self-affirming instead of soul-destroying, and which allows individuals to build a sense of community and collegiality on the basis of the common purposes and shared decisions of their efforts, can we not then envision work as a place where we are "at home"? If we define the family, or some sort of "private life," through stark contrast with the rest of social life (work, community, politics, etc.), we give up the ground that connects desire for a rich and rewarding life with socialism. For we then accept the contemporary bourgeois worldview that human meaning and fulfillment can, indeed must, be centered on personal life, that public life is necessarily impoverished. Instead, we need to argue for the possibility of radically changing the competitive, individualistic, and hierarchical organization of work and community life. Extension of the values now located exclusively in family life—solidarity, respect, and a commitment to others' development—across a society requires the elimination of "the family" in its meaning as a special place for those values.

Kinship, love, and "good things to eat" tend go together in our society; but they are tendentially connected.[22] How, then, do we want to deconstruct the family? Should households take responsibility for children and the daily needs of adults, or should we meet more of our needs outside the place where we sleep and enjoy privacy? What kinds of spaces will we live in? What kinds of bonds will connect the people who share living spaces? Where will children live and how will they be cared for? In a brief for radical deconstruction, Michèle Barrett and Mary McIntosh have argued the benefits of a society where most emotional and physical needs are met outside of households.[23] In her generally positive review of their book, Judith Stacey asserts that households formed by people whose economic and emotional needs are guaranteed elsewhere have little concern for commitment and stability. "Whatever view one takes about the desirability of long-term emotional commitments among adults, it seems cavalier to ignore the possibility that relational and residential decisions we make might conflict with the needs and interests of children."[24]

We would argue the virtues of separating the pooling of resources for day-to-day support from questions of intimacy and parenting. The fear that without emotional or economic necessity people will have no patience for working at their relationships assumes the bourgeois ideology of fundamentally anti-social human nature and the Smithian world of the invisible hand. The weight of the psychological evidence in this regard points in the direction of relationships impossibly distorted by lack of alternatives, rather than made more rewarding by them. This is not to say that after the advent of socialism no one will ever be jealous or hurt by lost love, or that the demands of a parent's life (e.g. to relocate) will never conflict with the interests of a child (e.g. in staying put). But why not assume that in a society where men and women lead rich and rewarding lives, the decision to have a child will be made far more freely than it is in our society (for women especially)? Those who choose to be parents will do so only if they are willing to accept the necessary trade-offs, which in any case will be far less stark than they now are. Moreover, when relationships break up, or someone moves, the pain of loss must surely be much less for children (and adults for that matter) who have many loving relationships and their own place in the world.[25]

The Family versus the State

For left conservative-feminism, the family and private life preserve a private sphere of individual choice and a defense against overweaning collective power. Elshtain, for example, claims that women's maternal thinking is a source of pacifist resistance to militarism; the family and traditional solidarities (ethnic, religious) are protectors of democracy, of the individual against domination.[26]

Elshtain's invocation of maternal thinking draws upon a significant body of work in feminist theory asserting distinct male and female worldviews (either biologically or socially determined, or both). The work of Carol Gilligan and Sarah Ruddick is best known.[27] In contrast to male morality organized around abstract rights, female morality is based on concrete human need. In contrast to a male drive for mastery stands the female commitment to nurturance and protection of human life. Elshtain simply ignores the conservative and destructive side of women's traditional family roles.[28] There is nothing automatically oppositional in women's involvement with and care for their own children. The considerations that may lead women to peace movements—the interest in preserving the lives of their children—may also lead them to support military build-up and strong defense. Concern for one's family can lead to a willing ignorance about public issues and a disregard for the people belonging to other families (e.g. women in neighborhood-based anti-bussing movements).

But even if our goal is to generalize maternal thinking to society, it won't be done by maintaining the family as a launching pad for maternal campaigns for peace and justice. Only radical democratization of public life can integrate care and nurturance into social decisions. The problem with public life is not so much that it is dominated by "male thinking," but that there are no institutions for active participation of individuals in making the decisions which affect their lives. The preservation of the family as a sphere supposedly protective of individual needs over against a public sphere organized for social needs simply guarantees that public decisions will continue to reflect the private interests and public purposes of dominant groups. The issue is one not of values but of power and decision-making. Even a public power more attuned to needs could not function to meet them without this. Needs are not obvious; not all needs can be met; nor are all needs compatible. The full participation of all in decision-making is crucial. In making women in the family no longer solely or even primarily responsible for caring, we will not lose nurture but rather ensure that public actions more fully reflect individual needs.

On the same grounds, we reject left conservative-feminism's critique of demands for expanded public services, in which they argue that feminism has accelerated individuals' reliance on social engineering experts, increasing vulnerability to technocratic control.[29] Again, their argument ignores the other side of the process. While women may become dependent on the welfare state (as workers in it, as well as clients), they are less dependent on individual men and thus in a better position to engage in political activity and public life, including organizing together to improve the quality and extent of public services. We do not have to defend, indeed we should not defend, the elitist and bureaucratic character of the existing welfare state. The appeal of socialist compared to liberal reforms lies in our demand for public services that are worker- and client-controlled, democratic, and integrated into the communities they serve.

Socialist-feminists are understandably hesitant to embrace a vision of democratic and collective life which reconciles needs of individuals and the group. The failure of twentieth-century revolutions to maintain individual freedom has produced considerable skepticism about the possibility of reconciling individual autonomy with collectivity. In this context, Judith Stacey points to the "potential hazards in an excessively collectivized existence," preferring instead an approach which acknowledges "the dangers of intolerance and social pressures to conform" and creates "more space for privacy, even anonymity," providing "relief from the onerous aspects of community."[30] This is a timely warning. But in our view, it cannot be implemented by stripping the family of its patriarchal and anti-social elements while preserving it as a place to come home to.

To defend family as a realm of privacy protected from societal interference or obligation replicates the bourgeois division between state and civil society in which individual autonomy is only guaranteed negatively—that is, as the right to be left alone to act without interference—rather than positively—that is, as the right to have certain kinds of choices made available. Rather than counterposing private to public life, we would argue that individual autonomy can only be guaranteed by a radical democratization of the social order. We need not assume that with socialism the obligations of the individual to the collective will disappear, nor that the interests of individuals and the group will automatically be similar. We need only claim that decision-making in all areas of life—schools, neighborhoods, workplaces, broader economic decisions, management of resources, uses of wealth, military questions, and so on—will be organized so that individuals and groups who have different ideas can argue for and defend them, that political minorities are guaranteed the opportunities and resources necessary to organize. In addition, democratization requires structures through which the obligations of the individual to the community can be negotiated; it further requires that compulsory action be limited as far as possible, that available choices be maximized.

Family as a Source of Resistance

Family ties can and have contributed to the self-organization of oppressed groups. In general, however, familial ties cut in the opposite direction—toward fragmentation and away from building political organization and collective struggle. This is especially the case today with extended family networks attenuated and not constituent of broader communities (as was previously the case, say, in the ethnic communities around mills and factories). While the family based on a monogamous bond between two adults who undertake to care for themselves and their own children is not a contractual relationship, it fits well into an atomized society of contracting individuals. Families change the war of each against all into a war of twos against twos. Commitment to one person does not automatically exclude solidarity with others. Yet, because other kinds of solidarity normally appear so much more tenuous (and they are), building and protecting family resources—emotional and economic—appears a reasonable strategy for survival. Under normal conditions of life in capitalist society—competition in a labor market, insecurity, political atomization—familial ties become a substitute for wider networks and communities. Without those broader networks, people have no way or hope of changing the rules of the game. Playing within the rules means surviving on one's own, often at the expense of others. Thus, for example, it is not surprising that married people are far less sympathetic to expanding social services than are single people. In the 1984 election the marriage gap exceeded the gender gap.[31]

Family and other more traditional ties (ethnicity) have fueled and supported collective political organization only when inserted into oppositional movements.[32] These movements define solidarity in terms which, unlike that of the family, do not fit into an individualistic worldview. Oppositional movements are premissed on the need for broader long-term commitments (beyond purely personal connections) and on collective struggle. In the context of these other solidarities, family ties of kinship and marriage may contribute to building collectively. But it is the nonfamilial connections which make possible transformed consciousness. Struggle opens people to social and cultural innovations which break through the fundamental individualism of the family. Collective and communal forms of societal organization appear as logical extensions of the relationships individuals construct in social movement—they do not flow directly from the practices of family life.[33]

Abortion and Women's Rights

Feminists have often posed their demands as demands for women's rights, focusing most attention in recent years on the right to abortion. Not only has this particular demand been attacked, but the whole notion of women's rights has been criticized by left conservative-feminists as individualistic and presupposing a bourgeois political framework. For example, Betty Friedan's "discovery" that feminists were mistaken to focus on abortion when the "real issue" is the right to have children (as if the two can be separated) is echoed by Wendy Brown in an article critical of the politics of the reproductive rights movement.[34] For socialists, she argues, the abortion issue should be approached from communitarian, collective values, not from the values of bourgeois society. Rather than minimizing the pain and grief of abortion, as Brown claims many feminists do, we should cease to focus on the inherently limited concept of women's rights and concentrate instead on the social changes that will allow women to enjoy fully their capacity for nurturance. Although we agree that liberal feminists define the issue too narrowly,[35] we will argue, against left conservative-feminists, that posing feminist demands as women's rights is perfectly valid, and, specifically, that women's right to abortion is and always will be fundamental to a good society.

Although talk of rights often reflects a liberal perspective, it need not. Most philosophers agree that to say people have a right—for example, a basic human right to food—is just to say that they ought to have food and that no one ought to prevent them from having it; or, more coercively, that others ought to do what they can to enable them to have the food they need. Thus, rights can be understood as moral claims and moral judgments can be understood as claims about rights.

As socialists, we think that workers do have (in the moral sense) and should have (in the legal sense) the right to control collectively the means of production, their labor, and the product of their labor. One way of describing socialism is to say that under socialism the working class has this right, whereas under capitalism capitalists do and workers do not. Workers' right to control the means of production is a right that they can have as a group, but not as individuals. Since they can't individually control the means of production, this is a right the class possesses *as a class*, not as individuals.

However, rights can also be individual, which is how liberals exclusively define rights. For example, the right to self-development would be a claim that all members would have on the group. In both capitalist and socialist societies, rights are meaningful and important, not inherently individualistic in a bad sense of a liberal concept of right. This latter is true of abortion rights.

Women have a right to abortion because it is essential to their self-determination—individually and collectively. Partly this is due to the biological fact that they bear children. But it is also due to mutable social and historical conditions: viz., that women are expected—indeed forced—to assume primary responsibility for children they bear. In a sexist society like our own, women need to assert their rights to control their reproduction, since others would unilaterally deprive them of this control and thus compel women to be sexual and domestic servants. If present social/historical conditions changed so that women no longer had primary responsibility for rearing children—imagine a nonsexist, truly democratic society—would each individual woman still have the right to abortion? In other words, is the right to abortion an individual right in a nonsexist society as well as in sexist ones? Since having children or not having children has implications for society as a whole, even for future generations, if society would assume responsibility for caring for children, then should each individual woman have the exclusive right to decide whether or not to have children, as we believe she does now?

In such a society, which would entail genuine community and collective decision-making, the issue of obligation to the collective to which our critics like to appeal has more validity. Nevertheless, it is still the individual woman who would have to bear a child or to undergo an unwanted abortion. That seems to keep the right to abortion an individual right. On the other hand, one could argue, such a democratic socialist society would have the right to expect various commitments from individuals; individuals could not simply do what they want all the time no matter how it affected the rest of the society. Is bearing a child or refraining from having a child so much different from the labor of defense such a society might democratically require of its members (and which could involve risks equal to pregnancy or abortion)? If there is no fundamental difference, then should society have the right to make reproductive decisions, in the way that decisions about production or defense are made? But that means abortion would no longer be women's right.

We find it difficult to resolve this dilemma. We might be willing to say that in such a society abortion would not be an individual right. However, we think it would still remain a right of women collectively. That is, there ought to be democratic structures by which women collectively could decide important matters that particularly affect women and would still particularly affect them even in these changed social conditions. Even in the best of societies women would still need rights over their reproduction. Marx said that rights are limited because they are the application of an equal standard to individuals who are necessarily unequal—that is, not the same.[36] In the case of reproduction, the fact that, despite individual differences among them, women are equal to each other while being unequal to—that is, different from—men, determines that they (and not men) have these rights. Only women would be in a position to appreciate both the needs of the society as a whole and what reproductive rights would mean to the individual woman.

In fact, however, we think there would be very few circumstances in which women as a group would be justified in intruding on an individual's reproductive choices. If women's real interest as to whether or not to have children were not in conflict with the interests of the rest of the society, then their desires, or at least actions, would probably be in accord as well—or could be brought into accord by social pressure, moral persuasion, and material incentives. The cases where these would not work would be too insignificant to do much damage. More problematic would be the situation where there is a genuine conflict of individual and group interest—where, say, individuals want more children than there are resources to support.[37] However, this situation would be decidedly rare in a socialist society, and a variety of noncoercive measures would most likely be effective. If not, it would still be worse on the whole to coerce women to have children or abortions than it would for society to have too many or too few children.

Socialist-Feminist Strategy

In conclusion, we reject the counterposition of a "politics of rights" to a "politics of human needs." The crux of the issue is not whether to be for women's rights but how we define rights, how we argue for them, and how we organize around them. A socialist-feminist approach can be distinguished from a liberal-feminist strategy precisely by focusing on that counterposition between autonomy and community which liberal-feminism ignores and which lies at the heart of the anti-feminist backlash. Today women (and men) are forced to sacrifice one human need in order to fulfill another. Our politics ought to center on concrete reforms which allow people to get beyond these dilemmas. Further, the reforms we demand and the way we organize for them (the kinds of movements we build) ought to prefigure the social/personal relationships and reordered priorities we want to achieve through socialist revolution.

We can reappropriate "control" and "choice" if we locate them in a political framework emphasizing the social and economic changes necessary to provide women with real choice and real control. For example, liberal-feminism defends abortion as a woman's "right to choose," in terms of her right to make the decision by herself, her "right to privacy." A socialist-feminist strategy locates abortion on demand within a broader constellation of "reproductive rights" which create the conditions for women to choose *to be* or *not to be* mothers. Real choice depends on "having money, a room, a job, some help, and also the ability to reflect, to analyze."[38] The conditions for choice include, in addition to abortion, safe, effective contraception; an end to sterilization abuse (especially prevalent against women of color and poor women); quality medical care and childcare; adequate housing; a living wage; adequate maternity/paternity leave; shorter workdays for parents with no loss in pay; freedom to express sexual preference.[39]

Reproductive rights are claims women have on the society. The reproductive-rights program includes reforms which increase women's capacity to have and raise children outside of the traditional family—by themselves, with another woman—as well as creating the work environments and social services necessary to support men's more equal involvement in childrearing and women's more equal involvement in public life. Finally, by forcefully including the right to have children, reproductive-rights politics allow us to defend more effectively women's decision not to have children. This is crucial if feminists are to resist a pro-natalism that implicitly denigrates women without children and capitulates to compulsory motherhood.[40]

A similar argument can be made for a socialist-feminist approach to the family. The question is not, are we for or against the family, but how can we address the complex of issues raised by "family politics" in a way that strengthens the alternatives to the family/household as a privileged source of support and nurturance? In general we agree with Barrett and McIntosh's proposal for a political strategy which: (1) works for immediate changes to increase the range of available choices; (2) works towards collective institutions for accomplishing the tasks at present allocated to private family life—especially income maintenance, the work of making meals, cleaning and housekeeping, and the work of caring for children, the old, and the sick or disabled. Maternity leave, higher wages, and child-care subsidies, for example, will begin to increase women's independence, access to public life, and choices about our living arrangements. Caring in a lively and sociable setting not shut away in isolated apartments and houses, meals available at school and work, neighborhood cooperatives for adults to share childcare, dinner time, and socializing—all help to undercut the special attraction of privatized family life.[41]

In the end, though, no particular set of reforms will automatically reconcile our need for autonomy *and* community. The key lies in using the fight for reforms to shape a socialist-feminist politics and movement around women's participation in a public life that is both challenging and supportive, democratic and nurturant. We cannot allow the difficult personal choices we are all forced to make or the conservative environment we face to rob us of our capacity to envision a different world, to insist that our vision is, finally, the only way out of the contradiction between autonomy and community, and to use our vision to explain and motivate the reform struggles in which we engage. To lose our nerve at this point is to regress to subordination.

[*1985*]

Notes

1. Lasch is more anti-capitalist than feminist, and Friedan more feminist than anti-capitalist. We are here addressing as "Left" conservative feminism that subset of all these writers' propositions which are troubling to socialist-feminists. For an excellent summary and critique of the whole literature, see Judith Stacey, "The New Conservative Feminism," *Feminist Studies* 9, no. 3 (Fall 1983). See also, Michèle Barrett and Mary McIntosh, "Narcissism and the Family: A Critique of Lasch," *New Left Review* 135 (September–October 1982), 35–48.
2. See, e.g., Jean Bethke Elshtain, "Feminism, Family, and Community," *Dissent* (Fall 1982), 442–49.
3. Ibid., 445–46.
4. See Myra Marx Ferree, "Working Class Jobs: Paid Work and Housework as

Sources of Satisfaction," *Social Problems* 23, no. 4 (April 1976), 431–41; and Judith Baker Agassi, *Comparing the Work Attitudes of Women and Men* (Lexington, Mass., 1982), 219.

5. Lois Wladis Hoffman, "Effects on Child," in Lois Wladis Hoffman and F. Ivan Nye, eds., *Working Mothers* (San Francisco, 1974), 132–33.

6. See, for example, Peggy Reeves Sanday, *Female Power and Male Dominance* (Cambridge, 1981), chap. 6.

7. Philip Blumstein and Pepper Schwartz, *American Couples* (New York, 1983), 53–54. Working-class women gain more power from going to work than do middle-class wives, in part because they bring in a higher percentage of total family income when they work; see Stephan J. Bahr, "Effects on Power and Division of Labor in the Family," in Hoffman and Nye, eds., *Working Mothers*, 178–85.

8. Elshtain, "Feminism, Family, and Community," 445.

9. "American Feminism in the Age of the Body," *Signs* 10, no. 1 (Autumn 1984), 119–25

10. For a critique of the "sex debate" which begins to define a middle ground, see Ann Ferguson, "Sex War: The Debate Between Radical and Libertarian Feminists," *Signs* 10, no. 1 (Autumn 1984), 106–12; and Ilene Philipson, "The Repression of History and Gender: A Critical Perspective on the Feminist Sexuality Debate," 113–118. For further specification of a strategic approach to these issues, see Ann Ferguson, "The Sex Debate in the Women's Movement: A Socialist-Feminist Approach," *Against the Current* (September–October 1983), 10–16.

11. Jean Bethke Elshtain, "Antigone's Daughters: Reflections on Female Identity and the State," in Irene Diamond, ed., *Families, Politics, and Public Policy: A Feminist Dialogue on Women and the State* (New York, 1983), 300–311; and Christopher Lasch, *The Culture of Narcissism: American Life in an Age of Diminishing Expectations* (New York, 1978), 224–32.

12. Lasch, *Haven in a Heartless World: The Family Beseiged* (New York, 1977), 174–83.

13. Elshtain, "Antigone's Daughters," 307.

14. "Feminism, Family, and Community," 448.

15. In addition to quality daycare, reducing the amount of time parents must work is essential to alleviating these hardships.

16. *New York Times*, September 4, 1984, 12. See also Alice Clarke-Stewart, *Daycare* (Cambridge, Mass., 1982), 63–67. The quality of care, especially the ratio of adults to children, makes an important difference. Kagan et al., for example, argue that three children to one adult is an upper limit for the care of children under three years old. They find in general that "a child's attendance at daycare staffed by conscientious and nurturant adults during the first two and one-half years of life does not seem to produce a psychological profile very much different from rearing totally in the home." Jerome Kagan, Richard B. Kearsley and Philip R. Zelazo, *Infancy: Its Place in Human Development* (Cambridge, Mass., 1978), 260–66.

17. Carol B. Stack, *All Our Kin: Strategies for Survival in a Black Community* (New York, 1974); on childrearing, see chap. 5.

18. While the domestic networks Stack studied included non-relatives, they were organized primarily around kinship relationships. For a discussion of this point,

see Martha A. Ackelsberg, "'Sisters' or 'Comrades'? The Politics of Friends and Families," in Diamond, ed., *Families, Politics, and Public Policy*, 339–56, esp. 348–49.

19. There are actually a variety of kibbutzim whose practices have changed over time. The most thoroughly studied group have done childrearing as described. See A. I. Rabin and Benjamin Beit-Hallahmi, *Twenty Years Later: Kibbutz Children Grown Up* (New York 1982). One major deficiency from a feminist perspective is that women, the mother, and (female) metaplot appear to be major caregivers for the first year.

20. Bruno Bettelheim, *The Children of the Dream* (New York, 1969); and M. E. Spiro, *Children of the Kibbutz* (Cambridge, Mass., 1958).

21. See Rabin and Beit-Hallahmi, *Twenty Years Later*; and Uri Leviatan and Elliette Orchan, "Kibbutz Ex-members and their Adjustment to Life Outside the Kibbutz," *Interchange* 13, no. 1 (1982), 16–28.

22. Michèle Barrett and Mary McIntosh, *The Anti-Social Family* (London, 1982), 159. See also Jane Collier, Michelle Z. Rosaldo, and Sylvia Yanagisako, "Is There a Family? New Anthropological Views," and Rayna Rapp, "Family and Class in Contemporary America: Notes Toward An Understanding of Ideology," in Barrie Thorne with Marilyn Yalom, eds., *Rethinking the Family: Some Feminist Questions* (New York, 1982), 25–39 and 168–87 respectively.

23. *The Anti-Social Family*, passim.

24. "Should the Family Perish?", *Socialist Review*, 14, no. 2 (March–April 1984), 121.

25. Kagan et al., for example, argue that even children who suffer extreme maternal deprivation or disruption in early years (e.g., orphans) recover when placed in a benevolent and supportive environment; *Infancy*, 141–44.

26. Elshtain, "Antigone's Daughters," 307–10.

27. Carol Gilligan, *In a Different Voice* (Cambridge, Mass., 1982); and Sarah Ruddick, "Maternal Thinking," *Feminist Studies* 6, no. 2 (Summer 1980), 342–67. See also Nancy C. M. Hartsock, *Money, Sex and Power: Toward a Feminist Historical Materialism* (New York, 1983), esp. chap. 10; and Sandra Harding, "What Is the Real Material Base of Patriarchy and Capital?", in Lydia Sargent, ed., *Women and Revolution: A Discussion of the Unhappy Marriage of Marxism and Feminism* (Boston, 1981), 135–63.

28. Ruddick, on the other hand, does recognize this other side of mothering.

29. This is the assertion of Lasch, *Haven in a Heartless World*, xiv–xvi; and Elshtain, "Antigone's Daughters," 303, and "Feminism, Family, and Community," 447. See also Betty Friedan, *The Second Stage* (New York, 1981), 241, 306–7.

30. Stacey, "Should the Family Perish?", 123.

31. Reagan voters: 61 percent of men, 57 percent of women; 65 percent of married men, 60 percent of married women; 53 percent of unmarried men, 50 percent of unmarried women. *New York Times* (8 November 1984), 11.

32. For example, Herb Mills has described the relationship between waterfront, neighborhood, family, and union which built the Longshoreman's Union in San Francisco. In Harry C. Boyte and Sara M. Evans, "Strategies in Search of America: Cultural Radicalism, Populism and Democratic Culture," *Socialist Review* 14, nos. 3–4 (May–August 1984), 73–100, esp. 87, the authors emphasize the process of working together in constructing collectivity out of grassroots organizing. We would put equal weight on the purposes and political

objectives around which people struggle. Transformed consciousness arises from a process of politicization within the context of collective action, but it does not arise automatically from collective action itself.

33. This is not to deny that the impetus for participation may come out of family needs or the defense of family resources: for example, the entry of the coal miners' wives into the 1984–85 British coal strike which changed the women's relationship to politics, and to the union (and, perhaps, to their husbands). See Angela Weir and Elizabeth Wilson, "The British Women's Movement," *New Left Review* 148 (November–December 1984), 74–103, esp. 101.

34. Friedan, *The Second Stage*, 258–9; Wendy Brown, "Reproductive Freedom and the Right to Privacy: A Paradox for Feminists," in Diamond, ed., *Families, Politics, and Public Policy*, 322–38.

35. For a nice discussion of the limitations of the liberal approach, see Rosalind Pollack Petchesky, "Reproductive Freedom: Beyond a 'Woman's Right to Choose'," *Signs* 5, no. 4 (1980), and the further development of these arguments in her *Abortion and Women's Choice* (New York, 1984).

36. In a society where everyone got what s/he needed, hence where there would be no conflict of interest, the concept of rights would not apply. Marx makes this point in the *Critique of the Gotha Programme* as a means of clarifying the inherently limited nature of rights—but not in order to dismiss the need for rights short of "pure communism."

37. The conflict in China between the government's efforts to keep down population and the peasants' efforts to have more children would seem a case in point. In our view it is not. However, the Chinese case raises a host of complex issues beyond the scope of this essay, including the problem of building socialism in an underdeveloped country; whether reproductive, or indeed any, decisions are democratically made in China; whether China is a socialist society; as well as the more general difficulty of how to handle conflicts of interests between present and future generations.

38. Denise Riley, "The Serious Burdens of Love? Some Questions on Childcare, Feminism and Socialism," in Lynne Segal, ed., *What Is To Be Done About the Family?* (London, 1983), 133.

39. See Committee for Abortion Rights and Against Sterilization Abuse (CARASA), *Women Under Attack: Abortion, Sterilization Abuse, and Reproductive Freedom* (New York, 1979). For a discussion of reproductive rights politics and feminist theory on sex, reproduction, and the family, see Linda Gordon, "Why Nineteenth-Century Feminists Did Not Support Birth Control and Twentieth-Century Feminists Do: Feminism, Reproduction, and the Family," in Thorne, *Rethinking the Family*, 40–53, esp, 49–52.

40. "Reproductive rights" also breaks from Friedan's attempt to excise "sexual politics"—lesbianism and abortion—from feminism as the condition for alliances with all those "including anti-abortion Catholics, who want to fight for our right to have children." *The Second Stage*, 103–111.

41. Barrett and McIntosh, *The Anti-Social Family*, chap. 4. For a discussion of the contradictions in welfare state policy and how feminists might deal with them, see Fran Bennett, "The State, Welfare, and Women's Dependence," in Segal, *What Is To Be Done About the Family?*, 190–214.

Chapter 8

Democracy, Community, and Care

"Every oppressed group needs to imagine through the help of history and mythology a world where our oppression did not seem the pre-ordained order.... The mistake lies in believing in this ideal past or imagined future so thoroughly and single-mindedly that finding solutions to present-day inequities loses priority, or we attempt to create too-easy solutions for the pain we feel today." [1]

In two great utopian novels of the 1970s, *Woman on the Edge of Time* and *The Dispossessed*,[2] Marge Piercy and Ursula LeGuin, respectively, drew on anarchist—that is, radically democratic collectivist—ideas while exploring in depth those areas of life that have been feminism's particular focus. They imagined how children would be parented and educated, whether gender would even exist, how individuals would experience and express sexual desire, what human relationships would be like. Both novels assumed, as did feminists of the time, that the privatized, heterosexual nuclear family household was antithetical to radically democratic, egalitarian social relations. They imagined worlds where gender was no longer a central social category, where homosexual desire was treated no differently from heterosexual desire, and where monogamous relationships were not mandated but freely chosen. They envisioned children and parents embedded in a supportive, democratic community, men and women equally involved in caregiving, the essential chores/ pleasures of daily life (cooking, eating, laundry, etc.) taking place in communal rather than private spaces. Their concepts of parenting and of education challenged dominant ideas about children's need to be protected from the demands of the adult world. Education ought to be based in learning by doing as children participated in meaningful work. They envisioned more democratic, less authoritarian, relationships

between adults and children. Challenging the idea of a benevolent necessity for adult control, they argued that children had much greater
capacities for self-regulation and responsible decision-making than adults
gave them credit for. They also argued that involving children in productive work had to begin early, so children would appreciate the
pleasures and rewards of contributing to the common good. In a society
where labor is organized through profoundly democratic decision-
making and for meeting human needs, workplace "efficiency" would
encourage, even demand, making a place for apprenticeship—not to
mention flexible (and shorter) working hours to free people up for
activities of nurture, leisure, and citizenship. These utopian visions grew
out of some of the core struggles of second-wave feminism, particularly
its radical liberationist wing. Compared to feminists today, feminists
then, facing a patriarchal family/household system that appeared firmly
entrenched, felt more free to reject the family wholesale. And, in a
period of relative prosperity and economic security, they were also more
free to experiment with alternative forms of living.

My generation of socialists and socialist-feminists who took part in
and were inspired by the great postwar waves of rebellion against
exploitation, oppression and colonial rule, have been fundamentally
shaped by our historical experience, an experience of enormous political
gains but also dashed hopes, profound disappointments, and some bitter
defeats. The postmodernists' hostility to "grand narratives" (feminist as
well as Marxist) draws support from not only the bankruptcy of Communism but also the exhaustion of the radical political organizations
(Marxist, anti-racist and feminist) of the 1960s and 1970s which embodied the revolutionary aspirations of our generation.

The 'prefigurative' communes and political collectives of the New
Left, including feminist groups, who hoped to bridge the present and
the postrevolutionary future have almost all splintered and died.
Attempts to legislate personal relations and group life, to "live according
to political principle" defined in rigid, narrow terms, bred intolerance,
sectarianism, factionalism, and splits. Yet the questions we tried to
address are still with us. It's time to dust ourselves off and return to
those imaginative visions, informed but not defeated by our failures.
"Prefigurative" communities (political groups, community-based organizations, collectively run workplaces and living spaces) are an important
ground for winning new people to socialist ideals. They allow us to
practice being in different kinds of relationships, to experience our
capacities for cooperation, solidarity, and democracy.

From the perspective of the 1990s, the battle against the bourgeois family, against the stultifying, consumerist, conformist, privatistic, patriarchal household, might seem anachronistic. There are strong political forces attempting to reimpose the traditional male-breadwinner/female-caregiver family ideal; and we have been forced to spend far too much political energy beating them back. But there are strong countercurrents, appearing perhaps more in how people live than in the political system, where well-organized conservative minorities have influence far beyond their numbers. Many children spend some time in a single parent, generally single-mother, family; in almost 25 percent of two-earner households in the U.S. women earn more than men; increasing numbers of blended families create many new kinds of kin relationships; new reproductive technologies are exploding concepts of "natural" motherhood, and lesbians and gay men are more accepted as parents and are more out as families.[3] And insofar as their circumstances allow it, many men and women are trying to break old gender patterns, sharing both income-earning and responsibility for everyday caregiving within their families. It is no longer compelling to assert that only one kind of family is natural, normal, or even preferable. But important as they are, these changes have, if anything, strengthened the family's hold on popular social and political imaginations. While families may be more internally democratic, they are also even more private than ever before, one of the few remaining places people expect to give and receive support.

The harsh political and economic shifts in the society surrounding the family have closed off the space for imagining different kinds of community. Instead of organizing for a revolutionary alternative to welfare-state Cold War liberalism, we find ourselves battling simply to preserve a minimal welfare state. But the issues we confronted are still there. If anything, life in this center of global capitalism seems ever more contradictory. On the one hand, there are increasing opportunities for self-expression through consumption of a giddy array of commodified identities; on the other, there are frightening economic insecurity and worries about what the future might hold. On the one hand, there is increasing sexual autonomy for women; on the other, we witness the abandonment of single mothers and their children, now forced to survive alone in the low-wage labor market. At a time of increasing economic and political opportunities for women, there is a crisis in caregiving inside and outside family households.

The communitarians and religious authoritarians are trying to convince Americans that we have too much freedom and too much individualism. They argue that security, support, and nurture can only emerge when obligation and duty are enforced by social norms, law, and the reallocation of resources to encourage desirable and discourage undesirable individual choices. However much the communitarians may criticize capitalism for its rampant individualism and commodification of every sphere of life, their utopian vision is antithetical to feminism. They denigrate the value of "chosen" interdependencies (friendship, intentional communities) and privilege bonds of obligation that rest on a bedrock of blood relations—the primordial "born into" communities whose webs of interdependence are never questioned and therefore never really chosen, only accepted.[4]

Feminists of color have confronted more directly than white feminists the strengths and weaknesses of "born-into" communities. Contrasting families in communities of color to those of the white middle class, Black and Latina feminists argue that the extended kin (and fictive kin) sharing networks linking women and children across families, and the norms of communal responsibility for children, especially strong in Black communities, offer an alternative to the possessive and exclusive relationships of the bourgeois family.[5] This positive revaluation of disparaged family forms emphasizes the communal values and cooperative institutions which undergird resistance to white supremacy and provide a basis for women to claim authority in their community. However important this analysis is as a corrective to the early feminist critique of a supposedly universal male-breadwinner household, it still left only dimly illuminated another side of racial solidarity in a patriarchal, capitalist society: the suppression of women's sexual desires, the limitations on their exercise of public power, the onerous responsibilities for others that left little room for self, the webs of sometimes overwhelming financial and emotional dependencies, the corrosion of relationships weighted down with too much to carry. In ground-breaking work opening up possibilities for exploring sexism within communities of color, lesbian-feminists of color explored the painful terrain of their marginalization within their home communities. They described the enforced silences, the regulation and self-regulation of women's sexuality as a political strategy, the fears of betrayal projected onto women's bodies and sexuality, the powerful pressures toward conformity and the suppression of individual needs/desires in the name of group solidarity.

> We believe the more severely we protect the sex roles within the family, the stronger we will be as a unit in opposition to the anglo threat. And yet, our refusal to examine all the roots of the lovelessness in our families is our weakest

> link and softest spot.... Family is *not* by definition the man in a dominant
> position over women and children. Familia is cross-generational bonding, deep
> emotional ties between opposite sexes, and within our sex. It is sexuality,
> which involves, but is not limited to intercourse or orgasm.... It is finding
> familia among friends where blood ties are formed through suffering and
> celebration shared. The strength of our families never came from domina-
> tion. It has only endured in spite of it—like our women.[6]

In challenging the narrow ground of solidarity that has dominated
the culture and politics of their home communities, lesbian-feminists of
color have been among the most eloquent voices articulating, in accessible language and with emotional immediacy, the case for a radically
democratic anti-racist and feminist-socialist politics in the U.S.

The American public's refusal to be horrified by Clinton's extra-
marital affairs indicates that backward-looking moralists remain a
minority. Yet, conservatives have also captured political ground by taking
aim at one of contemporary capitalism's weakest points: the pervasive
anxiety about how we will take care of ourselves, each other, our elderly,
and our children, and a simmering resentment about the toll that this
caregiving is taking. Family households are more burdened and perhaps
more isolated from other sources of support than ever before. In one of
the most blatant examples of political hypocrisy in our time, the last
remaining public institutions through which some kind of societal responsibility for our elderly and our children is expressed—social security
and public education—are under ruthless attack. In the current political configuration, where government and the public are savaged and
the market extolled, the family household remains the only place where
people can envision non-contractual relationships, claims on others for
support, and an unquestioned right to have one's needs met. The
romance of the capitalist market, of a society organized around individualistic striving, can only work if families are there to pick up the
pieces.[7] Affluent families are increasingly substituting paid services made
affordable by service workers' low wages. Working-class families get by
in other ways (drawing on female relatives for childcare, working different shifts so parents can trade-off being home, having fewer children).
But even with these accommodations, responsibilities for others, in
addition to children, remain: the elderly parents, the brother who can't
find work, the sister who can't make it alone as a single mother.

The situation produces a downward spiral: the more people must
rely on family, the more focused they become on increasing their individual resources and maximizing their own family fortunes, the less

willing to support other people's families, other people's children. New, more inclusive ideals of family are contesting compulsory heterosexuality and male dominance within the household. But they do not, in themselves, challenge the ideal of the family household itself as a haven in a heartless world. New, reformed and more democratic family ideals can coexist with an intensification of familistic political ideologies and individualistic survival strategies.

One of the weakest points of the current economy is its failure to support families. So it would seem that one of the best arguments against the assaulting forces of the capitalist juggernaut is to point out the contradiction between corporate power and family needs. Many progressives are taking just that tack: the name of New York State's newest effort at creating a third party, the "Working Families Party," is a case in point. To form a politics around "working families" is terribly limited and ultimately conservative. To be clear, I am not arguing against campaigns, such as the UPS strike, which protested the widespread use of part-timers on the ground that many UPS workers had families to support. But a politics centered on "working-families" simply reproduces bourgeois morality in which working is a sign of deservingness and family a sign of need—as if single individuals are or ought to be "self-sufficient." And it reinforces the ideal of the family/household as the privileged site of economic, emotional, social support and care. Further, a program of demands organized around the needs of "working families" obscures the ways in which different kinds of communities are systematically disadvantaged. Some communities have more nonworking families than others. Finally, assimilating gay/lesbian families to straight families by focusing on their commonalities as "working" or "economically productive" or "stable/coupled," leaves little room for the liberatory demands of sexual politics. This is not simply a matter of including rights of sexual expression as a fundamental democratic demand. A radical vision of community has to recognize the sexual/erotic bases of human connection, challenging both the repressiveness of traditional conservatism and the "repressive desublimation" of the contemporary sexual order. Queer politics creates a space for articulating this, partly because queer sexuality has not been harnessed so directly as heterosexuality to procreation and thus to the institutions of social reproduction. As lesbian-feminists of color have demonstrated, through writing and political activism, fear of or shame about having the wrong kind of sexual desire fuels a defensive repressiveness which spreads throughout a community. In contrast, appreciation for our

unruly desires makes them less threatening, we have less need to regulate ourselves and others, opening up more possibility for empathic
connection and thus solidarity.

Familistic politics is attractive in part because communities are weaker
than ever before. But "community" is itself an amorphous concept. We
speak, at least in the U.S., of the business community, or the therapeu-
tic community, in the same way we speak of neighborhoods or socially
homogenous spaces. Community as a particular kind of public space,
a space for communication, democratic decision-making and cooperation around crucial tasks and decisions, is understandably undeveloped in advanced capitalist societies. In the capitalist political
economy, communities are formed primarily out of their common
position with regard to markets (e.g. for housing, for jobs) and to various institutions that regulate the distribution of resources (e.g. local
government, the welfare department, the education system). Community appears as an arena of voluntary relationships over against the
necessary and more obligatory ties of family and the commands of
capitalist employers. So while there is a kind of "romance" of community, and even perhaps a real longing for community, in the U.S.
today there is little space for people to create or sustain communal
institutions. On the other side, in both American myth and historical
experience, the potentially arbitrary and repressive power of communities looms large. This can only be countered by a vision of radically
democratic communities that allow space for variation in the ways that
individuals can live and participate.[8] From a feminist perspective, democratic community is built not only out of particular kinds of political
structures, but also by particular kinds of people—people who have the
ability to negotiate inevitable tensions between collective demands and
individual needs. These capacities are first learned in relation to our
early caregivers and continue in how we experience ourselves in relation
to others.

Feminists have long argued that childrearing by women within the
context of an isolated family/household creates particular kinds of
gendered personalities but also fundamental difficulties around dependence for both men and women. The hyperindividualism of bourgeois
society is reproduced in personality via family structure. Personality is
shaped both directly and indirectly (through how parents, teachers, and
other caregivers envision the goals of child development) by a capitalist
culture that denigrates dependence and over-values individual independence (understood as freedom from ties to others). But fears about

dependence arise also from forms of parenting that especially intensify dilemmas of development. These dilemmas arise out of a human reality: the long period of dependence and inequality of power in relations of infants/children to adults who care for them. Whatever the existential limits or grounding of developmental dilemmas in human physiology, social structures shape both their character and resolution. For children reared by isolated, disempowered mothers and distant fathers in patriarchal family households, developmental struggles center around individuation from a female caregiver, conflicting desires around autonomy and merger, conflicting fears about being left alone and about being taken over.[9] Having the capacity to bring these fears and desires into some kind of balance, to resolve them in at least a "good enough" way is necessary for individuals to engage well in the give-and-take of democratic group life—to be able to share power, to recognize others' needs and, at the same time, to be able to assert one's own views against pressures toward group conformity, to tolerate conflict.

Feminists have thought quite a bit about this question, especially about how a rigid, defensive, masculinity constructed through the denigration of the feminine reinforces drives toward domination, expressed in both the micro-politics of relationships and the macro-politics of the economy and the state. Feminists have also, at least tentatively, explored how women's fears of separation create over-enmeshment, inability to distinguish others' needs from one's own, conflict avoidance and inability to tolerate differences within a group, and projection of aggressive impulses onto sons, husbands, and fathers.[10] These analyses all point toward rearranging family life in very fundamental ways. A key change, feminists have argued, is for men to become equally involved with the daily routines of caregiving for young children. This is important not only to change how boys and girls come to acquire gendered identities. It is also crucial to creating reciprocity and equality among adults who have to negotiate with one another in ways that a more gendered division of labor does not require. And men develop skills—the ability to tolerate and respond to helplessness, to recognize and respond to others' emotional states, to anticipate wants and needs—which carry over into their relationships with adults—with their partners as well as their colleagues and friends.[11]

Feminist utopian visions, though, go further than rearranging the gender division of labor within the household. They reject family households as the basic unit of social reproduction, of reciprocal exchanges of emotional and physical caring necessary to renew life. The reasons are both social and psychological. First, more collective forms of every-day living expand the sphere of social solidarity and exert a counter-vailing pressure against the privatistic and exclusivist bonds of sexual/affectional partnership and parent–child relations. Second, although it is important for children to have intense, affectional bonds with some particular others, it seems that these ties can be made more problem-atic where parents don't share caregiving with other adults. In more communal forms of living, children can use other adults as a buffer in negotiating conflicts/tensions with their parents. And, participating in a broader supportive community, parents may find it easier to treat their children as separate individuals rather than extensions of them-selves. In other words, situated within a broader caring community, children and parents might not experience conflicts around autonomy/separation and dependence/merger as intensely as we do today. Further, affective ties that extend beyond the mother–child dyad, the Oedipal triangle, or even sibling relationships lay the basis for individuals to develop psychic structures incorporating a broader set of social identi-fications.

Comparative studies of childrearing practice already indicate the importance of culturally produced understandings and the social organization of caregiving for defining paths of child development.[12] Segura and Pierce argue that the particular family constellation within which Chicano and Chicana children are cared for, characterized by nonexclusive mothering and significant cross-generational ties between grandmothers and granddaughters, explains, in part, why Chicanos and Chicanas develop strong group identities.[13] Mahoney and Yngvesson make the point that how a society defines the process of development affects interactional patterns between adults and children. For example, among the Ilongot people of the Philippines the developmental process is understood as a gradual acquisition of knowledge (and thus of in-creased autonomy) through an extended network of interactions (expe-riences) with multiple caretakers. In contrast, they argue, among the Anglo-American middle class, development is seen to be a struggle for autonomy envisioned as breaking away from a confining dependence on a primary parent.[14]

What are some implications of these ideas for political action? In-stead of a political focus on protecting and supporting families, we should argue for expanding, supporting, and reviving communities, and investing resources in local, democratically controlled institutions for providing care. The entry (both chosen and forced) of women into paid work has drastically undermined the basis for traditional community: the unpaid labor of women. The crisis of caregiving and the burdens on individual family households are a compelling point of entry for a prefigurative politics which proposes new kinds of sharing relationships and new kinds of public places, such as co-housing, community gardens, daycare cooperatives, democratized schools and recreation centers.

Such experiments and reforms would provide a space for envisioning a rich, local, public life and identifying the kinds of resources individuals will need in order to participate. For instance, parents can't belong to daycare cooperatives if they can't afford to leave work to fulfill the volunteer time requirement. And they can't understand or appreciate what's happening with their older children in public schools if employers won't pay them for their time off work. Making schools more democratic, and convincing teachers to share power with parents, requires that parents have the time and resources really to participate in the work of the school.[15] Living patterns are constrained by social institutions but also by the built environment. Without capital to renovate old housing, most people can't participate in new kinds of living arrangements, like co-housing. Co-housing communities combine individual households with communal living spaces. Members are expected to participate in a committee responsible for some collective activities and daily life is organized around sharing of responsibilities like providing adult supervision for children after school and cooking dinner. Co-housing communities offer new possibilities for expanding the circle of adults who care for children and for each other. They make it more possible for individuals to participate in childrearing without necessarily producing their own child. And they allow adults to share the burdens and pleasures of caring for each other. Taking the sting out of living single, co-housing community creates a ground for real choice about coupling up. These experiments should be encouraged and subsidized with public funds, rather than being available only to those who have the money to try them.[16]

Recreating community, rebuilding a supportive infrastructure for caregiving that does not rely on exploiting women's unpaid labor, points in the direction of new kinds of public investment: not only new public jobs (more recreation directors, childcare workers, etc.) but resources for building new kinds of relationships between those who provide services and those who use them. Democratized public schools, daycare centers, and community centers, as cooperative institutions, require workers, parents, children, and other neighborhood residents to participate and work together. And, because community institutions are part of a larger public system of provision, participatory norms can be extended upward—in a council-type system of governance. This is a particularly important point, for local control can also have a narrow, even conservative, side. To counter parochial tendencies, community institutions have to be embedded in a broader set of democratic decision-making relationships with each other. Posing an alternative to the top-down and top-heavy bureaucracy of the capitalist welfare state, the fight for democratic communal caring effectively challenges the rightist ideologues who contend that only privatization can provide real control and choice.

There are many different entry points for the political initiatives I am proposing. In the U.S. some of these would be: the fight to defend the public schools against voucher systems, the movement to shift federal spending from the military to human services, efforts to defend single mothers driven into low-wage jobs, battles about urban development and attempts to reshape the built environment, local government use of federal funds for public housing. In these and many other arenas, we can pose alternatives to the overburdened, isolated family household through an attractive vision of cooperative, democratic ways of caring for adults and children.

One of the many ironies of our present is that, at least in the U.S., the expanding space for more inclusive, more diverse, more tolerant, and more respectful social relations in personal life coexists with a narrowing space for public democracy, a cynicism about public life. This irony reflects not just the defeats but also the successes of the liberatory movements of the 1960s—their cultural and political legacy. However bleak the political terrain on which we struggle today, we cannot afford to lose the communal, egalitarian visions those movements created; nor to suspend attempts to prefigure these visions through the kinds of organizations we build, the reforms we propose, and the ways we argue for them. If, last time around, prefigurative politics informed by utopian visions often became oppressive, we can learn from our mistakes. To turn away defensively from dreaming because we are so afraid of being disppointed, to wish for less because we fear we cannot win more, will impoverish and undermine our efforts to build more radical political struggles. We can speak to the real dilemmas, the practices, and the yearnings of working-class people. The crisis in caregiving haunts everyday life, creating a political space for the left as well as the right. We can enter that space with political discourses and, as far as possible, practical proposals for new kinds of communal institutions that express our vision of deeply and thoroughly *democratic* community.

[*2000*]

Notes

1. Cherrie Moraga, *Loving in the War Years* (Boston: South End Press, 1983), 129.
2. Marge Piercy, *Woman on the Edge of Time* (New York: Ballantine Books, 1976); Ursula K. LeGuin, *The Dispossessed* (London: Harper & Row, 1974). The novels are also different. LeGuin's subtitle, "an ambiguous utopia," reflects her exploration of repressive tendencies in communal society, a problem that is not at all foregrounded in Piercy's novel. The two novels also reflect, perhaps, generational differences in radical post war feminisms. If Piercy's theoretical touchstone is Shulamith Firestone (*The Dialectic of Sex*), LeGuin's would be de Beauvoir (*The Second Sex*).
3. Just to be clear: of course the changes have very real downsides. Single mothers are impoverished; reproductive technologies have opened up new avenues for controlling and exploiting women's bodies, two-thirds of the closing of the gender gap in wages has occurred not because women are making more, but because men are earning less.
4. Michael Sandel, *Liberalism and the Limits of Justice* (Cambridge: Cambridge University Press, 1982), 150–52; Jean Bethke Elshtain, "Feminism, Family and Community," *Dissent* (Fall 1982).
5. Patricia Hill Collins, *Black Feminist Thought* (London: Routledge, 1990), esp. chap. 6.
6. Moraga, *Loving in the War Years*, 110–11; see also, Evelynn M. Hammonds, "Toward a Genealogy of Black Female Sexuality: The Problematic of Silence," in M. Jacqui Alexander and Chandra Talpade Mohanty, eds., *Feminist Genealogies, Colonial Legacies, Democratic Futures* (London: Routledge, 1997), pp. 170–182.
7. Michèle Barrett and Mary McIntosh, *The Anti-Social Family* (London: Verso, 1984).
8. Much of our thinking about collective living is preoccupied with the problem of "free-riders" on the one hand, collective despotism on the other. These are important questions. But that they loom especially large for us says more about our own society than it does about universal human propensities toward power and exploitation. The evidence from social relations in egalitarian hunter-gatherer societies indicates that they are able to achieve a balance in which individual idiosyncracy and differential abilities to contribute to the group or engage in the group's social life are tolerated. Conflicts are resolved through dialogue; rifts are acknowledged and, at least temporarily, repaired, through games, clowning and communal ritual. See, for example, Colin M. Turnbull, "Mbuti Womanhood," in Frances Dahlberg, ed., *Woman the Gatherer* (New Haven: Yale Universisty Press, 1981), 205–220.
9. Jessica Benjamin, *Bonds of Love* (New York: Pantheon Books, 1988).
10. Lynne Segal, *Slow Motion* (New Jersey: Rutgers University Press, 1990), 264–68; Valerie Miner and Helen E. Longino, eds., *Competition: A Feminist Taboo?*

(New York: The Feminist Press, 1987), esp. 21–37, 195–208.

11. Scott Coltrane, *Family Man* (Oxford: Oxford University Press, 1997), 117–20; Barbara Katz Rothman, *Recreating Motherhood* (New York: W.W. Norton, 1989), 223–28.

12. Coltrane, *Family Man*, 180–92.

13. Denise A. Segura and Jennifer L. Pierce, "Chicana/o Family Structure and Gender Personality: Chodorow, Familism, and Psychoanalytic Sociology Revisited," *Signs* 19, no. 1 (Autumn 1993), 63–91. The authors also explore the relationship between these childrearing patterns and "machismo."

14. Maureen A. Mahoney and Barbara Yngvesson, "The Construction of Subjectivity and the Paradox of Resistance: Reintegrating Feminist Anthropology and Psychology," *Signs* 18, no. 1 (Autumn 1992), 44–73.

15. David Levine et al., eds., *Rethinking Schools: An Agenda for Change* (New York: New Press, 1995).

16. Kathryn McCamant and Charles Durrett, *Cohousing* (Berkeley: Habitat Press, 1988).

Part IV

Class Politics and Feminist Strategy

Chapter 9

Meeting the Challenge
of the Political Right

Being a socialist-feminist activist has never been easy. We occupy a
stony ground between the popularity of liberal (and social-democratic)
feminism's apparently practical reformism and the heady appeal of
radical-feminism's claim to a female moral/spiritual superiority.
Especially in these not so very revolutionary times, to write about the
meaning of revolutionary change from the point of view of socialist-
feminism seems to be more an exercise in mythmaking than analysis,
more an expression of utopian hope than an outlining of political strategy.
Ironically, just at the moment that socialist-feminists are trying to cope
with what we experience as a decline if not the defeat of feminism, or
at least of feminism as a grassroots movement within which radicals
could organize, some on the left are finding in feminism—and other
"new movements"—revolutionary subjects to replace the working class.

Feminism certainly has much to contribute to expanding what Marxism understands to be human liberation and to creating the kind of
movement that could possibly bring it about. Feminism insists that we
take as a field for theory and political intervention domains of social
life that Marxism has fundamentally ignored: sexuality, intimacy, raising
children, the care and nurture of adults. In so doing, feminism has
allowed us to think far more extensively than before about the material
basis of socialism—about the best way to organize social life to "make"
socialist people and to foster relationships of equality and respect. In
confronting the pain and rewards of motherhood in contemporary
society, and in understanding mothering as a kind of work, feminism
has allowed us to redefine what we mean by both alienated and unalienated labor. In revaluing those human capacities and activities that
have been defined as belonging primarily to women, feminism has

fundamentally challenged any vision of socialism that fails to reintegrate the dimensions of human life that capitalism has so radically separated. Feminist theory has helped to undermine the system that Marxist theory had become: its economic reductionism, its productivism and uncritical approach to technology; its narrow definitions of work, worker, and working class; its reification of the capitalist split between "public" and "private" and the privileging of the public as an arena for theoretical analysis and political organization; its impoverished understandings of consciousness, particularly its inattention to the way that emotional needs shape political understandings, the relationship between gender identities and the construction of political and economic "interests." Feminism, in its theory and in its political practice has been a rich resource for the renewal of Marxism—for recapturing and developing its radically democratic liberatory vision.

Feminist organizations have wrestled with questions that the Marxist left rarely recognized: the tension between process and product, between leadership and inclusiveness, between building collectivity and encouraging critical debate, between creating consensus and appreciating differences, and so forth. Certainly, in our struggle to find "pre-figurative" forms of organization, the feminist movement hasn't come to easy answers. Indeed, most of the questions feminism raises can only really be answered through a broad process of dialogue and experiment engaging the creativity and experience of many diverse communities of resistance. But if these tensions can't be easily resolved, confronting them has allowed feminism to develop ways of discussing, acting together, and deciding (or deciding not to decide) that could help to counter the bureaucratic tendencies that have plagued left organizations, small and large.

The Contribution of "New Movements"

Contemporary left critics[1] who draw inspiration from the "new movements" and argue for a politics based on radical democracy rather than on class exploitation have identified a crucial question facing revolutionary socialists: how to move the demand for democratic participation and the struggle against forms of domination other than class from the margins of socialist politics.[2]

Further, while they aren't the only ones making this point, these critics are certainly right, I think, to argue on the one hand for the subversive potential of protests against domination, ecological destruction, nuclear annihilation, and on the other hand that a revolutionary socialist bloc is a political creation: no demand, including the demand for democratic participation, is necessarily subversive and any struggle can be articulated to an incorporationist project as well as to a revolutionary one.

Laclau and Mouffe argue:

> All struggles, whether those of workers or other political subjects, left to themselves, have a partial character, and can be articulated to very different discourses. It is this articulation which gives them their character, not the place from which they come. There is therefore no subject—nor, further, any "necessity"—which is absolutely radical and irrecuperable by the dominant order, and which constitutes an absolutely guaranteed point of departure for a total transformation.[3]

Many of us would agree with their salutary focus on the political, on the constructed and contingent character of revolutionary consciousness. But what are the strategic conclusions to be drawn? Because there is no subject which is necessarily radical, does that mean that revolutionary worldviews are as likely to be constructed and adopted by one social group as another? To be sure, needs and interests are socially and historically constructed and counterhegemonic worldviews are part of this process. Radical discourses redefine needs and identify interests in ways that illuminate the interconnection of different needs and interests and link those needs and interests to a vision of transformed society. But worldviews are carried by groups who by their social location and experience, their everyday experience as well as their experience in reform movements, are more or less open to one set of ideas or another.

Moreover, the struggle against exploitation and the struggle against domination ought not to be counterposed. If the new movements have shown us the importance of other dimensions of oppression and other identities as sources of radical protest, their evolution has also demonstrated how structures of capital accumulation, when unchallenged (either politically or economically), limit and distort these possibilities. While there are still some activist "new movement" groups, in general the new movements have failed to extend their social base and, at least in the U.S., increasingly rely on strategies such as lobbying and providing expertise within existing political structures. Their move toward more conservative reform strategies cannot be explained simply by a failure of political imagination. The leaderships of these movements have responded to a political climate whose hostility to reform is definitely shaped by an international capitalist offensive against labor and the defeat and disorganization of the trade unions.

These pressures—and their political consequences—are quite clear in the successes and failures of feminism. A consideration of this one new movement perhaps can make clear the enduring necessity for socialist revolutionaries to base our politics (organizations and activities, as well as program) on the self-activity of those people we can broadly call the working class.[4]

Feminism after the Second Wave

In the 1960s and 1970s feminism had a historic role to play as a "cross-class" movement for democratic rights. For it is only in our time and through feminist organizing that the bourgeois revolution has been completed and women have become not only citizens but also owners of their own person and truly free sellers of their own labor power. The entire edifice which legislated women's subservience in marriage, denied us control over our bodies and reproductive capacity, and legalized our economic marginalization has been substantially dismantled. This victory has helped to force a reorganization of the gender order—materially, culturally, and politically. The terms of this reorganization are now a matter of contest. In this struggle, women face not only a reactionary right that romanticizes the patriarchal family but also a modernizing right that celebrates meritocratic values and individual choice, understood to reside in the market.

As its opponents are changing, so too is feminism. Feminism began as a real social movement. The autonomous, grassroots, local organizations which were the hallmark of second-wave feminism—and the locus of its creative genius—have been replaced by feminism as organized interest group. While feminists (in the broadest sense of advocates for women) have entered and begun to affect conservative as well as liberal and social-democratic parties, business and professional organizations as well as trade unions, the major contemporary inheritor of second-wave feminism is to be found in what I would call "social-welfare feminism"—a loose network of individuals and organizations inside and outside the state apparatus who seek to represent the interests of women, including working-class and racially oppressed women. Feminism in advanced capitalist countries today is much more a network of organizations for lobbying than for grassroots organizing. The membership provides money, sometimes votes, sometimes letters and phone calls, but very little local activism.

Like their counterparts in the trade unions, although perhaps even less organizationally tied to their social base than trade-union officials and staff, the women who make their living one way or another as representatives of women's interests (what Australian feminists have called "femocrats") have particularly strong connections to the political parties that have historically supported the expansion of the welfare state—the social-democratic parties (and the Democratic Party in the U.S.). While feminists have been able to wield considerable influence within these parties, and within their governments when in power, they have also been bounded by their dependence on these parties and the state apparatus, and by the vulnerability of their own organizations with their relatively weak social base. Thus, in general (and depending on the relative strength of the political parties to which they are tied) feminists have been pushed onto the defensive politically.

Where, then, lies feminism's transformative promise? I would argue that the same social, economic, and political changes that have led to the institutionalization of feminism and its cultural incorporation have created the possibility of a new kind of feminist organization—one based on the self-activity of working-class women. Rather than a cross-class movement for democratic rights, such a women's movement would be based in organizations of and for women which are allied to and part of other struggles and located organizationally within working-class movements, whether these are based in communities or workplaces. Such a movement would not necessarily be revolutionary—any more than trade unions or other working-class organizations are. Nonetheless, by both their structural position and experience working-class women are best placed to create and respond to a political practice that does go beyond reformism to bridge socialism and feminism. The realization of this potential depends in part on whether the revolutionary socialist left will embrace, in its vision of revolution and modes of organization, the insights and experience of feminist theory and practice.

The Impact of Increasing Class Divisions among Women

As an organized self-conscious political movement, feminism has been largely middle class and white. Women of color certainly made crucial contributions to feminist theory in their writing and to feminist politics in their community organizing. But only in the 1980s and mainly through the trade unions have working-class women become organized with a consciousness of their special capacities and needs. This is not to deny the participation of women workers, both unionized and not, such as teachers, in the feminist movement of the 1960s and 1970s, but only to argue that organized feminism remains overwhelmingly white and middle class.

In the 1960s and 1970s working-class women (white women and women of color) entered politics as members of families and communities. They were at the core of the civil rights, welfare rights, school integration, tenants, and other movements. In those struggles, women often transformed their consciousness, developed a sense of their personal effectiveness and their right to respect in personal and public life, learned to value women's leadership, and some even contested with men in their movements over program, demands, and strategy. But they did not, for the most part, identify their organizations and struggles with feminism or women's rights. They spoke as women of an oppressed class, or race, or community, while the feminist movement spoke of Woman.

This feminist movement, for its own part, made historic gains for women, including working-class women. But working-class women were not the major actors in making reform nor its primary beneficiaries. Feminist demands for equality have been culturally incorporated and institutionalized as the right to compete and to contract. Old assumptions about the natural basis of the sexual division of labor have been challenged. Women are free to negotiate relationships and parental responsibilities with men, to choose "lifestyles" and "careers." This new gender ideal reflects real changes, especially in the lives of middle-class women who have the resources to negotiate the class- and race-biased systems of education, cultural formation, employment, and so on. Indeed, women have become more class divided—and it is even less the case today that a middle-class movement can speak for all women.[5] Although almost all working women have double responsibilities, either because they do not get equal participation from male partners or because they are single parents, women in managerial and professional work can find individual solutions to combining waged work and family care. Their higher incomes makes it possible to buy their way out of household responsibilities and especially to have quality childcare; they have more bargaining power as individuals to negotiate benefits like paid parental leave; they have more control over their job conditions, and thus more flexibility at work; their higher status jobs place them in less dangerous and vulnerable positions.[6]

The majority of women cannot achieve equality through individual solutions. Most crucially, so long as caring for other people is the private responsibility of individual households, women will find it difficult to break out of the vicious cycle in which their relatively low wages reinforce the sexual division of labor within the family, and their domestic responsibilities disadvantage them in the labor market. In addition, for most women, single parenthood will continue to spell hardship and poverty. It is hardly surprising if many working-class women, even those who share feminist aspirations for respect and equality, feel very ambivalent about feminism. Women's increasing freedom seems to have come at the expense of decreasing protections; in a society of atomized individuals who regard each other as means to an end, many women can only be the losers. The drudgery of a double day is hardly liberation; and identities realized in expanded consumption, in appropriating marketed lifestyles and images, can't fill our need for social recognition and effective participation.

However, the reforms necessary to promote most women's equal participation in work and public life and thus women's equality in personal life, have proven to be much more difficult to win than the legal and cultural changes that are the legacy of second-wave feminism. As a movement for legal reform, feminism was able to make gains in the 1960s and 1970s without really taking on capitalist class power. That is not to say that it was easy to force managers to stop discriminating in hiring or to pay women and men equally for equal work, or to legalize abortion. Nor is it to say that these gains are even today uncontested. But a movement that was predominantly based in the middle class—educated women, students, affluent housewives, professional women—could still compel legislatures to pass anti-discrimination law, and compel the police and the courts to enforce it.[7]

To change the situation of working-class women, however, will require a significant redistribution of resources. Working-class women require, at minimum, quality affordable childcare (and eldercare) and paid time off for parental responsibilities (including meeting children's educational and emotional as well as physical needs) and in the longer run, shorter work days—not only so that parents can enjoy relating to their children but also so that they have time in their lives for activities other than meeting responsibilities in paid work and domestic work. Most crucially, women need time for organizing a politics to rediscover, rename, and combat women's oppression.

Yet any substantial reorganization of social reproduction represents a serious claim on surplus wealth—and therefore runs up against the interests and demands of capital (expressed in both the power of individual employers and the resistance by the state to providing the material basis for women's equality). Even in relatively wealthy countries with strong social-democratic parties, state provisions—family allowances, paid parental leave, state-subsidized childcare—are still not extensive enough to undercut the logic of a sexual division of labor. One year paid parental leave, and a week or two's worth of paid family leave a year, makes doing two jobs easier, but households still need lots of unpaid labor to sustain themselves. Responsibility for dependent people (children, the ill, the elderly, etc.) requires time, emotional effort, and physical work from household members. While some women can demand equality of sacrifice from male partners or manage well alone, most end up in arrangements where they are the primary caregivers, achieving a decent living standard through the contributions of male partners whose greater income-earning capacities underwrite their privileged primary "breadwinner" status. Moreover, the scope of subsidies and government provisions is always constrained by the demands of capital accumulation: economic downturns lead to state cutbacks, often most severely in highly labor-intensive areas of personal services and in those services that meet the needs of the least politically well-mobilized constituencies—in other words, in those services most important to women and especially mothers.[8]

I am not arguing that the persistence of the sexual division of labor in the occupational structure and the household is simply the outcome of rational responses by men and women to material difficulties they face. Clearly, women's life goals, their desire for children, their sense of responsibility for elderly parents are socially shaped, and women enter into and stay in relationships with men for reasons other than economic survival. Further, had women not to contend with men's resistance, the possibilities for changing the sexual division of labor in the household or workplace would be much greater even within the limits set by the protection of capital accumulation and the privatization of social reproduction. Nonetheless, these structural limitations are important barriers to women's self-organization and points of resistance to feminist projects.

The Political Drift to the Right

Once we consider this point, it becomes easier to understand why a fundamentally minoritarian political movement, the New Right, has been so successful a counter to feminism. The appearance of a right-wing opposition was only to be expected in reaction to feminism's challenging the traditional gender order. However, there is nothing inevitable about the right's capacity to define the terms of political discourse, to put feminism on the defensive, especially because most women reject the right's vision. Indeed, the right appears so influential not because it reflects majority sentiment but because there is no politics and no political organization that articulates a compelling alternative worldview. Without the capacity to construct personal dilemmas as political issues, feminism is necessarily on the defensive as it confronts an opposition whose political influence reaches far beyond its numbers. Rejecting a mainstream feminism that overvalues male-defined success, accepts the competitive and hierarchical structures of capitalist society, uncritically supports the technocratic welfare state, and yet repelled by the right's repressive moralism, most women have turned away from participation in organized political life. It is not only the pressures of everyday survival but the barrenness of politics that pushes women to seek solutions in a perfected personal life.

Still, feminism remains very much alive, institutionalized in a vast network of organizations which together create a kind of "woman's lobby." Configurations reflect national political structures. In the U.S., this network includes organizations that are part of government at local and national levels—women's commissions and task forces, affirmative action offices, parts of the social welfare bureaucracy, and so on; traditional political organizations (e.g., the Congressional Women's Caucus, the National Women's Political Caucus, organizations within the Republican and Democratic Parties, the National Organization for Women); lobbies for almost every women's issue from welfare rights to tax reform to abortion; organizations that work in and around the judicial system, primarily lending legal support to anti-discrimination and other hopefully precedent-setting cases. The lobby also includes groups that are not explicitly political, such as the official associations of predominantly women professions (social workers, librarians, nurses, etc.); women's caucuses and organizations of women in traditionally male professions; organizations of women trade-union officials; organizations of social service providers, and so on. This women's lobby functions as a traditional political interest group, aligned primarily with the Democratic Party.

Of course, political differences remain within mainstream feminism. The old-style liberal feminism, focused primarily on legislating equal treatment rather than expanding state services, unwilling to address class and race differences among women, is still quite powerful. Indeed, this brand of feminism has been increasingly incorporated into political discourses of the center and all but the extreme right. The debate about whether mothers should work, whether children should be in day care, whether women ought to be able to compete with men in economic and political life, has been pretty much won by the "feminist" side. The argument now is over whether the state should take responsibility for creating the conditions for "equal opportunity" or whether that can all be left to the competitive incentives of the marketplace.[9] In North America, for instance, the debate on childcare legislation revolves around not whether mothers should work, but how much the government should spend on daycare, and for whom, and whether the state should subsidize private providers (through vouchers or tax credits, for instance) or develop public childcare.[10] Social-welfare feminists argue for state intervention and effort, and many have come to elaborate a politics that looks to the state for much more than anti-discrimination legislation and enforcement.[11] If not by their own experience, then through the lives of women they try to help, and, perhaps most important, through pressure from organizations of trade-union women and Black women, these social-welfare feminists have organized campaigns for government intervention to help working-class women: for example, paid parental leave, quality childcare, subsidized health care, pay equity.

However, given (a) the tremendous resistance to expanding government spending in general, (b) the powerful industrial and regional interests who defend the current distribution of state funding (e.g., the military-industrial complex), and (c) the much greater political resources of middle-class as compared to working-class/poor constituencies, most of these efforts have either been completely defeated or the legislation finally passed has benefited primarily middle-class women and has had a negligible or in some cases even deleterious impact on working-class and poor women.[12] Moreover, facing these very powerful constraints, social-welfare feminists (who because of their political worldview and structural location are in any case much more at home with legislating benefits for women than with helping women to organize themselves) have failed to expand their grassroots activist base.

Without that kind of support, they have been especially vulnerable to pressures from the right. This is nowhere more visible than in the attempt to reappropriate "the family" from the right, primarily by recasting demands for expanded state benefits for women as a program to strengthen the family.[13] In the spring of 1988, for example, Representative Patricia Schroeder, co-chair of the U.S. Congressional Women's Caucus, organized a "Great American Family Tour," in which she and other speakers campaigned across the U.S. for parental leave, childcare, housing, and health care legislation. In conjunction with Schroeder's campaign, the Coalition of Labor Union Women (CLUW) organized a demonstration in Washington, D.C. on these same issues, calling the demonstration "Celebrate the American Family: Working Together for Change." This strategy has been especially disastrous in marginalizing the issue of compulsory heterosexuality on the feminist political agenda and thereby strengthening the influence of conservatives on issues such as abortion, teenage sexual rights, lesbian/gay rights, and AIDS.[14] Organizers of the CLUW demonstration refused to include gay/lesbian rights or abortion rights as family issues, would not accept speakers from organizations involved in those campaigns, and attempted to keep gay/lesbian organizations from displaying their literature at the rally.[15] Demands for reform that increase women's sexual independence and that directly contest male domination in personal relationships cannot be so easily recast as "really" programs to improve the lives of children and men—which is what "pro-family" politics is all about. Moreover, justifying benefits to women in this way further delegitimizes women's claim to autonomy, self-development, and individuality, undercutting the very ground on which the project of women's liberation has to rest.

From this analysis, the counterposition of feminism and Marxism, of the feminist movement to the trade-union movement, appears particularly absurd. Feminism as a mass reform struggle with radicalizing potential cannot be renewed on the basis of its old middle-class constituencies but depends on the rebuilding of working-class self-organization. By working-class self-organization, I mean the collectively structured process of engaging in resistance to and making demands on corporate capital, whether that is done directly (strikes) or indirectly (campaigns for government intervention), by people who do not exercise power in their daily working lives and who are situated economically so that they don't control very much of their own time on the job or off it. Without the capacity, *in practice*, to take on the limits set by the demands of capital accumulation in a period of increasing international competition, feminism will continue to be vitiated of its radical potential, capitulating to the right, and unable to mobilize broad layers of women.

The Self-organization of Working-class Women

The fate of feminism as an actual *movement,* then, is tied to the fate of trade unionism and other forms of collective resistance to corporate capital. If it was possible for "new movements" to flourish in the 1960s and 1970s alongside an essentially bureaucratic and demobilized trade unionism, this is no longer the case. But the decline of the old trade-union movement is not the end of the working class, or of trade unions, as agents of social change. It is the exhaustion of a kind of unionism and a kind of industrial organization—the "social contract unionism" based in heavy industry that became dominant after the Second World War. To confront increasingly centralized and mobile capital, many organizers and activists look to a social and political unionism based in solidarities beyond the workplace—linkages with communities, across industries and sectors, and so on.[16] Obviously, one key strategic issue is how to rebuild involvement and organization at the base of a kind that can sustain militant resistance under conditions of an intense employers' offensive substantially underwritten by the state.

In this effort, working-class women can make a crucial contribution as organizers in communities and workplaces. Historically, trade-union women, and perhaps especially Black trade-union women, have fought for women's equality in their unions and in their workplaces; but so long as women were a minority within the workforce and therefore within the trade-union movement, they could be marginalized. Mainstream feminism's success in legitimizing the ideal of equality and the massive entry of women into waged work have created the conditions for the development of a working-class feminism, one that integrates itself not only politically but organizationally with other movements of the exploited and oppressed.

The action and politics of working-class women in their trade-union and community organizing have forced socialist-feminists to rethink our categories—even how we define "feminist". Are Black women organizing for better prenatal health care, or for neighborhood watches to prevent rape, doing feminist organizing, even if they locate themselves within the anti-racism movement and don't identify themselves as feminist? Are working women organizing for higher pay as family bread-winners feminists even if they define themselves as trade unionists? Out of these activities, many working-class women activists become conscious of their oppression and of their need to organize as women *not in opposition to but in relation to their membership in unions or oppressed communities.*[17]

They must therefore find forms of organization and political expression that reject the practice and politics of both the traditional left and feminism. Both movements have tended to find common ground by universalizing similarities ("we are all workers"; "we are all women") without recognizing and incorporating differences, whether these be differences of gender, race/ethnicity, or sexual orientation. What the organizational forms might be, it is hard to say. One model, perhaps, would be a geographically based (local, regional, national) confederation of grassroots women's groups based in unions, workplaces, and communities, that are organized around certain projects and which bring women together frequently to socialize, make decisions, and act.

At the moment, organized working-class women are in the minority. Still, they represent a potential leadership, not only for a renewed feminism but for a renewed trade unionism, one that no longer concerns itself only with public issues and public life, that no longer narrows its scope to workplace/industrial as opposed to community/personal issues.[18] Women's lives bridge, in ways that men's do not, the divide between work and community. Working-class women cannot create, as men have often done, a union culture that builds solidarity through exclusive bonds and loyalties and that regards families and communities to be auxiliary rather than central points of support and power.[19] Dependent on sharing networks of kin and neighbors to negotiate their double day, working-class women are likely to define independence in ways very different from men and to be less vulnerable than men to the bourgeois ideal of themselves as freely contracting citizen workers and independent wage earners. Finally, in their workplaces and occupations women are less racially segregated than they are in terms of where they live. At work, white women and women of color might find common ground as they discover that they share the experiences and dilemmas of meeting their obligations and interests not only as workers but also as kin, friends, and members of communities.

Reform and Revolution

An effort to elaborate a socialist-feminist reform strategy for a working-class women's movement, to contest the emerging leadership of women politicians and trade-union officials, and to develop grassroots organizations of working-class women that are prefigurative in their demands as well as in their organizational forms should be at the center of any discussion of revolutionary strategy at the turn of the century.

It may be that in the long run advanced capitalist societies could reorganize social reproduction in ways that would substantially decrease the burdens of care now carried by households and by women. But socialized forms of care would still inevitably be delivered, like other welfare state services, in a class- and race-biased and highly bureaucratic system. Nonetheless, such an expansion of the welfare state would substantially underwrite further change in gender relations and gender ideology.[20] In any case, it is certain that, while it may be possible for capitalism to absorb gender equality in the long run, significant shifts away from the privatization of social reproduction will have to be forced upon capital, in the same way that universal male suffrage, the recognition of trade unions, or the welfare state were won through struggle. And women's struggles to create the material basis for gender equality has the potential to go far beyond its incorporationist ends. That potential lies in the movement itself—in its creation of aspirations that transcend any particular reform—and especially in the capacity of revolutionary socialists to deepen grassroots organization and broaden the political understandings of women activists.

As a movement for equality and against male domination, feminism is not inevitably radical or socialist. Social-welfare feminism has a reform vision that can be very attractive to working-class women: a workplace attuned to family needs, a benevolent and expanded welfare state, and a democratized nuclear family. This vision is not contradictory to capitalism. It accepts the split between public and private in which the social relationships and culture of the workplace remain structured by hierarchy and competition. The mainstream feminist vision would reduce the penalties for losing and insure that women could fairly compete, but not change the essential organizational structures nor eliminate the labor market.[21]

The social-welfare feminist vision contains little critique of the bureaucratic welfare state and maintains a liberal faith in the welfare state's ability to equalize the unequal. Childcare might become a general entitlement, like public education. But, as with public education, class and race inequalities will produce vast differences in the quality of care and in the capacity of parents to negotiate the system, both to ensure that their children's needs are met and to protect themselves from unwanted intrusions. The modernizing right's attack on the welfare state draws heavily on these legitimate concerns.

Reforms that expand state supports for family households (subsidies to family caregivers, tax credits for childcare costs, etc.) assume that they will continue to be the primary units for providing care. While such policies might help the family (at least more families) better deliver on its promise of fulfillment and self-expression, they pose no challenge to the individualism and alienation that define our experience of public life in advanced capitalist societies. They thus reinforce the existing cynicism about the possibilities for participatory democratic alternatives.[22]

In order to address the central dilemmas in working-class women's lives—and in particular the felt counterposition between autonomy and collectivity, between freedom and security, between self-development and nurturance—we have not only to project an attractive socialist vision but also to develop a strategy for reform that transcends rather than capitulates to existing political worldviews. This strategy has to include, first, a reform program which is self-conscious about the changes called for, the language in which we justify our claims, and the necessity to link always short-run goals to visions of a radically reorganized society. Second, the strategy has to support and try to bring into being political organization and institutional reforms that allow individuals to develop and control collectively their own objectives and activities, to increase their personal capacities, and to enhance their sense that even larger changes would be possible if they joined their efforts with those of others. Commitments to a radically democratic and participatory society can more easily be built out of some practices than out of others.

Once we focus on this issue, however, the importance of revising Marxist theory to integrate socialist-feminist analysis also comes to the fore. Marxist politics, even in its most democratic and visionary tradition, does not speak to the key contradictions of women's everyday lives. Just think, for example, how much time the democratic socialist tradition in Marxist politics has spent debating workplace democracy, planning and participation, and addressing issues such as how to combine expertise with workers' control of production, authority with democracy. But hardly a word has been spoken on the problems of organizing social reproduction, the renewal of life daily and inter-generationally.

How, for example, do we provide security and continuity for children without replicating the intense, exclusive relationships of the nuclear family? We know that women and children need to be liberated from each other. But once we recognize that motherhood is not only oppressive but also a kind of skilled work and that parents derive pleasure from children, what implications does that have for how we organize participation in other work, in production? Does creative work require complete freedom from the obligations and restraints that caring for someone else necessarily entails? Finally, how can we organize collectivities in a way that reduces, if not ends, the tension between self-development and collective obligation? Ignored by Marxists, such questions have been extensively explored in socialist-feminist writing and politics.

In response to the right's romanticized evocation of *"the* family," socialist-feminists have argued for a strategy of "deconstruction." Kinship, love, and good things to eat tend to go together in our society, but that's not inevitable. How, then, do we want to "deconstruct" the family? Should households continue to take responsibility for children and the daily physical needs of adults, or should we meet more of our needs outside the place where we sleep and enjoy privacy? How might we differently arrange living spaces? What kinds of bonds will connect people who share them? Where will children live and how might they be cared for? Can we find inspiration in the open and fluid networks of adults and children cooperating across households that constitute the survival strategies of the very poor?

There is no feminist agreement on these issues, no socialist-feminist orthodoxy to be absorbed into Marxism.[23] But these debates have to be considered central questions on which any good Marxist must be well educated—as well educated as on debates in political economy. This is not only because socialist-feminist theory allows us to present a much richer and broader vision of what socialism might be. It is also because socialist feminists have been concerned with whole areas of human experience in capitalism that Marxism never really considered as a field for political action—sexuality, intimacy, motherhood, gender identity. Moreover, socialist-feminist analysis has demonstrated the profound impact of gender relationships, gender identity, and gender ideology on Marxism's traditional territory—trade unionism, parliamentary and extra-parliamentary politics, state policy. In defending feminist gains against the attack from the right, socialist feminists have been forced to confront, to analyze, and to try to respond to the powerful relationship between sexuality, gender identity, and political commitments and worldviews. In identifying the longings and anxieties on which anti-feminism draws, socialist-feminism has strengthened Marxist analysis of conservative politics and laid the ground for a more effective response.

[*1989*]

Notes

I'd like to thank Jan Haaken, Nancy Holmstrom, Alan Hunter, Leo Panitch, and Bill Resnick for their thoughtful comments. Although I couldn't respond to all of their suggestions, the essay has been much improved by their critiques.

1. For instance, Samuel Bowles and Herbert Gintis, *Democracy and Capitalism* (New York: Basic Books, 1987); Ernesto Laclau and Chantal Mouffe, *Hegemony and Socialist Strategy: Towards a Radical Democratic Politics* (London: Verso, 1985).

2. Thoughtful critiques by Ellen Wood, Alan Hunter, and Norman Geras have delineated most of the problematic aspects of these works. Ellen Meiksins Wood, *The Retreat From Class: A New "True" Socialism* (London: Verso, 1986); Alan Hunter, "Post-Marxism and the New Social Movements," *Theory and Society* 17 (1988–89), 885–900; Norman Geras, "Post-Marxism?", *New Left Review* 163 (May–June 1987).

3. Laclau and Mouffe, *Hegemony and Socialist Strategy*, 169–70.

4. Because the definition of working class is so contested these days, one can't assume a commonly held meaning. For the purposes of this article, I am using the term "middle class" as a catch-all to include groups often defined as "new middle class", such as higher salaried professionals, middle to upper managers, and the old middle class of the self-employed and small businessmen/women. By "working class," I mean all other wage and salary workers.

5. On this point for England, see Elizabeth Wilson, "Thatcherism and Women: After Seven Years," in Ralph Miliband, Leo Panitch and John Saville, eds., *Socialist Register 1987* (London: Merlin Press, 1987).

6. While sexual violence—sexual harassment, rape, wife-beating—is a cross-class and cross-race phenomenon, nevertheless income, occupation, age, and race certainly differentiate women's vulnerability.

7. Some of these programs, of course, were severely eroded under the conservative governments of Reagan and Thatcher—especially enforcement of anti-discrimination policy in education and employment. Still, overall, even under conservative regimes, the movement of women into management and the professions has continued, while in areas such as changing local police and court practices in cases of rape and domestic violence there has been marked improvement, at least in the U.S.

8. On the impact of welfare-state cutbacks on women, see Jennifer G. Schirmer, *The Limits of Reform: Women, Capital and Welfare* (Cambridge, Mass.: Schenkman, 1982), 133–35; H. Heclo and H. Madsen, *Policy and Politics in Sweden* (Philadelphia: Temple University Press, 1987), 165–73; A. Borchorst and B. Siim, "Women and the Advanced Welfare State—A New Kind of Patriarchal Power," in A. Showstack Sassoon, ed., *Women and the State: The Shifting Boundaries of Public and Private* (London: Hutchinson, 1987); Mimi Abramovitz, *Regulating the Lives of Women* (Boston: South End Press, 1988); Anna Yeatman, *Feminists, Femocrats, Technocrats: Essays on the Contemporary Australian State* (Sydney: Allen & Unwin, 1990), chap. 7. I am very grateful to Anna Yeatman for sharing her manuscript with me.

9. For an excellent analysis of Thatcherism's "modernizing" gender ideology, see Wilson, "Thatcherism and Women: After Seven Years."

10. On Canada, see Jane Stinson, "Window On The North: Women's Issues and

Labour in Canada," *Labor Research Review* 11 (Spring 1988), 46–47. On the U.S. see the comparison of Democratic and Republican party platforms on childcare in *Ms.*, October 1986.

11. Political/state structures have very much shaped the strategic issues facing "social-welfare" feminist organization and politics. As both Siim and Hernes point out, in the Scandinavian countries with highly corporatist systems, all parties have assumed that the state has a responsibility to help women cope with a "double day," but feminists (and women generally) have been marginal to the centralized decision-making structures within which state policy is crafted. Berte Siim, "The Scandinavian Welfare States—Towards Sexual Equality or a New Kind of Male Domination," *Acta Sociologica* 30, no. 3/4 (1987), 255–70; H. Hernes, "Women and the Advanced Welfare State—The Transition from Private to Public Dependence," in H. Holter, ed., *Patriarchy in a Welfare State* (Oslo: Universitetsforlaget, 1984).

12. For example, Child Support Enforcement has been the only major legislation coming out of the "feminization of poverty" campaign, which sought a broad range of programs: childcare, increased services and income for elderly women, increased access to quality health care for women and children, etc. Whatever their impact on increasing the collection of support awards from affluent men (and the evidence is mixed at best), these laws have led to increased harassment of women welfare recipients without any improvement in their level of income. See Wendy Sarvasy and Judith Van Allen, "Fighting the Feminization of Poverty: Socialist-Feminist Analysis and Strategy," *Review of Radical Political Economics* 16, no. 4 (1984), 89–110.

13. See, for instance, Betty Friedan, *The Second Stage* (New York: Summit Books, 1981); and Jean Bethke Elshtain, "Feminism, Family, and Community," *Dissent*, Fall 1982.

14. For an analysis of how this political adaptation undercuts the organization of poor Black women, see Barbara Omolade, *It's a Family Affair: The Real Lives of Black Single Mothers* (Kitchen Table: Women of Color Press, 1986).

15. Although the 1984 CLUW Convention reaffirmed support for women's reproductive freedom, the CLUW leadership obviously may choose when publicly to endorse reproductive rights. An organization of women trade unionists working *within* the structures of the AFL–CIO, CLUW is one of the most integrated women's organizations: 50 percent of its leadership and membership are women of color. Although it has/had tremendous potential for mobilizing rank-and-file trade-union women, CLUW is today, for the most part, little different from the highly bureaucratized union organizations of which it is a part. For a history of CLUW, see Diane Balser, *Sisterhood and Solidarity* (Boston: South End Press, 1987).

16. For a discussion of alternatives based on recent U.S. experience, see Phil Kwik and Kim Moody, "Dare to Struggle: Lessons from P-9"; Frank Bardacke, "Watsonville: A Mexican Community on Strike"; Eric Mann, "Keeping GM Van Nuys Open"; all in Mike Davis and Michael Sprinker, eds., *Reshaping the U.S. Left: Popular Struggles in the 1980s* (New York: Verso, 1988).

17. The grassroots organizing of women within the Nicaraguan agricultural workers' union (ATC) is one example. In addition to increasing the education and involvement of women in the union, and putting demands like paid maternity leave on the bargaining agenda, this project sent delegates to

national women's conferences and to international meetings. At the request of the Nicaraguan women, feminists in Spain mobilized to send Spanish language pamphlets about contraception, contraceptives, and instruments for performing abortion to women in the ATC (personal communication from Norma Chinchilla). On the potential and problems of working-class and peasant women in the Nicaraguan revolution, see Maxine Molyneux, "Mobilization Without Emancipation? Women's Interests, the State, and Revolution in Nicaragua," *Feminist Studies* 7, no. 2 (Summer 1985).

18. For some examples of women's impact on the trade-union movement in the U.S. and Canada, see *Feminizing Unions: Labor Research Review* 11 (Spring 1988). For an instance of the impact of women's networks on workplace organizing, see Karen Brodkin Sacks, *Caring by the Hour* (Urbana and Chicago: University of Illinois Press, 1988).

19. I wouldn't deny the historical importance of community ties—friendship, kinship, neighborhood—to men's trade-union militancy. But I would argue that these reinforcing ties outside the workplace and the union hall were both in practice and subjectively created in a separate and exclusive male sphere.

20. Some feminists, drawing on the experience of the Soviet Union and Eastern Europe, are sceptical that providing more social supports to working women will have much impact on gender inequality. This is an issue that can't be settled here. But I would make three general points: (1) these societies in fact are still very far from freeing households substantially from the burdens of providing for their members; (2) the lack of political freedom in general tremendously inhibits the self-organization of women; (3) the bureaucratic and coercive character of public life leads to a romanticization of family and private life as domains of freedom, undermining women's aspirations for alternatives to traditional gender roles.

21. For an elaboration of this point, see Chapter 4.

22. On this point, see especially Michèle Barrett and Mary McIntosh, *The Antisocial Family* (London: Verso, 1984), chap. 4.

23. See, for example, Chapter 7 above; Barrett and McIntosh, *The Anti-social Family*; Judith Stacey, "Should the Family Perish?", *Socialist Review* 14, no. 2 (March–April 1984); Martha A. Ackelsberg, "Sisters or Comrades? The Politics of Friends and Families," in Irene Diamond, ed., *Families, Politics, and Public Policy* (New York: Longman, 1983); Denise Riley, "The Serious Burdens of Love?: Some Questions on Childcare, Feminism and Socialism," in Lynne Segal, ed., *What Is To Be Done About the Family?* (Harmondsworth: Penguin, 1983).

Chapter 10

The Best of Times, the Worst of Times: U.S. Feminism Today

Here is one picture of feminism and women's experience in the contemporary United States: women advancing up the ladder in professions, public administration and management; making steady inroads into political office; changing attitudes and cultural images; winning legislation against discriminatory practices in education and employment; feminist scholarship transforming academic disciplines; local and national women's organizations effectively defending many different women's interests.

Here is another: deteriorating conditions in women's lives; enduring male domination in the home and outside it. Violence against women persists, perhaps is even increasing; sado-masochistic representations of heterosexuality are more widespread than ever; increasing numbers of women are impoverished; occupational sex-segregation continues; previous gains, like abortion rights and affirmative action, are under attack.

Both pictures are true.[1] What, then, can we conclude about the future? Can feminism be rebuilt as a mass movement? Are the recent mobilizations in defense of abortion rights the beginning of a third wave? Or are they an exception, the echo of past militancy in a backlash era? Will the fate of second-wave feminism be the same as the first: almost from the moment of greatest victory—winning the vote in 1920—feminism was politically marginalized over four long decades. One way to understand what has happened to feminism and to assess strategic possibilities is to locate ourselves in the frame of a broader historic transformation of the gender order and the political economy of U.S. capitalism. This transition is very like that of the 1920s, when previous decades of capitalist restructuring and political conflict congealed in a new cultural and social order which selectively incorporated feminist aspirations, while undermining the social base of feminist organization. It was left to the second wave of feminism to complete the central political project of the first wave: to attack and dismantle the web of discriminatory laws and exclusionary social norms which reproduced women's subordination in family, economic, and political life. This was the second wave's historic victory and its enduring legacy. Moreover, unlike the 1920s, in our time feminist organization has been institutionalized, not marginalized. And while there is no longer a radical, grassroots movement, it is still possible to mobilize women, particularly around issues of discrimination or violation of individual rights. In 1992, three-quarters of a million marched in Washington to demonstrate support for abortion rights. Thousands of women met in protest against the Senate's disregard of Anita Hill's testimony about her sexual harassment by Supreme Court Justice nominee Clarence Thomas.[2]

Women in an Epoch of Restructuring

It is clear that we are living through a period of capitalist restructuring on a world scale which has both accelerated the unraveling of the old gender order (for instance, through the disappearance of "family wage" jobs for men) and exposed the limits of the liberal-feminist project. While the gains of the second wave are still hotly contested by a reactionary right bent on restoring the old patriarchal system, during the 1980s feminist demands for equality were increasingly institutionalized and culturally incorporated as women's right to compete and contract free from limitations imposed on account of our sex. Assumptions about natural gender differences in intellect, character, or capacities have been widely challenged. Yet within the context of a rapidly restructuring economy and the (related) political collapse of welfare-state liberalism, the emerging gender order has brought new hardships as much as new freedoms to the majority of women. Increasing autonomy is matched by increasing economic insecurity; economic independence is purchased at the cost of doing a double day; greater personal freedom is accompanied by a frightening vulnerability to exploitation and abuse.

The dilemmas facing women in the new gender order for the most part cannot be resolved through expanding anti-discrimination legislation and enforcement, no matter how broadly sex discrimination is defined. Required solutions—significant redistribution of wealth, reordered priorities in and expansion of government spending and increased regulation of employer practices—directly threaten powerful capitalist interests. Feminist organizations, despite their success in defending and extending the accomplishments of the second wave, have here been frustrated at almost every turn. Second-wave feminism has come up against a deep impasse that stretches across U.S. politics, rooted in the decline of working-class organization in the face of the employers' offensive and the increasing centralization and mobility of capital.

In the 1960s and 1970s it was possible for feminism to make gains alongside a trade unionism that was for the most part bureaucratic and demobilized. Today, feminism's fate is tied to the fate of trade unionism and other forms of collective resistance to corporate capital. But the organizations for mobilizing such resistance are weaker than ever before. Competitive demands in an internationalizing economy have generated capitalist attacks on working people and their institutions. Meanwhile, the Democratic Party has no strategy for or interest in confronting corporate capital, and faces no pressure from below that might even push it in that direction. Feminist organizations, along with the other interest groups—trade unions, civil rights organizations, environmental and peace groups—have tended to rely on building relationships with the Democrats in order to wrest concessions from the state. Now they find themselves tied to a party abjectly capitulating to capital. And they are powerless to stop the attack on working-class standards of living and the rollback of pro-working-class state interventions demanded by corporate capital in order to protect profit in an intensely competitive global economy.[3] Working-class women and communities of color have born the brunt of this assault. The solution to the political impasse facing feminism cannot come from feminists alone. It will require a serious and disruptive challenge to capital, a broad and militant "rainbow movement," including new, more social and political forms of trade-union struggle and national political organization independent of the Democratic Party.

Capitalism and the Gender Division of Labor

From the founding of the Republic, women's subordination (like precapitalist exploitation) was organized through explicit constraints legitimated by an ideology of inherent gender differences in talents and capacities. Women's assignment to the care of dependent individuals within the private household and their exclusion from public life were reproduced actively and directly by various exclusionary rules and practices (governing education, political participation, and the labor market) as well as marriage and property law and legalized male violence against women. The historic victory of first-wave feminism was to make women citizens. The historic victory of the second wave has been to make women fully free sellers of our own labor-power, by substantially dismantling the legal and normative edifice which had mandated women's subservience in marriage, denied us rights in our bodies and reproductive capacity, and legitimated our economic marginalization. This victory has helped to force a reorganization of the gender order— materially, culturally, politically. In the emerging gender order, women's subordination continues to rest on a gender division of labor, but one that is reproduced (like the exploitation of wage labor) "behind the backs" of women through an ostensibly gender-neutral system of contractual relationships—in education and employment, in sexual intimacy, in household formation. Women are more free to negotiate their relationships and responsibilities with employers and with men. And some—indeed a significant stratum of affluent, well-educated women— strike relatively good bargains. On the other hand, most women negotiate from a one-down position.

Increasing opportunities are real—evidenced in the widening *variation* in women's life chances across race and class lines. But real, too, are the constraints that shape women's individual choices: most fundamentally, the continued location of primary responsibility for caregiving in family households. In a capitalist economy, households are not only arenas of privacy, intimacy, and sexual pleasure. They are also the basic unit of survival. Through pooling resources of money and labor-time in households adults meet their own and others' routine and extraordinary needs for care. Solidarities formed through intimacy and sexual pleasure are relied upon to cement the social relationships through which material and emotional support are shared.[4] Capitalist societies vary in the extent to which the state subsidizes households or provides services to supplement household responsibility. In the U.S., with one of the most undeveloped of welfare states, households are left substantially on their own to negotiate the market. Women's relatively lower wages make reasonable a family strategy based on a gender division of labor in which men specialize in income earning, while "helping out" around the house, and women specialize in caregiving while also working for pay.[5]

But even in relatively wealthy countries with strong social-democratic parties, state provision is still not extensive enough (nor the normal workday short enough) to undercut the logic of a gender division of labor in the household.[6] Moreover, economic downturns always lead to cutbacks in state provision, especially in labor-intensive services (education; health care; childcare; care of the elderly, mentally ill, disabled) and services which meet the needs of the least politically well-mobilized constituencies—in other words, those services most important to women and mothers.

Of course, the gender division of labor is not simply the outcome of rational responses by men and women to material difficulties. It also reflects women's and men's interests and desires. Women's attachment to motherhood and their sense of responsibility for elderly parents, thus their decisions about balancing education and paid work with other commitments, are socially, not just economically, shaped. Women enter into and stay in relationships with men for reasons other than economic survival, although the hardships of single parenthood and impoverished old age also shape these decisions. Men resist sharing domestic work and women's entry into their occupations not only to protect economic and political advantage but also to defend the boundaries of gendered identities. Male violence against women and the fear of male violence constrains women's choices about occupations, about living singly, and shape the compromises they make in their relationships with men. The institutions of compulsory heterosexuality close off possibilities of finding intimacy, love, mutual support, shared parenting with women rather than with men.

While breaking down the gender division of labor will require changes across this whole spectrum, a substantial reorganization of how we meet human needs for care and nurture is fundamental. Otherwise, individual and family survival strategies will tend to reproduce a gender division of labor in the household, while women's greater domestic responsibilities will continue to disadvantage them in the labor market. This disadvantage has an individual and a collective aspect. At the individual level, women make strategic choices that limit their educational investment, interrupt their labor-force participation, direct them into less competitive and highly rewarded areas of occupations and into part-time employment.[7] At the collective level, the double day undermines women's capacities for self-organization in both economic and political arenas, accounting at least in part for the persistently lower wages of female-dominated occupations. Historically, women's rates of unionization have been much lower than men's.[8] Female-dominated professions have not achieved the sort of political clout that has enabled male-dominated professions such as medicine, law, and engineering to use the state to protect their interests as employees as well as entrepreneurs.[9]

Straight, direct sex discrimination persists throughout the economy and in the political system, but it is increasingly contested. Indeed, the existence of that contest—in the absence of a broader and more successful assault on the structural bases of the gender division of labor—reinforces the illusion that, because women have more opportunities in education and jobs, the persistence of a gender division of labor must reflect their own choices and preferences. The visible stratum of successful women who have broken into male jobs and negotiated more egalitarian relationships with men further confirms the illusion. Even when the problems posed by women's entry into paid work—their double day, their low wages and poverty, the widespread "crisis in caregiving"—are recognized, this only generates endless debates in politics, on talk shows, in books and advice columns about the pros and cons of different individual survival strategies, often pitting "career-first" women against those who put "family first." Collective strategies are rarely part of the discussion, because possibilities for fundamentally shifting the terms of women's choices appear to be so remote. In this situation, it is not surprising that second-wave feminists, looking back at the 1920s, are haunted by the fear that another forty years must pass before the contradictions of the new gender order explode into a radical movement of organized resistance.

Does History Repeat Itself?

In many ways the 1980s were like the 1920s: periods of political reaction and capitalist innovation. With capital on the offensive against the working class, both decades saw fundamental economic dislocations, increasing affluence and misery, celebration of hyperconsumerism and self-seeking individualism, creating a sense of spiritual and political disorientation in the majority and a marginalized left. In both decades working-class organization was decimated by transforming productive structures: the skilled craft unions undermined by mass-production industries, the industrial unions by an increasingly mobile and internationalized corporate capital. In both periods the organization of gender—actual relationships between men and women as well as their cultural representation—changed dramatically. And in both instances, this reorganization of gender was consistent with economic reorganization while also responding to women's struggles against the old gender order.[10]

Turn-of-the-century political and social movements, including various feminist currents, challenged the nineteenth-century cult of true womanhood, opening the door for another feminine ideal—the "new woman" of the 1920s. In contrast to the purity, piety, and asexuality of middle-class Victorian women excluded from public life, the "new women" of the white middle class entered higher education, lived independently and worked in female professions, at least until marriage, were encouraged to seek heterosexual pleasure within companionship marriage, and offered fulfillment through modern wifehood and motherhood, now reconfigured as parallels to male careers. Through informed consumption of professional expertise and new commodities the modern housewife/mother could participate in the modern world. In the 1920s, rising middle-class incomes and the rapid expansion of consumer goods made it possible for white middle-class women to live the new lifestyle; but the new woman was not simply corporate capital's creation, however much she was shaped by its drive toward mass consumption. This modernization of domesticity incorporated as well as defeated middle-class women's aspirations for equal participation in education, employment, and politics.[11]

Second-wave feminism developed within the same economic order— a powerful and expanding U.S. economy centered in mass production and mass consumption—whose emergence contributed to the demise of first-wave feminism in the 1920s. The post-Second World War economic boom based in U.S. world hegemony brought accelerated demand for middle-class women's employment in health, education, and social services (supported by expanded public spending) and encouraged their re-entry into wage work.[12] The expansion of public higher education encouraged their entry into colleges and universities.[13] Women professionals were key players in mainstream feminist organizations, while the radical organizations of the second wave found a social base, facilities, and institutional resources in and around colleges and universities.[14]

The "new woman" of the 1980s, the all too familiar superwoman, like her counterpart of the 1920s, responded to the new opportunities and experiences of affluent middle-class white women and selectively incorporated feminist aspirations. She also reflected the changing realities of working-class women's lives due to the dislocations of a restructuring capitalist economy. The long-term demand for female labor, declining wages of working-class men, and the rise of industries marketing downscale as well as upscale services, further commodifying personal life, have increased the number of mothers working a double day. The new gender order promises to transcend the oppression of the male-breadwinner nuclear family and the gender division of labor in private and public life. In place of gender roles legitimated on biological grounds, the modern ideal family is made up of freely contracting autonomous individuals negotiating exchanges to meet each other's material, emotional, and sexual needs and to care for their children. Women (and men) can make their own identities, competing on the labor market and choosing lifestyles, limited only by talent, drive, personal resources and the ability to calculate the timing of marriage, motherhood, and career moves. The reality, of course, is a bit different: the drudgery of a double day, the impoverishment of single parenthood, the emptiness of identities realized in expanded consumption are hardly liberation. But if the new gender order makes promises that will not be delivered, the question remains whether, as in the period from the 1920s to the 1960s, women will experience the lived contradictions of gender arrangements as personal failures rather than as issues to be resolved by collective action.[15]

Yet, even in this worst of times, U.S. feminism has neither been forced underground nor definitively marginalized as in the 1920s. No longer a social movement, feminism can still mobilize women in a way that would never have been possible in the 1920s (or the 1930s, 1940s or 1950s, for that matter). Demonstrations for the ERA held simultaneously in Washington, D.C. and Los Angeles in March 1986 mobilized a hundred thousand women. Recent marches in the Capitol to defend legal abortion had huge turnouts of six hundred to seven hundred and fifty thousand—the largest women's rights demonstrations ever held in this country.

The difference between first- and second-wave feminism lies in this: second-wave feminism has made the transition from a social movement to a broadly institutionalized and effective interest group. First-wave feminism did not. First-wave feminism was organized through middle-class women's female world of educational, charitable, social, and religious activities. The networks built in that female world were translated into political organization and action. Leadership came from well-educated women, often with inherited money, some married, many single, who had been excluded from the political and professional organizations through which middle-class men sought to secure their interests. These "independent" women had been forced to build their own institutional base: women's colleges, settlement houses, charitable organizations, and professional associations.

By the 1920s, this female world had been fundamentally undermined by the semi-incorporation of middle-class women as a subaltern group in education, professions and political life and by the changing conditions in the lives of middle-class married women. As middle-class wives and mothers moved from producing to consuming, from providing services such as medical care to purchasing them, they relied less on the reciprocal helping relationships around which so much of middle-class women's social life had turned. "Volunteerism" brought middle-class women out of their increasingly privatized and self-sufficient family households but in the service of their husbands' and children's advancement. In the "modernization" of separate spheres, middle-class women lost the institutions that had nurtured their self-organization, but retained their economic dependence on men.[16]

The legacy of second-wave feminism—as well as the social and economic changes that produced it and that it helped create—have been very different. Women's broad integration into paid work and their increasing access to independent income has created a pool of financial and political resources to support a "women's lobby," a vast array of feminist organizations representing "women's interests" in bourgeois politics. In addition to the explicitly political feminist organizations, such as the National Organization for Women and the National Women's Political Caucus, contemporary middle-class professionals and women workers have organized around their interests as wage-earning women. Trade unions, professional associations, Women's Studies programs in colleges and universities, social-service organizations, women's bookstores, bars and coffee shops, provide an infrastructure for information sharing, education, and mobilization. Feminism is no longer a mass movement based on grassroots, local, voluntary political activism. But women organized to advocate for women are part of the political scene to a degree unprecedented in our history.

Moreover, compared even to the height of the feminist movement from the late 1960s through the mid 1970s, the self-organization of women reaches more deeply into the ranks of working-class women and women of color, especially through the feminization of the trade unions, although the majority, even of unionized women, are not active.[17] While mothers and especially single mothers are doubly burdened, small families and delayed childbearing have increased the pool of working-class and middle-class women who can participate.[18] Feminists may be on the defensive and they will certainly lose battles, but they simply cannot be driven from the field.[19]

Feminism in Popular Consciousness

Although poll data always have to be taken with a grain of salt, public opinion surveys seem to demonstrate strong support not only for feminist ideas but for women's self-organization. In 1985 the majority of women felt they did not have an equal chance with men in becoming business executives or entering prestige professions. More women felt that they were excluded from leadership responsibilities (46 percent) in 1985 than in 1970 (31 percent). In 1974, 64 percent of women had agreed that being taken care of by a loving husband was more important than making it on one's own, compared to 48 percent of women in 1985. Although most women are working to support themselves and their families, the majority (66 percent) would continue to work even if they didn't have to. A marriage where husband and wife share responsibilities is preferred to the male-breadwinner family by 57 percent of all women.[20] But many women are also conscious of men's resistance to this idea: more than half agreed that "men are willing to let women get ahead, but only if women still do all the housework at home."[21]

These national averages hide apparent generational differences. Younger women seem to be more supportive of the women's movement and more confident about their own futures than older women. For instance, women aged eighteen to twenty-nine working full time were as likely as men their age to call their work a career. Women under forty-five were less likely than women over forty-five to believe that "men still run almost everything and usually don't include women when important decisions are being made." About 25 percent of the younger women, far more than in older groups, agreed that "nothing is slighted when a woman combines work, marriage and children."[22] And even more of the women under forty-five (71 percent) than over forty-five (60 percent) agree that "a strong women's movement to push for changes that benefit women" is necessary.[23]

If most women support a "women's movement" and the majority do not want to return to the traditional family, they are ambivalent about the changes that have taken place. Almost half of the women interviewed in a *New York Times* poll felt that "women have had to give up too much in order to gain better jobs and more opportunities than twenty years ago." Working women feel extremely pressed, especially when they work full time and have children. Sixty-eight percent of wives who work full time and 84 percent of those with children under eighteen said they did not have enough time for themselves. A large majority of these women said they, not their husbands, did most of the housework and childcare and 42 percent felt their husbands did less than their fair share of chores.[24]

As working women have become a larger and more differentiated market, as women stay single longer and have more discretionary income, as "niche marketing" strategies become more effective and media outlets more variegated, representations of gender have also become more diverse. Jockeying for the "career woman's" attention and her disposable income, advertisers support television shows that feature self-sufficient single working women and nontraditional families (some have even experimented with positive depictions of lesbian and gay relationships). On the other hand, more traditional images of male and female sexuality are displayed in men's magazines and ads on televised sports programs, while women's anxieties about their bodies and sexual attractiveness are exploited almost everywhere. Films with very different representations of gender are produced and marketed with specialized audiences in mind.[25] This cacophony of images creates a far more diverse popular culture than the hegemonic celebration of female domesticity and middle-class family life that helped to marginalize feminism after 1920. Competing representations reflect and reinforce the contestation over gender identities that second-wave feminism opened up.

Six new national women's magazines were founded in the 1970s to reach the new, younger, and more affluent working woman. They were joined in the 1980s by more than fifty new regional women's publications, such as *New York Woman*, targeting professional/managerial women.[26] The names of the new national journals evoke their content and the images they project: *Self, Savvy Woman, Working Woman, Working Mother, New Woman*, and of course *Ms.*—compared to the "seven sisters," the traditional women's magazines: *Family Circle, Woman's Day, Good Housekeeping, Better Homes and Garden, Ladies' Home Journal, Redbook* and *McCalls*. The median personal income of the new magazines' readers in the late 1980s ranged from $16,254 to $20,574, compared to readers of the seven sisters, who earned from $14,414 to $16,079 on average.[27]

Most women still read the traditional women's magazines (which have a combined circulation of forty million compared to three million for the newer magazines).[28] But the seven sisters also reflect the new realities of women's lives and shifting constructions of womanhood.[29] *Good Housekeeping* began its "New Traditionalist" campaign ("for the contemporary woman who has made a new commitment to the traditional values [husband, children, home] that some people thought were old-fashioned") by glorifying the past: "My mother really knew what she was doing." But the campaign quickly evolved to feature well-educated women who have quit "fast track" for slower-track careers: working as consultants, or establishing their own business in order better to combine career with motherhood, hardly a return to the traditional family. A recent ad showed a divorced and remarried mother working full time in a traditionally male blue-collar craft job (another unrealistic image, given that only 2 per cent of those jobs are held by women).[30] While the seven sisters counsel women to deal with conflicts between waged and unpaid work by "putting family first," the new magazines promise "career women" that market forces are on their side: companies will become more flexible, offer more benefits such as childcare, in order to hold on to their highly valued, highly educated and experienced women workers.[31]

Class Divisions and Feminist Politics

Combining work and motherhood is an issue for all women in the U.S., but women's resources for coping differ widely by race and class. In fact, over the 1980s the disparities in the lives and life chances of women grew.[32] Educated women reaped the benefits of the struggle for equal access to education and employment that feminists waged in the 1970s. The restructuring economy created increased demand for workers in professional and managerial jobs and expanding places in professional schools. But without other changes, economic restructuring alone would simply have increased opportunities for men in management and the professions.

Instead, higher-education institutions were forced to drop their sex bars. In 1973–74 women constituted 2 percent of graduating dentists, 7 percent of Masters of Business Administration, 11 percent of law school and medical school graduates. By 1986, they were 23 percent of graduating dentists, 31 percent of medical school graduates and of MBAs and almost 39 percent of law school graduates.[33] Since these schools are major gatekeepers, equal access to education helped to promote greater access to higher-paid occupations.

Affirmative action and anti-discrimination legislation also directly opened formerly all-male areas to women. "Blind auditions," in which performers play behind a screen, have helped women into the major U.S. orchestras, from 18 percent of the players in the late 1960s to 28 percent in 1985; women accounted for 47 percent of players in metropolitan orchestras.[34] In 1972, 11 percent of local television news anchors were women, compared to 36 percent in 1982; and in 1985, 11 percent of news directors were women, up from 1 percent in 1972.[35] Between 1975 and 1986, women moved from 15 percent to 39 percent of all employed economists; from 15 percent to 34 percent of computer systems analysts; from 7 percent to 18 percent of all lawyers; 1.8 percent to 4.4 percent of dentists. In 1975 women were 27 percent of all professional/managerial workers, and 40 percent in 1985; in 1975 women were 22 percent of all managers, and 54 percent in 1986. The proportion of all women workers in professional and managerial employment rose from 27 percent to 32 percent, while for men the proportion declined from 34.6 percent to 29.4 percent. And this increase was not due simply to expanding employment in traditional women's professions: schoolteaching, social work, nursing.[36] The average earnings of professional/managerial women increased faster than those of professional/managerial men between 1975 and 1986: 10.9 percent compared to 8.3 percent.[37] It appears that women took a larger share of the better-paid professional/managerial jobs in the 1980s.[38]

Relative to the men of their class, educated women in upper-income jobs have hardly achieved equality. Women doctors and lawyers are more likely to be in the lower-paid and less prestigious specialities and less likely to be in private practice where the most money is to be made.[39] Women television news reporters get less airtime than their male peers.[40] In general, women are not well represented in positions that wield power over men. Thus, while women are almost half of all metropolitan orchestras, there are almost no women conductors. While 25 percent of all associates in law firms are women, only 6 percent are partners.[41] Only 3 percent of top management positions in large corporations are held by women. Moreover, a large proportion of top women managers do not have children, compared to a very small proportion of men.[42] Women are hitting their heads on a "glass ceiling" that subtly or directly stops their rise up the hierarchy. In addition to outright discrimination and men's resistance to putting women into positions of authority,[43] women are having problems competing equally with men because of the persisting gender division of labor and women's continuing responsibility for children (and other family members).

In spite of these barriers, the proportion of women workers who are highly paid increased dramatically, especially in the 1980s. At the end of the 1970s, 6.8 percent of all full-time women workers were earning over $30,000. By 1986, 10.3 percent (2.9 million women) earned more than $30,000, adjusted for inflation. (For the workforce as a whole, 25 percent earned over $30,000.) At the other end of the spectrum, almost 18 percent of women working full time earned less than $10,000— about the same proportion as at the end of the 1970s.[44] In addition, 28 percent of employed women worked part time, and earned even less— about one-third of full-time women workers' pay. The reciprocal of increased opportunity for highly educated women over the 1980s was the rapid growth of contingent work (part-time, temporary, and contract employment without benefits) primarily in retail and service industries.[45] Following a historic pattern, women of color are overrepresented among the low-paid workers who fill the service and retail sales jobs which expanded in the 1980s to meet new needs generated by women's increased participation in paid labor (e.g. supermarkets and department stores open seven nights a week, fast-food outlets, childcare, nursing homes).[46]

While the career paths of professional/managerial women might not match those of the most successful men, hitting your head on a glass ceiling is not the same as falling into the basement. Women in the higher professions and upper management can use their high salaries to hire domestic help, and their relatively good bargaining positions to negotiate with employers for paid maternity leave and quality childcare.[47] Divorce and single parenthood may bring downward mobility but not descent into poverty.[48]

The differential experiences and resources of women workers are reflected in the market. There are upscale and downscale versions of fast food and frozen food, childcare, health care and business wear. For example, in 1988 fees at Harvard University's seven childcare centers averaged $750 a month, while the average clerical worker earned only $1,500.[49] Management employees at Campbell Soup Company's headquarters office, dissatisfied with the quality of childcare provided by Kindercare, a for-profit chain, forced the company to set up an in-house program. The new program provided more parental input, smaller group sizes, and increased pay for staff. Many working parents lack the clout of these managers. About 25 percent of all children under five in daycare are in childcare centers. For-profit chains like Kindercare—which operates 1,700 centers with low wages, high children-to-staff ratios and high turnover—are taking an increasing share of the market.[50]

Given their class location and their experience, it is not surprising that many professional/managerial women continue to provide money and personnel for liberal-feminist organizations and campaigns.

Emblematic of this group is former Labor Secretary Elizabeth Dole, who, even as the Bush administration was opposing legislation to strengthen anti-discrimination claims, announced that the Labor Department would undertake a "glass ceiling initiative" to speed promotion of women and minorities into top corporate posts.[51] However, this effort had little to offer the working-class and poor women whose conditions of life had been deteriorating so rapidly over the 1980s. Recognizing that many working women require more than a "level playing field," other mainstream feminist politicians and organizations have articulated a "work/family" reform agenda. These "social-welfare" feminists argue that government ought to provide women with resources as well as protecting them from discrimination. Their political perspective reflects their personal experience and occupational interests. Women trade-union staffers and the vast numbers of women employed in education, health, and social services which depend directly or indirectly on state funding, are the base of social-welfare feminism.[52] Directors of childcare centers, social workers, teachers, nurses, administrators, advocate for their programs in the name of the working-class women and women of color whom they serve.

Although social-welfare feminists appear to speak to the interests of working-class women and women of color, their worldview and strategic orientation place them squarely within a liberal not a socialist (or social-democratic) political tradition.[53] Nonetheless, liberal-feminism and social-welfare feminist approaches differ. They each draw on different aspects of that complex and in many ways internally contradictory political phenomenon, U.S. liberalism.

Liberal-feminism rests on the strand of liberalism that looks primarily to the regulatory arm of the state to ensure free and fair competition. This aspect of liberal thought has both a radical and a conservative side. Women's claim to "individual liberty" as a fundamental right has been used to challenge patriarchal privilege and power. The demand on the state to guarantee women's right to bodily autonomy has undergirded campaigns for legalizing abortion and criminalizing male violence against women within marriage as well as outside it. Feminists have been very creative in expanding the definition of sex discrimination to include unequal pay for work of comparable value, sexual harassment, and denigrating representations of women (in speech, text, or pictures) in workplaces and schools. Many working-class women have benefited from successful feminist campaigns for abortion rights, affirmative action programs in education, job training, and employment.

On the other hand, a politics which focuses *exclusively* on discriminatory treatment is inevitably class- and race-biased because it ignores women's differential resources for competing in the market. Liberal-feminists do not necessarily support an expanded welfare state. A survey of women voters "displeased by defeat of the ERA" (i.e. feminists of some sort) found that women from high-income families and white women were more likely than women from lower-income families and Black women to think that too much was spent on welfare and food stamps and that government ought not to guarantee jobs.[54]

Although liberal-feminism is clearly opposed by the reactionary right, which wants the state to legislate traditional patriarchal gender relations, it is quite compatible with the other major wing of U.S. conservatism: the "moderates" of the Republican Party. Over the past decade, feminist claims to equal treatment have been increasingly incorporated into their modernizing right discourse, which opposes "status-based" discrimination as a violation of market principles and accepts government intervention where necessary to guarantee meritocracy and equality of opportunity.[55]

Social-welfare feminists share the liberal-feminist commitment to individual rights and equal opportunity, but go further. Like the welfare-state liberalism of which it is a part, social-welfare feminism looks to the state to compensate for the inequalities generated by the capitalist market. Seeking to address the problems of working women, to ease the burden of the double day, and to improve women's and especially mothers' position on the labor market, social-welfare feminists call for expanded state programs for paid parental leave, universal health care, and quality childcare. All of these initiatives have been pretty well defeated (although the health care reform story isn't over yet). In the current period, the order of the day is welfare-state contraction, not expansion. Social-welfare feminists' major strategy—contesting for influence within the Democratic Party apparatus and electing sympathetic Democratic Party candidates to office—has left them dependent on this party and powerless to counter the Democrats' abandonment of the New Deal. While advocating for working-class women and women of color, social-welfare feminism has failed to alleviate the hardships so many women face. Not surprisingly, the majority of working-class women and women of color do not see political activism as an avenue for improving their own lives. They hold on to feminist aspirations and, like spectators at a football game, can be roused from time to time to cheer their side. But until they come onto the field to play, victories will be few and far between.

The Women's Lobby

Social-welfare feminist and liberal-feminist currents are represented on the political scene by a vast and extremely diverse network of organizations that has been called the "women's lobby." Because the courts are such a central avenue for legal change in the U.S., institutionalized liberal-feminism includes by now well-recognized and well-funded organizations working the judicial system, primarily by litigating precedent-setting cases.[56] While they depend on individual donations as well as corporate and foundation contributions, these organizations do not mobilize constituencies. They raise funds through membership and mailing lists of their parent organization and/or other organizations in the lobby.

Like other interest groups, organizations of the women's lobby work the legislative system: they contribute to election campaigns, identify issues for legislative action, draft proposed laws, write briefs and gather expert testimony, hire lobbyists to track the bills, mobilize constituencies to influence the vote. At the national level they have entry to Congress through the Congressional Caucus for Women's Issues and a network of experienced lobbyists and legislative "insiders."[57] At state and federal levels, organizations and their lobbyists form ad hoc coalitions whose membership shifts with different legislative efforts.[58]

Technical expertise for developing policy and proposed legislation is provided by nonprofit education and research organizations funded through direct-mail appeals to individuals and grants from foundations and other women's organizations. In addition, there is at least one research/policy organization for every women's issue imaginable.[59] Agencies providing services to women are organized nationally in order to lobby Congress for favorable legislation and federal funds.[60]

Membership organizations are the major route through which women are recruited to send money to candidates, postcards and petitions to Congress supporting legislation, and are mobilized for public action: lobby days at the state capital, testimony before legislative committees, protests before the city council, even sometimes marches and rallies. These organizations include far more than the explicitly feminist political groups—the National Organization for Women, the National Women's Political Caucus, and the National Abortion Rights Action League, for example—formed in the second wave. Many "women's" organizations such as the American Association of University Women, the YWCA, United Methodist Women, and the National Council of

Negro Women, participate in coalitions and on a broad range of political issues.[61] While organized primarily for educational, social, and charitable activities, they also mobilize members for political actions, principally lobbying legislators and working to elect sympathetic candidates.[62]

In addition to formal organizations, informal networks provide the personnel and financial resources which are crucial to building constituencies at state, local, and national levels. Women professionals and administrators in government agencies and in associated nonprofit organizations which contract state services use their institutional position to build political networks. Feminists working in educational systems (curriculum integration projects, affirmative action and sex equity in education programs), health care (teenage pregnancy programs, community health-care programs for working-class and minority women), and social service programs directed toward women (job training and publicly funded childcare for single mothers), advocate for women as part of their jobs. They testify at legislative hearings in favor of legislation to expand the funding or mission of their programs, go to city council meetings to lobby for increased funding or to protest cuts in services, lend organizational resources (office space, photocopiers, staff time) to ad hoc coalitions formed around issues. Professional alliances are drawn on to recruit a show of force when programs need to be defended.

The offices and staffs of women's professional and business associations disseminate information and solicit political and financial support.[63] Their major purpose is to advance their professions or women within their professions. Like any other professional association, these organizations engage in politics where they think their own interests are affected. Some organizations take a relatively narrow view of their political interests, concentrating on professional issues such as licencing and practice regulations.[64] But others range more widely. In 1983, for example, representatives from the American Nurses' Association joined those from the Women's Vote Project and the National Abortion Rights Action League to initiate the drive to nominate a woman for vice-president on the 1984 Democratic ticket.[65] In the early 1990s, feminist lawyers organized within the American Bar Association to pass a resolution putting the ABA on record in support of legal abortion.

Of course, the major, visible, feminist organization in the U.S. is the National Organization for Women. During its first decade, NOW was more open, locally controlled, and decentralized than traditional interest-group organizations. Like many of the new second-wave organizations, NOW had no national center and almost no national staff. Local chapters relied on their own funds and volunteers and determined their own political agendas. Following a bruising factional election in 1975, NOW began to reorganize along the lines of mainstream political organizations—ironically, under the leadership of Ellie Smeal, whose faction had come to power with the slogan "Out of the mainstream, into the revolution." The number of officers was reduced, paid staff positions were created, three national offices were consolidated into one—in Washington, D.C. The drive for the ERA, NOW's national priority between 1977 and 1982, also encouraged centralization.

The decision to concentrate so much effort on the ERA reflects key features of NOW's political and strategic orientation. First, NOW prefers to organize around issues that seem to transcend class differences—all women would benefit from writing sexual equality into the Constitution. Second, ERA cuts across political divisions between social-welfare and liberal-feminists and across parties (by the early 1970s both Democratic and Republican parties actively supported passage of the ERA).[66] Third, because the ERA has a broad constituency, the campaign to pass it promised to build NOW membership significantly. At first, the campaign did invigorate local chapters as NOW members organized for ratification in their states. But as the campaign wore on, concentrating on the unratified areas, local activity waned and the national office took over. Money to run campaigns in states that hadn't ratified the Amendment was raised by national direct-mail appeals, not by local chapters. National-level, high-visibility actions, such as the 1978 march in Washington for an extension of the ratification deadline, were controlled and organized by the national office. By the early 1980s, as a result of the push for the ERA, NOW's membership had grown to 220,000, though few were active in local chapters. Following the defeat of the ERA, however, NOW membership declined to about 160,000 in 1988. Then, in 1989, the Supreme Court's anti-abortion-rights *Webster* decision opened a new opportunity for the kind of single-issue nationally orchestrated campaign that NOW prefers. Members and their dues' dollars poured into the organization, raising membership to 270,000 and the budget to $10.6 million.[67] Even so, NOW's activist base remains very small relative to the total membership. Members can be mobilized for single events or actions around highly visible issues, such as the massive demonstrations for abortion rights held between 1989 and 1992. Otherwise, the relationship between members and organizations is similar to that of traditional interest groups—most members pay dues in order to be represented in Washington by paid staff, lobbyists, and sympathetic legislators.

Academic Feminism and Politics

Colleges and universities are still a political resource, teaching feminist ideas to new generations of undergraduates and providing a base for activism. A 1984 survey found that 68 percent of universities and 49 percent of four-year colleges offered Women's Studies courses (courses dealing with women and/or gender). By 1990, among the 3,000 universities and colleges, 621 had established a Women's Studies program.[68] While their numbers continue to grow (there were 276 in 1977), Women's Studies programs tend to be relatively small and marginal academic units.[69] Less than one-third (187) of the programs were permitted to offer an undergraduate degree.[70] On the other hand, most Women's Studies programs are securely established, sufficiently supported by students, administrators and other faculty to withstand the feverish "political correctness" attacks launched by conservatives over the past few years.

Women's Studies programs and campus women's centers politicize students, who in turn provide an audience for feminist ideas and a market for feminist books and journals. This market forged a feminist breakthrough in publishing in the 1970s and early 1980s, the years before academic feminists could get a hearing in the journals and presses controlled by their male peers. The rapid growth of programs and courses has sustained an explosion in the publication of books on women/gender. Academic feminists have established organizations within their disciplines to challenge male domination in the profession and to support feminist scholarship, holding annual conferences and founding feminist journals. These journals, along with several interdisciplinary publications, are crucial supports for feminist scholarship and thus for the careers/jobs of feminist faculty.[71] The interconnected networks of feminist faculty, Women's Studies programs and centers for research on women, professional associations, and publications create the institutional space for feminism in academia. In this space, oppositional and marginalized faculty (radical/socialist/Marxist-feminists, "out" lesbians, women of color) can sometimes find shelter. And from this space, feminist scholarship has begun to permeate the disciplines, graduate education, and undergraduate coursework.[72]

The institutionalization of academic feminism has not come without costs. Women's Studies program offices and women's centers continue to recruit young women into feminist political organizing.[73] However, the process of establishing and defending scholarly legitimacy has tended to depoliticize academic feminism. Research on women and gender is becoming acceptable, so long as it conforms to academic norms. Feminist faculty no longer need to connect to student activism or women's politics outside the academy to defend themselves. Meanwhile, the rewards of collegial recognition, the opportunities for institutional influence and, therefore, the demands of career-building, have increased exponentially. Academic feminists are insulated from the (healthy as well as destructive) challenges around issues of elitism, political relevance and commitment that they were forced to confront in the 1970s. As the lifeworld of feminist scholars narrows to the campus and the profession, their intellectual interests and identities (what it means to be a feminist, to do feminist work) veer away from involvement in radical grassroots organizing or even in mainstream forms of contestation in the public world.[74] For all the calls to pay attention to race/ethnicity and class, many feminist scholars have no connection with working-class women, whether white or women of color. At most, working-class women are subjects of study, almost never comrades in struggle.

For all that, academic feminism retains a political cut. The impact of a feminist teacher on students should not be underestimated. And feminist faculty are far more likely than other faculty to be politically active off-campus. Women academics and professionals contribute their knowledge as consultants and advisors to women's programs and political organizations, helping to develop legislation and policy recommendations and providing the "scientific expertise" necessary to justify and sell reforms: feminist social workers in making the "feminization of poverty" a political issue; feminist economists and sociologists in expanding the concept of equal pay to include equal pay for jobs of "comparable worth"; feminist psychologists in promoting an analysis of domestic and sexual violence that shifts responsibility from women and children to men; feminist lawyers in challenging "equal treatment" divorce policies around custody, alimony, and child support.

Working-class Women and Women of Color

Working-class women and women of color are less well-represented than academics and professionals, but their organizations are another source of institutional support for the women's lobby. Poor people's advocacy groups with women of color in leadership—for example, the National Welfare Rights Organization (whose membership at its height reached ten thousand in 1968) and the National Congress of Neighborhood Women (founded in 1975)—have pushed social-welfare feminist perspectives. The largest organized presence for women of color has been African-American women's groups, which represent a tradition of Black social-welfare feminism that extends back for more than a century.[75] Trade unions with large female memberships as well as caucuses and committees for women within unions are another resource for the "women's lobby." By the mid-1980s women constituted 41 percent of all union members, up from 25 percent ten years earlier (partly because of the rapid loss of jobs in the male-dominated industries with high rates of unionization). At local level, the proportion of women in leadership has increased substantially.[76]

The Coalition of Labor Union Women, with seventy-five chapters and eighteen thousand members, is the most integrated women's organization in the country. Half of CLUW leaders are women of color. In CLUW's early years, an intense battle was waged between socialist-feminist rank-and-filers and women trade-union officials. The socialist-feminists wanted CLUW to accept working women not yet organized into unions as members, to take on its own organizing projects, and to challenge directly the male trade-union officials around union policies and priorities. The women trade-union officials, who won the fight, focused CLUW's efforts on training women for leadership and promoting them into union office.[77]

However, craft unions and unions in heavy industry remain fairly hostile to female leadership and feminist efforts to put "women's issues" on the bargaining table and union legislative agendas. It is in unions with large or majority women memberships that women have been able to fight their way into leadership and force union support for feminist initiatives—affirmative action, comparable worth, hiring women into traditionally male jobs, bargaining for parental leave and other "family benefits." In the 1980s, along with the more progressive (and feminized) unions, CLUW supported comparable worth and a "pro-family" bargaining and legislative agenda which included government subsidies for health care, childcare, parental leave, as well as legislation for pay equity. Worried about alienating the male trade-union leadership, CLUW was at first reluctant to take on "sexual politics." While formally endorsing a pro-choice position, CLUW did little organizing within the unions around abortion rights, gay/lesbian issues, or sexual harassment. However, by the end of the 1980s CLUW's stance had shifted. The 1988 CLUW national convention affirmed support for abortion rights and CLUW initiated a "pro-union, pro-choice" campaign—to argue that women's right to choose is a "union" issue and that unions should go on record for abortion rights. CLUW has expanded work on sexual harassment, providing materials and training women to take the issue into their unions as well as their workplaces and issued a pamphlet entitled *Pride at Work: Organizing for Lesbian and Gay Rights in Unions.*[78]

The Legislative Balance Sheet

The strengths and weaknesses of the women's lobby are reflected in the legislative record of the 1970s and 1980s. Gains were made primarily when legislation did not require significant increases in government spending and focused on issues of discrimination (unequal treatment). They include the Pregnancy Disability Act of 1978, which overturned a Supreme Court ruling that allowed companies to exclude pregnancy from comprehensive insurance plans (although the Act did not require companies without sick leave or health benefits to provide them for pregnant workers); the Child Support Enforcement Amendments of 1984 and 1988, which help ex-wives, especially those who can't afford lawyers, to collect from their ex-husbands the child support awarded them by the courts;[79] the 1974 Equal Credit Opportunity Act and the Business Women's Act of 1988, which require banks to apply the regulations of the 1974 Act to women seeking business loans; the Civil Rights Restoration Act of 1988 and the Civil Rights Bill of 1991 (in coalition with labor and civil rights groups), which had to pass with a two-thirds majority in order to override the president's veto;[80] 1991 legislation permitting (but not requiring) women in the military services to fly combat missions.[81] The failure of the Equal Rights Amendment in the early 1980s, although a significant loss, did not reflect decreased support for anti-discrimination legislation. Requiring three-quarters of the states to ratify, a constitutional amendment can easily be defeated by a minority—in this instance missing the three-quarters mark by only one state. Except for Illinois, which required a three-fifths majority to ratify the amendment, all the states that refused to support the ERA were either rural or had large fundamentalist (or Mormon) minorities.[82]

In comparison to liberal-feminist initiatives, social-welfare feminist legislation addressing work/family dilemmas or women's poverty has languished almost entirely.[83] The Medical and Family Leave Act, which only requires businesses employing more than fifty people (about 5 percent of all firms) to grant *unpaid* leave to employees to care for children or other family members, stalled for failure to override the Reagan/Bush vetoes, but finally passed after Clinton's election. On the other hand, legislation requiring or subsidizing *paid* leave has not even been proposed. The 1990 Act for Better Childcare provided three years of block grants to states to aid some three-quarters of a million children in low-income families, barely scratching the surface of the ten million children under the age of six who need childcare.[84] Legislation that would improve women's incomes such as requiring private employers to pay equal wages for comparable jobs or raising the minimum wage significantly has got nowhere, and proposals to increase welfare benefits were rejected completely in legislation "reforming" the welfare system, the Family Support Act of 1988.[85]

Feminists in Electoral Politics

The National Women's Political Caucus, the National Women's Education Fund (to train women to be candidates and campaign managers), and the National Women's Campaign Fund were created in the early 1970s to increase the number of women candidates, to ensure their election, and to increase the number of women holding appointed as well as elected office. By 1984 there were twenty national and local political action committees (PACs) established to fund women candidates.[86] Over the 1980s the number of women running for and being elected to state and local office increased steadily. By 1991 women were 18 percent of state legislators compared to 4.8 percent in 1974 and 17.1 percent of the mayors of cities larger than thirty thousand compared to 1 percent in 1971.[87] In 1990, a record eighty-five women received major party nomination for state-wide office and fifty of them won election, bringing the number of women holding state-wide offices to a new high of fifty-nine.[88] Thus, by 1992, many more women were poised to challenge for national office. Contrary to the image of the 1992 women candidates as "outsiders," most were experienced activists with political credentials and party connections.[89] On the other hand, 1992 opened unusual opportunities for women candidates: the retirement of many incumbents, redistricting, and a surge of contributions from many women who previously had not donated to electoral campaigns increased the women's chances to win in both primaries and the general election.[90] In 1992, a record 108 women ran for Congress; 47 were elected to the House (an increase of 19 seats), 5 to the Senate (an increase from 2 to 6 seats). Of course, women are still grossly underrepresented in Congress (6 percent of the Senate, 11 percent of the House).[91]

While Democratic Party candidates tend to be social-welfare feminists, Republicans are more likely to be liberal-feminists.[92] Not atypically, the president of ERA Illinois ran for state senate on the Republican ticket in 1982 pledging to work for "public assistance only for those truly in need" and "a balanced state budget." Despite their moderation, from the late 1970s liberal-feminists in the Republican Party were politically marginalized by the right.[93] On the other hand, the party leadership has considered it necessary to increase women's participation in order to compete with the Democrats. During the early 1980s, when anti-feminist politics formed a centerpiece of Republican rhetoric and the official platform, women gained representation at all levels. Forty-eight percent of the delegates at the 1984 Republican Party convention were women—party leaders exerted steady pressure to persuade men originally selected as delegates to step aside for women. The Women's Division of the Republican Party, reconstituted in 1983, sponsored several projects to help develop candidates and prepare speakers. A third of the major speakers at the 1984 Convention were women. In 1988 the proportion of women delegates fell back to 35 percent, perhaps reflecting the increasing control of state party organizations by the right. Serious arm-twisting by the White House in 1992, although apparently begun rather late in the game, did push the number of women delegates back up to 43 percent. Efforts were then made to do better in 1996.[94] In 1986, more women ran for Congress as Republicans than as Democrats (37 against 33).[95] It appears, though, that the political dominance of the right has retarded the emergence of Republican women candidates. By 1992, the number of women Republican candidates for Congress remained at 37, while 71 women ran on the Democratic ticket.[96]

From the early 1970s, NOW, NWPC and NARAL organized to wield influence in the Democratic Party. Rules adopted in 1976 mandated that women would be half of the delegates. At the 1980 convention, 20 percent of the delegates were members of either NOW or NWPC, and by 1984 feminists had clear control of the party platform.[97] In 1988, partly because of rule changes, feminists faced more significant opposition, but they actually won a platform fight with Dukakis forces.[98] However, Dukakis, like many other Democratic candidates, did not campaign on the platform. Following the November election, disaffection with the Dukakis campaign and the party was running deep among NOW militants. In addition to the marginalization of feminist issues in the campaign, the NOW leadership was concerned by the clear commitment of the Democratic leadership to undercut the power of "constituencies" within the Democratic Party and return control to party elites. Molly Yard, president of NOW, caused a brief flap by calling for the formation of a women's party. Yard had no intention of leaving the Democrats, but was attempting to increase feminist leverage by threatening to bolt. NOW members, however, took her proposal seriously. NOW has the most radical and best-organized membership of any of the mainstream feminist organizations. Chapters are relatively small and they vary politically. But chapter activists go to the annual conferences and elect the national officers. Responding to the militants (and perhaps recognizing an opportunity to pressure the Democratic Party from the outside), at the 1989 national conference the NOW leadership supported a resolution to investigate the possibility of forming a third party based on an "Expanded Bill of Rights for the 21st Century."[99] At the NOW annual conference in the summer of 1992, the membership voted to endorse the formation of the "21st Century Party—The Nation's Equality Party" and recommended that NOW Political Action Committee contribute funds. The resolution emphasized that NOW PAC should continue to support feminist candidates of all political parties and that nothing in the resolution "will prevent or inhibit NOW members from endorsing and working for women's rights candidates of other parties, or prevents NOW members from affiliation or activity with other political parties." This wording makes clear that NOW is pursuing an "inside/outside" strategy, which centers on shifting the Democratic Party to the left rather than breaking from it. In the months between the convention and the November elections, NOW PAC ploughed money into the campaigns of Democratic women candidates.[100]

Indeed, the 1992 campaigns raised absolutely unprecedented funds for women candidates. For example, Emily's List (Early Money Is Like Yeast), founded in 1985 to funnel money to women Democratic candidates, raised $1.5 million in 1990 but jumped to $6 million in 1992.[101] The excitement and visibility of the 1992 races arose from women's anger at the Supreme Court's attack on abortion rights, the Senate's arrogant treatment of Anita Hill and confirmation of anti-abortion Supreme Court nominee Clarence Thomas. The urgency of assuring that the Senate would not appoint another anti-choice justice, the importance of preventing state legislatures from passing ever more restrictive abortion bills, the possibility of Congress enacting a Freedom of Choice Act guaranteeing women's access to abortion, encouraged women to run, roused their supporters to action, and significantly improved their chances of winning. The women's lobby has mobilized much more effectively around the threat to abortion rights than it has around other threats to women's lives—the crisis of the inner cities, lack of health care and childcare, low wages—clearly indicating the strength of liberal-feminist and the weakness of social-welfare feminist politics.

Abortion Politics: The Right-wing Backlash

In demanding safe, legal abortion, second-wave feminism appealed to the principle of individual liberty, arguing that women have a funda-mental right to bodily autonomy ("keep your laws off my body") and, more broadly, that control over reproductive capacities is necessary for women to be self-determining. That today so many women understand abortion rights this way is an accomplishment of the women's move-ment. On the other hand, fears about women's sexual and social autono-my have been central to the anti-feminist backlash and the growth of the New Right. The New Right first discovered sexual politics as an organizing tool in their fight against the Equal Rights Amendment, when they argued that the ERA would force women into the draft, legalize homosexual marriages, and guarantee "abortion on demand."[102] STOP ERA mobilized the same sorts of women subsequently so promi-nent in the campaign against legal abortion, whose activists are 80 percent female: housewives/mothers and women with strong religious convictions.[103] While the anti-abortion forces grew in organization and visibility, most women felt their right to abortion would be protected by the Supreme Court's 1973 *Roe* v. *Wade* decision making unconstitutional laws limiting a woman's right to abortion in the first two trimesters of pregnancy.[104] Feminist activism around abortion dropped off, leaving the field open for the anti-abortion forces. The "pro-life" movement made consistent gains in passing restrictive legislation at the state level and, perhaps more importantly, successfully reframed the public dis-course on abortion.

In 1977 Congress passed, and President Carter refused to veto, the Hyde Amendment, which excluded abortion from the free health care available to women on welfare. That law was found constitutional by a pre-Reagan Court. Only thirteen states have passed legislation directing the state government to replace the lost federal funds for poor women's abortions. Parental notification and consent laws, some more punitive than others, were passed in thirty-seven states. Several states passed legislation banning publicly funded hospitals from performing abortions.[105] The Reagan administration promulgated a "gag rule," prohibiting health-care providers who receive federal funds from discussing abortion as an option with pregnant patients.[106] Such laws and regulations predominantly affect young women and poor women who are dependent on public institutions rather than private doctors for their health care. In rural states threats against local doctors have pressured them into refusing to perform abortions. Women have to travel hundreds of miles to the one abortion clinic available, usually in the main city.[107] Blockades, occupations, and bombings of abortion clinics were widespread during the 1980s, and forced clinics to close, again mostly in smaller cities and rural areas.[108] Thus the anti-choice movement has been most successful in denying or limiting access to abortion for the most politically powerless women: rural women, young women, poor women, women of color.

In 1989, the Supreme Court, in *Webster* v. *Reproductive Health Services*, upheld a Missouri law restricting women's access to abortion. Webster was quickly followed by two more decisions (*Hodgson* v. *Minnesota* and *Ohio* v. *Akron Center for Reproductive Health*) which ruled constitutional state laws requiring abortion providers to notify one or both parents of a pregnant woman under eighteen before performing an abortion. With these decisions, the Court signaled that *Roe* v. *Wade* would be progressively undermined and possibly overturned—and this galvanized an outpouring of "pro-choice" activism: marches, rallies, speak-outs, letter-writing campaigns, fundraising from bake-sales to banquets, noisy demonstrations, street theater, and visits to legislators' offices.

Pro-choice forces have demonstrated considerable strength. It seems clear that the current Supreme Court will not strike down *Roe*. In deciding on a restrictive Pennsylvania law, three Reagan/Bush appointees—O'Connor, Kennedy and Souter—joined *Roe* supporters Stevens and Blackmun in striking down a spousal notification provision and argued against overturning *Roe*. The justices acknowledged that their decision was affected by the visible waves of protest. Arguing that an "entire generation has come of age free to assume Roe's concept of liberty in defining the capacity of women to act in society and to make reproductive decisions," a reversal would, they said, cause "significant damage to the stability of the society" as well as "profound and unnecessary damage to the Court's legitimacy." It was therefore unlikely that they would find constitutional the state laws criminalizing abortion due to come before them in 1993. On the other hand, O'Connor, Kennedy and Souter left the door open for many different kinds of restriction, arguing that the states could regulate abortion at any time during pregnancy in order to protect fetal life, even if the effect was to make it "more difficult or more expensive to procure an abortion," as long as the regulation did not impose an "undue burden." This new "undue burden" standard was interpreted to uphold provisions of the Pennsylvania law which required a minor to have parental consent, mandated a 24-hour waiting period and a so-called "informed consent" requirement that physicians must inform a pregnant woman seeking abortion about the medical risks associated with carrying the pregnancy to full term, inform her of the possible detrimental effects of abortion, show her state-prepared materials that include pictures of fetuses, lists of alternatives to abortion, and explain that the father is legally required to assist in supporting the child.[109]

Clinton's victory ensured that no more anti-abortion judges would be appointed to the Court for the next four years, but abortion rights remained very much a live issue in state legislatures and Congress. Anti-abortion forces continue to press for more restrictive laws, while pro-choice forces organize to pass laws guaranteeing abortion rights at state and national level.

It is impossible to predict how these battles will turn out. Pro-choice candidates won in several close gubernatorial races; attempts to pass new anti-abortion legislation were countered in several states; Maryland, Connecticut, and Washington have passed new laws protecting abortion rights in the event *Roe* v. *Wade* is overturned; many legislators who had been anti-abortion or who had avoided taking a position switched to a pro-choice stand. Between June 1989 and December 1990, the number of state legislatures which were likely to vote to keep abortion legal increased dramatically.[110] While the 1992 elections continued this trend, the overall picture remains cloudy at best. In 1990, only twenty states were solidly pro-choice (both houses supporting legal abortion), while seventeen could be expected to pass legislation outlawing abortion if *Roe* v. *Wade* were overturned. In a much larger number of states, the anti-abortion forces seem strong enough to pass parental consent, waiting periods, biased counseling requirements, and other laws restricting access to abortion.

The anti-abortion forces have been so successful because they locate abortion within a broader conservative worldview and political movement. In contrast, over the two decades since *Roe*, the mainstream organizations defending abortion rights have adopted a single-issue strategy. The "right to choose" about motherhood has come to be defined narrowly as the right to abort an unwanted pregnancy. Many have also abandoned the rhetoric of the second-wave movement, which demanded abortion rights as a condition of women's self-determination and sexual autonomy. Instead, they have assimilated the language of the *Roe* decision, which established a constitutional "right to privacy." The campaign of the National Abortion Rights Action League asks: "Who Decides?" Arguing that no other person has the right to make "so personal and private" a decision except the pregnant woman, NARAL, Planned Parenthood, and ACLU hope to appeal to the widely held conviction that individuals should be protected from interference by the state in private life. This rhetorical shift is problematic for many reasons, not least of which is that the ideal of "family privacy" can be used to shield men from scrutiny about their sexual and physical abuse of women and children.[111] Other mainstream women's organizations, prominently the National Organization for Women and the Fund for the Feminist Majority, have been more willing to confront the right wing directly over the connection between safe, legal abortion and women's equality.[112] Charging the conservatives with waging a "War Against Women," they organized a national mobilization around the slogan "A Woman's Life is a Human Life." While more militant in defense of women's right to control our own bodies, even the "feminist" wing of the pro-choice coalition has insisted on framing the issue of "choice" as a matter of individual rights in general and of avoiding an unwanted pregnancy in particular.

The Demand for Reproductive Rights

However important legal rights to abortion may be for all women, for most women *real choice* about childbearing requires much more than the right to make decisions about carrying a pregnancy to term. It is understandable that, facing a movement which wants to make motherhood compulsory and to control women's sexual expression, feminists have emphasized women's right to avoid pregnancy. For the young, white, women college students and college graduates who have flooded into the pro-choice movement, being denied access to abortion is so enraging precisely because it is a flagrant violation of the privileges and opportunities they have come to assume are theirs. But for working-class women, poor women, and women of color, the right to be mothers is also under attack. Lack of quality health care and childcare, homelessness, low wages, the social isolation and poverty of single parents, pressures on women in the welfare and public health-care system to get sterilized, all deny many women the material conditions necessary to have children and to raise their children in dignity and health.

The "reproductive rights" wing of the pro-choice movement, initiated during the 1970s by socialist-feminist activists and represented most forcefully in the 1980s by organizations of women of color such as the National Black Women's Health Project, has argued for linking women's right to control our own bodies to a broader set of demands that would empower women economically and socially. In addition to safe, legal, accessible, and affordable abortion, reproductive rights include the right to safe, effective, affordable contraception; "pro-sex" sex education; an end to sterilization abuse; universal health care, including preventive health care; care for children, the sick and the elderly in lively, sociable settings; good housing; a living wage; paid parental and family leave; shorter workdays for parents with no loss in pay; freedom to express sexual preference, including the right to be a lesbian mother.[113]

The mainstream organizations argue that a multi-issue strategy will splinter unity and weaken the movement. But supporters of a reproductive rights strategy counter that it is imperative to shift the terms of political discourse now centered entirely on a counterposition between women's rights and fetal rights.[114] A "pro-choice" movement that appears to ignore the material difficulties facing working-class women and women of color will not motivate their participation.

And only a movement with a broad political agenda can respond to the deep ambivalence about abortion that the anti-abortion movement has both fostered and exploited. While fewer than one in five women and men in the United States want to ban abortion entirely, only 31 percent will agree that abortion should be legal under any circumstances. Those in the middle believe that women pregnant from rape or incest, and women whose pregnancies threaten their physical health or life, ought to have the right to abort. The exceptions for rape and incest indicate clearly how anxieties about women's sexual autonomy shape the way people think about abortion: only women who are forced to engage in sexual intercourse should be freed from bearing the consequences of an unwanted pregnancy.[115] Fears about women abandoning their caregiving roles are also expressed in the pervasive sense that abortion should not be too easy or too available. Fewer than half of those polled agree that in cases where "the woman feels she can't care for the child" or "the pregnancy interferes with work or education" a woman should be allowed to get an abortion.[116]

The fight over abortion is not only about whether women should or should not have the right to make a decision. It is about the conditions under which women make decisions, the reasons women make these decisions, and the consequences of these decisions. And it is the symbolic focus of a much broader conflict. One can hardly imagine a more compelling representation of vulnerability than the defenseless and innocent fetus. Invoking women's responsibilities to the "unborn child" and decrying "convenience abortions," the anti-abortion movement manipulates real concerns about caregiving, real fears about economic survival, real anxieties about the loss of community and the alienation of daily life in late capitalism.[117] The right wing's vision—a return to the "world we have lost"—is so compelling, in part, because it is the only other worldview available. Many women reject the anti-abortion movement's reactionary model of community based on traditional family households and gender roles. But they are also suffering in the "world as it is." Rather than offering women an alternative vision, the single-issue pro-choice movement has tried very hard to narrow the debate, to shift attention away from "complex" and "controversial" questions of moral obligation and social responsibility, of the distribution of social and economic resources, of the apparently inevitable losses that women are experiencing in moving from traditional to new gender roles. Yet these concerns are at the center of many women's lived experience. In place of compulsory motherhood, late capitalism offers the insecurities of an increasingly predatory and competitive economy, disintegrating neighborhoods, impoverished public institutions. In place of unpaid care by wives, daughters, and mothers in the family it offers "Kentucky fried childcare," children left too much on their own, the isolation of single people, an abandoned old age. In place of sexual repression and hypocrisy, it offers the commodified sexuality of MTV, date rape, and teen pregnancy.

A politics centered exclusively on women's right to make decisions about our bodies doesn't begin to address these dilemmas. Yes, bodily

autonomy is fundamental. However, it is only a necessary, not a sufficient, condition for most women's self-determination. The outpouring
of activism to keep abortion legal has opened opportunities for building
a more inclusive and effective movement on the basis of a broader
political agenda. It would be possible to radicalize new activists, expand grassroots organizing around the full range of reproductive rights,
and strengthen the coalitions that are necessary to win reforms. But the
leadership of the pro-choice movement remains wedded to a single-
issue strategy. Even if this strategy succeeds in preserving legal abortion,
it will not significantly shift the terms of the abortion debate.

As the U.S. economy spirals downward, as competition among groups
intensifies, the conservative movement will continue to mobilize on the
basis of resentment and fear. Without the will even to present an alternative vision of community, let alone the capacity to win reforms that
speak to the real dilemmas of women's lives, feminism will not inspire
the levels of commitment and activism necessary definitively to defeat
the right.

The Debate over Difference

While it is important to call for an alternative to actually existing capitalism and to insist that autonomy for women and caring for people do
not have to be counterposed, the gap between what we can win and
what we can envision remains daunting. The real barriers to changing
the material conditions of working-class women's lives shape wrenching
political dilemmas for feminists. These dilemmas have fueled a decade
or more of debate in theory and politics over "equal treatment" versus
"special treatment" strategies.

Classic liberalism argues that women are not essentially different
from men and that equality depends on women's capacity to compete
and contract freely, thus requiring equal treatment—that is, without
prejudice or favor. This claim has undergirded real gains for women:
not only through dismantling exclusionary practices[118] but also by
expanding the definition of discriminatory behavior—for instance, to
include unequal pay for comparable male and female jobs and sexual
harassment.[119] In the mid-1970s feminist organizations launched a long
educational and legal campaign to define sexual harassment as a form
of sex discrimination in employment and education covered by the 1964
Civil Rights Act. The first speak-out, organized by Working Women
United, a grassroots group in Ithaca, New York, was held in 1975; in

1977 NOW established a project on sexual harassment in education; in 1980 women's organizations prevailed upon the EEOC to issue guidelines and regulations against sexual harassment for employers. The Supreme Court ruled in 1986 that "sexual harassment" is a form of sex discrimination, making employers and educational institutions liable for incidents.[120] Yet feminists have also discovered that equal treatment does not always establish the conditions for equality.

In a recent case the Supreme Court ruled unconstitutional a "fetal protection" policy in which Johnson Controls barred women, but not men, from certain (higher-paid) jobs working with lead, on the ground that lead posed a risk to normal fetal development, should the woman become pregnant while employed. Pre-menopausal women had to agree to sterilization if they wanted the jobs.[121] The Court argued that women workers had the same right as men workers to decide whether they wished to incur risks. The Court did not rule that the employer had any obligation to reduce the dangers of the job itself. The decision equalized women's access to the better-paid jobs, but forced them to choose between reproductive hazards and higher wages.[122] The Johnson Controls case is not unique—similar treatment often produces unequal outcomes, and may even appear to increase women's vulnerability to exploitation. For example, most states abolished or severely restricted alimony in divorce, on the grounds that laws requiring men but not women to support their ex-spouses were discriminatory.[123] The "tender years" doctrine, by which custody of young children was always awarded to the mother, has been abandoned on the ground that automatic preference for the mother violates the principle of equal treatment before the law.[124] On the argument that all workers should be treated equally, employers have resisted laws mandating maternity leave; and under women's equal right to contract, lawyers have defended surrogacy, the practice of hiring women to bear children for infertile couples.[125] In response, some feminists have argued against equal-treatment strategies on the ground that women are different from men and their special needs and capacities should be recognized and protected. They argue that asserting the value of the mother–child bond or the uniqueness of pregnancy would defend women's claims to maternity leave, alimony, and child support, and the rights to have custody of their children in divorce or surrogacy cases.[126] Opponents of special-treatment strategies have argued that they tend to reproduce the gender division of labor in the home and reinforce an essentialist ideology of sexual difference. Proponents claim, however, that equal-treatment approaches accept male-defined, abstract standards of justice and attempt to assimilate women to male norms.

Trying to transcend this counterposition, some feminists have argued for result-equality rather than rule-equality strategies. Equality, it is argued, cannot be achieved by holding everyone to the same abstract standard—similar treatment. Rather, equality can only be secured by recognizing that people are different in many different ways. If our goal is to enable everyone to have the same opportunity to participate, then it is necessary to accommodate people's differences, to "denormalize the way institutions formulate their rules by revealing the plural circumstances that exist, or ought to exist, within them," as Iris Young has argued.[127] Gender-neutral approaches which neither assimilate women to a male standard (equal treatment) nor universalize gender differences (special treatment) have been argued as a way out of the dilemma.[128] Men do not get pregnant and pregnancy is not an illness. But men are likely to experience other conditions which affect their participation at work. Justice requires all employees to receive temporarily changed job assignments or paid time off when changed circumstances require it, not dismissal or lost wages. The demand for paid *parental* leave assumes that men as well as women have family responsibilities. It also recognizes that employees are different—some are raising children, some are not. These differences should be recognized rather than holding all employees to the same standard—treating them as if they had no responsibilities for children (or as if the employer had no responsibility for subsidizing and supporting the raising of children). In divorce a rule that gave preference for child custody to the "primary parent" would not assume a special mother–child bond. It would also prevent men from using contested custody as a lever against their ex-wives, because in the vast majority of cases wives are mainly responsible for caring for their children.[129]

While feminist lawyers, philosophers, and social theorists attempt to work out consistent worldviews, the real force that fuels the debate is not so much opposing promises and assumptions about the definition of equality or whether women have a distinct nature but the political and economic barriers to transcending the counterposition between equality and difference. Special-treatment strategies are attractive when they can secure advantages for women that cannot be won any other way. In California, for example, a law requiring employers to provide pregnant women (unpaid) leave and guaranteeing them their jobs back was passed as a substitute for a gender-neutral parental leave law that was strenuously opposed by business and could not get sufficient votes.[130] As in the feminist debate on protective legislation in the early twentieth century, it often appears that immediate remedies can only be secured at the cost of long-term disadvantages. In an era where employers are demanding and getting concessions, and the welfare state is underfunded and under political attack, universal programs are especially difficult to win. Special-treatment strategies can sometimes draw on a broader base of support. The same commitment to the "sanctity of motherhood" that justifies their opposition to abortion leads right-to-life organizations and the Catholic hierarchy to support maternity leave and to oppose legalizing surrogate pregnancy. There is no easy choice between making alliances with these forces or leaving women unprotected. If women's jobs paid better, were respected and gave them real control over their working conditions, it might not be necessary to criminalize prostitution or ban surrogacy—far fewer women would wish to be surrogate mothers or prostitutes. If the value of caregiving work were recognized, quality childcare and eldercare would be subsidized and paid parental leave would be available; paid time off for doing things with children or other people in our care would be available to men as well as to women. Women would then be less likely to structure their employment decisions around their childcare responsibilities, and would not be penalized by caring for children and end up having to depend on husbands and ex-husbands for support. But these conditions are hardly on the immediate horizon. So the pressures in favor of special treatment strategies are intense. Still, most women approach these issues in a pragmatic way, adopting whatever arguments and strategies seem to work. The same woman might argue an equal-treatment position in relation to demanding women's access to military combat positions but a special-treatment position in relation to legislation for paid maternity leave. Crafting a consistent strategy out of these contradictory impulses is unlikely to happen until there is a movement that can shift the balance of political forces, challenge corporate interests, and make it more possible to win "gender-neutral" policies.

The Challenge from Women of Color

Over the 1980s the interests and worldview of white heterosexual professional/managerial women continued to dominate mainstream feminism. But their hegemony has been challenged, especially in academia but also within mainstream feminist organizations. Powerful texts by feminist women of color exposed the assumptions of universality in feminist theory and forced a profound rethinking of feminist conceptual frameworks and feminist analysis.[131] Older Black women's organizations such as the National Council of Negro Women, and new organizations of African-American, Latina, Asian-American and Native American women that sprung out of the civil rights and feminist movements of the 1960s, have pushed NOW and other mainstream feminist organizations to be more inclusive.[132] The Jesse Jackson campaigns, especially the campaign of 1988 in which the militants in the mainstream feminist groups, and particularly NOW, were more marginalized in the Democratic Party and therefore more willing to join Jackson's primary bid, helped to push in the same direction. The National Congress of Neighborhood Women, the National Welfare Rights Union, the National Black Women's Health Project, and women of color from CLUW have pressured the women's lobby to consider issues of concern to women of color and poor/working-class women. Feminist organizations, inside and outside academia, have responded, but in somewhat limited ways.[133] There is often more lip service paid than substance to the idea of diversity.[134]

Women of color have historically been caught between a middle-class white feminist movement and a male-dominated civil rights movement. Sexism in the Black community has held back coalitions between feminist and civil rights organizations; on the other hand, the racism of the white women's movement has made it very difficult for Black feminists to build ties and coalitions at the grassroots level.[135] At the 1984 Democratic Party National Convention, the National Women's Political Caucus and NOW disbanded the whip system they had built to organize delegates once Geraldine Ferraro had captured the vice-president slot on the ticket. In demonstrating loyalty to the party leadership (in return for Ferraro's nomination) the white feminists abandoned the Jackson forces, who wanted to continue to press the leadership around platform planks and other issues of concern to the poor and people of color. Angry Black women delegates formed the Black Women's Political Congress.[136] The Thomas/Hill hearings raised these issues in the most intense way. Experts, commentators, and representatives of political organizations defending Hill—the spokespeople for the feminist side— were overwhelmingly white, while Black opponents of Thomas were almost always Black male professionals, academics and civil rights leaders. Black women's voices in support of Hill received scant notice in the media, while African-American men and women decrying Hill's "disloyalty" were far more prominent. Kimberle Crenshaw makes the point that white feminist defenders of Anita Hill explained her silence only in terms of her fear that her career would be ended, a fear she would share with similarly placed white women. "Content to rest their case on a raceless tale of gender subordination," white feminists "missed an opportunity to span the chasm between feminism and anti-racism." They failed to address the fact that many Black women stay silent for fear that their stories might be used to reinforce stereotypes of Black men as sexually threatening, and/or for fear of ostracism from other Black people if they do speak out.[137] In a moving and impressive ex-pression of solidarity and political commitment, 1,603 Black women signed a statement, "No one will speak for us but ourselves," defending Hill and protesting the Thomas appointment as part of a broad-based attack on working people.[138] Their ability to mobilize so quickly and their willingness to speak out publicly reflects the growing organization and confidence of Black feminism. Their initiative reminded us, once again, that the hegemony of white feminism cannot be overcome with-out a strong, self-organized Black feminist presence. It also signaled that combating racism, on the part of white feminists, has to go beyond self-examination to include active support, material as well as political, for the self-organization of women of color.

Although feminist organizations and publications have come to re-cognize relations of domination and privilege among women in terms of race, many tend to treat this as a problem of psychology and prejudice—"unlearning racism" workshops are very popular. Increased awareness of how racism affects interaction and decision-making is im-portant, and consciousness-raising very useful. However, white feminists have yet to confront sufficiently questions of political practice and political organization: whether their organizations will share political resources (money, access to the media, authority to speak) and decision-making with those of women of color; whether their organizations will take responsibility for struggles around issues of vital concern to women of color and working-class women even though those issues are not defined as feminist issues (e.g. environmental racism, community pro-tests against factory closings); and whether an inclusive movement would have the same political understandings and strategies as the current feminist movement—for instance, how feminists evaluate and talk about motherhood, what is meant by reproductive "choice," the stance taken toward the police and the courts as remedies for violence against women.[139]

The Lesbian Challenge

After two decades of powerful writing and consistent organizing, lesbian feminists have begun to break down heterosexism in the mainstream women's movement. In 1981, Betty Friedan could still write that lesbianism was a "lavender herring," a diversion for feminism.[140] However, by the end of the 1980s the growing political strength of the gay rights movement and lesbian activists' organizing within women's organizations brought a shift in attitudes.[141] In 1988, the National Women's Studies Association annual convention presented its first plenary session on lesbian studies. In 1989 NOW organized its first National Lesbian Conference, and the national convention of the American Association of University Women recognized its first lesbian caucus. These gains are especially important in light of the strength of homophobia in society. Homosexuality is still not protected by any national civil rights legislation (discrimination by race, national origin, religion, sex, age, and disability are all illegal—although conservative appointees in the federal courts as well as the Supreme Court have undermined the effectiveness of these laws). In fact, the country has become far more polarized on the issue, as gains in acceptance are matched by increases in organized violence against gay people and political mobilizations against gay rights.

The reactionary backlash put mainstream feminism on the defensive. Accused of encouraging "family breakdown," "divorce, drugs and delinquency," feminists have attempted to reappropriate the family from the right by putting "family" at the center of their own politics, with unfortunately conservatizing consequences.[142] There has been a disturbing tendency to counterpose "family issues" to sexual politics and women's rights. A spate of books and articles have appeared, written by feminists, accusing the movement of paying too much attention to issues of individual equality and not enough attention to the "real needs" of most women: help with negotiating their double day.[143] This counterposing of "sexual politics" to "pro-family politics" recapitulates the sterile debate between equal-rights feminism and social feminism which tore through the women's movement in the early decades of the twentieth century. There, also, the battle was waged over the "class" character of individual rights, whether individual rights were meaningful for working-class women. Rather than separating the demand for formal civil rights (the right to be free from discrimination) from the demand for substantive social rights (claims on the community for support), it makes sense to focus on their interconnection.[144] At the very least, this means breaking with traditional definitions of the family, insisting that alternative households—those formed by single mothers, lesbian/gay couples, and non-related individuals—are functional, sane, healthy, good for children and adults. Further, they deserve the same economic and social support from the community that we are demanding for heterosexual couple families. More broadly, it requires that we assert the value of freely chosen sexual and parental relationships, while demonstrating how both sexual autonomy and access to material resources (not least, time and money) are fundamental to achieving them. This strategy has yet to be adopted by mainstream feminists.

Although mainstream organizations have gone on record in support of lesbian and gay rights, they have tended to keep the issue out of other organizing efforts. This is partly the result of their preference for single-issue strategies—for instance, pro-choice groups will not include gay/lesbian rights any more than they would include childcare as an issue in campaigns defending legalized abortion. But lesbianism has also been marginalized in social-welfare feminism's central multi-issue strategy, the "work–family" agenda. Congresswoman Pat Schroeder supports civil rights legislation for gays/lesbians, but has not incorporated "domestic partnership" legislation into her legislative "work–family" agenda. Although the Coalition of Labor Union Women officially supports gay/lesbian civil rights, organizers of their 1988 demonstration in Washington for "pro-family" legislation which included parental leave, childcare, housing, health care, and pay equity, not only failed to include domestic partnership legislation in the demands but also refused to allow representatives of lesbian/gay organizations to speak at the rally. CLUW's practice may be changing. Its recent actions in support of lesbian/gay rights may indicate that the organization will take a more inclusive stance in the future.

Over the past four years, as the conservative movement has successfully organized against lesbian/gay rights and used the issue to increase its political strength at state and local levels, mainstream groups, concerned about the right's growing political influence, have been forced to take a stand in favor of lesbian/gay rights. During the 1992 elections, anti-gay ballot measures in several states and cities were opposed by extremely broad coalitions, which included mainline Churches, trade unions, civil rights organizations, civic and even employer organizations. As support for lesbian/gay rights becomes more politically acceptable, mainstream feminist organizations may be less fearful of integrating lesbian issues into their actions and discourse.

The Autonomous Women's Movement

From the 1960s up through the mid 1970s, the women's movement was divided between "insiders" and "outsiders"; between liberal-feminist groups oriented toward gaining position and power within existing state institutions, including political parties, and the autonomous women's movement oriented to revolutionary change, including radical-feminist, lesbian-separatist, socialist-feminist and anarcha-feminist currents. "Insiders" were divided between moderates and militants. Moderates tended to rely on building influence at elite levels and on court suits using the Civil Rights Act of 1964. The militants (primarily the National Organization for Women) used those tactics but were not afraid of "grassroots" organization and popular mobilizations—rallies, marches, and speak-outs.

As the autonomous movement declined and many women active in those groups became part of the women's lobby, they helped to build social-welfare politics and organizations. Over time, insiders have become more politically diverse, while the remaining outsiders are more marginal, although also more integrated into other radical and counter-cultural movements than in the 1960s and 1970s. The grassroots, locally controlled organizations, depending primarily on volunteers and self-generated funding, that were the hallmark of the autonomous women's movement have pretty much disappeared. The only organizations that survive provide a product or service, supported through the market or government and charities. More than a hundred cities have a women's bookstore, but most are privately owned. The feminist women's health clinics, which started as collectives, have mostly become ordinary businesses. The battered women's shelters and sexual violence crisis lines are supported by a combination of community fundraising, grants from charitable foundations, state government funds (generated, in a nice irony, by legislation levying a marriage license tax) and federal funds (generated, in a not so nice irony, by conservative "victims' assistance" and "anti-crime" programs). In contrast, the women's peace movement, which galvanized so much action in the early 1980s, has faded, along with the anti-pornography groups, the Take Back the Night organizations, the local women workers' organizing projects, local feminist newspapers and newsletters.

In this relocation of feminist organization, efforts to influence legislation and state policy are increasingly cut off from grassroots activism, so those who work within the political system have had to accept (and ultimately come to justify) vastly diminished expectations and demands. All the insiders, whether radical-feminists and socialist-feminists schooled in the autonomous women's movement or newcomers, face similar difficulties.

First are the obvious conservatizing pressures on individuals trying to hold on to their jobs or their organizations, often in very tenuous institutional positions, and without an organized and committed grassroots following to support them. Second, the programs feminists run, however limited, do serve women and are desperately needed, so the pressures to preserve them by any means necessary are intense. The less confident feminists are of being able to defend themselves by mobilizing a base, the more concerned they become to find powerful allies, and the more they have to argue for and structure their programs in terms acceptable to those forces. For example, we find childcare advocates defending state subsidies not on the ground that quality care by adults in addition to mothers frees women and is healthy for children but because mothers are "forced to work." Maintaining alliances requires reciprocity—being careful not to criticize publicly a "law and order" district attorney who enforces restraining orders against batterers but fails to discipline racist police officers; endorsing a powerful legislator who supports state programs for vocational training to "displaced homemakers" but opposes pro-labor legislation. Third, powerfully situated individuals are reluctant to deal with organizations that can't control their rank and file, whether they are students, employees, volunteers, or union members. This puts pressure on leaders to monitor participation carefully to ensure that people who are too naive, not part of the team, or possibly irresponsible, are not empowered to make decisions which would potentially disrupt carefully nurtured relationships. The dangers of too broad a participation gradually overwhelm the earlier feminist commitment to eliminating hierarchy and creating fully democratic structures—not that the tensions inherent in trying to build these egalitarian structures were ever or could ever be resolved, but now they are seldom even struggled with. This is the experiential context within which the political currents of the autonomous women's movement have evolved.

From Socialist-Feminism to Social-Welfare Feminism

The rise of social-welfare feminist politics in the women's lobby owes something to the collapse of the revolutionary left and of the socialist-feminist collectives and organizations which were part of it. The

generation of socialist-feminist activists who became social-service workers and schoolteachers, trade-union staff, organizers and officials, public administrators and lawyers, health workers and so on brought with
them a commitment to represent the needs and interests of working-
class women and women of color. They have helped to develop and
organize for social-welfare feminist politics within many different
arenas.[145] But the pressures of working on the inside, under conditions
of ascendant corporate power and working-class demobilization, have
led to a subtle shift in focus from organizing to advocacy, a displacement of goals in which feminists aim to get something from the state
for women rather than to encourage the self-organization of women.[146]
For example, socialist-feminists working as researchers and trade-union
advisers and organizers were instrumental in developing campaigns for
"comparable worth"—equal pay for comparable male and female jobs.
The concept of revaluing women's jobs inspired many working women
and union activists, potentially questioned hierarchies of pay and market ideology, and appeared to open up radical possibilities for organizing women workers.[147] Instead, most efforts to implement these policies
for government workers at the state level became focused on fairly
technical negotiations over job evaluation schemes, which engaged
academic experts, management, and union representatives and went on
pretty much over the heads of the workers.[148]

The strategic vision of social-welfare feminism projects a cross-class
alliance usually spoken of as "building unity out of diversity." Casting
what are in reality often conflicting interests (at least in the short run)
as "diversity of experience" allows social-welfare feminists to minimize
the difficulties in forging these alliances.[149] The language of "empowering women" fills feminist discourse, but doesn't necessarily address those
instances when the empowerment of one group of women requires
another group of women to cede power. For instance, in attempting to
improve their own wages and working conditions by controlling the
labor supply, registered nurses have organized against programs to
upgrade the skills of lesser-educated practical nurses and nurse's aides,
while organizing for legislation to expand subsidized health care to the
working poor, women, and children.[150] To take another example, claiming professional expertise has been a central strategy through which
women working in health, education, and social services have tried to
protect their autonomy from management. But because they have so
much invested in their professional status, they tend to devalue the
client's point of view, experience, or expertise.[151]

Of course, alliances between professionals/administrators and working-class women can be fruitful—but only under conditions of radical mobilization and community organization in which the "clients" (parents of children in schools or daycare centers, welfare recipients, clinic patients) advocate for themselves and break through the middle-class assumptions and patronizing relations which normally characterize interactions between women professionals/service workers and their clients.[152]

More generally, the distinction between a revolutionary (socialist-feminist) and a reform (social-welfare feminist) strategy lies not in whether one organizes to wrest some concession from the state but in how that effort fits into an overall strategy. Unfortunately, the feminist debate over the state has rarely been posed in this way, but rather as a choice between being outside or inside the state, between working for reforms or working to build alternative institutions.[153] Feminists inside the state gain personal and institutional points of influence/power that can be an asset for constituencies trying to win something from the state. But these very routes of access to political resources impose their own logic on those who try to use them. This logic shapes not only what is understood to be possible but also what is understood to be desirable. Without a counterforce, this logic will come to dominate reform efforts.[154]

A socialist-feminist strategy takes the primary goal of fighting for reform to be the creation of a counterforce. The main point of organizing people around their immediate needs is to develop the capacities of women activists, their critical understanding and confidence in collective action, their commitments to ways of organizing social life that are democratic and participatory. This focus is difficult to sustain when activism is at a low ebb, and therefore gains seem to come, if at all, through institutional positions and influence. But the strategic choice to put building grassroots networks and solidarities first is even more important at such times. For the more dependent feminists are on influential individuals and politically powerful organizations, the more vulnerable we are to the conforming pressures such alliances inevitably bring with them.[155]

Radical-Feminism and the Movement against Sexual Violence

Radical-feminism's early focus on adventure, autonomy, individuality, sexual pleasure, and power reflected the optimism of an era of collective challenges and real victories. At its origin, the movement against sexual violence emphasized self-defense and collective empowerment as strategies against male violence. Women should learn how to fight, police their communities, support and advocate for victims, organize for increased social, economic and political power, and challenge cultural representations that sexually objectify women. The current politics which emphasizes women's victimization and need for protection also reflects a reality—of women's increasing impoverishment and continued vulnerability to exploitation. If heterosexuality is potentially pleasurable as well as dangerous, its dangers loom very large these days, especially given the apparently unchangeable material conditions of women's lives. Making matters worse, in the early 1980s the movement was racked by a highly factionalized "sex debate" that reflected but utterly failed to resolve this dilemma.[156] By its rancour, the fight between the "anti-pornography" and "pro-sex" factions undermined enthusiasm and activity, further weakened the grassroots support available to the programs providing services and advocacy on the issue of violence against women, and increased the felt isolation of those continuing to work in the area.

From the late 1970s the shelters and crisis lines had struggled to survive as federal and state money, much of it from the last remnants of the poverty program—community block grants and CETA—declined. But as funding for social programs dried up, money became available through anti-crime programs, like the Law Enforcement Assistance Act and victims' assistance programs.[157] Feminists had always seen the need to challenge the practices of police and courts, which tended to protect rather than punish perpetrators of sexual violence. But that challenge was never expected to constitute the cornerstone of the strategy to stop male violence, any more than was protesting the sexual objectification of women in the media. The empowerment of women, not their protection, was the key. As confidence in the movement's ability to win the material and political conditions of power for women ebbed, reliance on the coercive arm of the state came to play a more central part in the aims and accomplishments of those advocating around the issue.

In alliance with social-work professionals and law-and-order advocates, feminist organizations have successfully pressured for changes in both judicial and police practices.[158] In 1986, 46 percent of police departments serving jurisdictions of populations greater than 100,000 had a pro-arrest policy, compared to only 10 percent in 1984.[159] Nine states have passed legislation making arrest of the batterer mandatory, whether or not the victim files a formal complaint.[160] The judicial process for wives to obtain restraining orders (prohibiting men accused of battering their wives from entering their homes or workplaces, harassing them, and so on) has been simplified. Many urban police departments automatically arrest batterers for violating a restraining order. Most states have revised or enacted new rape statutes, prohibiting cross-examination of the victim about her previous sexual history, and eliminating the traditional requirement for corroboration—a witness or proof of physical resistance.[161] By the mid-1980s twenty-three states had made it a crime for a man to force his wife to have sexual relations.

The impulses that have framed this state response are contradictory, marrying feminist analysis to paternalistic protectiveness and repressive attitudes toward sexuality. Feminist standpoints are articulated in the mix but do not predominate. At first the right wing opposed legislation funding shelters for battered women, which were, according to one conservative senator, nothing more than outposts for feminist "missionaries who would wage war on the traditional family."[162] But by the mid-1980s Eagle Forum (one of the major anti-feminist organizations of the far right) had formed its own Coalition for Abused Women, to compete with feminist organizations for funding. In 1985 the Eagle Forum protested award of a Department of Justice grant to the National Coalition Against Domestic Violence for an education project on the grounds that NCADV was a "subversive group of radical lesbian feminists." Attorney-General Meese banned the use of the word "lesbian" in all publications for the project and required the coalition to submit all work to the Department of Justice for approval.[163] The NCADV terminated the agreement rather than submit to censorship. The next year, Schlafley's group received $625,000 to study the effects of domestic violence on "traditional women."[164]

As right-wing women move onto what had been a feminist political terrain, and as feminists find their political options narrowing, it has been more common to find the two groups on the same side, rather than on opposing sides, of an issue. While asserting their support for the traditional patriarchal family, right-wing women have organized to defend women and children against men's abuse of their patriarchal power. They want to use the state to discipline men as well as women, to enforce the traditional family bargain on men, to ensure that men provide protection and support to "good" women (i.e. those who provide men with the wife/mother services which are rightfully theirs). Feminists, however much we would like to free women from this exchange, find that persistent social, economic, and political gender inequalities often leave women without many alternatives to dependence on men. So, for instance, conservative and feminist women's groups have both organized for government programs to collect the child-support owed women by their ex-husbands, for higher mandated child-support awards, and for the re-establishment of alimony.[165]

This blurring of the differences between feminists and conservatives is especially clear in the area of sexual violence. In spite of the legal changes feminists have won, many rapes are still not prosecuted because the district attorney decides they are "unfounded" (i.e. too hard to prove—this is especially the case where the rapist and victim are acquainted), batterers under restraining orders kill their wives, the shelters turn away many more women than they take in, and the crisis lines are asked for more help than they can provide. Women advocating for victims of sexual violence feel that they are in a war and losing. And that desperation may lead them to feel that they have better allies in district attorneys who order the police to arrest "johns" as well as prostitutes than in feminists who want to decriminalize prostitution. They may find more common ground with conservative women's groups who want to close down nude-dancing joints than with feminists who oppose restrictive laws but offer little that can protect women from exploitation in an expanding sex industry.[166] We live in a world where sexual autonomy carries the price of insecurity, while protection is available only at the cost of sexual repression. Neither choice is liberating for women.

Feminist Politics on the Margins

There is still a thriving women's culture closely tied to and supported by urban lesbian communities and by feminists in the countercultural "left" milieu. Alternative health care (feminist naturopathy, chiropractic and massage, feminist therapy, midwifery), women's spirituality groups and women's bookstores, as well as national feminist newspapers and magazines, rely on the organization, funds, and participation of lesbians.[167] Much of "women's music" could not survive without the energy of the lesbian community. They are the disc jockeys who play the music on community radio stations, the producers who bring the performers to town, the organizers and audiences at women's music festivals that provide national exposure for new musicians and groups.[168] This culture is "woman-identified" but not separatist, although in it are expressed the whole range of radical-feminist politics, including lesbian separatism.

Most of the local feminist newspapers and newsletters are gone, but a few national feminist publications that are informed by radical-/socialist-feminist ideas have survived: *Sojourner* and *Off Our Backs* publish regularly with circulations around twenty-five thousand.[169] Here you can still find debates about pornography, separatism, racism in the women's movement, about whether feminists should support legalizing prostitution or surrogacy or adopting babies from the third world, about whether a book reviewed or an article printed was "classist." Here you find stories about welfare mothers, poor women, working-class working women, women of color, lesbians, community organizing projects, union drives, and successful protests. Here you will see profiled women who are community organizers and activists rather than businesswomen, politicians or administrators. These papers give expression to a radical sensibility but their relatively small readership signals the marginal status of that politics.

The decline of the political organizations and activities that infused women's culture with radical-feminist content has encouraged the substitution of lifestyle for politics, community building as an end in itself rather than a strategy for changing the world. "Cultural-feminism" has replaced radical-feminism as the hegemonic world-view in what remains of the autonomous women's community.[170] Cultural-feminism turns the radical-feminist slogan "the personal is political" on its head, assuming that personal transformation and immersion in a gynocentric community are the same thing as political empowerment. The polarization of "male" to "female" ways of being, knowing, feeling, and thinking that is fundamental to cultural feminism encourages a politics of salvation through womanly virtue; this leaves little room for the pragmatic, limited, ambivalent, and conflictual political practice of coalition-building among women divided by race, ethnicity, sexual orientation, not to mention with organizations of working-class and oppressed people which include men.[171]

Yet the women's spirituality movement, which claims to recover ancient pre-patriarchal women-centered communalism, has a political cut. *Woman of Power*, a journal of the women's spirituality movement (with a growing circulation not too far from that of the second-wave socialist-/radical-feminist publications *Sojourner* and *Off Our Backs*), was founded as a journal of spirituality *and* politics. Feminist/anarchist witches like the writer and speaker Starhawk have large followings. Her political paganism introduced many to an anti-capitalist critique, and asserted the value/possibility of a participatory and democratic social, economic, political life. Although political activism may be a minor current and the dominant voice in the women's spirituality movement is cultural-feminism, the same women who organize a summer solstice ritual might organize an all-women affinity group that joins a Take Back The Night march, a protest against nuclear weapons or a chemical dumping site.

Along with women's spirituality, ecofeminism emerged in the 1980s as an important ideological current outside mainstream feminism. From early on, radical-feminist theorists connected male domination to the "rape of nature." In *Gyn/ecology*, Mary Daly called on women to identify with nature against men and referred to herself as an ecofeminist. The identification of woman and nature as victims of male violence has also been given a positive valence by the women's spirituality movement, which promises to re-establish the connection between the human and natural worlds associated with the Goddess-worship of the ancient "earth religions." Ecofeminism is not a coherent body of theory and practice— it includes radical-feminists and anarcha-feminists, lesbian-separatists and feminists active in the left wing of the green movement. While all ecofeminists put social relations of domination at the center of analysis, they differ in how they understand domination and how they connect preservation of the natural world to revolutionizing social relations. Some, for instance, reject any notion of a "natural" or eternal "male" drive toward domination or female capacity for nurturance, arguing a more socially constructed view of gender and acknowledging that capitalism's systemic dynamic toward growth cannot be reduced to an expression of male psychology or values.[172] The politics of most ecofeminist activists, like the radical ecology movement in general, tends toward an anti-industrial rather than anti-capitalist analysis, identifying primarily with cultures and peoples who have not yet been corrupted by the industrial world. The poisoning of farmworkers or industrial workers, pollution in urban/suburban working-class communities, especially white working-class communities, are issues that have not yet captured the imagination of most ecofeminist activists. Ecofeminism also shares radical-feminism's deep ambivalence about the relationship of feminism to movements that include men. With the exception of the left greens, there is no discussion among ecofeminists about building links to working-class organizations. Insofar as the ecofeminist and women's spirituality movements address racism at all, they think of it as a problem of white women's supremacist attitudes, rather than as an axis for coalition-building with community organizations that include men.

Currents outside mainstream feminism always had a relatively narrow social base: countercultural communities, young people, students. This is even more true now. Feminists and feminism have real influence within the radical wing of the peace/anti-imperialist/anti-nuclear/ecology movements.[173] But there is a huge gulf between these radical movements and the rest of U.S. political life.

What Next?

In this best and worst of times, second-wave feminism has come up against a political impasse which fundamentally shapes its trajectory. The way out of this impasse seems both straightforward and impossible. Straightforward because it seems obvious that only a serious and disruptive challenge to state and capital can force the redistribution of wealth necessary to improve the lives of most women. Impossible because this challenge depends on the renewal of working-class self-organization, yet so much of our experience points in the opposite direction. The signs of demobilization are too familiar: the shrinking ranks and militancy of the trade unions, the decimation of urban communities of color and their institutions, the bitter sectoral conflicts over state budgets, the increasingly intense pressures of daily survival and the individualistic strategies most people pursue.

In the face of the severe constraints on the reforms that can be won under the current political balance of forces, the survivors of the second wave, the organizations of the women's lobby, have conceded to intense conservatizing pressures. These pressures will only be reversed when feminists can challenge in practice the now dominant interests in the state. However, this challenge cannot be organized by feminists alone nor with old forms of feminist organization. It requires a broad and militant mobilization from below incorporating movements for democratic rights that are far more inclusive, new more social and political forms of trade-union struggle, and national political organization(s) independent of the Democratic Party. We have no choice but to stake our future on this possibility. To limit our political horizons otherwise leaves us defenseless against conservatizing pressures and will blind us to the instances of creative resistance, albeit molecular and disparate, that, as we know from past experience, are the seedbeds of a larger mobilization.

The democratic aspirations that flamed so strongly not only in the student, civil rights, and women's movements, but also in the workers' rank-and-file rebellions of the 1960s and early 1970s, have not been extinguished. They simmer below the surface, held in check by the anxieties and fears of a social and economic crisis which cry out for the restoration of stability and order. For all but a narrow layer of relatively privileged women, greater personal freedom comes at the cost of increased isolation and exploitation, decreased protection and support. Mainstream political currents—the possessive individualism of the moderate Republicans, the repressive communitarianism of the religious right, the technocratic and defensive welfarism of the new Democrats—express but cannot transcend the apparently irreconcilable conflict between material security and individual liberty.

Yet even in this period of demoralization, defeat and passivity, there have been moments of broader struggle. Jesse Jackson's impressive showing in the 1988 presidential primary depended on and reflected the strength of the different movements on the ground who came together in local Rainbow Coalitions. The Rainbow potentially opened a space for cooperation and dialogue, an opportunity for transforming and broadening the political understanding and practice of the activists from all the different movements who participated in it. In particular, the Rainbow opened the possibility for building a permanent political organization and a broad left reform agenda that offers a way out of the dilemmas that now seem so intractable. Limited by its electoralist constraints and dependence on Jackson, who was seeking to maintain credibility within the Democratic Party, the Rainbow failed to fulfill this promise. Lacking a programmatic and organizational basis for unity, the movements today are politically much weaker than the potential of their numbers.

The Rainbow's defeat has not eradicated possibilities for a massive coalition movement that would break the political impasse. However, neither the time and form of this breakthrough nor the specific issue, campaign or strategic intervention that might galvanize it can be known. What I would like to end with, then, is not a strategic solution but a strategic stance, an approach to feminist organizing that looks toward a third wave of feminist struggle which, in concert with other movements, will build on the historic victories of the second wave while transcending its limitations.

Toward the Third Wave

The impulses that brought movement activists together in the Rainbow Coalition continue to express themselves in creative new forms of trade-union organizing (worker/community alliances), in new forms of environmentalism (labor/environmental solidarity networks and joint projects), in new forms of feminism. In the 1980s and into the 1990s, working-class women, in and outside the trade unions, organized around their multiple identities—as workers, members of oppressed communities, as women. To take just a few examples: welfare-rights groups are not *women's* organizations, yet their leadership and activists are mostly women who organize against and name as sexist and racist the oppressive regulations of the welfare system. The women-of-color health projects are explicitly women's organizations but not explicitly women's rights organizations, yet they organize women of color to defend abortion rights. Latina textile workers and Asian women garment workers have established women's groups that organize simultaneously in the workplace and the community. Rural women have formed support groups that protest plant closures, organize to relieve community poverty, and combat rising levels of male violence. All these forms have in common a feminist practice that organizes *women around their interests/ needs as women* not in separation from but in relation to their needs and interests as workers and members of oppressed communities.

Although feminist academics and activists increasingly acknowledge that there is no such entity as Woman, few have addressed the question of how to act on that understanding. The now obligatory invocation that "gender, race, and class intersect" is a good beginning, but does not constitute a political strategy. The feminist practice of working-class women does point in a strategic direction. However, because many groups are still small and local and do not command the political resources that organizations of the women's lobby look for in their allies, mainstream feminists have pretty much ignored these grassroots efforts. This is unfortunate and short-sighted. In these initiatives are located the possibilities for developing a feminist coalitional politics which speaks to the majority of women, because it responds to both sides of our human need—for personal autonomy and supportive community.

Whatever the arena of our political organizing (the academy, the legislature, the media, the workplace or the street), our reform demands and ways of arguing for them have to transcend rather than capitulate to existing political worldviews. We need to develop a politics that combines the liberatory moments (the demand for individual self-expression, self-determination, and democratic participation) of the movements for democratic inclusion (feminism, civil rights, gay/lesbian rights) with new struggles over material needs (for health care, for childcare and paid parental leave, for living-wage jobs, for a clean environment). Although we are forced to play on an ideological terrain we have not created, we can use the language of conventional discourse to infuse all our organizing with a radically democratic vision.[174]

First, we can reappropriate the concepts of choice and control from the right, which has so effectively counterposed the market and the family (as spaces where individuals exercise power) to the welfare state. In addition to organizing to defend and expand public services, we should argue for democratically run (worker and client controlled), decentralized and collective alternatives to the unpaid domestic work of women. For example, working-class mothers have good reason to feel ambivalent about turning their children, or their elderly parents, over to underfunded and bureaucratic state services or to the explotative profiteering of the marketplace. Women from oppressed racial/ethnic communities have every reason to regard with suspicion institutions that systematically deny the value of their culture, suppress their history, and undermine their children's self-regard. But neighborhood child-care centers cooperatively run by parents and workers support and require participation and involvement. And democratized public institutions cannot function without changes in the organization of paid employment, including more flexible working hours and paid time off.

In the liberal lexicon, choice is only guaranteed negatively, as the right to act without interference. For affluent middle-class women, negative freedom may be sufficient. But most women need much more. We should define choice positively, as the right of every woman to have good alternatives to choose from, ensuring that good choices for some women don't rest on the exploitation of others (working-class women and women of color) as domestic servants, low-paid service workers, fetal incubators, test cases for new contraceptives, and so on.

Second, we have to integrate women's need for autonomy, self-knowledge, and self-development into every argument for reform. Liberal-feminists defend women's right to autonomy, but in a language of contracts and limited liability which fails to address most women's interest in and need for a supportive community. Conservatives invoke the values of interdependence and long-term commitments but only within the confines of a patriarchal family and community. Caught between these two poles, and on the defensive, social-welfare feminists have tended to argue for childcare or living wages for women on the basis of necessity (their husbands don't make enough, they have no husbands, therefore women "need" to work), implying that there is nothing problematic about the privatized nuclear family organized around a gender division of labor and we would return to it if we could. This is a mistake, for the feminist critique of the patriarchal family remains valid and the dangers of women's economic dependence on men are very real. Instead, we should argue the value of broadening responsibility for the care of children and adults to a democratized public sphere. Our goal is not to "free" women from the long-term commitments and obligations now located so exclusively in the family, to narrow the terms of relationship, but to create the conditions under which women can enter relationships from a position of equal access with men to economic survival and political power.

Finally, we have to recapture the radical potential of sexual politics *and* integrate these issues into other struggles for reform. The defensive distances that separate movements organizing to meet human needs (such as trade unions, community and "poor people's" organizations, social-welfare feminism) from those organized to demand individual rights to sexual expression must be bridged. Abortion and lesbian rights evoke deep anxieties because they so directly challenge gender identities and the social order built upon them. Recognizing these anxieties, and responding to the growing conservative mobilization around them, even the newly militant movements for abortion and lesbian/gay rights have tended to narrow their politics to the confines of an assimilationist liberal framework, emphasizing privacy rights and tolerance. Rejecting these limits, the radical "direct action" wings of the abortion and lesbian/gay rights movements (WAC, WHAM, Queer Nation, and Lesbian Avengers) are "disruptive" in theory and practice.[175] Their expressive activism may amuse, anger or shock, but their defiance also undermines the conservatives' power to dominate the terrain of political discourse. Like their 1960s' counterparts, however, contemporary sex-radicals draw on a political tradition of radical individualism that is itself limited. The assertion of an individual right to sexual self-expression can be more easily marginalized by conservatives when the movements promoting it are silent about the ways in which late capitalism consistently denies the conditions of self-determination to most people.

In this worst and best of times there is contest and resistance—in daily life, as individual women confront the various powers they face, in the multiple, creative efforts of organized resistance that continually spring up in mainstream feminism and outside it. The contradictions will not be resolved, the dilemmas will persist—and so will the well-springs of a radical challenge and a third feminist wave.

[*1993*]

Notes

I deeply appreciate the many contributions to this work made by Jan Haaken, Barbara Laslett, and Bill Resnick. I am also grateful to Perry Anderson and Ellen DuBois, whose critical reading certainly improved the essay.

1. Although there have been interesting developments in feminism and in women's overall situation since 1993, when this essay was first published, the contradictory picture it describes is fundamentally unchanged. In the early twenty-first century, feminism continues to attract young women, changes in gender relations in the workplace and especially within personal life are apparent, and opportunities for women to enter previously all-male domains are greater than ever before. On the other side, the political hold of the modernizing right is stronger than ever, abortion and lesbian/gay rights are still potent issues that the reactionary right exploits politically, many women struggle with the burdens of a double shift, the conditions of life everyday life for working-class women, white and of color, are deteriorating as the safety net shreds, as public services are cut back, as real wages stagnate and economic insecurity intensifies.

2. In New York City, "Women Tell the Truth: A Conference on Parity, Power and Sexual Harassment," hastily planned by a coalition of more than 150 women's organizations after the Hill–Thomas hearings, was attended by 2,000 while another 2,100 were turned away for lack of space. *New Directions for Women*, July–August 1992, 3.

3. The Clinton victory, or perhaps more accurately the Bush defeat, was welcome. However, behind the rhetoric, Clinton's program exemplifies this capitulation to corporate interests. Proposed spending on job creation, social services, and education is quite small. Clinton's reservations about the environmental and labor impacts of the North American Free Trade agreement are minimal. Clinton garnered business support unprecedented for a Democrat, partly because he promised government investment in the domestic economy and an aggressive trade policy, while Bush seemed ready to sell everything off to the multinationals.

4. The degree to which these solidarities are formed around heterosexual marriage varies by race, class, and sexual orientation. Cross-household networks including biological and fictive kin are more typical of African-American communities. The networks are organized around a gendered division of labor, with women assuming primary responsibility for making and maintaining caregiving relationship. Lesbians and gay men may rely on friendship networks more than family networks, although the drive to legalize same-sex marriage and to force employers to provide benefits to "domestic partners" as well as married couples reflects the importance of the household as a survival unit.

5. In 1988, 35 percent of married women with children under six were employed full time, while 18 percent worked part-time, and 47 percent were not working

for wages at all. Of course, this represented a phenomenal increase in work-force participation by mothers of young children. In 1960, only 17 percent of women in two-parent families with children under six were employed. Sara E. Rix, ed., *The American Woman, 1990–91* (New York, 1990), Table 17.

6. On this point, see Linda Haas, *Equal Parenthood and Social Policy: A Study of Parental Leave In Sweden* (Albany, 1992). The structure of careers also shapes choices about taking leave and working part-time. For instance, in Sweden more men take parental leave in the industrial and mining area of the north than in the predominantly white-collar south.

7. However, as many feminist economists have pointed out, differences in human capital can account for at most 50 percent of the wage gap between men and women. Francine D. Blau and Marianne A. Ferber, *The Economics of Men, Women and Work*, 2nd ed. (Englewood Cliffs, 1992), 193–95.

8. In 1985, 22 percent of men and 13 percent of women wage and salary work-ers belonged to unions, "Union Membership of Employed Wage and Salary Workers, 1985," *Monthly Labour Review*, May 1986, 45. Historically, men's rate of unionization has been substantially higher than it is today.

9. This is not to ignore the lack of support and outright opposition from men that women have faced when organizing. I am only arguing that overcoming this opposition is more difficult because of women's double day.

10. For this point, on the 1920s, see Rayna Rapp and Ellen Ross, "The 1920s: Feminism, Consumerism, and Political Backlash in the United States," in J. Friedlander et al., eds., *Women in Culture and Politics: A Century of Change* (Bloomington, 1986); on the 1980s, Judith Stacey, "Sexism by a Subtler Name? Postindustrial Conditions and Postfeminist Consciousness," *Socialist Review* 96, November–December 1987, 7–30.

11. I focus on middle-class women because they were the major social base for feminist organization. For more on this point and on how these changes af-fected working-class women and Black women, see Chapter 2.

12. Between 1950 and 1965, the labor force participation of older women in-creased dramatically, from 37.9 percent to 50.9 percent for women aged 45–54 and from 27.0 percent to 41.1 percent for women aged 55–64. By com-parison, increases in the proportion of younger women working for wages between 1950 and 1965 (i.e. women whose children were not yet in their teens) were much smaller (from 34 percent to 38.5 percent for women 25–34 and from 39.1 percent to 46.1 percent for women aged 35–44. Sara E. Rix, *The American Woman, 1988–89* (New York, 1988), Table 10.

13. Between 1960 and 1968 the number of women receiving college degrees doubled. Jo Freeman, *The Politics of Women's Liberation* (New York, 1975), 29. By the late 1960s almost half of all women high-school graduates continued on to institutions of higher education and almost one-quarter of all women 20–21 years old were enrolled in school. National Center for Educational Statis-tics, *Digest of Educational Statistics*, 1979, Table 5; and 1992, Table 171.

14. Educated working women who had participated in the surviving women's organizations of the 1950s were key organizers of the early mainstream move-ment. Leila J. Rupp and Verta Taylor, *Survival in the Doldrums: The American Women's Rights Movement, 1945–1960* (New York, 1987). At the National Wom-en's Conference in 1977, 70 percent of the delegates were employed either by government or by non-profit social welfare organizations, 63 percent were employed full time, 15 percent had bachelor's and 39 percent had graduate

degrees. Alice S. Rossi, *Feminists in Politics* (New York, 1982), 81. Women professionals in social work and mental health mobilized resources for the battered women's movement at both local and national levels. Kathleen J. Tierney, "The Battered Women Movement and the Creation of the Wife Beating Problem," *Social Problems* 29, no. 3 (February 1982), 207–220. For more on this point, see Chapter 2.

15. For one perspective on contemporary white working-class women's experience and consciousness, see Judith Stacey, *Brave New Families: Stories of Domestic Upheaval in Late Twentieth Century America* (New York, 1990).

16. White middle-class women's organizations with commitments to advancing women's equality were never extinguished; but they had no mass base. Even in those instances, such as the New Deal administration, where an elite of professional and activist women were well positioned politically, they could not turn personal influence and expertise into legislative or policy victories. For a more complete discussion of this point, see Chapter 2.

17. Rayna Rapp, "Is the Legacy of Second Wave Feminism Post-Feminism?", *Socialist Review* 3 (January–March 1988), 1–37.

18. They don't yet have children or their older children demand less time. In 1988, 33 percent of all children born were born to mothers in their thirties compared to 19 percent in 1976. *New York Times*, June 22, 1989.

19. That *Backlash: The Undeclared War against American Women* (New York, 1991), Susan Fauldi's biting liberal-feminist tract delineating the gains of the conservative counterattack against feminism, could also be a very successful bestseller graphically expresses the balance of forces more recently.

20. Ethel Klein, "The Diffusion of Consciousness in the United States and Western Europe," in Mary Fainsod Katzenstein and Carol McClurg Mueller, eds., *The Women's Movements of the United States and Western Europe* (Philadelphia, 1987).

21. *New York Times*, August 20, 1989.

22. Of course, that so many women still perceive work/family conflicts tells us nothing about how they respond to the dilemma. Some may conclude that women have an obligation to "put their families first," while others may believe that women deserve more help from employers, government, and spouses.

23. *New York Times*, August 20, 1989. Black women were more supportive of a strong women's movement than white women (85 percent to 64 percent). In a 1989 survey, 62 percent of women polled agreed that feminism has been helpful to women, although only 33 percent considered themselves feminists. *Time*, December 4, 1989.

24. *New York Times*, August 21, 1989. Women living alone may also feel isolated and insecure, as Deborah Rosenfelt and Judith Stacey argue, "Second Thoughts on the Second Wave," in Karen V. Hansen and Ilene J. Philipson, eds., *Women, Class, and the Feminist Imagination* (Philadelphia, 1990). On the other hand, there is some evidence that single motherhood reduces women's domestic burdens, since they no longer must take care of husbands in addition to children. Heidi I. Hartmann, "The Family as the Locus of Gender, Class and Political Struggle: The Example of Housework," *Signs* 6, no. 3 (Spring 1981), 366–94.

25. 1980s youth culture, AIDS notwithstanding, incorporated and legitimized an ideal of female sexual assertiveness. Like the flapper and the vamp, young women of the 1980s seem to have embraced feminist demands for sexual self-

determination but forgotten the feminist critique of male power. Yet unlike the 1920s, even in the dominant male domains of rap and rock, male power has not gone unchallenged, as contemporary Black women rappers and white women rockers confront their male counterparts on issues of violence against women and abortion rights. *Ms.*, July–August 1991, 93.

26. "What Women Want to Read," *Newsweek*, February 23, 1987; Sara E. Stern, "Working to Meet Women's Multiple Roles," *Advertising Age*, October 3, 1985.

27. 1988 figures.

28. *Newsweek*, February 23, 1987. In 1990, *Ms.*, floundering politically and losing money, was reorganized as an ad-free, reader-supported publication, with a relatively high subscription and cover price. It has more than survived, claiming a circulation of 150,000, well above the "break-even" point of 75,000 readers, but well below the readership of the other magazines. Deirdre Carmody, "Power to the Readers: *Ms.* Thrives without Ads," *New York Times*, July 22, 1991.

29. Patrick Reilly, "Service Magazines Adapt to Market," *Advertising Age*, March 7, 1988.

30. *Time*, December 4, 1989; *New York Times*, May 10, 1990.

31. Karen Rubin (founder, publisher and editor of *Making It! The Careers Newsmagazine*): "Now that a select group of companies have begun to introduce flexible policies, and women in valued positions are setting precedents, observers predict that the varied options will filter down throughout organizations, and from top companies to up and coming firms until they are finally entrenched as part of the American way of life." *Ms.*, March 1987.

32. These disparities exploded in Clinton's face when he was forced to back away from his nominee for attorney-general, Zoe Baird, once it was disclosed that she had illegally employed undocumented workers as live-in servants. Typically, mainstream feminists leapt to Baird's defense on the ground that she had little choice and suffered from the same difficulties as any other working mother seeking quality care for her child. This opened the way for a completely inauthentic, but effective, anti-feminist attack by conservatives in the name of the majority of working mothers.

33. Rix, *The American Woman, 1988–89*, 363. By 1990, women were 31 percent of graduating dentists, 34 percent of medical doctors and MBAs, 42 percent of lawyers. *Digest of Educational Statistics*, 1992.

34. Rix, *The American Woman, 1988–89*, 222.

35. Rix, *The American Woman, 1987–88*, 218.

36. In 1989 44 percent of women professionals worked in five predominantly female professions compared to 59 percent in 1970. Blau and Ferber, *The Economics of Men Women and Work*, 123.

37. Barnet Wagman and Nancy Folbre, "The Feminization of Inequality: Some New Patterns," *Challenge*, November–December 1988, 56–59.

38. During the 1970s, the incomes of highly educated women workers increased at the same rate as their male counterparts. But during the 1980s, women's incomes rose much faster than men's. For instance, among full-time workers over twenty-five years old with four years of college, between 1970 and 1979, women's median income rose 65 percent, men's median income 69 percent. Between 1979 and 1989, women's median incomes almost doubled, while men's incomes rose 72 percent. See *Digest of Educational Statistics*, 1991, U.S.

Department of Education, Table 357.

39. Rix, *The American Woman, 1990–91*, 217. According to a *Business Week* survey, entry-level jobs for women MBAs paid 12 percent less than those of their male counterparts.

40. Rix, *The American Woman, 1987–88*, 216–17.

41. *ABA Journal*, March 1989, 8.

42. One study of female executives found 20 percent never married, 20 percent were separated or divorced, and 46 percent had children; while 99 percent of male executives were married and 95 percent had children. *Ms.*, 1987, 31.

43. Tamar Lewin, "Partnership Awarded to Woman in Sex Bias Case," *New York Times*, May 16, 1990. Throughout the 1980s accounting and law firms had argued that partnership involves such special personal relationships that courts cannot intervene in a firm's decision-making. The Federal Court found in favor of the woman plaintiff, who had been denied partnership in Price Waterhouse, one of the nation's largest accounting firms—although she had brought in more business than any of the other eighty-eight all-male candidates—because the partners considered her "unfeminine."

44. Wagman and Folbre, "The Feminization of Inequality."

45. Among women 20–54 years old working part time, 19 percent of white women and 39 percent of Black women were involuntary part-timers who wanted but could not obtain full-time employment. Some 33 percent of women, compared to 11 percent of men, put together full-time work schedules by combining part-time jobs. Polly Callaghan and Heidi Hartmann, *Contingent Work*, Economic Policy Institute 1991, 22, 23, 38.

46. Blau and Ferber, *The Economics of Men, Women and Work*, 122; Evelyn Glenn, "From Servitude to Service Work: Historical Continuities in the Racial Division of Paid Reproductive Labour," *Signs* 18, no. 1 (1992), 1–43.

47. Barbara Basler, "Putting a Career on Hold," *New York Times Magazine*, December 7, 1986. Deborah Graham, "It's Getting Better, Slowly," *ABA Journal*, December 1, 1986, 54–58. According to the director of the American Bar Association's Commission on Women in the Profession, increasing numbers of lawyers who worked part time as associates have achieved partner status. *New York Times*, August 3, 1990.

48. The household incomes of women married to higher-income men tend to drop the most following divorce or separation. But, on average, these women have substantially higher household incomes than divorced women from less affluent households when married. Robert S. Weiss, "The Impact of Marital Dissolution on Income and Consumption in Single-Parent Households," *Journal of Marriage and the Family*, February 1984, 115–24. Race differences are also large. Following a divorce or separation 11 percent of white women and 33 percent of Black women had living standards below the poverty line. Greg J. Duncan and Saul D. Hoffman, "A Reconsideration of the Economic Consequences of Marital Dissolution," *Demography* 22, no. 4 (1985).

49. Kenneth B. Noble, "Union Seeking Affordable Day Care at Harvard," *New York Times*, February 28, 1988.

50. *New York Times Magazine*, January 29, 1989. In 1988, the National Child Care Staffing Study found the average hourly wage for chains was $4.10 per hour and the average annual turnover of staff 74 percent. *New York Times*, June 27, 1991.

51. *New York Times*, July 30, 1990. A study of pro-choice activists in California found that over half earned incomes in the top 10 percent of all working women, and 10 percent had an annual personal income in the top 2 percent. A total of 37 percent had undertaken some graduate work, 18 percent were doctors, lawyers, or PhDs. Kristin Luker, *Abortion and the Politics of Motherhood*, Berkeley 1984, 195.

52. Between 1960 and 1980 human services employment accounted for 41 percent of the increase in employment of women; 39 percent for white women and 58 percent for Black women compared to 21 percent for men. Women in the professions are more than twice as dependent as men on social welfare employment. It is estimated that 60–70 percent of all human services employment is directly or indirectly generated by state-sector spending. Steven P. Erie et al., "Women and the Reagan Revolution: Thermidor for the Social Welfare Economy," in Irene Diamond, ed., *Families, Politics and Public Policy* (New York, 1983).

53. Of couse, this reflects the political configuration of the U.S. more generally. In countries with social-democratic parties and political traditions, the sort of women who are social-welfare feminists in the United States are social democrats. See, e.g., Hester Eisenstein, *Gender Shock: Practicing Feminism on Two Continents* (Boston, 1991).

54. Ethel Klein, "The Diffusion of Consciousness in the United States and Western Europe," in Katzenstein and Mueller, eds., *The Women's Movements of the United States and Western Europe*, 31–32.

55. For more on the "modernizing right," see Bill Resnick, "The Right's Prospects: Can it Reconstruct America?", *Socialist Review* 2, no. 2 (March–April 1981), 9–37.

56. Major players include the Women's Legal Defense Fund, Women's Rights Project of the American Civil Liberties Union, the Center for Reproductive Law & Policy, NOW's Legal Defense and Education Fund, and the National Women's Law Center. The Puerto Rican Legal Defense and Education Fund (Latinas' Rights Initiative), the Mexican American Legal Defense and Education Fund, and the NAACP Legal Defense and Education Fund are also active litigators on issues pertaining to minority women.

57. The Congressional Caucus for Women's Issues represents the Women's Lobby in Congress. Formed as the Congresswomen's Caucus in 1977, the group changed its name to the Caucus for Women's Issues and opened membership to men in 1981 when several Republican women refused to join after Reagan's election, while others who did join refused to challenge the president. In order to coordinate better with the Caucus, in 1985 major organizations of the Women's Lobby established a "Council of Presidents" that establishes a Women's Agenda for the Congressional session. Rix, *The American Woman, 1990–91*, 281–82.

58. Twenty-six states have Women's Agenda Projects, which coordinate lobbying in the state legislatures and encourage women to run for office. *Ms.* 1, no. 1 (July–August 1990), 90.

59. Multi-issue Washington-based organizations include the Center for Women's Policy Studies, founded in 1972, the National Women's Law Center (1981), the Women's Research and Education Institute (1977); and the Institute for Women's Policy Research (1987).

60. For example, the National Coalition Against Domestic Violence, founded in 1978, represents about three-fourths of the 1,200 crisis lines, battered women's shelters, and safe home networks in the country. Wider Opportunities for Women, Inc. advocates for a network of three hundred employment and training programs for women in forty states; the National Women's Health Network represents five hundred women's and health organizations.

61. Older women's organizations were important conduits for the women's lobby in the early years of the second wave. They include the League of Women Voters, successor to the National Woman Suffrage Association, founded in 1920; the National Federation of Business and Professional Women (1919); the American Association of University Women (1882). Although not as radical as the second-wave activists, many of these organizations were founded originally for feminist reasons (and were repoliticized in the 1970s). For instance, the National Council of Jewish Women was established in 1894 after Jewish women wishing to participate in the Columbia Exposition's Parliament of Religions were admitted only as hostesses. United Methodist Women was established to sponsor single-women missionaries, after male church leaders banned them from missions. Anne N. Costain, "Representing Women: The Transition from Social Movement to Interest Group," in E. Bonaparth and Emily Stoper, eds., *Women, Power and Policy*, 2nd ed. (New York, 1988), 26–47. The National Council of Negro Women was founded in 1935 to give political voice to Black women's numerous social, professional, and educational organizations. Paul Giddings, *When and Where I Enter: The Impact of Black Women on Race and Sex* (New York, 1984), 205.

62. In 1989, for instance, the AAUW's volunteer Capitol Hill Lobby corps made more than a thousand visits to congressional offices. Some 1,500 AAUW members visited congressional offices in June to lobby for the family leave bill; fifty AAUW division presidents lobbied their members of Congress to pass the Civil Rights Act of 1990. AAUW, *Outlook*, 84, no. 3 (Fall, 1990), 16.

63. For example, the American Nurses Association; the National Federation of Specialty Nursing; the American Medical Women's Association (for women physicians and medical students); the National Association of Social Workers; Women in Communications; the National Association of Women Judges; Association of Women in Science; the National Association of Women Deans, Administrators, and Counsellors; the National Association for Female Executives. Six hundred organizations were founded in the 1980s. *Time*, December 4, 1989.

64. For instance, midwives and nurse practitioners have organized to challenge doctors' total control of health services by expanding the kinds of practice they are licensed to provide.

65. Susan M. Hartmann, *From Margin to Mainstream: American Women in Politics since 1960* (Philadelphia, 1989), 174.

66. In the 1920s, equal-rights feminists initiated the drive to pass the ERA but were opposed by social-feminists concerned about its impact on legislation protecting working women. This split continued into the 1940s when the Republicans (in 1940) and the Democrats (in 1944, over the objection of the trade unions, including women trade unionists) adopted ERA in their platforms. By the late 1960s trade-union women had dropped their opposition to the ERA, partly because the 1964 Civil Rights Act was already being inter-

preted to nullify gender-specific labor laws. U. Mansbridge, *Why We Lost the ERA* (Chicago, 1986), 8–19. By 1980, right-wing Republicans had forced the party to come out in opposition to the ERA. However, many Republican women voters still favored the ERA and worked for its passage in their states.

67. *Oregonian,* July 1, 1990. The first mobilizations were held in the spring of 1989, even before the decision, in anticipation of an unfavorable ruling.

68. There are also 63 centers for research on women and 360 women's centers (providing services to students).

69. Perhaps not surprisingly, the public universities have been more hospitable environments than the elite private universities and private colleges in general. The oldest, most well-funded and largest Women's Studies programs are located in public universities. Student interest is more likely to determine curriculum (and thus the introduction of Women's Studies courses into departments) in those institutions where departmental funding is enrollment-driven.

70. A total of 425 programs offer a minor, certificate, or area of concentration. Similarly, while programs are rapidly expanding at the graduate level, from 23 in 1986 to 102 in 1990, almost all of these programs offer a minor or concentration to accompany a graduate degree awarded through a traditional department.

71. The main interdisciplinary journals are *Signs, Feminist Studies, National Women's Studies Association Journal,* and *Frontiers.*

72. As with feminism more generally, the glass is half empty and half full here. There is disagreement about how well feminist scholarship is doing and how "feminist" is the scholarship that has been accepted into the disciplines. Whatever the case, most would agree that autonomous organizations and journals are still crucial for protecting and promoting feminist scholarship.

73. Students and college graduates are the social base of the direct action groups (Women's Health Action Movement, Women's Action Coalition) and the "Third Wave" (a New York-based organization aspiring to be a national young women's group) that have sprung up in response to the right-wing attack on abortion rights. Campuses also supply volunteers for shelters and crisis lines, mainstream organizations such as the National Abortion Rights Action League, and electoral campaigns of feminist candidates.

74. On the tensions between academics and activists in the National Women's Studies Association, see Robin Leidner, "Stretching the Boundaries of Liberalism: Democratic Innovation in a Feminist Organization," *Signs* 16, no. 2 (1991), 263–89.

75. Founded in 1896, the National Association of Colored Women represented fifty thousand women in 28 federations and over a thousand clubs by 1916. Organizations founded in the second wave—for example, the National Black Feminist Organization (1973) and the National Coalition of 100 Black Women (1981) were self-identified as feminist, but also conscious of their political differences with mainstream white women's organizations. Giddings, *When and Where I Enter*, 95, 344, 353.

76. By the late 1980s, in the American Federation of State, County and Municipal Employees, 33 percent of local union presidents and 45 percent of local union officers were women. Women were presidents of 15 percent of Communication Workers of America locals and 12 percent of IUE locals. The number

of United Auto Workers of America locals with women presidents doubled between 1979 and 1987. Ruth Needleman, "Women Workers: A Force for Rebuilding Unionism," *Labor Research Review* 7, no. 1 (Spring 1988), 6.

77. Although it has tremendous potential for mobilizing rank and file trade-union women, until now CLUW activists, for the most part, have been staff and local officials. For a history and analysis of CLUW, see Diane Balser, *Sisterhood and Solidarity* (Boston, 1987).

78. *CLUW News* (March–April and May–June 1992).

79. In 1987 only 50 percent of ex-husbands paid the full amount owed their ex-wives, while 25 percent paid nothing. Improved enforcement makes the most difference in living standards for women with more affluent ex-husbands, since the amount of the award varies according to the husband's earnings. In Oregon in 1991, a father earning $18,000 paid $372 per month, compared to $1,283 for a father earning $70,000. *Oregonian*, July 29, 1991. Given Black men's economic marginality, Black women are least likely to benefit from higher mandated payments or more vigilant enforcement of court orders. Mary Jo Bane, "Household Composition and Poverty," in Sheldon H. Danziger and Daniel H. Weinberg, eds., *Fighting Poverty: What Works and What Doesn't* (Cambridge, Mass., 1987), 231.

80. The Civil Rights Restoration Act overturned a Supreme Court ruling that permitted educational institutions to continue receiving federal funds although they had been found guilty of discrimination (within three years of the ruling the Department of Education had dropped or curtailed more than five hundred discrimination complaints). The 1991 Civil Rights Act expanded remedies available to victims of job discrimination and reversed several recent Supreme Court decisions that have made it more difficult to prove discrimination in employment. However, the Act places a cap on the amount of punitive damages plaintiffs can be awarded in cases of sex, although not race, discrimination.

81. In 1948 Congress enacted legislation excluding women from all combat duties. The new law would not affect combat jobs in the infantry or other ground units, or aboard warships.

82. Mansbridge, *Why We Lost the ERA*, 13–14.

83. The picture below the federal level is a bit better. For example, by August 1987 twenty states and 166 localities had implemented some kind of comparable worth adjustments for government employees (at an average cost of 2–4 percent of state payrolls) and an additional twenty-six states had begun to investigate wage disparities among comparable jobs. Intersecting networks of female leaders have been important in the passage of pay equity laws. Sara Evans and Barbara Nelson, *Wage Justice: Comparable Worth and the Paradox of Technocratic Reform* (Chicago, 1989), 164, 173.

84. *New York Times*, October 7, 1992. There are still no national standards for staffing and facilities. Federal standards are important because state standards vary widely, depending on the balance of political forces in each state. For instance South Carolina requires only one adult for every eight infants; Kansas and Maryland one for every three infants. Texas requires one adult for every seventeen three-year-olds; but in New York and North Dakota there must be an adult for every seven three-year-old children. Tamar Lewin, "Small Tots, Big Biz," *New York Times Magazine*, January 29, 1989. Clinton has pro-

posed increased funding for the HeadStart program (childcare for poor pre-school children), but even in the very unlikely event his proposal were to pass, HeadStart would not be fully funded to serve all the potentially eligible children until 1998. Moreover, current per-capita funding is not sufficient to guarantee programs of adequate quality.

85. Nearly two-thirds (63.4 percent) of all minimum-wage workers are women, and 40 percent of all women paid at hourly rates and maintaining families work in jobs that pay at or just above the minimum wage. National Women's Law Center, *Minimum Wage and Women* (March 1989). Over the last twenty years, the average welfare grant has declined 27 percent in real dollars. "'88 Welfare Act is Failing Short, Researchers Say," *New York Times*, March 30, 1992. Clinton's proposals for welfare reform similarly neglect this issue.

86. Hartmann, *From Margin to Mainstream*, 78. Some organizations simply promote women candidates, while others, like the National Women's Political Caucus, endorse only women candidates who are "pro-choice, support public funding for abortions and birth control information, passage and ratification of the ERA and publicly and privately funded childcare programs." *CAWP News & Notes* 9, no. 1 (Winter 1993), 16. NOW generally funds women candidates, but will also support pro-feminist men. For example, NOW endorsed Democrat Barney Frank rather than Republican Margaret Heckler for Congress and stayed neutral in the 1990 Democratic Party primary race between Diane Feinstein and John Van de Kamp for governor of California. (NOW supported Feinstein's campaign against Republican Pete Wilson.)

87. *New York Times*, May 24, 1992; Rix, *The American Woman, 1990–1991*, 387; National Women's Political Caucus 1988 Convention Brochure.

88. *AAUW Outlook*, February–March 1991, 10. Women have done better at state-wide appointed office than elections, holding 23 percent of all state cabinet appointments. National Women's Political Caucus, "Governors' Appointment Survey, 1989–91," April 1992.

89. *CAWP News & Notes*, 1–2. Of the twenty-four women newly elected to the House of Representatives in 1992, seventeen had held elected office at the local or state level; three had held appointed political offices. CAWP Fact Sheet, *Women in the U.S. House of Representatives 1993*.

90. Most of the newly elected senators and representatives did not run against incumbents. Of the five new women senators, three were elected to open seats and one defeated an interim senator. In the House, twenty-two of the twenty-four women candidates who won election did not run against incumbents, while twenth-three incumbent women won re-election. Center for Reproductive Law & Policy, *Reproductive Freedom News* I, no. 10 (November 1992), 3–4. On the surge of new donors, see *Wall Street Journal*, January 6, 1992.

91. In 1992, 2,373 women ran for state legislature (1,399 Democrats and 961 Republicans). Of these, 1,374 won election (59 percent of the Democrats; 57 percent of the Republicans), increasing their proportion of state legislators to 20 percent. CAWP Fact Sheet.

92. In 1992, only six of the fifty-four Republican women candidates running in the primaries for the House of Representatives opposed abortion. *New York Times*, May 24, 1992.

93. At the 1992 convention, women party activists unsuccessfully organized to challenge the anti-abortion plank in the party platform. In addition to form-

ing an organization, the National Republican Coalition for Choice, they established a Republicans for Choice PAC (to fund and endorse candidates) and a new fund-raising group, WISH (Women in the Senate and the House), to raise money for Republican pro-choice candidates. Although Bush's defeat will probably open up some opportunities for the moderates, the right wing is very well-entrenched at the grassroots of the party.

94. Jo Freeman, "Whom You Know versus Who You Represent: Feminist Influence in the Republican and Democratic Parties," in Katzenstein and Mueller, eds., *The Women's Movements of the United States and Western Europe*, 232. Personal communication from Karen Johnson, National Federation of Republican Women.

95. Ruth B. Mandel, "The Political Woman," in Rix, *The American Woman, 1988–89*.

96. Although half of the Democrats won election, only one-third of the Republican women candidates won. *CAWP News & Notes*, 24.

97. Freeman, "Whom You Know versus Who You Represent," 230, 234.

98. In 1988 49 percent and in 1992 49.7 percent of the delegates were women. Democratic National Committee Office, personal communication.

99. The Bill of Rights outlines a broad social-welfare agenda including freedom from discrimination based on sex, race, sexual orientation, religion, age, disability; rights to a decent standard of living, a clean and protected environment, and freedom from violence including the violence of war.

100. In 1992, NOW PAC contributed funds and staff to Lynn Yaekel's successful "come from behind" primary race against a conservative Democrat. Yaekel went on to lose narrowly to Arlen Specter, who led the prosecution of Anita Hill during the Senate confirmation hearings on Clarence Thomas. NOW contributed funds and volunteers to African-American feminist Carol Moseley Braun, who defeated incumbent Alan Dixon in the Illinois primary election for Senator. Dixon was one of two northern Democrats who had voted to confirm Clarence Thomas. Patricia Ireland, "The State of NOW," *Ms.*, July–August 1992, 27. Overall, NOW contributed more than a half-million dollars to women Democratic Party candidates in the 1992 elections. *CAWP News & Notes*, 11.

101. There are now forty-two PACs which either give money predominantly to women candidates or have "a predominantly female donor base." There are eleven national PACs. Four of the thirty-one state/local PACs focus on women of color (HOPE PAC, Latina PAC in California, Ain't I a Woman PAC in Pennsylvania, and African-American Women's PAC in Los Angeles). In 1990 women's PACs contributed $3.1 million, 68 percent to female candidates. In 1992 the PACs raised $11.8 million, 98 percent for female candidates. *CAWP News & Notes*, 10–11.

102. Although the right has successfully organized a constituency through sexual politics, the country is not more anti-abortion or anti-gay than in the past. Despite the highly visible attacks on abortion clinics and the unprovoked attacks by youth gangs on gay men in many cities, despite the hysteria around AIDS, almost two decades of legal abortion and the gay rights movement have moved attitudes in a more tolerant direction. Two-thirds of adults under forty-five (compared to only one-third over forty-five) know someone who had an abortion; 58 percent of them favored keeping abortion legal as it is now.

E.J. Dionne, Jr., "Poll on Abortion Finds the Nation is Sharply Divided," *New York Times*, April 26, 1989. Opinion polls taken since 1977 show support growing for equal job opportunities for gays and lesbians—71 percent in 1989 compared to 59 percent in 1982 and 56 percent in 1977. On the other hand, homophobia is still quite strong: only a minority said homosexuals were appropriate as high school teachers, clergy or elementary school teachers (47, 44 and 42 percent, respectively), although these levels of approval are also higher than in 1977. *New York Times*, October 25, 1989. Again, national data conceal important variations. While protestant fundamentalist churches are at the center of anti-gay political mobilizations, the Episcopal Church recently approved the ordination of a lesbian living in an open "committed monogamous relationship." Peter Steinfels, "Lesbian Ordained Episcopal Priest," *New York Times*, June 6, 1991. Campaigns to extend employee benefits to include "partners" (gay and heterosexual) as well as spouses have won in some instances with private employers and local governments. Phyllis Kriegel, "Making a Federal Case: Lesbian and Gay Couples Gain Spousal Benefits," *New Directions for Women*, May–June 1991, 1. Four states—Connecticut, Massachusetts, Wisconsin and Hawaii—have passed gay rights laws. *Sojourner*, May 1991, 29.

103. Luker, *Abortion and the Politics of Motherhood*, 138; Hartmann, *From Margin to Mainstream*, 143. Religiosity (measured by frequency of church attendance and whether respondents think religion is "very important" or "extremely important" in their lives) is one of the strongest predictors of opposition to abortion. M. Combs and S. Welch, "Blacks, Whites, and Attitudes Toward Abortion," *Public Opinion Quarterly* 46 (1982), 510–20.

104. *Roe v. Wade* argued that the state had a "compelling interest" in fetal life only in the last trimester of pregnancy. Regulation of abortion in the second trimester was allowed, but only to protect the health of the pregnant woman.

105. Unenforceable while they were making their way through the courts, these laws were found constitutional in Webster.

106. In 1991 the Supreme Court found this regulation constitutional. Legislation to overturn the gag rule passed both houses, but without the two-thirds majority to overrule Bush's veto. In a lame attempt to placate "pro-choice" forces, President Bush amended the regulations to allow doctors but not other providers to discuss abortion. One of Clinton's first acts as president was to rescind the gag rule.

107. For instance, none of the 1,200 physicians in North Dakota will perform abortions. The one abortion clinic in North Dakota, located in Fargo, the only metropolitan area, has to fly doctors in from Minnesota. Isabel Wilderson, "In North Dakota, Option of Abortion is Limited," *New York Times*, May 6, 1990, 33. Almost one-third of women of childbearing age live in a county with no clinic or hospital providing abortion. In ten states more than 20 percent of the women who had abortions in 1988 left the state to have them performed. *Oregonian*, March 20, 1992.

108. In 1985, 47 percent of abortion providers were harassed. Marlene Gerber Fried, ed., *From Abortion to Reproductive Freedom: Transforming a Movement* (Boston, 1990), 195. Between 1985 and 1988 the number of abortion providers declined in thirty-three states. NARAL, *Who Decides! A State-by-State Review of Abortion Rights* (Washington, D.C., 1991), 186.

109. In 1983, similar restrictions had been found *unconstitutional* by a different

Supreme Court (*Akron Center for Reproductive Health* v. *City of Akron*). The concept of "informed consent" originated with the patients' rights and women's health movements. In this instance it has been coopted and distorted by the anti-abortion forces.

110. In 1989, 11 state senates and 13 state assemblies were likely to vote for legal abortion, but by 1990, 22 state senates and 24 assemblies were in the yes column. NARAL, *Who Decides?*

111. The limitations of "family privacy" as a defense were also clear in the Court's Hardwick decision. Following the logic of *Roe* and *Griswold*, which ruled unconstitutional state limits on married couples' access to contraceptives, the Court *upheld* Georgia's criminal statute against sodomy (when practiced by homosexuals) on the ground that privacy rights inhered only in "family, marriage, or procreation." R. P. Petchesky, *Abortion and Woman's Choice*, rev. ed. (Boston, 1990), 315. For discussion of the progressive and conservative aspects of "privacy" see R. P. Petchesky and Rhonda Copelon, "From Privacy to Autonomy: The Conditions of Sexual and Reproductive Freedom," in Fried, ed., *From Abortion to Reproductive Freedom*.

112. The Fund for the Feminist Majority, founded by former NOW president Ellie Smeal, recently received $10 million from a wealthy supporter to organize for abortion rights. As the abortion issue heated up, Smeal used Fund resources to organize two national campaigns, one against parental notification and consent laws and another for legalization of RU486, the abortion pill currently banned because of pressure from the right. Both campaigns were run in the top-down method Smeal pioneered in NOW.

113. In the narrow constitutional sense of individual rights, many of these demands—for example, the right to a living wage—are not rights at all. The strategic decision to stretch the concept of rights to include the material conditions of self-determination reflects the dominant political discourse of the U.S., where the idea that individuals have fundamental rights is widely held and deeply legitimated.

114. The foregrounding of the fetus, the backgrounding of women to the point of being reduced to a womb, the treatment of pregnant women and fetuses as separate and antagonistic persons extend to other forms of restriction on pregnant women such as the incarceration of pregnant addicts and forced Caesarian births. Ruth Hubbard, "Fetal Protection Policies: Using Pregnancy to Control Women," *Sojourner: The Women's Forum*, October 1990, 16–17. Between 1981 and 1988 there have been at least twenty-one cases in which hospitals sought court orders to force a pregnant woman to undergo a Caesarean and in all but three cases the courts have granted the order. "Update on Women," *New Directions for Women*, January–February 1988, 14. Of the orders sought, 81 percent were against Black, Asian, or Latina women. Fried, ed., *From Abortion to Reproductive Freedom*, 159.

115. See Petchesky, *Abortion and Woman's Choice*, for a development of this point.

116. The right-wing attack on lesbian and gay rights combines similar elements. On the one hand, anxieties about maintaining sexual boundaries and sexual order are expressed in the constant invocation of homosexuality as promiscuous and perverse (i.e. not tied to reproduction). On the other hand, campaigns focus on gay schoolteachers and adoptive parents, invoking images of "innocent" children and our responsibility to protect them (from the presumed

dangers of homosexual recruitment and sexual abuse).

117. For more on this point, see Alan Hunter, "Children in the Service of Conservatism: Parent–Child Relations in the New Right's Pro-Family Rhetoric," Institute for Legal Studies, University of Wisconsin–Madison, Working Papers Series 2, April 1988. On how these dilemmas bring women into the anti-abortion movement, see Faye D. Ginsburg, *Contested Lives: The Abortion Debate in an American Community* (Berkeley, 1989); and Luker, *Abortion and the Politics of Motherhood*.

118. Most recently, Congress agreed to allow women to fly combat missions—a first step toward opening combat roles to women in the military.

119. In 1984 only four states had carried out pay equity adjustments for state workers and twenty-seven had taken no action; by 1988 twenty had begun to make adjustments and only seven had taken no action at all. National Committee on Pay Equity, 1988, 14. Pay equity legislation that would apply to private sector workers has made no headway at either the state or the federal level. Rix, *The American Woman, 1990–91*, 392.

120. Anita Hill's nationally televized testimony raised awareness among both employers and women, even though the senators appeared to disbelieve her. Following the hearings, complaints to federal and state regulatory commissions increased substantially, while many employers began or expanded programs to educate management and workers about the issue. *Washington Post*, 12 March 1992.

121. These policies have been widespread. Twenty percent of the large chemical and electronics companies in Massachusetts restricted women's but not men's employment options on the grounds of possible risk to their reproductive health in 1988. Rix, *The American Woman, 1990–91*, 50.

122. This case was brought by the United Auto Workers Union, which argued that both men and women should be protected from the harmful effects of lead, and no one should have to choose between their health and their job. But because the case was fought and decided substantively on the issue of "protection" versus "equality," at least some feminists did not regard the decision as a victory. See Ruth Rosen, "What Feminist Victory in the Court?", *New York Times*, April 1, 1991; and Nancy Reeves, letter to the editor, *New York Times*, April 24, 1991. For an overview, see Cynthia Daniels, "Gender Difference, Fetal Rights, and the Politics of Protectionism: Workplace Issues," in Fried, ed., *From Abortion to Reproductive Freedom*.

123. For instance, Delaware's 2/20 law limited alimony to a maximum of two years if a couple had been married for less than twenty years. A coalition of women attorneys, the Women's Section of the American Bar Association and the state Women's Commission drafted and successfully passed a revision that set the allowable years for alimony at 50 percent of the marriage's length. *AAUW Outlook*, January–February 1989, 20–21.

124. Martha Fineman, "Dominant Discourse, Professional Language, and Legal Change in Child Custody Decisionmaking," *Harvard Law Review* 101, no. 4 (February 1988), 738–39. The impact on women is not primarily that they lose custody of their children (although fathers appear to be winning more contested custody cases than in the past) but that the possibility of winning custody has given men increased leverage in bargaining divorce settlements with their ex-wives. Ellen Lewin, "Claims to Motherhood: Custody Disputes

and Maternal Strategies," in Faye Ginsburg and Anna Tsing, eds., *Negotiating Gender in American Culture* (Boston, 1990). Obviously this hits women from the middle and upper class hardest, since most working-class and poor families have little property or wealth to bargain over, although working-class women do have to bargain about the amount of child-support awards.

125. Corporations challenged a California law requiring employers to grant unpaid maternity leave on the ground that employers who did not provide similar benefits for other workers with other kinds of temporary disabilities would be discriminating against male and in favor of female employees. In *California Savings and Loan Association* v. *Guerra*, the Court upheld the maternity leave law. Lise Vogel, "Debating Difference: Feminism, Pregnancy, and the Workplace," *Feminist Studies* 16, no. 1 (Spring 1990), 9–32. On surrogacy, see Carmel Shalev, *Birth Power: The Case for Surrogacy* (New Haven, 1989).

126. For representative arguments see Phyllis Chesler, *The Sacred Bond* (New York, 1988), and *Mothers on Trial* (New York, 1986).

127. Iris Young, *Throwing Like a Girl and Other Essays in Feminist Philosophy and Social Theory* (Bloomington, 1990), 134.

128. Deborah L. Rhode, "Definitions of Difference," in *Theoretical Perspectives on Sexual Difference* (New Haven, 1990).

129. On alimony and custody, see Fineman, "Dominant Discourse, Professional Language, and Legal Change," 770–74; and Fineman, "Implementing Equality: Ideology, Contradiction and Social Change: A Study of Rhetoric and Result in the Regulation of the Consequences of Divorce," *Wisconsin Law Review* 789 (1983). On pregnancy and employment, see Vogel, "Debating Difference." A "gender-neutral" approach would not rule out taking into account biological differences. For instance, Barbara Katz Rothman argues that pregnancy is a social relationship, that expectant fathers as well as expectant mothers can participate in that relationship, but that the pregnant woman is the primary parent because she has the closest and most consistent relationship to the developing fetus. On this ground, she would support custody rights for birth mothers in cases of adoption and surrogacy agreements. *Recreating Motherhood* (New York, 1989).

130. By 1990, only four states had passed "family leave" laws requiring employers to grant unpaid leave to male or female workers. Congressional Caucus for Women's Issues, *Update*, June 1990, 12.

131. For an overview of feminist writing by women of color, see Gloria Anzaldua, ed., *Making Face, Making Soul, Haciendo Caras: Creative and Critical Perspectives by Women of Color* (San Francisco, 1990); Patricia Hill Collins, *Black Feminist Thought: Knowledge, Consciousness, and the Politics of Empowerment* (Boston, 1990). For the impact of feminist women-of-color writers on feminist theory, compare, for instance, the first and second editions of the feminist theory text, *Feminist Frameworks*, by Alison Jaggar and Paula Rothenberg (New York, 1978 and 1984).

132. Eleanor J. Bader, "NOW Confronts Racism," *New Directions for Women*, November–December 1990, 3. Progress has been slow, partly because, although mainstream organizations have made efforts to recruit and promote women of color within their organizations, they have proved quite resistant to sharing power with organizations of women of color. For example, women-of-color reproductive rights groups protested their exclusion by NOW in planning

the April 1991 March for Women's Lives. Their statement, distributed at the march, is reprinted in *Radical America* 24, no. 2 (June 1992).

133. Chela Sandoval, "Feminism and Racism: A Report on the 1981 National Women's Studies Association Conference," in Anzaldua, ed., *Making Face, Making Soul, Hacieno Caras*. A protest over the firing of the only African-American member of the National Women's Studies Association staff rocked the 1990 annual meeting. When negotiations collapsed after two days, many members of the Women of Color Caucus resigned from the organization and later founded the National Women of Colour Association. The director of NWSA subsequently resigned; and the 1991 annual meeting was canceled. The new director, an African-American woman, and a new national board have worked quite hard to reshape NWSA in response to the criticisms expressed. Protests by women of color also forced racism onto the agenda of the 1991 founding convention of the National Organization of Lesbians.

134. As Bernice Johnson Reagon put it, "You don't really want Black folks, you are just looking for yourself with a little color to it." "Coalition Politics: Turning the Century," in *Home Girls: A Black Feminist Anthology* (Albany, 1983).

135. Barbara Omolade, "Black Women and Feminism," in Hester Eisentein and Alice Jardine, eds., *The Future of Difference* (New Brunswick, 1985).

136. Hartmann, *From Margin to Mainstream*, 177. As noted above, mainstream organizations are more willing to recruit women of color than they are to share power with organizations of women of color, and NOW has an especially poor record on this account. "Who's Sorry NOW? Women of Color Protest Pro-Choice March," *Ms.*, July–August 1992, 88–89.

137. "Whose Story is it, Anyway? Feminist and Antiracist Appropriations of Anita Hill," in Toni Morrison, ed., *Race-ing Justice, En-gendering Power: Essays on Anita Hill, Clarence Thomas, and the Construction of Social Reality* (New York, 1992).

138. The statement was written by a group of two dozen African-American women, mostly academics. In addition to the signers, four to five hundred others sent contributions. The result was a full-page ad in the *New York Times* and several ads in African-American weeklies across the country. The statement is now available as a poster, and the signers have formed a national network called African-American Women in Defence of Ourselves. *New Directions for Women*, January–February 1992, 14; March–April 1992, 20.

139. Elsa Barkley Brown, "'What Has Happened Here': The Politics of Difference in Women's History and Feminist Politics," *Feminist Studies* 18, no. 2 (Summer 1992), 295–312.

140. Betty Friedan, *The Second Stage* (New York, 1981).

141. The huge march in Washington for gay/lesbian/bisexual rights in the spring of 1993 (estimates varied from six hundred thousand to a million) reflected the breadth, political self-confidence, and organization of queer activism.

142. Recently, Congresswoman Pat Schroeder joined the "new Democrats" of Clinton's Progressive Policy Institute and conservatives of the Family Research Council in support of "braking mechanisms," such as mandated waiting periods, before couples with children can obtain a divorce. *New York Times*, May 1, 1991.

143. Two representative, and widely read, texts are Sylvia Ann Hewlett, *A Lesser Life: The Myth of Women's Liberation in America* (New York, 1986), and Suzanne Gordon, *Prisoners of Men's Dreams: Striking Out for a New Feminine Future* (Boston,

1991).

144. Patricia Hill Collins (*Black Feminist Thought*) has called this a "both/and" politics. See also Ann Ferguson, *Sexual Democracy* (Boulder, 1991), chap. 11.

145. For instance, DSA co-chair, writer Barbara Ehrenreich, was a key propagandist for the "feminization of poverty" campaign which sought to convince mainstream feminists that poverty is a "woman's issue." Barbara Ehrenreich and Karin Stallard, "The Nouveau Poor," *Ms.*, July–August 1982.

146. There are still many socialist-feminists active in grassroots projects organizing women as workers, welfare recipients, health-care consumers, and community members (e.g. the Women's Economic Agenda Project in California; Muheras Obreras in New Mexico; Women's Health Action Movement in New York; reproductive rights projects in Boston, Detroit and Portland; movement publications such as *Labor Notes* and *Rethinking Schools*). But they are too small in number, too isolated from each other, too strapped for money, at least for the moment, to affect the larger political scene.

147. Rosalind Feldberg, "Comparable Worth: Toward Theory and Practice in the United States," *Signs* 10, no. 2 (Winter 1984), 311–28.

148. Evans and Nelson, *Wage Justice*; Joan Acker, *Doing Comparable Worth* (Philadelphia, 1989).

149. For a representative case of such conlicts of interest, see Guida West, "Cooperation and Conflict among Women in the Welfare Rights Movement," in Lisa Albrecht and Rose Brewer, eds., *Bridges of Power: Women's Multi-cultural Alliances* (Philadelphia, 1990), 149–71.

150. Nona Y. Glazer, "'Between a Rock and a Hard Place': Women's Professional Organizations in Nursing and Class, Racial and Ethnic Inequalities," *Gender and Society* 5, no. 3 (September 1991), 351–72.

151. See, e.g., Sandra Morgen, "'It's the Whole Power of the City Against Us!' The Development of Political Consciousness in a Women's Health Care Coalition," in Ann Bookman and Sandra Morgen, eds., *Women and the Politics of Empowerment* (Philadelphia, 1988).

152. Ann Withorn, "For Better and For Worse: Women Against Women in the Welfare State," in Rochelle Lefkowitz and Ann Withorn, eds., *For Crying Out Loud: Women and Poverty in the United States* (New York, 1986).

153. See, for instance, Frances Fox Piven, "Women and the State: Ideology, Power, and Welfare," in ibid.

154. See, for instance, Alice Kessler-Harris's candid exposition of how the rules of the game at the university pressure Women's Studies directors to jettison the interests of nontraditional, community-based scholars in order to advance those of the tenure-track faculty. See also Hester Eisenstein's delineation of the pressures on "femocrats," feminists working in the Australian state bureaucracy: *Gender Shock: Practicing Feminism on Two Continents* (Boston, 1990).

155. Although Ann Bookman and Sandra Morgen's volume, *Women and the Politics of Empowerment*, is not directly concerned with this strategic issue, many of the essays document the vitality of working-class women's trade-union and community organizations.

156. For a summary of the debate and an unusually balanced and sensible intervention in it, see Ann Ferguson, "The Sex Debate in the Women's Movement," *Against the Current*, September–October 1983, 10–17, and *Blood at the Root: Motherhood, Sexuality and Male Dominance* (London, 1989), chap. 10.

157. Kathleen J. Tierney, "The Battered Women Movement and the Creation of the Wife Beating Problem," *Social Problems* 29, no. 3 (February 1982).

158. Elizabeth Pleck, *Domestic Tyranny: The Making of Social Policy Against Family Violence from Colonial Times to the Present* (New York, 1987), 200.

159. Traditionally, police called to the scene of a domestic dispute tended to "cool off" the batterer and leave, except in cases of severe injury or death. In a pro-arrest policy, officers called to a domestic dispute will make an arrest if there is any evidence at all of physical abuse. A 1982 study in Minneapolis found that arresting batterers significantly reduced recidivism, even if the batterer was never formally charged or received court punishment. Rix, *The American Woman*, 1988–1989, 298–99.

160. Hartmann, *From Margin to Mainstream*, 170. Stiffer arrest policies were also encouraged by large damage awards to victims of domestic violence who sued local governments for not providing them with adequate police protection.

161. Although rape convictions, especially where the victim and perpetrator are acquainted, are still difficult to obtain, as juries often prefer to believe the accused rather than the woman's story. See, for example, the acquittal of three white fraternity members at St. John's University who sodomized a Black woman student. According to Manhattan sex crimes prosecutor Linda Fairstein, however, conviction rates are improving, ranging from 50 to 75 percent. E. R. Shipp, "Bearing Witness to the Unbearable," *New York Times*, July 28, 1991.

162. Pleck, *Domestic Tyranny*, 197.

163. But some members of the NCADV opposed that decision and split off to form a group called the National Women's Abuse Prevention Project, which compromised on the lesbian issue and received the funding.

164. Congressional Caucus on Women's Issues, *Update*, October 20, 1986, 11.

165. There is every reason to hold men responsible, but it is necessary to do so in a way that does not reinforce the traditional marital bargain. Child-support enforcement legislation does little to increase the incomes of women formerly married to low-income men or women receiving state benefits, who are allowed to retain only $50 a month of the child-support collected from their ex-spouses. Given the severe political and economic constraints under which feminists are working, there has been little energy for devising alternative strategies for ensuring divorced women and single mothers an adequate standard of living and empowering women and children within the family.

166. The gap between academics and activists on this issue is truly vast. Radical-feminist analyses of sexuality and strategies for ending male violence dominate popular writing and thinking in the anti-violence movement. In contrast, the now extensive feminist literature analysing sexuality from social constructionist and psychoanalytic perspectives is often inaccessible in style and, even more important, takes very little responsibility for movement strategy, for outlining how in the short run as well as the long run feminists can organize to defend women against sexual violence and sexual exploitation.

167. As Arlene Stein points out, urban lesbian communities are no longer so unitary, politically or spatially, as they once were. "Sisters and Queers: The Decentring of Lesbian Feminism," *Socialist Review* 22, no. 1 (January–March 1992). Despite this diversity, lesbian organizations and networks still play a critical part in maintaining the women-identified institutions that sustain this

women's culture.

168. There seems to be some concern that expanding opportunities for women in the mainstream are undermining the production, distribution and performance of women's music. Jennifer Einhorn, "Women's Music, Where Did it Go?", in *Sojourner*, September 1991, 34–35.

169. Two New York area-based publications, *New Directions for Women* and *On the Issues*, have circulations almost twice as large, and the new *Ms.* probably about four times as large. They are difficult to characterize, because their content is fairly eclectic. However, they are certainly self-consciously *political* and feminist and clearly to the left of the other women's magazines.

170. Hester Eisenstein, *Contemporary Feminist Thought* (Boston, 1983); Alice Echols, *Daring To Be Bad* (Minneapolis, 1990).

171. See, for instance, the interview with lesbian separatist Sonia Johnson, "Sonia Johnson: Breaking Free," in *Sojourner*, January 1988, 16; and the critical response by Angela Bowen, Terri Ortiz, Jennifer Abod, and Jacqui Alexander, "Taking Issue With Sonia," *Sojourner*, February 1988, 14.

172. Janet Biehl, *Rethinking Ecofeminist Politics* (Boston, 1991).

173. Barbara Epstein, *Political Protest and Cultural Revolution: Nonviolent Direct Action in the 1970s and 1980s* (Berkeley, 1991).

174. For a more extensive discussion of this point, see Chapter 8 above.

175. Lisa Duggan, "Making it Perfectly Queer," *Socialist Review* 22, no. 1 (January–March 1992).

Conclusion

Intersections, Locations, and Capitalist Class Relations: Intersectionality from a Marxist Perspective

In feminist theory "intersectionality" has emerged as an analytic strategy to address the interrelation of multiple, crosscutting institutionalized power relations defined by race, class, gender, and sexuality (and other axes of domination). Most intersectional analysis focuses at the level of social location, a "place" defined by these intersecting axes of domination, and asks how a social location shapes experience and identity. In the first part of this essay I follow such an approach. If feminism is to become a powerful movement again, working-class women will have to organize across the divides of race/ethnicity and sexuality. Therefore, it is of political importance to understand how class locations, in intersection with race/ethnicity and sexuality, shape women's survival projects, their strategies for claiming self-worth and exercising public authority, their uses of motherhood as an identity, and their responses to cultural constructions of their sexuality. I explore class differences within racial/ethnic groups as well as class similarities across racial/ethnic divides as a route toward delineating the potential common ground for a working-class women's politics and for a feminist politics of class.

In the second part of the essay I move from class as social location to class as social relations of production. Here I show how the possibilities for resistance in different class locations develop within a political context which is in turn shaped by capitalist relations of production, by the dynamics of the capitalist economy and the powers of the capitalist class. Coming back to themes of earlier essays in this volume, I argue that global capitalist restructuring has reconfigured the political terrain in the U.S. with profound strategic implications for feminism and other movements of liberation.

Class Locations and Intersections

Intersectional analysis, developed primarily by feminist women-of-color scholars and writers, demonstrates that race and gender oppressions do not build on each other in any simple additive way. White feminists' failure to understand this has contributed significantly to missed opportunities for building an inclusive feminist movement. An exemplary instance of this failure occurred in the positions taken by mainstream feminists in the politics around Anita Hill's testimony at the Senate confirmation hearings for Supreme Court nominee Clarence Thomas. By claiming Anita Hill's experience as representative of all professional women's experience of sexual harassment, white feminists fundamentally eliminated her specificity as a Black professional woman.[1] They thereby missed an opportunity to publicly acknowledge the existence and impact of racial oppression. Anita Hill did not experience or respond to her harassment as a gender assault separate from experiences of the racial discrimination she might have faced in her efforts to succeed as a professional. Positioned by her race, Anita Hill had to deal with her harassment under constraints that white professional women do not face. She had to be a credit to her race. If her success came at a personal cost of enduring harassment, she had to weigh that cost against a more collective one: disappointing all those who counted on her success and who had supported her along the way. White feminists interpreted her long silence about the harassment as the consequence of the isolation and self-blame that many middle-class white women experience in similar situations. In so doing, they not only ignored the history of Black women's understanding and awareness of their sexual vulnerability in the public world; they also minimized the particular dangers confronting Black women who publicly resist sexual exploitation. Black women's representations in the dominant culture as sexually voracious and promiscuous threatened not only to discredit Anita Hill individually but to vitiate one very crucial purpose of her professional striving—to recuperate Black women's image by refuting what everyone believes about *the* Black woman. Finally, her silence came out of a long history of racial solidarity. Thus, Anita Hill's silence as well as her speaking out, the uses to which her speech was put by white feminists and the ways in which her speech was discounted by (mostly but not entirely) male spokespeople for the Black community, were emblematic of the difficulties as well as potentials of Black women's location at the intersection of race and gender.

Women-of-color feminists have also drawn on gender/race inter-sectionality to critique sexism in their communities and male dominance in organizations and movements against racial oppression both histori-cally and today.[2] As in the case of Anita Hill, male leaderships decide what is and is not called for in the name of racial solidarity. Kimberlé Crenshaw offers this telling example: "while gang violence, homicide, and other forms of Black-on-Black crime have increasingly been dis-cussed within African-American politics, patriarchal ideas about gender and power preclude the recognition of domestic violence as yet another compelling incidence of Black-on-Black crime."[3]

Perhaps the most well-explored instance of race/gender intersection-ality has been the different locations of white women and women of color in the work of social reproduction. Historically and today, whether in the private household (domestic servant and her employer) or in the public sphere (hotel maids/nurses' aides/kitchen workers and profes-sionals/supervisors/administrative support staff), women of color do the most menial, difficult, and dirty work. As Glenn puts it, "this racial construction of gendered labor has created divisions between White and racial ethnic women that go beyond difference in experience and standpoint. Their situations have been interdependent: the higher status and living standards of White women have depended on the subordi-nation and lower standards of living of women of color."[4] Although Glenn terms this an analysis of race/gender intersectionality, class and capitalism lurk in the background. All white women are not upper middle class—indeed the majority are working class and don't employ either nannies for their children or domestic workers to clean their houses. And the majority of poor women are white women, even though white women are far less likely to be poor than women of color. At the same time, class differences appear to have increased among women of color. In the post-civil-rights era, opportunities for some women of color to enter the middle class of managerial and professional workers have expanded even as working-class women of color have lost ground, with the most vulnerable pushed even further into poverty. Glenn's contri-bution to feminist theory is substantial and groundbreaking. Here I want to build on her insights to indicate the importance of integrating class into analysis of race/gender intersections. Class analysis is crucial to understanding how and why different groups of women adopt differ-ent survival projects which shape and are shaped by possibilities for collective action.

Women, class, and resistance

Class locations are difficult to define, especially when we attempt to capture how positions in the economy create bundles of individual experiences and group affiliations which might give rise to distinctly different identities, or interests, or worldviews. There is a very large literature debating how to draw these lines or to deal with those many class locations that seem to be contradictory in terms of their attributes. Defining class locations becomes especially fraught for intersectional analysis, because in most instances we are not comparing those who own capital with those who do not, but are trying rather to understand relations of power and relative privilege among those who do wage and salaried work.[5] For the purposes of this essay, I use "middle class" to mean roughly salaried professionals and managers, divided between those at the upper reaches who are closer to capital and those at the lower end who are closer to working-class occupations. I use "working class" to mean blue-, white-, and pink-collar waged workers and those who never access permanent employment. I am interested here in two aspects of class/race intersectionality in shaping women's resistance strategies: class differences within racial/ethnic groups and class simi-larities across the racial/ethnic divide. First, drawing from a rich historical literature on Black women's political organization and resist-ance, I lay out some of the ways that class differences among Black women created lines of conflict as well as alliance. Second, I explore how class location shapes similar dilemmas of gender identity for working-class women across their racial/ethnic differences.

From reconstruction through the civil-rights era Black women, whether working class (domestic and service workers, married to blue-collar men or sharecroppers) or middle class (schoolteachers, nurses, social workers, or married to them) or members of the Black elite (af-fluent professionals and business people), shared in the development of community institutions, and a "collective wisdom" passed down from one generation to the next. Based in the educational, occupational, and housing segregation that organized racial oppression in the U.S., a Black civil society emerged that gave Black women a field for collective action and the development of distinct identities as "race women." Most edu-cated and professional Black middle-class women were relegated to the segregated institutions of their communities—Black schools and colleges, Black social service agencies, and so on. Rather than separating them-selves from their working-class sisters, they created and sustained a tradition of reform work for racial uplift.[6] Within this very strong and honorable reform tradition, however, there were class tensions and conflicts. More than one "culture of resistance" could be found in Black civil society. These different cultures of resistance arose from different class locations.

Deborah Gray White documents how the class location of middle-class (and "elite") Black women reformers shaped their worldviews, organizational practices, and political strategies.[7] They arrived at their political choices not only as an expression of their class-based worldview, but in response to the avenues open to them for exercising political influence. The emergence of the Black women's club movement coincided with the formation of a new urban Black middle class and the opening up of new terrains for Black political organization, terrains which came to be dominated by middle-class men and women.[8]

Elsa Barkeley Brown argues that the development of gender identities was integral to this process: "[t]hrough discussions of manhood and womanhood, middle-class men and women constructed themselves as respectable and entitled, and sought to use such constructions to throw a mantle of protection over their working-class brothers and sisters."[9] The duty of the middle-class club woman was to provide not just social services for the poor but services that in one way or another educated the Black working-class, and particularly Black women, on the means and benefits of achieving respectability.

Just as many early twentieth-century white women reformers carved out a political space for themselves in social housekeeping, so also Black middle-class women found a public role in the moral uplift of African-American working-class and poor women.[10] Black working-class women, like their immigrant working-class counterparts, often resisted and resented being defined as in need of improvement. Despite these parallels, however, it is necessary to be very clear that the class tensions and conflicts between Black elite/middle-class and Black working-class/poor women were significantly different from the intersecting class and race divisions that brought middle-class white women reformers into relation to working-class and poor women from other racial/ethnic communities. The "Americanization" projects that motivated Anglo white middle-class women reformers had different roots and the effects of their strategies different (and more negative) consequences, politically and economically, for working-class and poor women.[11] Shared racial oppression and more closely shared economic circumstances than those that characterized white middle-class reformers and their clients led Black middle-class women to organize programs and advance political views that better reflected the needs of the women they were trying to serve.[12]

Furthermore, Black middle-class women's anxieties about proving respectability and virtue were themselves a response to white supremacist representations of super-sexualized Black womanhood. These cultural figurations of Black women were so threatening because they legitimated the social, economic, and political power structures through which Black women's labor was exploited, their motherhood denied, their bodies abused and invaded. These representations were also, and especially, galling to Black middle-class women, as they were often used to justify Black women's exclusion from white middle-class society and from social positions of honor and leadership, positions for which they were eminently qualified by virtue of their educational attainment and social comportment. However, Black clubwomen's strategic choice—to build a counter-identity on chastity, virtue, community service, and cultural refinement—also reflected gender and class relations *within* the Black community.[13] Deborah Gray White points out that in making chastity the foremost requirement for middle-class status, "club women established an orthodoxy bound to drive a wedge between themselves and the masses of black women."[14] For Black working-class women were in the process of developing and defining their own strategies for claiming self-worth. In the next section I discuss how different groups of women within the Black working class negotiated the dilemmas surrounding their sexuality and gender identity.

Black working-class women had as much, if not more, than Black middle-class women to fear from white supremacist constructions of their sexuality. Black women workers were threatened and bedeviled by their white male employers; sexual harassment, attempted and completed rape, were endemic occupational hazards of factory work and domestic service. Thus, it was not only middle-class Black women who adopted a "culture of dissemblance." Black working-class women also felt compelled to hide any expression of their sexuality from public view.[15] On the other hand, as interviews with Black women workers in domestic service show, many Black working-class women made clear distinctions between how they had to present themselves to the white world and who they really were.[16] Within their own urban communities, working-class Black women, especially young women, resonated to a feminine identity quite different from that which the middle-class wished to impose: the explicit sexual self-assertion of the women blues singers of the 1920s. Performing in working-class clubs and finding a mass audience for their recordings among urban workers, men and women, the blues singers challenged dominant ideals of respectable womanhood and defied the silencing of Black women's sexuality. They sang openly about the pleasures as well as the dangers of Black women's heterosexual relationships; they engaged in and made recordings about lesbian affairs.[17]

As Robin Kelly notes, to appreciate fully Black working-class resistance to racism it is necessary to look "underneath" formal organizations—unions, churches, civil rights organization—to what he calls the "infrapolitics" of Black street life and culture. He characterizes the resistance in Black working-class popular culture as "alternative" rather than "oppositional."[18] This seems to be true of the Blueswomen and their working-class clientele. Subcultures create a space for developing and expressing worldviews that defy the conventions of the dominant society. On the other hand, once members of an oppressed group attempt to enter into that world, to contest for power or place, they become vulnerable to pressures toward conformity. And the more dependent they are on winning allies from powerful groups, the more vulnerable they are to these pressures. Only when oppressed people have a base in powerful social movements, can they fully challenge hegemonic worldviews and create their own.

The Blueswomen expressed one side of Black resistance and reflected, in culture, what many working-class women coming into the city expressed in their daily lives as they took advantage of new opportunities for work and for leisure. In their own communities, working-class Black women and men were more free to discount and defy white and middle-class norms of respectability. While opening up space for sexual expression, the Blueswomen's defiance could not constitute a basis for contestation with the surrounding white supremacist order. Indeed, they threatened to undermine the claims to respectability so central to the politics of the Black middle class.

Not surprisingly, the Blueswomen met strong opposition from the clubwomen and other Black middle-class spokespeople. The growing numbers of Black working-class women migrating to the cities, their increasing assertiveness, discretionary income, and, most particularly, their enjoyment of dance halls and cabarets, fueled what amounted to a moral panic in the Black middle class.[19] According to Hazel Carby, "the migrating Black woman could be variously situated as a threat to the progress of the race; a threat to the establishment of a respectable Black middle class; a threat to congenial Black and white middle-class relations, and a threat to the formation of Black masculinity in an urban environment."[20] Kimberley Phillips makes the further point that this "politics of displacement" was also a reaction to the intensified racism and rising tide of segregation experienced by the Black community during this period. The black middle class and elites responded to the increased threat by displacing blame from whites, whom they could not control, onto the Black working class, whom they could hope to manage.[21]

There were other strategies of resistance besides the defiance of the Blueswomen and the uplift organizing of the middle-class African-American clubwomen. Black working-class women also formed women's organizations.[22] These organizations, in contrast to those of the Black middle class, approached working-class communities less through projects of moral education and social service and more through projects of collective self-organization—consumer cooperatives, mutual aid and benevolent associations, housewives' leagues, and consumer boycott campaigns (such as the "Don't Buy Where You Can't Work" campaign), and women's auxiliaries to labor unions.[23] In spite of these different organizing strategies, working class women's organizations appear also to have adopted collective identities that emphasized respectability and women's contribution to the race through family and community work.[24] The need to contain and control Black women's sexuality in the interest of race advancement continued to be a theme of both working-class and middle-class Black women's organizations throughout the twentieth century. The Black women's organizations of the 1950s had much the same negative response to rock and roll as their predecessors had to the Blueswomen.[25]

Working-class Black churches, like their middle-class counterparts, were also caught up in the surveillance of women's sexuality and sexual autonomy.[26] Yet, in other respects, working-class churches broke with middle-class norms. Working-class congregations were crucial sites of support for labor organizing in contrast to the Black middle-class churches, whose congregants tended to have ties to white urban elites—philanthropists, businessmen, and politicians.[27] Even more striking, there was far more room in working-class churches for women to play leadership roles, including as preachers. However, despite their rebellious stance toward the Black middle class and toward white employers, working-class churchwomen adamantly sought to police other Black women's sexual expression.[28]

Both middle-class and working-class Black women struggled to create a feminine identity over against white supremacist cultural constructions of their bodies as degraded and dangerous and adopted some of the same strategies. But these strategies appear to have expressed somewhat different dilemmas. For the Black middle class, the referent of their actions with respect to and on behalf of the poor was the white world they aspired to enter. They made alliances with white elites when they could, they acted as brokers across the race divide, and they had a strong interest in ensuring that the Black working class did not threaten their hard-earned and fragile social positions.[29] Black working-class churchwomen's efforts at sexual containment had less to do with matronizing moral uplift or with a "politics of displacement" than with a real contest between men and women within the working class over the claims that women could make on men. The life of the street, of public spaces away from home and church, offered freedom to women but also to men.[30] The strains of poverty made it difficult to keep families together and the consequences of separation were far more harsh for women than for men. Offering the church as an alternative site for emotional expressiveness and release, these working-class women may have hoped to bind men more closely to them. Where they stressed responsibility, commitment, and community, the culture of the street celebrated a break from the constraints of alienated work and perhaps even family obligation. On the other hand, the clubs, dance halls, and bars where Black working-class men and women pursued pleasure and leisure also provided income (licit and illicit) for working-class women. And, for many young women, these were arenas for sexual experimentation and courtship.[31]

Working-class as well as middle-class Black women counterposed to the individualistic self-expression of sexuality and the street a more communal ideal of maternal authority based in caring for family and community. The image of the strong Black mother has powerfully shaped Black women's struggle for self-definition. In her book *Fighting Words*, Patricia Hill Collins criticizes what she terms the paradigm of individual sacrifice for women that can border on exploitation. Norms of racial solidarity have placed Black women in the position of being traitors to the race if they appear to put themselves first.[32] Black women have been more successful in naming and challenging the gender, race, and economic exploitation and discrimination they suffered at the hands of white-dominated institutions than at disentangling the gender oppression that weaves through the respect, admiration, personal influence, and even social power conferred on them by their roles as community workers and strong Black mothers.[33]

Class, motherhood and sexuality

The strong mother/community-worker roles of Black women are replicated, in different guises, in other communities of color but also in
white working-class communities. In this next section I explore the
similarities, across racial/ethnic divides, in working-class women's strategies for making gender identities. I argue that the same tension between claiming respect on the basis of motherhood, on the one hand,
and women's sexual self-expression, on the other hand—a tension which
has historically shaped Black women's struggle for self-definition—is
also present in white working-class women's lives. In this context, I
trace out some connections between working-class women's investments
in maternal honor and the heterosexism that working-class lesbians have
so painfully experienced and described.

There are, of course, historically constructed differences in the
cultures, family/household patterns, and maternal roles of different
racial/ethnic communities. For example, as Patricia Hill Collins and
Paula Gunn Allen argue, Native Americans and African Americans have
carried with them, from their precapitalist communities of origin,
communal traditions that women could draw on, traditions that gave
them more ground for exercising autonomy in the public worlds of
their communities.[34] The extended kin networks of Chicano and Asian-
American communities, like those of Southern white and many European immigrant communities, had origins in more patriarchal agrarian
economies.[35]

Women moving into community work and public roles have faced
more or less opposition from men depending, at least in part, on these
differences within the cultures of their communities.[36] But all working-
class people, white as well as people of color, have needed to rely on
cross-household networks to organize exchanges of goods and labor as
a fundamental strategy for survival.[37] Because these networks are based
on combining waged and unwaged work and especially rely on women's
labor and social skills, they are a material base for the development of
gender identities and a working-class community culture which confers
honor on women as strong mothers who endure. White working-class
women have not been "angels in the house." And as Dorothy Allison
makes so poignantly clear, the women in her family have felt pulled to
support their men, over against a world which disempowers and
disrespects them, even at the women's own expense, in a tangle of
sympathy for men and a need for men's income.[38]

All women of color are sexual Others in white supremacist culture, defined, in one way or another (geisha, squaw, tropical bombshell, hot mama) as (hetero)sexually available. Men of color are made Other by being hyper-masculinized (Blacks and Latinos) or emasculated/feminized (Asians).[39] Class difference, on the other hand, is a much less central theme in contemporary representational culture and other public discourses. In the hegemonic cultural construction of class in America, there are only three classes: the (white) rich, the (white) middle class, and the (Black and brown) poor. Class is so thoroughly racialized that white poverty (and even the working class as a distinct group) virtually disappears. Yet, for this very reason, "white trash" remains a powerful slur that haunts white working-class women.

The connections between erotic fantasy, desire, fear, and relations of domination in Western culture are too complex to take on here. So also is the exploration of "trash" identity and how it works as a cultural discourse. I just want to point out that the cultural denigration of poor people and the sexualization of poor women works as a "controlling image" for white working-class women in ways that are parallel, although not identical, to the "controlling images" that women of color have confronted and resisted in their struggle for self-definition. I want to suggest that the powerful identification with and use of mothering by working-class women is constructed out of both the opportunities for exercising authority internal to the community and the dangers of claiming sexual desire, inside and outside it. Additionally, sexuality and motherhood are culturally constructed as oppositions. So for women to build identities around socially valorized ideals of motherhood and caring work inevitably pushes them in the direction of sexual self-denial. Assertion of sexual desire (especially sexual desire outside its containment in romantic love and marriage) is also an acknowledgement of self-need that threatens to disrupt the basis of personal authority located in women's caring for others first.

Evelynn Hammonds argues that the silencing and self-silencing of Black women's sexuality makes Black lesbians outsiders in their own community.[40] Patricia Hill Collins speculates that one of the sources of resistance to Black feminism among Black women is its association with lesbianism, interpreted as a desire to separate from men. The significance of Christianity for African-American women and the thoroughgoing homophobia of Black nationalist politics reinforce women's rejection of homosexuality.[41] Without denying the influences Collins identifies, I think that Hammonds has captured something powerful in linking the suppression of female sexual desire more generally to Black women's fear of lesbian sexuality. Several Chicana writers make a similar argument about the splitting of femininity between the maternal and the sexual in Chicano culture. In her maternal body, the Chicana is honored and trusted. In her sexual body, the Chicana is dangerous, a potential traitor to her people.[42] If embracing the maternal requires a denial of sexual desire and agency, then the lesbian, who is defined by her desiring, and by her lack of sexual interest in men, represents what must be suppressed—a female sexuality that is not under the control of or in the service of men. Although the madonna/whore split is pervasive in Western culture, it takes on another layer of meaning in working-class and racially oppressed communities where motherwork holds people together and group loyalty is crucial for survival.

White working-class women's association, in the dominant culture, with dangerous, perverse sexuality similarly privileges maternal strength and endurance over against sexual self-expression as the locus of adult women's identities. As Bev Skeggs shows in her longitudinal ethnographic study of a group of white working-class women she first met in a vocational training course, working-class women have to negotiate a difficult path to becoming respectable *and* heterosexual.[43] For working-class women, living in the shadow of their "white trash" figurations, heterosexuality produces simultaneously normalization and marginalization. The distinction between women who enjoy and are in control of sex and those who are more innocent maps onto the distinction between respectable and unrespectable women. Not all of the women negotiated these dilemmas in the same way. Still, they all had to confront and work through the conflation of class shame and sexual shame.[44]

The women's class affected their identities primarily in the ways that they actively disidentified with being working class. Unable either to leave their class position or to engage in a collective resistance to their conditions of life, the women turned to "respectability and responsibility as a means of establishing a valued and legitimate way of being and of being seen."[45] This strategy in turn, Skeggs argues, placed lesbian sexuality even further off limits. To take up a lesbian identity, particularly insofar as lesbians were seen to be part of a "middle-class" sexual counter-culture which affirmed individual choice and sexual self-expression, woud run counter to women's prior investments in caring, family, and motherhood.[46]

Dorothy Allison, writing from a different context—growing up poor white in the South—explores with compassion and insight the consequences of what Skeggs describes as the "inability *to be* without shame, humiliation and judgement." It was only once Allison's family left the South Carolina Piedmont's rigid class structure, where opportunities for "passing" or "moving up" were nonexistent, that she came to realize possibilities beyond being locked into her "white trash" identity. The women in Skeggs's study had more, but not much more, room to negotiate their identities. Their vocational training and occupations—as daycare workers, home health workers, nurses' aides—provided a vehicle for, and in fact encouraged, them to see themselves as skilled, responsible, and therefore respectable. The women in Allison's family could not get out from under being the "bad poor."[47] They understood that their sexuality had exchange value, and found ways to use it, on the job as well as off it. This, of course, further undermined their possibilities for claiming sexual virtue and respectability. It was one of the reasons, Allison argues, that they clung so fiercely to their racism. They worked as waitresses and counter girls, but they refused to work as maids. Participating in a rigid racial division of gendered labor, they used avenues open to them by institutionalized racism and white supremacy to create self-worth and claim respect.[48]

These examples highlight the connection between collective group organization and identity formation. They also show how social structures constrain the possibilities for collective organization and therefore constrain the range of understandings and ways of positioning oneself available for any individual in the group to take up.[49] Individual women's biographies and particular experiences shaped how they managed the dilemmas and contradictions that they faced in developing their gender identities. But the range of interpretations that could make sense of their dilemmas—and the feelings/emotions they generated—was shaped by the culture and everyday relationships of their social life, the groups of people with whom they lived and worked, and on whom they relied for day-to-day survival. And the culture of the group was, in turn, shaped by the history, the successes and failures, of broader collective struggle, as well as the possibilities for collective action in the present. Constructions and accounts of oneself which reverse the judgements of the dominant society—in the case of white working-class women, the bourgeois ideology that holds individuals responsible for their positions in the economic, social, and cultural hierarchy—are only possible in the context of lived, socially supported, collective resistance.

In their struggle to assert self-worth and claim respect, women of color can draw on collective identities which are reproduced and reinforced not only in everyday life but through political organization and contestation. However differently inflected by class, discourses of race and ethnicity, negative and positive, are central in contemporary culture and politics. Although weakened and divided (more on this below), organizations defending people of color are visibly part of the political scene. For white working-class women, by contrast, there is much less support for challenging hegemonic cultural constructions. There is no working-class-based politics, no broad-based working-class movements, not even in recent memory, and thus no powerful counter-discourse through which to claim a valued working-class identity. There is still, of course, resistance. The working-class women in Skeggs' study found ways to support each other in defending themselves from "put downs" and making fun of people who thought they "were better than us." Nonetheless, in the absence of a working-class oppositional culture, the possibilities for white working-class women to make a radical break with white, middle-class definitions of respectability and self-worth are narrow indeed.

For the white working-class women examined here, trade unions were not an important part of their work or community worlds. In trade unions, women workers can develop cultures of solidarity and group support for feminine identities which challenge middle-class denigration of their life choices and self-presentation. Of course, there is nothing automatic about such a development. At least historically, the masculinist culture of the male-dominated trade-union movement has tended to support the association between sexual virtue and respectable white working-class womanhood. On the other hand, trade unions have also from time to time provided an arena for women to struggle with working-class men about gender roles. And there are examples from labor history of working-class women publicly enacting an unruly sexuality, sometimes with support from their "brother" unionists: notably, within the context of militant trade-union struggles where women were present not only as supportive wives but as workers themselves.[50]

White working-class women, like women of color, have struggled not only with men but with each other about the meanings of their sexualities within a context shaped profoundly by their class location. They have resisted and accepted, redefined and denied, hegemonic constructions of their sexual selves within life-worlds shaped by their working-class kin, friends, and communities. Conflicts around the sexual containment of women have been intimately bound up with individual and group strategies for responding to their class-based economic, social, and political exclusion and marginalization.

It is certainly crucial that feminists investigate the relations of power and privilege created by institutionalized racism so that we can address them. However, it is also crucial to incorporate class into feminist analysis far more thoroughly than has yet been done.[51] To ignore white working-class women in feminist theorizing of intersectionality and to fail to address the *specificity* of working-class women of color inhibits our political imagination. It highlights those divisions among women which provide the *least* potential common ground—the division between white middle-class (especially upper professional and managerial) women and poor and working-class women of color. An intersectional analysis that includes class location as a key term can open up new fields for cross-race coalition-building and feminist theorizing. It leads us to see that welfare rights and immigrant rights organizing can be feminist projects.[52] It makes trade-union organizing campaigns, workplace organizing around issues of race/gender discrimination, cross-border organizing support campaigns, protests against the institutions of the new world economic order, such as the World Trade Organization, key sites of feminist political work.[53] It brings working-class women's community struggles—for example, over housing, toxic waste and pollution—and the possibilities for coalition-building across communities around these issues into the center of feminist politics.[54] But developing an anti-racist working-class feminism is not only about the issues we organize around—for example, economic issues in contrast with sexual politics. After all, working-class women get breast cancer, need abortions, and are sexually assaulted. An anti-racist working-class feminist politics is defined by how activists organize around any issue. The way we understand the problem, who we see as allies, the solutions we propose, must address the concerns and interests of all working-class women.

The development of an anti-racist working-class feminist politics is the only basis for a renewed feminist movement. As I have argued at various points in this book, the great mobilization of the second wave achieved historic gains without directly confronting capitalist class interests. This was true also of the civil rights movement. Today, both movements face a similar impasse. In the next section, I consider how the dynamics of the capitalist economy and the powers of the capitalist class have shaped the political prospects of our movements.

Capitalist Class Power and the Politics of Resistance

The civil rights and feminist movements combined revolutionary and reformist aims, their radical wings seeking to redistribute economic and political power. Though falling far short of this goal, the movements did dismantle the old gender and racial orders and opened the field for other movements against oppression (for example, gay/lesbian rights, disability rights). They have made it possible for a new left challenge, when it develops, to be far more self-consciously and powerfully anti-racist, anti-sexist, and anti-heterosexist than any that has gone before.[55] On the other hand, by almost any measure, neither racial oppression nor male domination have disappeared from the scene. They have, however, been fundamentally reorganized. Both operate, now, not through an explicit, legally and culturally authorized system of exclusion, but through a process of incorporation that systemically reproduces disadvantage. Elsewhere in this book I have made the argument for this claim in the case of male dominance. Here, I briefly recapitulate it, and then lay out the parallel for the reorganization of institutionalized racism.

The exclusion of women from higher-paid occupations and the male-breadwinner/female-housewife family, which underwrote patriarchal power, have been overturned. Yet male dominance continues, because feminism has been signally unable to win significant changes in the organization of social reproduction. Caregiving remains the privatized responsibility of family/households. No matter how women restrict their childbearing, the needs of adults and children continue to weigh heavily on their shoulders. Women in the upper reaches of the class structure—women in the higher professions and management positions— can buy their way out of responsibilities, but most women cannot. Men and women are negotiating different kinds of bargains about how to share caregiving responsibilities.[56] But so long as these responsibilities remain individual rather than social, households will be forced to organize a division of labor around them and women will continue to be disadvantaged relative to men in the labor market. Further, so long as solo motherhood remains so very difficult, while women will choose it when they need to, the double burdens of being a breadwinner and caregiver will continue to underwrite not only a backward-looking political and cultural nostalgia about the nuclear family but also women's investments in and tolerance for reformed, but still "patriarchal," bargains in family households.[57]

The forces arrayed against changing this underpinning of male dominance are formidable. To make social reproduction a more collective responsibility would require a serious redistribution of wealth. Thus, I argued, feminism's next wave will have to make common cause with and be part of a broad, anticapitalist, rainbow movement, including trade unions that are truly social-movement organizations.

In her analysis of the impasse facing Black feminism, Patricia Hill Collins argues similarly that the gains of the civil rights and feminist movements have contributed to a reorganization of the racial order rather than the demise of institutionalized racism and racialized politics. Although successful in breaking down the explicit, legalized, and culturally sanctioned segregation that defined the horizons of Black life for over a century, the civil rights movement, like the feminist movement, has not been able to improve significantly the lives of the majority of Black people, while opening up previously unthinkable opportunities for a relatively small group. Class divisions among Black women have grown wider. The upward mobility of the Black middle class has weakened the community base of the civil rights movement, and the visible success of some Black women obscures and mystifies the continuing systemic and institutionalized racism that disadvantages the majority. Increased access to political, residential, and employment spaces for some Black women, she argues, is paired with the intractable impoverishment of the majority. Further, the breakup of Black civil society—the loss of institutions that developed in the segregated communities which defined Black life up through the civil rights era—have undermined the practices, such as community work, that fostered a Black women's tradition of resistance.[58]

To address this new impasse, Collins says, Black feminists have to recommit themselves to supporting, organizing for, and representing the needs of working-class and poor Black women. She argues secondly for a break from the sexism and homophobia that have infused Afrocentrism, calling for a racial solidarity that is sensitive to Black heterogeneity and difference and prepared to engage in principled coalitions.[59]

Thus, the problems facing the feminist and civil rights movements are parallel. In both instances, tremendous gains for the middle class are matched by continuing difficulties for an increasingly impoverished working class.[60] My point is not at all to refocus our attention on class to the exclusion of race or gender. The persistence of race and gender discrimination is well documented, even for the middle class.[61] Many African Americans' foothold in the middle class is certainly more tenuous than that of white men. While having moved out of the urban ghettos, Black people live in segregated suburbs that are less affluent than white suburbs.[62] Still, the rise of a Black intelligentsia, of Black professionals, political office holders, corporate managers, and high-level state administrators is a historic change. The question remains, though, why hasn't it been possible for the Black working class to take advantage of the same openings? For the African-American working class to reach even the distressed levels of the white working class would require a serious redistribution of income and wealth, through expansion of public investment in communities and housing, in schooling and access to higher education, and by the creation of living-wage jobs. If the potential for state intervention to end Black poverty was undermined by racism during the 1960s,[63] it surely will not be fulfilled until the political balance of forces is shifted decisively leftward and with a much more heightened awareness of how institutionalized racism has scuttled previous efforts. The way out of the impasse facing the Black working class cannot be found in reinvigorating the political thrust of the single-issue politics of the 1960s. At least in its assimilationist goals, that strategy has come up against structural and political limits. The successful political campaigns against affirmative action; the re-invigorated racist political discourses around crime, welfare, and immigration; the cutbacks in spending for social services and housing—these are not a simple "political backlash," a pendulum-swing to the right which is bound to move back. They are the political effects of profound changes in the economy. The drift of politics in the U.S. steadily to the right over the past twenty years will only be halted by a broad-based, multi-issue movement that combines the forces of many different groups in order to confront capital's formidable political and economic power.

The civil rights revolution failed to carry the majority of Black people into the mainstream of the U.S. economy because, to put it simply, by the time the Black working class finally got a ticket to ride the train that had carried other excluded groups into the mainstream, the train was no longer running. As Karen Brodkin so persuasively shows, in the post-Second World War era, the combination of government intervention (especially the GI bill and housing programs) and unprecedented economic growth and prosperity laid the basis for the men of previously denigrated and excluded ethnic groups, and particularly Jews, to "become white."[64] The war against fascism had perhaps helped to undermine popular anti-Semitism, but we should not put too much weight on this factor. In many communities prejudice toward Jews remained quite strong, even after the war. Yet although the anti-communist right fulminated against Jews, by the early 1950s, in the context of a booming economy and what amounted to an affirmative action program which addressed broad segments of the working class, their anti-Semitism had little political purchase. However, Blacks were systematically denied access to the government programs that provided suburban home-ownership, college education, and thus occupational upward mobility for many working-class ethnic males.[65] The gains made by ethnic groups of European origin, accrued in the 1950s, were passed down to the next generations and then used to sustain racist myths about the inferiority of Black culture.

By the time the civil rights movement finally won for Black people even a small part of the kind of consistent federal support that had propelled Jews and other "Euro-American" men into the middle class and across the color line, the economic conditions that had allowed for such upward mobility were about to disappear. Almost as the movements were coming into their own—from the mid-1960s through the early 1970s—the U.S. economy was entering into a sea change which culminated in the current reconfiguration and dominance of capitalist class power. As the postwar hegemony of U.S. corporate capital began to give way with the rise of new and quite powerful international competitors, profit margins began to narrow, and the corporations launched an offensive on wages and working conditions as a strategy to restore profits.[66] The bureaucratized labor unions were totally unprepared for this "new class war" and unwilling to take the risks involved in breaking away from the corporatist strategies that had allowed them to build their organizations in the period of prosperity.[67] The employers' offensive sparked defensive rank-and-file revolts and an upsurge in militancy in the early 1970s. But, with the exception of the Black revolutionary union movements in Detroit, these revolts only rarely connected with the student, civil rights, feminist, and antiwar movements of their time. And they failed to shift fundamentally the "business union" strategies of their ossified union leaderships. By the 1980s, many corporations had turned away from squeezing manufacturing workers to simply dumping them altogether. Deindustrialization in the old centers of production, movement of manufacturing to the south and overseas, then the emergence of more flexible production processes and outsourcing—all pushed organized workers further onto the defensive.[68] There were many inspiring struggles by working-class communities in these years.

And some activists, as they reached out across the country for support, found new allies among the other movements, in the course of their struggle expanding and even radicalizing their own political world-views.[69] But these battles were almost all lost. Plants just shut down. And if they didn't, the employers were able to force workers into harsh bargains that included wage cuts, changes in work rules, loss of control over schedules, speed-ups, and so on. Between 1980 and 1984, union membership in the private sector declined from 20.1 percent to 15.6 percent of the workforce. By 1996 only 10.2 percent of workers in private industry were unionized.[70]

As the old industrial centers died, so did the communities dependent on them. This was, of course, especially fateful for Black urban communities dependent on stable, unionized working-class jobs.[71] During the 1970s, while affirmative-action policy and anti-discrimination legislation was opening up opportunities for higher education and professional/managerial employment to middle-class white women and people of color, good blue-collar jobs were disappearing. Urban renewal and deindustrialization, along with expanding opportunities for residential mobility for Blacks who had the means to move out further, undermined the economic base of inner-city neighborhoods. White flight and suburbanization did the rest of the job, so by the time Black urban residents were able to use the political muscle won through their civil rights struggle, they found themselves holding power in cities with a shrinking economic base in states where legislatures were increasingly hostile.

The political hostility, the intensified and racialized conflict between suburb and city, and the movement of white working-class communities away from the Democratic Party also had their roots in the employers' offensive.[72] The civil rights and women's movements really did threaten white male monopolies. Although this challenge would have always produced resistance, economic expansion, such as in the post-Second World War years, which saw real improvements in the standards of living of almost all working-class people, would also have softened the blow and helped to undercut the racist appeals of the right. Instead, working-class communities faced declining wages, job loss, shrinking opportunities, and increasing economic insecurity. Increasing economic competition intensifies reliance on existing group solidarities, solidarities that arise out of the ways that people come together to organize their everyday survival. These survival projects, organized through kin and other social networks as well as in the workplace, will in the ordinary course of events reproduce rather than disrupt the occupational and residential racial/ethnic segregation which is the basis for racial/ethnic conflict. To be clear: this is not an argument against anti-racism political strategies or for supposedly "universal" as opposed to "targeted" government programs. It is rather to say that economic and political conditions are related, that the past gains were made under conditions which will not return, and that a new anti-racism offensive will only be possible if it is tied to an anticapitalist politics—allied to a broad coalition for economic and social justice.

Without the capacity to organize a collective response to the employers' offensive, white working-class people inevitably were mobilized to hold onto whatever advantages they could command, displacing their anger and fear onto the most vulnerable and powerless segments of society. Obviously, this is not the first time racist appeals and scapegoating have successfully divided U.S. working people.

In the absence of a more collective and inclusive response to economic instability, group resentment and political mobilization on the basis of narrow group interests are the order of the day. Omi and Winant make the point that even if white racism is deeply rooted, nonetheless a white backlash was not inevitable. "A more comprehensive series of reforms, for example, might have extended to redistribution initiatives and full-employment commitments, which could have cushioned the blow that whites located in marginal neighborhoods, school districts, jobs, etc. received when affirmative action and similar programs increased competition for semiskilled work, public education, and affordable housing."[73] Of course, the major cause of white workers' deteriorating living standards was the employers' offensive against workers' wages, jobs, and working conditions, an assault which weighed even more heavily on the Black working class. However, the policies and programs that would have helped protect workers from the consequences of this assault were certainly not in the cards. As the economic room for contesting corporate power shrank, so did the political space for countering corporate interests. A full-employment policy, proposed during the 1970s and 1980s by the trade unions to soften the blows of dislocation and to strengthen the bargaining position of workers, never got off the ground. Instead, federally enforced legal protections for organizing were gutted.[74]

The right's mobilization of racist feelings and ideologies took form not only in an attack on aggressive state intervention to redress racial discrimination (especially campaigns against affirmative action, bilingual

education, etc.) but also in an attack on the public sector more generally—both public-sector workers and users of social-welfare programs
(especially clear in welfare reform and anti-immigration legislation). The
mobilization of anti-immigrant sentiment has not been limited to the
white working class; increasing competition between nonwhite racial/
ethnic groups and increasing class division within them has also been
the basis for attacks on immigrants as part of a broader assault on the
"undeserving" poor.[75]

As the drift to the right has gained momentum, conservative interest
groups have been able to capture increasing shares of the state budget.
Thus, not only was funding for public services—especially those directed to the poor (in the hegemonic figuration of the class system, an
"underclass" made up predominantly of people of color)—generally
under attack. The 1980s and 1990s also saw increasing shifts away
from social spending and toward spending on the coercive arm of the
state—a rise in military spending as a portion of the federal budget and
the rapid growth of prisons to the point that it makes sense to speak of
a prison-industrial complex.[76]

This rise of the right through a politics of opposition to the "liberal"
welfare state also has its origins in the employers' offensive. The expansion of the welfare state began in the 1950s but accelerated in the
1960s as a response to the urban rebellions and the increasingly well-
organized groups making claims for state services.[77] Increased government spending, whether at the federal, state, or local level, was never
financed by serious transfers of wealth. After averaging 45 percent in
the 1950s, corporate tax rates began a sharp decline in the 1960s,
reaching 24 percent in 1994.[78] Effective tax rates on the incomes of the
wealthy were only very mildly redistributive and since the mid-1970s
have become much less so.[79] The burden of funding for the U.S. welfare
state falls on wage and salary incomes—a system of financing which
emerged from the defeat of more interventionist strategies. Although
during the 1930s there was real debate in policy circles over strategies
to manage the economy, by the end of the Second World War an interventionist model of the state had been decisively marginalized in
favor of what has been called "growth liberalism."[80] In this approach,
government's role is confined to using fiscal power—its capacity to tax
and spend—to maintain purchasing power and to fuel economic expansion. Management of the economy through wage-setting, powerful
regulatory institutions, or publicly owned production was rejected in
favor of demand stimulation and restrained social welfare spending. In

comparison to the social-democratic regimes that emerged in many other capitalist economies, the postwar accord between labor and capital created a segmented system of income security, pensions, and health benefits. Unionized workers earned pension and health benefits through their contracts, leaving those in the lower tiers of the working class dependent on the public sector.[81]

This system worked relatively well during the prosperous postwar boom years. A rising tide did lift all boats, although not equally, and it was possible to build a "guns and butter" state through taxing the working class and middle class. With real income rising, taxation did not loom large as a political issue. The employers' offensive, however, quickly exposed the fundamental weaknesses of this foundation for welfare-state liberalism. During the 1970s, while median real family income declined by 16 percent, taxes increased as a proportion of workers' income. The revolts against property taxes in the late 1970s were simply the beginning of a successful conservative mobilization around the issue of taxation and spending.[82]

The conservative movement that emerged in the 1970s but took over U.S. politics in the 1980s was an alliance of two overlapping but distinct political movements. The religious right created its strength out of the Christian churches and on the basis of a backlash against feminism and gay/lesbian rights movements. The modernizing right has staked its claim much more firmly in a classic liberal political worldview. Thus, their neoliberalism has incorporated the individual-rights discourses of the civil rights movements rearticulated as the right to fair competition on the market. Although the religious right has caused feminism and the gay/lesbian movement a lot of pain, the real conservative success story lies in the dominance of the modernizing right's worldview. Clinton's rhetoric on welfare in the 1992 campaign captured this shift very well, particularly the celebration of work as a moral issue (working mothers are good role models who break the "cycle of dependence"), which reproduced rather than challenged the now standard and pervasive representation of Black poor single mothers as undeserving welfare queens. The modernizing right's discourse depends on the contrast between the deserving—those who wish to make it through their own efforts (a hand up)—and the undeserving—namely, those who argue for group support (a hand out). Efforts by the government to improve the lives of people collectively are delegitimized by this framing. Instead, the role of the state is to "help" those who need it to enter into the market and to enjoy the supposedly equal opportunities for upward

mobility awaiting those willing to make the effort. While New Democrats put a slightly more populist spin on this basic conservative mes-
sage, they have essentially adopted it. As civil rights and women's
organizations are forced to struggle on this terrain, they have pragmati-
cally adapted to the limits of available discourses, reproducing rather
than challenging the conservative terms of the debate.

As I argued in my analysis of the political consensus on welfare
reform, the "middle-class" representatives advocating for communities
of color—directors of nonprofit organizations, social-service providers,
public health workers, and so on—shifted their political strategies in
response to the rapid decline of support for government investments in
their communities. Navigating within increasingly conservative political
waters and without a politically mobilized social base, they adapted
their political rhetoric and demands to suit the times. Mainstream civil
rights organizations have joined with Black conservatives and Black
nationalists to justify social-service programs in terms of their value for
morally uplifting the Black working class, now redefined as an underclass. This shift has also been fueled by a masculinist political current
that has been historically dominant in communities of color.[83] The crisis
of the Black male, like the panic about (Black) teen pregnancy, comes
to justify state funding for services that target behavioral reform.[84]
Whatever successes advocates may have in grasping some of the shrinking state funds for their own programs, they pay for these gains in
reinforcing the very ideologies which have justified funding cutbacks in
the first place. That is, the focus on the "bad character" of the "underclass" supports eliminating hard-won public programs, now disparaged
as entitlements that breed "dependence" in favor of the bracing independence and self-help of the market economy. At the same time, as
Barbara Omolade argues, political statements, such as the Million Man
March, which mobilize around themes of Black male responsibility,
strike a responsive emotional chord among women who struggle with
single parenthood and extremely conflictual gender relations.[85] Here,
too, we see the political consequences of our movements' failure to
wrest concessions from the state that would lighten women's burdens of
caregiving.

Advocates' failure to move resources into their communities leaves
their working-class base stranded.[86] The pattern of dramatic class cleav-
age within the Black community has been repeated in many others as
a consequence of global capitalist restructuring, and the recent wave of
immigration to the U.S., particularly into "Asian" and "Latino" com-

munities. Bringing very different cultural capitals and economic resources with them, and in certain instances benefiting from large federal subsidies, some new immigrants have done quite well, while many others have filled the ranks of the expanding working class.[87] At the same time, political openings in the state apparatus and elective offices increase opportunities for individuals to play a brokering role as representatives of their respective racial/ethnic groups. New relationships between the local state and urban racial/ethnic enclaves have created more complex power structures internally, while at the same time increasing competition among racial/ethnic groups jockeying for position with regard to public spending and investments.[88]

The working classes in these communities have spoken politically and sporadically through riots/rebellions, mobilizations for immigrant rights, community–labor coalitions around union organizing drives, and other grassroots struggles.[89] But their voices are muted compared to those of their middle-class spokespeople.[90]

To understand, then, both the gains and impasses of the civil rights and women's movements, their ability to challenge so thoroughly and to change ways of thinking about race and gender and their inability to sustain this challenge, it is helpful to put them in the context of the periods of capitalist economic transformation. The economic changes that were already reshaping the political landscape in the 1970s and 1980s accelerated in the 1990s: the expansion of markets and production, the increase in labor migration both within and across national borders, the flexibility and mobility of investment/production, the penetration of global firms into the U.S. economy not only in goods but in services, the increasing freeing of global firms from control and regulation by national states. The capitalist restructuring that first undermined the conditions of blue-collar workers in core manufacturing industries now threatens security and stability of jobs in many sectors—from middle-managers and supervisors to production workers.

At the core of these changes are not simply globalization but capital's increasing flexibility, mobility, and concentrated power, as well as the intensity of capitalist competition and the employers' drive to squeeze ever more out of the workforce. A highly competitive and turbulent economy now dominates life in the U.S. As in the significant periods of capitalist restructuring that preceded this one, the institutions of working-class political and economic defense that had been built up under the old paradigm and that might have worked (although not all that well) previously are now utterly unable to respond to new conditions.

Until some alternatives develop, the political hegemony of the modernizing right can be expected to remain in place.

Even if no quick or easy solution seems to be on the horizon, the situation is not without realistic hopes and expectations for renewed contestation and political organization. The U.S. working class has become more immigrant, more racially/ethnically diverse, more low-waged, and more female. And the trade unions, although weak in terms of the percentage of the labor force who are members of unions, are groping toward new, more militant, more democratic, more political, and more community-based modes of struggle. In response to global capital's vicious exploitation of the environment as well as the workforce, coalitions of environmental groups and trade unions have been formed.[91] Labor is changing partly because it has no choice, partly because new groups of workers have organized within the trade unions to make new demands: gay/lesbian workers have organized for their unions to take a stand on and contribute to campaigns for lesbian/gay rights; feminist union members have forced their unions to "come out" for abortion rights, to see support for these rights as a union issue; immigrants are organizing. Grassroots worker solidarity organizations, like Jobs With Justice, have built international labor solidarity and raised the consciousness of U.S. workers through cross-border organizing campaigns.[92] New community-based organizations which bridge trade-union organizing with struggles for racial justice have emerged.[93] For the first time there is a real possibility for a coalitional politics, for a rainbow movement organized around a broad agenda of social and economic justice.[94] Of course, there are currents running in a very different direction, and they are, right now, the stronger. Still, we, all of us who won't settle for what the powerful intend, have no choice but to stake our future on this possibility, engaging in the "visionary pragmatism"[95] that has animated resistance to oppression and the struggle for justice in every generation.

[*2000*]

Notes

I am very grateful to Kristin Barker, Tom Biolsi, Jan Haaken, Nancy Holmstrom, Barbara Laslett, Sally Markowitz, Frann Michel, and Bill Resnick for their generous comments and suggestions on earlier drafts of this essay.

1. For the following analysis, see Kimberlé Crenshaw, "Whose Story is it Anyway? Feminist and Antiracist Appropriations of Anita Hill," in Toni Morrison, ed., *Race-ing Justice, En-gendering Power: Essays on Anita Hill, Clarence Thomas, and*

the Construction of Social Reality (New York: Pantheon Books, 1992), 402–40; and Elsa Barkley Brown, "'What Has Happened Here': The Politics of Difference in Women's History and Feminist Politics," in Linda Nicholson, ed., *The Second Wave: A Reader in Feminist Theory* (New York: Routledge, 1997).

2. Barbara Omolade, *The Rising Song of African American Women* (New York: Routledge, 1994), 180–202; Deborah Gray White, *Too Heavy a Load: Black Women in Defense of Themselves, 1894–1994* (New York: Norton, 1999), 116–22; Elizabeth Martinez, *De Colores Means All of Us* (Cambridge, Mass.: South End Press, 1998), 172–81; Purvi Shah, "Redefining the Home: How Community Elites Silence Feminist Activism," in Sonia Shah, ed., *Dragon Ladies: Asian American Feminists Breathe Fire* (Boston: South End Press, 1997).

3. Kimberlé Crenshaw, "Intersectionality and Identity Politics: Learning from Violence Against Women of Color," in Mary Lyndon Shanley and Uma Narayan, eds., *Reconstructing Political Theory: Feminist Perspectives*, (University Park: Pennsylvania State University Press, 1997), 184.

4. Evelyn Nakano Glenn, "The Social Construction and Institutionalization of Gender and Race: An Integrative Framework," in Myra Marx Ferree, Judith Lorber, and Beth B. Hess, eds., *Revisioning Gender* (Thousand Oaks: Sage, 1999), 20.

5. For overviews of the issues here, see Erik Olin Wright, *The Debate on Classes* (London: Verso, 1989), and Joan Acker, "Rewriting Class, Race, and Gender: Problems in Feminist Rethinking," in Ferree et al., eds., *Revisioning Gender*, 44–69.

6. Patricia Hill Collins, *Black Feminist Thought: Knowledge, Consciousness, and the Politics of Empowerment* (Boston: Unwin Hyman, 1990), esp. chap. 7.

7. See White, *Too Heavy a Load*, e.g. 78, 132–33.

8. Elsa Barkley Brown, "Negotiating and Transforming the Public Sphere: African American Political Life in the Transition from Slavery to Freedom," in Cathy J. Cohen, Kathleen B. Jones, and Joan Tronto, eds., *Women Transforming Politics: An Alternative Reader* (New York: New York University Press, 1997), 358–62.

9. Ibid., 362.

10. White, *Too Heavy a Load*, 132–33; Robin D. G. Kelly, *Race Rebels: Culture, Politics, and the Black Working Class* (New York: The Free Press, 1994), 39, 45–47, 83.

11. Linda Gordon, *Pitied But Not Entitled: Single Mothers and the History of Welfare* (New York: The Free Press, 1994), 126–43.

12. For the modern period, see Cheryl Townsend Gilkes, "Building in Many Places: Multiple Commitments and Ideologies in Black Women's Community Work," in Ann Bookman and Sandra Morgen, eds., *Women and the Politics of Empowerment* (Philadelphia: Temple University Press, 1988), 57.

13. White, *Too Heavy a Load*, 69–73.

14. Ibid., 70.

15. Barkley Brown, "What Has Happened Here," 278–80, inc. nn. 25 and 26.

16. Collins, *Black Feminist Thought*, chap. 5.

17. Daphne Duval Harrison, *Black Pearls: Blues Queens of the 1920s* (New Brunswick, N.J.: Rutgers University Press, 1990); Angela Y. Davis, *Blues Legacies and Black Feminism* (New York: Pantheon Books, 1998).

18. Kelly, *Race Rebels*, 47.

19. See also Tera W. Hunter, "'Work That Body': African-American Women, Work

and Leisure in Atlanta and the New South," in Eric Arnesen, Julie Greene, and Bruce Laurie, eds., *Labor Histories: Class, Politics, and the Working-Class Experience* (Urbana: University of Illinois Press, 1998), 155–57; Kevin K. Gaines, *Uplifting the Race: Black Leadership, Politics, and Culture in the Twentieth Century* (Chapel Hill: University of North Carolina Press, 1996), esp. 88–93. For analysis of a similar white middle-class "moral panic" focused on young women in this same period, see Constance A. Nathanson, *Dangerous Passage: The Social Control of Sexuality in Women's Adolescence* (Philadelphia: Temple University Press, 1991).

20. Hazel V. Carby, "Policing the Black Woman's Body in an Urban Context," in Cohen et al., *Women Transforming Politics*, 153.

21. Kimberley L. Phillips, "Making a Church Home: African-American Migrants, Religion, and Working-Cass Activism," in Arnesen et al., eds., *Labor Histories*, 234–5. See also Gaines, *Uplifting the Race*, chap. 7. This class-inflected response to newcomers in the context of increasing racism is similar to the response of Jewish middle-class women in England to immigrants from Eastern Europere in the context of intensified English anti-semitism during the early years of the twentieth century. See Susan L. Tananbaum, "Biology and Community: The Duality of Jewish Mothering in East London, 1880–1939," in Evelyn Nakano Glenn, Crace Chang, and Linda Renie Forcey, eds., *Mothering: Ideology, Experience, and Agency* (New York: Routledge, 1994), 311–32.

22. Due to space considerations, I am not including Black working-women's organizations (e.g. professional associations, trade unions) in this essay.

23. See White, *Too Heavy a Load*, 163–68. Darlene Clark Hine, "The Housewives' League of Detroit: Black Women and Economic Nationalism," in Nancy A. Hewitt and Suzanne Lebsock, eds., *Visible Women: New Essays on American Activism* (Chicago: University of Illinois Press, 1993), 222–41; and on mutual aid associations, Kelly, *Race Rebels*, 38.

24. While claiming a working-class identity, the women of the Ladies Auxiliary of the Brotherhood of Sleeping Car Porters were in some ways more like, than unlike, the middle-class clubwomen. Many did not work outside the home; a significant number had college degrees. White, *Too Heavy a Load*, 171.

25. Ibid.

26. Phillips, "Making a Church Home," 246–47.

27. Ibid., 247–50.

28. According to Phillips, "The largely female congregation of the Jesus Only Church of God had an elaborate list of prohibitions, including 'adultery, fornication, lying and joking, backbiting, whoremongering, smoking, drinking, chewing tobacco, dipping snuff, dancing in public, wearing lipstick, earrings, beads or short skirts'" (ibid., 247).

29. Gaines, *Uplifting the Race*, 36–46.

30. Evelyn Brooks Higginbotham, *Righteous Discontent: The Women's Movement in the Black Baptist Church, 1880–1920* (Cambridge, Mass.: Harvard University Press, 1993), 204, and "Rethinking Vernacular Culture: Black Religion and Race Records in the 1920s and 1930s," in Wahneema Lubiano, ed., *The House that Race Built* (New York: Vintage, 1998), pp. 157–77. On the masculinist popular culture of the zoot suit years, see Kelly, *Race Rebels*, chap. 7.

31. Kelly, *Race Rebels*, 46–48.

32. Patricia Hill Collins, *Fighting Words: Black Women and the Search for Justice*

(Minneapolis: University of Minnesota Press, 1998), 30.

33. See also Kesho Yvonne Scott, *The Habit of Surviving* (New York: Ballantine Books, 1991).

34. Collins, *Feminist Thought*, 119–33; Paula Gunn Allen, *The Sacred Hoop: Recovering the Feminine in American Indian Traditions* (Boston: Beacon Press, 1992).

35. Bonnie Thornton Dill, "Fictive Kin, Paper Sons and Compadrazgo: Women of Color and the Struggle for Family Survival," in Maxine Baca Zinn and Bonnie Thornton Dill, eds., *Women of Color in U.S. Society* (Philadelphia: Temple University Press, 1994), 149–70; Karen Brodkin, *How Jews Became White Folks and What That Says About Race in America* (New Brunswick, N.J.: Rutgers University Press, 1998), 124–27.

36. Nancy A. Naples, *Grassroots Warriors: Activist Mothering, Community Work, and the War on Poverty* (New York: Routledge, 1998), 145–6, 152.

37. See Chapter 3 in this volume. See also Karen Brodkin Sacks, "Toward a Unified Theory of Class, Race, and Gender," *American Ethnologist* 16, no. 3 (1989), 534–50; Margaret K. Nelson and Joan Smith, *Working Hard and Making Do: Surviving in Small Town America* (Berkeley: University of California Press, 1999).

38. Dorothy Allison, *Skin: Talking About Sex, Class, and Literature* (Ithaca, N.Y.: Firebrand Books, 1994), 17.

39. Leith Mullings, *On Our Own Terms: Race, Class, and Gender in the Lives of African American Women* (New York: Routledge, 1997), chap. 6, and "The Pocahontas Perplex: The Image of Indian Woman in American Culture," *Massachusetts Review* 16 (1975), 698–714; Yen Le Espiritu, *Asian American Women and Men: Labor, Laws, and Love* (Thousand Oaks: Sage, 1997), chap. 5.

40. Evelynn M. Hammonds, "Toward a Genealogy of Black Female Sexuality: The Problematic of Silence," in M. Jacqui Alexander and Chandra Talpade Mohanty, eds., *Feminist Genealogies, Colonial Legacies, Democratic Futures* (New York: Routledge, 1997), 170–82.

41. Collins, *Fighting Words*, 69.

42. Aida Hurtado, "The Politics of Sexuality in the Gender Subordination of Chicanas," in Carola Trujillo, ed., *Living Chicana Theory* (Berkeley: Third Woman Press, 1998), 383–428.

43. Beverley Skeggs, *Formations of Class and Gender* (London: Sage, 1997), esp. chap. 7.

44. Ibid., 131–32.

45. Ibid., 95.

46. Ibid., 122–23.

47. Allison, *Skin*, 18.

48. Ibid., 26–27.

49. For an excellent example of a materialist approach to identity, see Paula M. L. Moya, "Postmodernism, Realism, and the Politics of Identity: Cherríe Moraga and Chicana Feminism," in Alexander and Mohanty, eds., *Feminist Genealogies*, 125–50.

50. See, for example, Jacquelyn Dowd Hall, "Disorderly Women: Gender and Labor Militancy in the Appalachian South," *Journal of American History* 73, no. 2 (1986), 354–72, 372–79; Nancy A. Hewitt, "In Pursuit of Power: The Political Economy of Women's Activism in Twentieth-Century Tampa," in Hewitt and Lebsock, eds., *Visible Women*, 199–221.

51. For a complementary analysis, see Delia D. Aguilar, "Questionable Claims: Colonialism Redux, Feminist Style," *Race & Class* 41, no. 3 (2000), 1–12.

52. On the gendered character of and link between the attacks on welfare recipients and on immigrants, see Grace Chang, *Disposable Domestics: Immigrant Women Workers in the Global Economy* (Cambridge, Mass.: South End Press, 2000).

53. As Nancy MacLean points out in her history of cross-race cooperation among white women and women (and men) of color in the struggle for affirmative action on the job. "The Hidden History of Affirmative Action: Working Women's Struggles in the 1970s and the Gender of Class," *Feminist Studies* 25, no. 1 (Spring 1999), 43–78.

54. Temma Kaplan, *Crazy for Democracy: Women in Grassroots Movements* (New York: Routledge, 1997).

55. On anti-sexist consciousness in new Latino/a student movements, see Martinez, *De Colores Means All of Us*, 216–17, 165–69.

56. Stephanie Coontz, *The Way We Really Are* (New York: Basic Books, 1997) chap. 3; Louise Lamphere, Patricia Zavella, and Felipe Gonzales, with Peter B. Evans, *Sunbelt Working Mothers: Reconciling Family and Factory* (Ithaca: Cornell University Press, 1993).

57. Judith Stacey, "What Comes After Patriarchy? Comparative Reflections on Gender and Power in a 'Post-Patriarchal' Age," and Linda Gordon and Alan Hunter, "Not All Male Dominance is Patriarchal," both in *Radical History Review* 71 (1998), 63–83.

58. Collins, *Fighting Words*, 30–32.

59. Ibid., 182–83.

60. White women's gains have been greater proportionally, because they are more evenly distributed within the class structure.

61. Sharlene Hesse-Biber and Gregg Lee Carter, *Working Women in America: Split Dreams* (New York: Oxford University Press, 2000), 40–52.

62. Dennis R. Judd, "Symbolic Politics and Urban Policies: Why African Americans Got So Little from the Democrats," in Adolph Reed, Jr., ed., *Without Justice for All: The New Liberalism and Our Retreat from Racial Equality* (Boulder, Colo.: Westview Press, 1999), 144–47.

63. Jill Quadagno, *The Color of Welfare: How Racism Undermined the War on Poverty* (New York: Oxford, 1994).

64. Brodkin, *How Jews Became White Folks*, chap. 1.

65. Ibid.; see also Judd, "Symbolic Politics and Urban Policies," 126–31.

66. Aaron Brenner, "Rank and File Rebellion, 1966–1975," Ph.D. dissertation, Columbia University, 1996, 30–49.

67. Ibid., 56–62.

68. Kim Moody, *Workers in a Lean World* (London: Verso, 1997), 51–113.

69. Ibid., 23–31; Neala J. Schleuning, *Women, Community, and the Hormel Strike of 1985–86* (Westport, Conn.: Greenwood Press, 1994).

70. Moody, *Workers in a Lean World*, 183; Mike Davis, *Prisoners of the American Dream* (London: Verso, 1986), 147.

71. On the impact of deindustrialization on the Black community in Los Angeles, Detroit, and Birmingham, see Mike Davis, "Los Angeles: Civil Liberties between the Hammer and the Rock," *New Left Review* 170 (July–August 1988), 37–60, esp. 47–52; Tomas J. Sugrue, *The Origins of the Urban Crisis: Race and Inequality in Postwar Detroit* (Princeton: Princeton University Press, 1996); Kelly,

Race Rebels, chap. 4, esp. 93–100.

72. I am interested here particularly in the inroads of the right in the working-class base, the ways in which race divided working-class people. This is not intended as an overall analysis of the rise of the right in U.S. politics.

73. Michael Omi and Howard Winant, *Racial Formation in the United States: From the 1960s to the 1990s*, 2d. ed. (New York: Routledge, 1994), 208 n.63.

74. Davis, *Prisoners of the American Dream*, 131–35, 138–40.

75. Martinez, *De Colores Means All of Us*, 200–01, 243–44.

76. Angela Y. Davis, "Race and Criminalization: Black Americans and the Punishment Industry," in Lubiano, ed., *The House that Race Built*, pp. 264–79.

77. Francis Fox Piven, "The Welfare State as Work Enforcer," *Dollars and Sense*, September–October 1999, 32–34.

78. Nancy Folbre and the Center for Popular Economics, *The New Field Guide to the U.S. Economy* (New York: The New Press, 1995), 5.12.

79. Lawrence Mishel, Jared Bernstein, John Schmitt, *The State of Working America, 1998–99* (Ithaca: Cornell University Press, 1999), 99–118; Joseph Pechman, *The Rich, the Poor, and the Taxes they Pay*, (Boulder, Colo.: Westview Press, 1986), 31–39.

80. Alan Brinkely, "The New Deal and the Idea of the State," in Steve Fraser and Gary Gerstle, eds., *The Rise and Fall of the New Deal Order: 1930–1980* (Princeton: Princeton University Press, 1989), 85–121.

81. For an analysis of labor's defeat and the emergence of this accord, see Nelson Lichtenstein, "From Corporatism to Collective Bargaining: Organized Labor and the Eclipse of Social Democracy in the Postwar Era," in Fraser and Gerstle, eds., *The Rise and Fall of the New Deal Order*, 122–52.

82. Michael K. Brown, "The Segmented Welfare System: Distributive Conflict and Retrenchment in the United States, 1968–1984," in Michael K. Brown, ed., *Remaking the Welfare State: Retrenchment and Social Policy in America and Europe* (Philadelphia: Temple University Press, 1988), 182–210.

83. Mullings, *On Our Own Terms*, 135–46; see also Martinez, *De Colores Means All of Us*, 172–81.

84. Willie M. Legett, "The Crisis of the Black Male: A New Ideology in Black Politics", and Preston H. Smith, "'Self-Help,' Black Conservatives, and the Reemergence of Black Privatism", both in Reed, ed., *Without Justice for All*.

85. Omolade, *The Rising Song*, chap. 5; see also Mullings, *On Our Own Terms*, 146–48.

86. The politics of urban regimes and the failure of even those controlled by Black mayors to shift substantial resources to the urban working class and poor is a complex issue. For a subtle and perceptive analysis of the politics and policies of Black office holders and public managers, see Adolph Reed, Jr., *Stirrings in the Jug: Black Politics in the Post-Segregation Era* (Minneapolis: University of Minnesota Press, 1999); on their adaptation to the political climate, see 204–05.

87. On the impact of "massive state assistance" for middle-class Cuban immigrants, as well as the class relations internal to the Miami Cuban community, see Alex Stepick III and Guillermo Grenier, "Cubans in Miami," in Joan Moore and Raquel Pinderhughes, eds., *In the Barrios: Latinos and the Underclass Debate* (New York: Russell Sage Foundation, 1993), 79–100. On differential fates of Asian immigrants, see Paul Ong, Edna Bonacich, and Lucie Cheng,

eds., *The New Asian Immigration in Los Angeles and Global Restructuring* (Philadelphia: Temple University Press, 1994). On class differences and the new immigration, see Jan Lin, *Reconstructing Chinatown: Ethnic Enclave, Global Change* (Minneapolis: University of Minnesota Press, 1998).

88. On divisions among communities of color, see, for example, "Melvin L. Oliver, James H. Johnson, Jr., and Walter Farrell, Jr., "Anatomy of a Rebellion: A Political-Economic Analysis," in Robert Gooding-Williams, ed., *Reading Rodney King, Reading Urban Uprising* (New York: Routledge, 1993); Alejandro Portes and Alex Stepick, "A Repeat Performance? The Nicaraguan Exodus," in Mary Romero, Pierrette Hondagneu-Sotelo, and Vilma Ortiz, eds., *Challenging Fronteras: Structuring Latina and Latino Lives in the U.S.* (New York: Routledge, 1997); Martinez, *De Colores Means All of Us*, 75–80. On the brokering role of the middle-class, see Reed, *Stirrings*; Yen Espiritu and Paul Ong, "Class Constraints on Racial Solidarity among Asian Americans," in Ong et al., *New Asian Immigration*, 295–321.

89. Eric Mann, "Class, Community and Empire: Toward an Anti-Imperialist Strategy for Labor," in Ellen Meiksins Wood, Peter Meiksins, and Michael Yates, eds., *Rising From the Ashes? Labor in the Age of "Global" Capitalism* (New York: Monthly Review Press, 1998), 100–09; Moody, *Workers in a Lean World*, 170–78.

90. On middle-class bias in Asian-American organizations, see Espiritu and Ong, "Class Constraints."

91. Martinez, *De Colores Means All of Us*, 108–16. For those of us participating in the truly massive demonstrations that disrupted the meetings of the World Trade Organization in Seattle, November 29–30, 1999, this potential for a broad coalition of labor, environment, and social justice groups seemed to be closer to reality than ever.

92. These grassroots organizations as well as the reform movements within the official trade unions, such as Teamsters for a Democratic Union, represent a force for challenging the economic nationalism of the trade-union officialdom (and for winning rank-and-file workers to more internationalist perspectives). For an analysis of these political prospects, see Kim Moody, "Global Capital and Economic Nationalism: Protectionism or Solidarity?" *Against the Current* 14, no. 3 (July–August 2000), 34–38, and "Global Capital and Economic Nationalism: Finding Protection in the Crowd," *Against the Current* 14, no 4 (September–October 2000), 25–29.

93. For example, the Workers Organizing Committee in Portland, Oregon, the Chinese Staff and Worker Association in New York City, the Bus Riders Union in Los Angeles, Black Workers for Justice in Rocky Mountain, North Carolina. Lin, 192–93, Mann, 103–06.

94. For explorations of such a coalitional politics, see Iris Young, "Polity and Group Difference: A Critique of the Ideal of Universal Citizenship," and Bernice Johnson Reagon, "Coalition Politics: Turning the Century," both in Anne Phillips, ed., *Feminism and Politics* (New York: Oxford University Press, 1998); Chela Sandoval, "Mestizaje as Method: Feminists-of-Color Challenge the Canon," in Trujillo, ed., *Living Chicana Theory*, 352–70.

95. I borrow this phrase from Stanlie M. James and Abena P. A. Busia, eds., *Theorizing Black Feminisms: The Visionary Pragmatism of Black Women* (London and New York: Routledge, 1993).

Index